Ivan Ava

The Communist Party in Canada

A History

McClelland and Stewart Limited

Copyright © 1975 McClelland and Stewart Limited

0-7710-0980-1

The Canadian Publishers
McClelland and Stewart Limited
25 Hollinger Road, Toronto

Printed and bound in Canada

Contents

335,43
A 945c
1975

Preface		v
Acknowledgements		vii
Abbreviations		ix
1	Sources of Canadian Communism	1
2	The 1920s	22
3	"Class against Class"	54
4	Towards a People's Front	96
5	From an "Imperialist" to a "Just" War	139
6	Spies and Others	167
7	The Cold War	180
8	Destalinization in Canada	218
9	Beyond the 1950s	236
Conclusion		272
Bibliography		284
Notes		288
Index		302

Preface

This is a study of a political party that has operated under different names for more than five decades in Canada. Older than the CCF-NDP and Social Credit, the Communist Party of Canada has continually differed in more ways than one from all its competitors in the political arena. From the beginning, its organizational structure, the nature of its links with the outside world, and its attitude towards a whole series of international and domestic problems created in the minds of its members, sympathizers and detractors an aura of uniqueness which pleased Communist spokesmen and provided ammunition for their enemies.

Although this uniqueness appeared much more clearly in some areas of Communist activity than in others, it determined the party's place in Canadian life, contributed to its occasional successes and more numerous failures, and accounts for the amount of attention devoted by government agencies to the CPC. This was true even after the Communists had failed to turn the CPC into a mass party and were unable to make an appreciable impact on the Canadian electorate. Their reputation as radical critics, skilful organizers and unscrupulous schemers was so widespread that they were seldom allowed to retire into the sort of obscurity that their limited numbers and successive defeats might have earned them. Liberal and Conservative administrations in Ottawa and the Government of Quebec found it necessary to keep them under surveillance, restrict their radius of action, and support those individuals and organizations that were prepared to fight the CPC and its subsidiaries.

The history of the CPC is the story of a small number of men and women who operated mostly on the fringe rather than in the mainstream of Canadian politics. Handicapped by the ethnic origin of much of its rank-and-file and by the social background of many of its leaders, as well as by the slogans the latter repeated and the allegiance they proudly proclaimed, the Communists advocated policies which most of the time the majority of Canadians found abhorrent, incomprehensible or at best irrelevant to Canadian needs. Who the Communists were, what views they held, and why they were not more successful in making converts, are the questions I now propose to answer, relying primarily on Communist sources, Canadian or otherwise.

Ivan Avakumovic
November, 1974

Acknowledgements

My thanks are due to many people: to the veterans of the Communist movement whom I interviewed or corresponded with, and especially to Harry Binder, Steve Endicott, Harry Fistell, William Kashtan, John Kolasky, Osmo Lahti, Sam Lipshitz, Tom McEwen, Nigel Morgan, S. B. Ryerson, J. B. Salsberg and Sid Sarkin; to those Communists who preferred to remain anonymous; to the late Earl Browder, Mr. T. C. Douglas, Prof. Theodore Draper, Mr. Graham Elliston, Prof. Michiel Horn, Mr. Jay Lovestone, Prof. J. E. Rea and Mrs. Walter Wiggins; to Mr. Cormac Quin, who scrutinized my manuscript, much to its advantage; and not least to my wife for her help and her patience.

I also wish to acknowledge my debt to institutions and libraries of whose facilities I made use, notably the British Museum in London, the Glenbow-Alberta Institute in Calgary, the Hoover Institution at Stanford University, the International Institute for Social History in Amsterdam, the Lenin Library in Moscow, the National Library in Ottawa, the university libraries of British Columbia, Manitoba and Toronto, the provincial libraries in Toronto, Victoria and Winnipeg, and the Public Archives of Ontario in Toronto.

Abbreviations

ACCL	All-Canadian Congress of Labour
AFL	American Federation of Labor
AUUC	Association of United Ukrainian Canadians
CCF	Co-operative Commonwealth Federation
CCL	Canadian Congress of Labour
CCW	Canadian Congress of Women
CCYM	Co-operative Commonwealth Youth Movement
CEC	Central Executive Committee
CI	Communist International
CIO	Committee for Industrial Organization
CLC	Canadian Labour Congress
CLDL	Canadian Labor Defence League
CLP	Canadian Labour Party
Comintern	Communist International
CPC	Communist Party of Canada
CPSU	Communist Party of the Soviet Union
CPUSA	Communist Party of the United States of America
CYC	Canadian Youth Congress
FO	Finnish Organization
FUL	Farmers' Unity League
IUMMSW	International Union of Mine, Mill and Smelter Workers of America
IWA	International Woodworkers of America
IWW	Industrial Workers of the World
Krestintern	Krest'yanskii Internatsional (Peasant International)
LDR	League for Democratic Rights
LPP	Labor Progressive Party
NATO	North Atlantic Treaty Organization
NC	National Committee
NDP	New Democratic Party

NEC	National Executive Committee
NFLY	National Federation of Labor Youth
OBU	One Big Union
PFEL	Progressive Farmers' Educational League
Profintern	Krasnyi Internatsional Profsoiuzov (Red International of Trade Unions).
PWM	Progressive Workers Movement
RILU	Red International of Labour Unions
SDPC	Social Democratic Party of Canada
SPC	Socialist Party of Canada
TLC	Trades and Labor Congress
TUEL	Trade Union Educational League
UAW	United Automobile Workers
UE	United Electrical, Radio and Machine Workers of America
UFA	United Farmers of Alberta
UFC (SS)	United Farmers of Canada (Saskatchewan Section)
UFM	United Farmers of Manitoba
UFO	United Farmers of Ontario
UJPO	United Jewish People's Order
ULFTA	Ukrainian Labor-Farmer Temple Association
USW	United Steelworkers of America
WLL	Women's Labour Leagues
WPC	Workers' Party of Canada
WUL	Workers' Unity League
YCL	Young Communist League

Chapter 1

Sources of Canadian Communism

Like all Communist parties outside the Soviet Union, the Communist Party of Canada (CPC) was composed of two distinct strands: the home-grown socialism of the years before and during the First World War, and the Bolshevik victory in Russia in November 1917.

Socialism reached Canada in the second half of the nineteenth century. Its first supporters were artisans and skilled workers, most of whom had been born in the British Isles or the United States. Concentrated mainly in Ontario and British Columbia, these pioneers and their successors faced difficulties not shared by their comrades in the industrially more advanced societies of North-West Europe.

The sheer size of the country presented a major obstacle to any attempt to organize workers across the Dominion. The lure of cheap land, the proximity of the United States, and the prospect of saving enough to start one's own business appreciably reduced the ranks of those who under different circumstances would have been inclined to listen to socialist agitators. The existence of a sizable French-Canadian community dominated by a Catholic Church hostile to the class struggle and to demands for nationalization made the task of spreading socialism in Quebec a thankless one. On the west coast the presence of oriental labour provided a source of controversy that for decades divided all workers, but particularly the miners.

Nor did the established order facilitate the task of those who challenged the status quo. Electoral laws, municipal regulations, the law courts, the police and, in some instances, the militia and the navy, were used against those who appeared to threaten law, order and private property.

1

More sophisticated but equally effective was the policy the Liberals and Tories followed most of the time in their dealings with those labour leaders who represented a potential force in provincial and federal politics. Consultation on issues of interest to organized labour, a modicum of social legislation, and a willingness to invite prominent trade unionists to stand as candidates of working men on the ticket of the "old line" parties, blunted the edges of class conflict and hampered the formation of a socialist party capable of gaining the loyalty of large segments of the working class. A popular press critical of socialist doctrines and slogans, a wide range of church organizations catering for the spiritual and emotional needs of the poor and millenarian elements of the population, employers who were unwilling to brook any interference with the way they ran their enterprises, and intellectuals who were not eager to sacrifice their careers in the service of socialism, were factors that completed the isolation of the small minority of artisans and workers that was fighting for social change.

Under those circumstances, it is understandable that the socialist movement should have at first been confined to small workers' associations and trade unions, which published short-lived newspapers, issued manifestoes, organized demonstrations and often quarrelled bitterly among themselves. Later, when successful strikes took place, the resulting improvement in working conditions, coupled with the enthusiasm of the socialist agitators, enhanced the popularity of social democracy and paved the way for the formation of socialist parties.

On the eve of the First World War socialists and radicals in Canada could choose between several left-wing parties. Branches of the New York-based Socialist Labor Party (SLP) had been established in the early 1890s. After a promising start, most of them had disintegrated by the end of the century. The few that survived played a minor role in the labour movement in B.C., Montreal and Ontario. They could not compete with the Socialist Party of Canada (SPC), the first major socialist organization in the Dominion. Founded in 1905, its chief strength lay in British Columbia and Alberta, though it had branches as far east as Nova Scotia. The Socialist Party of North America was largely confined to Toronto. It was led by those who left the SPC in 1910.

All these Marxist parties were appreciably weaker than the Social Democratic Party of Canada (SDPC), which had over 3,500 members and 133 locals in 1913.[1] In several provinces Labour and Independent Labour parties completed the galaxy of radical organizations. In Montreal, Toronto and Winnipeg, there were also small groups of anarchists, who denounced socialists and employers alike in their struggle for a stateless, classless and money-less society.

The bewildering profusion of radical organizations with impos-ing titles and short membership rolls stemmed from the major controversies which divided socialists and radicals in Europe and the United States. Many Canadian socialists had been drawn into these controversies before they had emigrated to Canada. Those who had worked in the United States had been influenced by Edward Bellamy's utopian romance *Looking Backward*, Daniel De Leon's Socialist Labor Party, Eugene Debs' Socialist Party, and the Industrial Workers of the World (iww). The emigrants from the British Isles included ex-members and sympathizers of the non-Marxist Labour and Independent Labour parties, admir-ers of Robert Blatchford, the influential socialist editor of *The Clarion*, and those who had been associated with Marxist organi-zations such as the Social Democratic Federation, the British Socialist Party and the Socialist Labour Party in Scotland. Recent immigrants from eastern Europe reflected the differences of opin-ion among socialists in Poland, Russia, the Ukraine and the Slav parts of the Austro-Hungarian Empire. The Finns alone came from a society in which the social democratic movement had time and again before 1914 demonstrated its ability to win the support of over a quarter of the electorate.

Although all these radical organizations in Europe and the United States denounced the capitalist world as corrupt, wasteful and hostile to labour, they disagreed publicly about the means to destroy such a society and build a new one based on the brother-hood of man and the abolition of private property. Some socialists, grouped primarily in the B.C. branches of the spc, stressed what they considered to be the Marxist interpretation of history. They believed that the socialists' most important duty was to teach the working class the principles of scientific socialism and thus prepare the workers for the task that awaited them. This emphasis on edu-cation was combined with great scepticism of any scheme to improve existing society. Their dislike of gradual reforms, which they dismissed as palliatives, made the spc unwilling to devote much effort to electioneering or to "bread and butter" trade union activities.

The dogmatic attitude of the spc leaders met with increasing opposition in spc locals across the country. The "undemocratic and arbitrary actions" of the spc executive in Vancouver brought matters to a head in 1910.[2] Twenty locals in Manitoba and

Ontario broke away and formed in 1911 the Social Democratic Party of Canada, in which immigrants from tsarist Russia and Austria-Hungary provided most of the rank-and-file, while Anglo-Saxons dominated the executive. The SDPC was less doctrinaire than the SPC, took a greater interest in elections, emphasized the need to fight for reforms within the framework of capitalist society, and joined other socialist parties of the world in the International Socialist Bureau, a move that the SPC had refused to take. The *Cotton's Weekly*, the mouthpiece of the SDPC, was for several years the most widely read socialist publication in Canada and displayed greater awareness of events abroad than the *Western Clarion* of the SPC.

The SPC also clashed with the moderate trade union officials of the Trades and Labor Congress (TLC), an organization made up of Canadian locals of international unions whose main strength lay south of the border. Confined almost exclusively to skilled workers, most of the international unions belonged to the American Federation of Labor (AFL). The AFL leaders did not support agitation by socialists, remained sceptical of any plans to organize semi-skilled and unskilled workers, and showed little interest in the unemployed.

Unlike the AFL, the TLC did not oppose independent political action. The formation of Labour and Independent Labour parties in Ontario and the West, with the encouragement of prominent trade unionists, testifies to the organization's belief that organized labour needed a political arm, and that the federal and provincial legislatures provided a useful forum for defending the rights of working men. Although their electoral performance was on the whole disappointing, the very existence of labour parties reflected a trend in Canadian politics and contributed to a shift in trade union thinking.

The TLC, however, did not represent the entire unionized labour force in Canada. As well as several trade unions independent of the TLC, Catholic unions in Quebec, and company unions created under the auspices of employers eager to prevent the emergence of a genuine trade union movement, the TLC also faced on the eve of the First World War a potential competitor in the Industrial Workers of the World (IWW). Founded by a group of American socialists impatient with the conservative approach of the AFL, the IWW advocated the formation of a single union for each industry, open to all those who worked in that industry regardless of individual skills. The Wobblies, as they were popularly known, preferred direct action in the form of strikes and violence to political manoeuvres. They also called for workers' control of industry, mines and transport, once the social revolution had succeeded.

Within a short period of time the IWW had aroused strong feelings among both the workers and employers. It won considerable support in mining and lumber camps in the western United States. IWW agitators, who included several future leaders of the Communist Party of the United States (CPUSA), were active in Alberta and B.C., where they took part in strikes. In eastern Canada the IWW was less successful, although here too it attracted some young workers who were impatient with the slow progress the socialists had made under moderate trade union leaders and budding socialist politicians.

Immediately prior to the First World War Canadian socialists had grounds for optimism. Since the beginning of the century, the stream of socialist and working class activity had increased steadily; there had been setbacks, some of them tragic, but on the whole by 1914 the socialists were more influential and the workers more militant than in the days of Sir John A. Macdonald.

The SPC and the SDPC had branches in over a hundred localities. Special organizations had been set up for socialist women and young people. Among Jews, Ukrainians and Finns the socialists represented a force that could not be ignored. Socialist slogans and arguments had penetrated a segment of organized labour. On the Prairies many farmers active in community affairs were sympathetic to several aspects of the socialist platform. The votes polled by socialist and labour candidates in the 1911 federal election and in several provincial elections before 1914 reflected the growing appeal of the radical ethic. So did the increase in the circulation of Canadian socialist publications and the import of socialist and anarchist literature from the U.S.A. and the United Kingdom.

The growing size of the socialist movement in Canada, however, could not hide its major weaknesses. The socialists had made little impact on French Candians, or in rural Ontario and most of the Maritimes. The proportion of organized socialists among Anglo-Saxon Canadians was significantly lower than among recent immigrants from eastern Europe. Women were as rare as university graduates in any socialist organization. The percentage of trade unionists in the Canadian labour force was rising only slowly. For ideological enlightenment Canadian socialists had to rely on works by their American and European comrades, because no Canadian socialist had written a book-length critique of the Canadian economy or a blueprint for a socialist society. The most the SPC could produce were some pamphlets, none of which contained an original idea or a memorable phrase.

More noticeable were the divisions among both those who considered themselves Marxists, as well as those between Marxist and non-Marxist socialists. The result was duplication of effort, bitter recriminations and numerous intrigues as militants jockeyed for position in the socialist parties and trade unions. The membership of socialist and labour parties fluctuated and overlapped a great deal as radicals searched for a haven and an effective instrument to change society. The disappointed and the fainthearted contributed to a fairly high rate of dropouts from the socialist movement. Those who persevered thundered against the existing order, insisted that labour and capitalism had nothing in common, called on the workers to prepare for the inevitable social revolution, and propounded socialist solutions varying in scope and attractiveness. The mentality of these Marxists explains their pro-Bolshevik sympathies once the outcome of the Russian Civil War was no longer in doubt. In the victorious Lenin many a Canadian Marxist found a kindred spirit, a leader who often used the same words in the same specific sense, who denounced the same institutions, and who advocated the same goals as they had done before 1914.

The outbreak of hostilities in 1914 came as a surprise to Canadian socialists, who had paid relatively little attention to the question of militarism, imperialism and war. Editorials in the radical press on the subject were as rare as the articles or the letters to the editor written by the militants. Even less attention was paid to the question of what the Canadian labour movement should do in time of war. The Canadian socialists expected that the workers in advanced industrial societies would prevent an outbreak of hostilities by means of their numbers, organization, political awareness and role in the modern economy. This reliance on the West and Central European proletariat is understandable in the light of the numerical weakness of the Canadian socialists and their belief that conflicts on other continents would not directly affect North America.

The Great War considerably narrowed the opportunities for socialist agitation in Canada. Appeals to patriotism, the pressure to volunteer for military service, the call for sacrifices to defeat German militarism, went hand in hand with higher prices, wartime shortages, restrictions on civil liberties, growing government interference in the economic life of the country, and widespread profiteering by those who would not allow the war to disturb "business as usual."

The SPC, SDPC and the Socialist Party of North America belonged to that minority of socialist parties which did not support the war effort of their respective governments. Although unwilling to align themselves with the established order on this crucial issue, the three Marxist parties in Canada did not organize a systematic campaign against Canadian involvement in the struggle against Imperial Germany, let alone try to subvert the loyalty of Canadian soldiers. Government regulations and the patriotic attitude of Anglo-Saxon Canadians in the first two and a half years of the war made it too too hazardous to launch an anti-war movement. The feeling of isolation most Canadian socialists experienced before 1917 also owed something to the fact that several prominent members of the SPC and SDPC withdrew from political activity while other SDPC leaders supported the Allied cause.

Those who did not abandon the views they held before 1914 argued that the Great War was an inevitable product of capitalism. They published reports about the stand which this or that socialist organization had taken in Europe. Special attention was paid to those socialist parties and groups in belligerent countries that were hostile to the continuation of the war and unwilling to join coalition governments. However, such activities were in addition to those in which the socialists had engaged before the outbreak of hostilities. Much effort went into ensuring the regular publication of socialist newspapers. Lectures and socialist Sunday Schools were also used as vehicles of socialist education. Here and there a candidate was put up in a municipal, provincial or federal election. Men who were active in trade unions before 1914 did not abandon their work after the beginning of the war. Given the outlook of most trade union leaders and of the bulk of the union rank-and-file, organized labour concentrated on preserving the standard of living of workers in general and of unionists in particular. Demands for conscription of wealth and strong opposition to military conscription formed part of the labour platform. The campaigns of organized labour, fought within the limits of wartime legislation, received a considerable impetus from the overthrow of tsarism in March 1917.

Canadian socialists and radicals shared the widespread view that tsarist Russia was a symbol of obscurantism, oppression and discrimination. Solidarity with the victims of tsarism was one of the planks of the socialist platform to which all socialists subscribed. Refugees from Russia after the unsuccessful revolution of 1905 had received a warm welcome in socialist circles, and had joined tens of thousands of other East Europeans who since the early 1890s had settled in Montreal, Toronto, northern Ontario and the West. Many of them came from the western parts of the Russian empire (present-day Finland, Poland, White Russia and eastern Ukraine), while others were Jews and Ukrainians from Bukovina, Galicia and Sub-Carpathian Ruthenia in Austria-Hungary.

Canada provided them with a haven and an opportunity to engage in the kind of political activity they had been denied in eastern Europe. Those who remained faithful to the socialist and revolutionary traditions of their youth formed political organizations such as the Finnish Social Democratic Party (1911) and the Federation of Ukrainian Social Democrats formed in 1911 and renamed the Ukrainian Social Democratic Party in 1914.[3] These two parties were affiliated to the SDPC.

At the same time the East European socialists set up newspapers in their native languages and founded benevolent and cultural societies. These attracted the attention of a fair number of immigrants. Many a newcomer was prepared to listen to radicals because he found life in Canada more complex and difficult than expected. The task of radicals was also eased by the fact that the traditional forces in the East European communities in Canada were appreciably weaker than they had been in a Ukrainian village in Galicia or in a ghetto in the tsarist Empire.

Many of the day-to-day activities of these East European Marxists followed the pattern of Russian rather than Canadian politics. Polemics and bickerings within ethnic groups took up an inordinate amount of time and energy, with the result that their political activities remained unknown not only to Anglo-Saxon and French Canadians, but also to those East Europeans who were busy assimilating themselves into Canadian society. The lack of toleration, the degree of factionalism and the amount of hairsplitting among these uprooted East European socialists owed something to the youthfulness of many radical leaders and activists. Youth went hand in hand with self-assurance as they fought three kinds of opponents in their ethnic communities: conservatives, supporters of the Liberal Party and those whose particular brand of socialism was antipathetic.

The First World War increased the spirit of alienation among many East Europeans in Canada. They felt little inducement to fight as Canada's soldiers and Russia's allies on a continent from which they had escaped. Many of them were still technically citizens of Austria-Hungary, an enemy of both the British Empire and Russia. Those who found jobs in industry were not grateful for the privilege of staying out of uniform. Harsh living and working conditions, and contact with tiny groups of Anglo-Saxons critical of Canadian participation in the war, strengthened the East Europeans' propensity for radicalism.

The authorities were aware of these sentiments and adopted measures which exasperated the radicals. The registration of enemy aliens and the internment of several thousand of them, the difficulties that East Europeans experienced in obtaining Canadian citizenship, and the abolition of Ukrainian schools in Manitoba, provided ammunition for men who felt and argued that the various layers of government in Canada were treating them just as the Habsburgs and Romanovs had in Europe. Anglo-Saxon support of the authorities' dealings with recent immigrants confirmed radical suspicions that Canadian society was hostile and oppressive.

The downfall of tsarism heightened their interest in events in Eastern Europe, and in the possibility of a compromise peace, at the very time when the conscription issue was dividing Canadians. Lenin's insistence on the need to end hostilities, his espousal of the principle of self-determination, and his identification with the demands for the transfer of power to workers', peasants' and soldiers' soviets (councils), after the Bolsheviks had become masters of Russia, appealed to many East Europeans.

The belief that the radicals in Russia had at last achieved a breakthrough in a world dominated by exploitation and war, and that their fellow-workers and farmers in Russia were laying the foundations of a new and far more progressive society than theirs in North America, was a tremendous inspiration to the Canadian Communist movement. The example of the Soviet Union sustained many a Canadian Communist at a time when public indifference, interspersed with hostility and ridicule, made it only too obvious how isolated and unpopular Communism was.

The pro-Communists among the East Europeans engaged in several kinds of activity. They collected funds and supplies to bring relief to the victims of the famine that engulfed parts of Russia in 1920-1922. The leaders of the Liberal and Tory parties joined in this campaign and called on Canadians to contribute to such organizations as the Save the Children Fund. More controversial were the various forms of agitation engaged in by pro-Bolshevik Canadians. They expressed their non-conformist views through their newspapers, resolutions they passed at public meetings, and through organizations they set up under the impact of events in Russia. Some of these organizations were ephemeral bodies with high sounding names, like the Soviet of Deputies of the Russian Colony in Winnipeg, whose representatives once called on the Chief Constable.[4] Other organizations proved more durable and attracted the attention of the police over a longer period of time. Among these were the Finnish Organization and the Ukrainian Labor Temple Association, (renamed in 1924 The Ukrainian Labor-Farmer Temple Association ULFTA).

At the same time pro-Bolshevik elements among the East European and English-speaking Canadians attacked any European and

American socialists who did not share Lenin's views. They publicized Bolshevik statements and proposals, and printed several of Lenin's articles. Much of what they published in their press was copied from pro-Communist newspapers and periodicals in Britain and the U.S.A.

Since news from Russia was scarce, biased and contradictory, it is not surprising that the readers of these Canadian publications shared the general Canadian ignorance of events and trends in eastern Europe. None the less, this propaganda worried the authorities. In an effort to reduce radical agitation the federal government used wartime legislation in September 1918 to ban several leftwing organizations, including the IWW and SDPC, to close down a dozen radical newspapers printed in English and other languages, and to put a seal on the property of several ethnic organizations run by Bolshevik sympathizers.

The policy of repression came under heavy criticism, although in some instances the ban was lifted before the end of 1918. In other cases the radicals carried on as best as they could through educational and other associations in which they were active, or had formed as a cover for their political activities. These included in Ontario the Labor Educational League and the Canadian Friends of Soviet Russia, the Labor College in Montreal, and the Workers' Alliance in Winnipeg. These and other organizations provided a forum for supporters of civil liberties, sympathizers of Lenin's Russia, and people who were disturbed by Canadian troops being sent to Siberia and northern Russia, where the Allies continued to fight the Soviet regime after the war with Germany had ended.

Demands for the withdrawal of Canadian troops from Russia were accompanied by a strike in Vancouver, in the course of which attempts were made to prevent the loading of a ship bound for Vladivostok. At the same time radical circles displayed broad sympathy for the Soviet form of government, which they identified with the dictatorship of the proletariat. The western labour conference in Calgary (March 1919) reflected this mood when it adopted a resolution favouring the "system of industrial soviet control by the selection of representatives from industries" as

> more efficient and of greater political value than the present form of government. This convention declares its full acceptance of the principle of 'Proletarian Dictatorship' as being absolute and efficient for the transformation of capitalist private property to communal wealth.[5]

The most diligent advocates of the Soviet cause were a tiny group of skilled workers whose enthusiasm for the Bolsheviks made up for their lack of experience in illegal activities, their lack of direct contact with the Communists in Russia, and their ignorance of what was involved in building a mass Communist movement. The pioneers included Tom Bell, a printer, William Moriarty, a draughtsman, and Tim Buck (after his return from the States in 1919). Early in 1921 they were joined by John Macdonald, who had been an Independent Labour Party candidate in the Ontario provincial election in 1919 and who became the first secretary of the CPC in June 1921. The backgrounds of these pioneers were all very similar. They were younger than the leaders of the socialist organizations that had existed in Canada before the Great War. They were relative newcomers to Canada, since they had only emigrated to the New World just before 1914. On arrival in North America, they had moved around a fair amount and had all worked at some point in the States. With the exception of Macdonald, none of them were trade union officials. Politically, they had been associated with several Canadian socialist organizations, without having played a leading role in any of them.

These pioneers were joined by Maurice Spector, who came from the Ukraine and was for a time on the executive of the SDPC. Several women also took part in the slow process of organizing those who saw the Bolsheviks as the wave of the future. The best known was Florence Custance, a teacher born in England and the wife of a prosperous and understanding accountant. Another agitator was Rebecca Buhay. She was of East European extraction and had been involved in radical politics in New York and Montreal during the First World War. An opponent of conscription, she and her brother Mike spoke from the same platform as Henri Bourassa, the French Canadian nationalist leader.

These Communists of British and Jewish descent were in touch with pro-Bolshevik Marxists of East European extraction, including Ukrainians John Boychuk, John Navis and Matthew Popovic (who combined politics with playwriting and amateur theatricals). Among the Finns J. W. Ahlqvist was the most prominent. Neither he nor the bulk of his supporters were natives of Canada.

The Popovics and Ahlqvists brought with them hundreds of followers, printing presses, flourishing weeklies, and buildings owned by pro-Communist organizations. Their colleagues operating among the Anglo-Saxons were not so fortunate in rallying support for a Communist party. They literally had to start from scratch. The underground groups they formed were very small, the leaflets they distributed against Allied intervention in Russia reached few Canadians, and the "one or two weeklies" at their disposal eked out, in the words of a Communist publication, "a precarious existence" and faced "an uncertain future."[6] The Communist pioneers of Anglo-Saxon and Celtic descent were aware of the uneven development of the movement to which they belonged. One of their organs, *The Workers Guard*, spoke the truth when it stated,

> Let us confess that we are not in the same class with these men [Finns and Ukrainians] when it comes to work – spade work – and perseverance. Let us retrieve ourselves and pull along the workers.[7]

Despite these difficulties, an attempt was made to form a Communist party soon after the end of hostilities in Europe. Much of the preparatory work was done by East Europeans who had been active in the SDPC. Information provided by an informer enabled the police to raid the meeting at which the Workers' International Revolutionary Party was to be launched in January 1919. Those arrested included Custance, who was set free. Others were not so fortunate. Mr. and Mrs. A. Ewert, who had been associated with the SPC during the war, were deported to Germany.

Police action set back the formation of a Communist Party in Canada for more than two years. The absence of a functioning Communist centre on Canadian soil drove a number of fledgling Communists in eastern Canada into the divided American Communist movement. Some became members of the illegal Communist Party of America, while others formed branches of the underground United Communist Party of America.[8] They defended their eagerness to join the American Communists on the ground that the forthcoming struggle required unity in Communist ranks regardless of where the activists lived in North America.

By becoming part and parcel of the split-prone American Communist movement the Canadian Communists learned the rudiments of Bolshevism from their American comrades and American Communist publications. Most of the key Bolshevik pronouncements were printed in the States before being printed in Canada. These documents, and American Communist newspapers and periodicals, found their way into Canada where they were avidly read in radical circles.

Occasionally, envoys of the two American Communist parties would pay brief visits to Canada, bringing news, directives and – according to the authorities – small sums of money. They also tried to find Canadians who would join American delegations to the Soviet Union. In two instances they succeeded. Joe Knight and George Cascaden attended the 1921 conference at which the Bolsheviks and their allies launched the Red International of Labour Unions (RILU), better known by its Russian name of Profintern. The stories they brought back from Moscow provided ammunition for the Communists as well as for their opponents in Canadian left-wing circles. Knight, a native of the United Kingdom and a fairly prominent member of the SPC during the war, defended Soviet policies on his return. Cascaden, a journalist born in Windsor, Ontario, complained of the way the Bolsheviks had manipulated the proceedings of the conference.

In their efforts to create a Communist party in Canada, the pioneers led by Bell and Spector received little guidance and support from Russian Bolsheviks until three emissaries of the Communist International or Comintern, founded in Moscow in March 1919, reached North America with instructions and funds in 1921. The mission of their visit was to end the factionalism among American Communists.

The question of whether the Canadian Communists were to remain part of the American Communist movement, as some American Communists had hoped, had to be settled before steps could be taken to create a separate Communist party north of the border. According to Buck, the proposal to form a separate Canadian Communist party was discussed in the Canadian branches of the two rival American Communist parties in the autumn of 1920. By spring, 1921, all those who mattered approved the proposal. The Communist International supported the move because it was in line with the Comintern organizational principle of one party for each country. The American Communist leaders also agreed when W. W. Weinstone, acting on behalf of C. E. Ruthenberg, the secretary of the Communist Party of America, spoke to Buck in New York in the spring of 1921. The Canadian Communists supported the proposal at special meetings. A joint committee representing the Canadian branches of the two parties ratified the decision. At last the Canadian Communists were in a position to make preparations for a conference at which the CPC would be officially launched.[9]

Such a conference had to take place in secret, because in the immediate postwar years the federal government continued to apply the wartime legislation against those engaged in illegal activities. The Communists fell into this category because of their denunciations of the existing order, their call for a social revolution and a Workers' Republic in Canada, and their expressions of solidarity with the Bolsheviks in Russia.

Government circles shared the fairly widespread fear that strikes would lead to disorders which, if unchecked, might degenerate into a Communist takeover in Canada. Events in Russia, revolutionary outbreaks in Central Europe, and labour unrest in Britain and the United States, provided additional ammunition for those who argued that vacillation in the face of Communist agitation would be fatal. Reports received by the police and armed forces from informers operating, or claiming to operate, within fledgling Communist groups, the evidence of genuine discontent with living and working conditions in urban centres, fears about the ability of the police and the army to put down riots, and doubts about the reliability of the army after several cases of insubordination among Canadian soldiers in Canada and abroad, made the authorities and a large segment of public opinion very jittery.

Their reaction to growing tensions, which culminated in the Winnipeg General Strike in the spring of 1919, can best be understood in the light of the widely held view that the demands for collective bargaining, and the strike itself, were merely the first step in a campaign to seize power in Winnipeg and ultimately in the country as a whole. The fact that the principal strike leaders were not among the pioneers of the Communist movement, but merely sympathetic to many of the aspirations of the Soviet regime, could be and was explained away by drawing attention to the large number of East European strikers who appeared to be very pro-Soviet. It was feared that just as Lenin had displaced the liberals and moderate socialists who ran Russia immediately after the downfall of tsarism, so would these East Europeans eventually take over.

Although the Royal Commission set up to examine the events in Winnipeg failed to find evidence to support this thesis, the General Strike played a major role in the development of the Canadian Communist movement. To strengthen the hands of the authorities, the federal government rushed amendments to the Immigration Act and the Criminal Code through Parliament. The former allowed the deportation of foreign-born citizens, while the latter defined "unlawful associations" as

> any association, organization, society or corporation whose professed purpose or one of whose purposes is to bring about any governmental, industrial or economic change within Canada by use of force, violence or physical injury to person or

property, or by threats of such injury, or which teaches, advocates, advises or defends the use of force, violence, terrorism or physical injury to person or property, or threats of such injury, or for any other purpose, or which shall by any means prosecute or pursue such purpose or professed purpose, or shall so teach, advocate, advise or defend, shall be an unlawful association.[10]

The threat of deportation and Article 98 of the Criminal Code became handy tools in the struggle against Communists, making them vulnerable by both place of birth and revolutionary phraseology.

Among the government institutions most feared by the Communists was the Royal Canadian Mounted Police (RCMP) and its predecessor, the Royal North West Mounted Police. The limited size of the RCMP and its varied duties did not prevent it from following assiduously the activities of the Communist leaders and activists. Like other police forces of the world, the RCMP had a number of informers recruited from among, or infiltrated into Communist circles. Some of these secret agents rose quite high in the Communist hierarchy. One of them, Leopold, alias J. W. Esselwein, attended many Communist conferences and briefings and served as a party official in Regina in the 1920s.

Communist awareness of the interest of the RCMP in their agitation, successes and plans, increased the strains under which party members worked in the 1920s and after. The need to check the antecedents and connections of anyone joining the CPC, or holding an important position in the Communist movement, took up valuable time. The fear that what was said, done and planned might immediately be reported, that undercover police agents would try to weaken or even smash the CPC from within, and that disgruntled party members and leaders would give away or sell to the authorities whatever information they might possess, was not conducive to rational debate among Communists.

The difficulties experienced by the Communist pioneers in the immediate postwar years did not prevent them from deriving some consolation and drawing several lessons from the Winnipeg General Strike. To those who were convinced that Marx and Engels had provided a scientific explanation of history, the events in Winnipeg were an additional proof of the relevance of Marxism. Something resembling a classic Marxist confrontation of industrial labour and the bourgeoisie had, after all, taken place in a major Canadian city.

The outcome of the General Strike also affected the thinking of radical trade unionists. Between 1919 and late 1921 American and Canadian Communists were disinclined to work in the international unions, which were dominated by moderates on both sides of the border. Instead, the Communists in Canada supported the formation of Canadian unions independent of the AFL and TLC. Of these new unions the most important and controversial was the One Big Union (OBU), launched on the eve of the Winnipeg General Strike in the spring of 1919.

The OBU's opposition to craft unions aroused the wrath of moderate trade union leaders. Its failure to espouse industrial unionism, as that term was understood before 1914, precluded a firm alliance between the OBU and the remnants of the IWW. The dominant wing of the OBU called on all workers in a city, regardless of trade and qualifications, to join a single union, which in turn would federate with similar organizations in other cities and areas of Canada. This form of organization was considered superior to craft unions and more likely to protect the workers' interests. In practice, however, the structure of the OBU proved to be a major drawback, and contributed to the swift decline of the OBU after its meteoric rise in 1919.

This organizational weakness was not immediately apparent to OBU supporters. For more than two years the OBU absorbed the energies of a fair number of SPC militants eager for action. These men, although sympathetic to the Bolsheviks in Russia, preferred to work within the OBU rather than in the small, clandestine Communist groups. It took some time before they became fully aware that the OBU was unlikely to regain the influence it had wielded in western Canada in 1919. Once they realized that the OBU had no future, they looked for another outlet for their talents. By the end of 1921 Malcolm Bruce, John Kavanagh and Joseph Knight, and others like them, had found niches in the Communist movement, in which they immediately rose to the top. Like Buck and Macdonald, they were all workers, and few, with the exception of Bruce, were native Canadians.

The absence of a closely knit revolutionary party to lead the strikers to success in Winnipeg could also be used as an argument for creating such a party. It was generally accepted by the pioneers of the Communist movement in Canada that the revolutionary party they envisaged would have to subscribe to the Comintern formulas based on the experience of the successful Bolsheviks. These were enshrined in a key document known as the Twenty-One Conditions of Admission to the Communist or Third International passed by the delegates to the second Comintern Congress in Moscow in 1920.

The Conditions of Admission provided general guidelines to fledgling Communist parties and to those who wanted to create such a party where none existed. The conditions contained a number of references to the need to oppose socialist leaders, parties, programs and methods of political and trade union activity. These were to be rejected without fail. In their place the Comintern advocated a new type of political organization, far more centralized than most socialist parties before 1914. Lenin and his collaborators insisted that

> all decisions of the congresses of the Communist International as well as the decisions of their executive Committee, are binding on all parties belonging to the Communist International. . . . All propaganda and agitation must be of a genuinely Communist character and in conformity with the program and decisions of the Communist International.

Parties belonging to the Comintern "must be based on the principle of democratic centralism" for the Communist party

> will be able to fulfil its duty only if its organization is as centralized as possible, if iron discipline prevails and if the party centre, upheld by the confidence of the party membership, has strength and authority and is equipped with the most comprehensive powers.

At the same time the Communist parties were told to carry out "systematic and persistent Communist activity" in mass organizations such as trade unions and co-operatives. Cells (also referred to as fractions, nuclei, or groups in Communist publications), were established in every organization the Communists created or joined, were "completely subordinate to the party as a whole," and represent one of the chief means enabling small groups of party members to play a role far out of all proportion to their numerical strength.

The Twenty-One Conditions created another major controversy in left-wing circles in Europe and North America. Some were prepared to accept the Conditions of Admission without any reservations, while others found it difficult to subscribe to them and moved away from the Bolsheviks. In Canada the debate over the Conditions of Admission contributed a great deal to the eventual demise of the SPC, which the Communist pioneers were most eager to win over as part of their campaign to rally all the Marxist organizations existing before 1914. Among these the SPC held a place of honour: it had a fairly high proportion of Anglo-Saxons among its rank-and-file; its members had understood Marxism and the class struggle, and cared less about gradual reforms than the SDPC; last but not least, members of the SPC were prominent in the OBU, a trade union that the Communists wanted to win over.

The text of the Twenty-One Conditions reached Canada via pro-Bolshevik publications in Britain and the U.S.A. before being published on the front page of the *Western Clarion* on January 1, 1921. Readers were told in the same issue that the executive of the SPC had agreed "to place the matter of affiliation" to the Comintern "before the party membership. . . . It is desired that before the matter is decided upon the Party members should discuss the matter of affiliation and on such matters as may relate to them . . . the date of the referendum will necessarily depend upon the discussion that arises, relevant to that matter."

The Winnipeg Local No. 3 of the SPC had actually begun to discuss the question of affiliation as early as October 1920. Although those who favoured joining the Comintern lost by 7 votes to 17, the matter was not resolved. Many a page of the *Western Clarion* was devoted to this subject, as supporters and opponents of affiliation marshalled their arguments in the first half of 1921.

Those who were eager to align the SPC with the Bolsheviks found a valuable ally in Albert Wells, the editor of the *B. C. Federationist*, published by the B. C. Federation of Labor. In February 1921 he began to serialize "*Left-wing Communism*" – *an Infantile Disorder*, written by Lenin in the summer of 1920. This work was a scathing critique of those Communists in western Europe whom Lenin considered sectarians. Much of what he had to say about them could also be applied to those who were in uneasy control of the SPC, who looked askance at some of the Bolshevik proposals and moves. They showed as little eagerness to join the Comintern as they had shown towards affiliating the SPC to the Second International of socialist parties in the days before the First World War.

The inability of the SPC leaders to take a definite stand on affiliation with the Comintern reflected the ambivalent attitude towards Bolshevism of many socialists in Europe and the United States in 1917-1921. Repelled by the methods used by Lenin and Trotsky to achieve and stay in power, and sceptical of the possibility of building socialism in a backward society like Russia, they were none the less prepared to give the Bolsheviks the benefit of the doubt. In public they defended Trotsky and Lenin against critics in the

West. They also condemned the Western powers for giving aid to those elements in the former tsarist Empire who were fighting Bolsheviks on the battlefield.

The views expressed by the leaders of the SPC did not go unchallenged. Some refuted them in lengthy articles in the *Western Clarion*. Others tried to convince their locals that affiliation with the Comintern was desirable. Some of these Marxists combined membership in the SPC with belonging to one of the two underground Communist parties. They believed that by staying and agitating within the SPC they would rally the bulk of that party to the Comintern, and thus avoid the disastrous split that tore apart the Socialist Party south of the border in 1919. However, another group of SPCers felt that there was no point in staying in the decaying organization. The number of its locals was down to 14 early in 1921, its membership was declining and the circulation of the *Western Clarion* fell from 8,000 in spring 1920 to 4,500 at the beginning of 1921.[11] Disillusioned, they transferred their loyalties to the illegal Communist movement or busied themselves in what remained of the OBU.

The SPCers who wrote and spoke on behalf of the Comintern included several future leaders of the CPC (Kavanagh and Moriarty). They emphasized the worldwide significance of the October Revolution, drew attention to the struggle in which the Bolsheviks were involved, and claimed that Lenin was laying the foundations of socialism in Russia. They also criticized the SPC for its activities before, during and after the First World War. They argued that educational work and propaganda in favour of socialism was not enough. What Canada needed was "a more virile type of working-class party." Only a "disciplined organization" could "ever expect to obtain political power on behalf of the working class." The time had come when "we must fall in line with other comrades who are conscious of what is needed."[12]

The opponents of affiliation to the Comintern hoped to strengthen their status as *bona fide* socialists by insisting that they had nothing in common with those European socialists who had supported their respective governments during the Great War. They even disassociated themselves from the well-known Marxist theoretician Karl Kautsky, who had not favoured the foreign policy of Imperial Germany. These statements were coupled with references to Lenin's Marxism, tributes to the spirit of initiative displayed by the Bolsheviks in 1917, and approval of their efforts to re-organize Russian society.

They offered many reasons to justify their unwillingness to join the Comintern. In common with many Marxists in other Western societies, they claimed that the Twenty-One Conditions of Admission meant "submission to the dictates of Moscow." The tactics laid down by the Comintern were "largely Russian in character." Conditions in a country like Russia were different from those in well-developed societies like Canada and the U.S.A.[13] In Canada there was no revolutionary situation in 1921. Voting patterns in recent elections had shown that few workers were prepared to support labour, let alone socialist, candidates. Hence a great deal of educational work remained to be done. The SPC would help the Bolsheviks more by educating the workers in Canada, than by frittering away limited resources in other activities.

"Educational facilities in reaching the masses" were to some extent dependent on whether the SPC could operate as a legal organization.[14] Affiliation to the Comintern would provide the government with a pretext to ban the SPC. The police had already infiltrated underground Communist groups with disastrous results for the Bolshevik cause in North America. The SPC, too, would be subjected to police infiltration, with all the attendant problems, if the party engaged in illegal activities. (Supporters of affiliation pointed out that the authorities would ban the SPC whenever it suited them, regardless of whether the SPC belonged to the Comintern or not).

Some contributors to the *Western Clarion* complained that the Communist International had not been sufficiently selective in its search for adherents in Europe and North America. They warned that Moscow had welcomed the support of socialists who were known as "opportunists." These the SPC could not stomach, either before or after 1914. The invitation to the IWW to join the Comintern was not conducive to harmony in the new International because the Wobblies' "concept of a Communist would be totally different to ours. We should then have two Third International groups struggling systematically to remove each other's choice."

The colonial and agrarian policies of the Comintern also came under criticism.

> To support all liberation movements in the colonies, is the policy of bourgeois nationalism and not the business of revolutionary socialism. This would call for support to Quebec Nationalists. . . .

The agrarian program of the Comintern, based on the distribution of land among the peasants, was not "compatible" with conditions in "highly developed countries." There, "the socialization of the land may be accomplished simultaneously with the socialization of industry."[15]

As the months passed, the controversy within the SPC and between underground Communist publications and opponents of affiliation with the Comintern became more acrimonious. After reading some of the attacks on him, W. A. Pritchard, a prominent SPCer, wrote about the "silly yappings of some neo-revolutionists." He contrasted the "work of proletarian education" that he and other SPCers had done "openly and publicly," with the illegal activities of "sewer pipe revolutionists of the rat hole persuasion."[16]

Pritchard's outburst came in the wake of the founding convention of the CPC. This was held in a barn outside Guelph, Ontario in late May and early June of 1921.[17] As was customary at the time, a Comintern envoy supervised the proceedings. Caleb Harrison, alias Atwood, had been active in De Leon's SLP and Debs' Socialist Party before embracing Lenin's brand of Communism.

The twenty-two delegates represented Communist and pro-Communist groups in Manitoba, Montreal and Ontario, and included an undercover RCMP agent. The desire to preserve secrecy and the failure to establish close links with small Communist circles elsewhere in the Dominion prevented the participation of Communist groups from west of Winnipeg. Despite a somewhat narrow range of representation, the delegates elected the first central committee of the CPC. Several of its members (such as Custance, Macdonald, Spector) were to lead the CPC in the 1920s.*

The founding convention also adopted a program based on that of the Communist Party of America, but without the latter's references to conditions in the States and the problems facing Communists south of the border. The program reflected basic Comintern tenets such as the "inevitability of and the necessity for revolution" and "the establishment of the proletarian dictatorship based upon Soviet power." The delegates endorsed the Twenty-One Conditions of Admission to the Comintern.

A Communist party had at last been launched. The difficult task of transforming the CPC into a truly revolutionary party with mass appeal still remained to be done. It was a task that was to preoccupy them in the years to come.

---

*According to Macdonald, "Buck was not even at the Convention where the Party was founded, nor was he a member of the first Executive." *The Vanguard* (Toronto, May 1936, p. 2.).

Chapter 2

The 1920s

The history of the CPC in the 1920s is that of a relatively small number of men and women busily carrying out Comintern directives and dodging the watchful eye of the security services while trying to convert their compatriots. The Communists' problem was all the greater as the Communist International proved to be a difficult taskmaster, the RCMP a skilful enemy, and the public far more susceptible to other influences than to Communist slogans and appeals, many of which originated in Moscow.

Every Comintern tactic, from "United front from below", which involved collaboration with the socialist rank-and-file, to demand for a "Workers' and Farmers' Government", was tried out in Canada. None improved the fortunes of the CPC and they were abandoned as soon as the general "line" of the Comintern changed in 1935.

The Communist International, besides issuing general guidelines, expressed its views on specific Canadian problems through the Anglo-American Secretariat, one of the organizational subdivisions of the Comintern. It was composed largely of American and British Communists working in Moscow, who followed events in Canada, read the minutes of leading CPC bodies and reports submitted by Canadian Communists on various topics. Periodically, Comintern officials discussed the affairs and problems of the Canadian Communist movement with delegates from the CPC. On the basis of these discussions and analyses, statements and advice in the form of directives, resolutions, telegrams, "Open Letters" and articles in the Comintern press reached the CPC. Material that could not be entrusted to the mails was sometimes delivered by the special courier service of the Comintern either directly from Europe or via the Communist Party of the U.S.A. Occasionally, in the years 1924-1927, the Comintern would use the facilities of the Soviet Trade Mission in Montreal.

All in all, the Anglo-American Secretariat lacked both the expertise and time to make a significant contribution to the activities of the CPC in the 1920s. Immersed in the affairs of the American and British Communist parties, diverted by the jockeying for power within the Comintern, and increasingly forced to generalize on the basis of the experiences of the Bolshevik party, the officials of the Anglo-American Secretariat often acted as a brake on whatever attempts Canadian Communists might have made to adapt general directives to specific Canadian conditions.

The reasoning behind the Comintern decisions on the CPC was seldom explained in detail to party activists in Canada. References to Canada and the CPC in Soviet and Comintern publications were few and far between, and dealt mainly with the struggle for supremacy between British and American capitalism in Canada, the plight of this or that segment of the Canadian economy, the nefarious role of big business in the Dominion, and potted accounts of what Canadians led by the CPC were doing in whatever campaign the Comintern and the CPC were currently engaged.

Nor did the Canadian Communist leaders respond by paying much attention to what was happening inside the Comintern and the Bolshevik party. Some, like Macdonald, were not very interested in the outside world. Others were too busy running the CPC and supervising the work of Communist auxiliary organizations. Very few of them, except for Spector, combined knowledge of Russia with enough intellectual curiosity to probe beneath the surface of Comintern and Soviet politics. Their faith in the Soviet experiment, and the pressures of day-to-day party work, made them unwilling to question, let alone challenge, any decision reached by those in Moscow whom they considered far superior to themselves in wisdom, skill and experience.

The problem facing the Communist pioneers after the convention at Guelph was the need to turn the CPC into a mass party. This meant contacting those who considered themselves Communists, but who had not been represented at the founding convention. It also meant winning over those left-wingers who were highly sympathetic towards many aspects of Lenin's Russia and were in broad agreement with the objectives of the Communist International, but who had reservations about this or that Comintern tactic. Divisive questions in need of resolution remained: specifically, whether or not to participate in elections to legislative bodies, whether or not to work within the existing trade unions, which were dominated by moderates critical of Lenin, and whether or not to model the Communist party in Canada on the Bolshevik party in Russia. Only by putting an end to these controversial issues and by rallying the disparate left-wing elements around the CPC could the new party become more than a number of pro-Soviet enthusiasts scattered across the Dominion.

The available evidence indicates that the appeal of Soviet Communism and the formation of the CPC provoked varying reactions among the leaders and activists of the pre-1917 Marxist organizations. According to Buck, "practically all the members" of the tiny Socialist Party of North America went over to the Communists.[1] The few Canadian locals of the Socialist Labor Party supplied a higher percentage of converts to Communism than did American locals. The SDPC was split mainly across ethnic lines. The Finns, the Ukrainians and the other East Europeans, including their leaders, had almost all gone over to the Communist movement by 1922. Most of the SDPC leaders and many of the activists of Anglo-Saxon origin remained aloof. In the SPC the two sides were more evenly matched, although even there East Europeans were more inclined to join the Communists than were the Anglo-Saxons.

In late 1921 the ranks of the still outlawed CPC were replenished by several prominent radicals who had played an important role in the SPC . They included Joe Knight, a leader of the OBU, who had been a delegate to the founding conference of the RILU or Profintern. He attended the Third Congress of the Comintern (June-July 1921) as an observer. On his return to Canada in September 1921, he described his impressions of Russia to audiences in Ontario and the West. For a time he acted as a representative of the Red Cross Society of the Russian Soviet Republic. In this capacity he frequently visited New York.

In Manitoba Hugh Bartholomew, a native of the United Kindom and one of the greatest socialist orators in the Prairies, also joined the CPC. He was to serve the Communist movement faithfully, although he never rose in the party hierarchy as high as his undeniable talents warranted. He was never able to shake off a charge of child molesting brought against him by his comrades. In despair, he committed suicide in 1931.

On the west coast the CPC won over several well-known members of the SPC. They included William Bennett, who became B.C. organizer of the CPC; Jack Kavanagh, who had played an important role in the OBU and was to play an equally significant one in the Australian Communist movement; and A. S. Wells, who as editor of the *B.C. Federationist* was arrested in September 1921 for serializing Lenin's *"Left-wing Communism" – an Infantile Disorder*. In a statement later published in one of the first legal Communist newspapers, Kavanaugh and Wells called on members of the SPC to join in launching a new workers' party.[2]

The support of these radicals increased the CPC's chances of winning over the OBU and the SPC. Although both of them were well past their prime as far as influence, numbers and drive were concerned, they still possessed several welcome attributes in the autumn of 1921. Both organizations claimed to speak on behalf of class-conscious workers; both had defended the Bolsheviks in their publications; and both claimed support in English-speaking Canada. Their supporters were all the more desirable because of their geographical location and ethnic background. The illegal CPC was stronger in Ontario and Montreal than among Anglo-Saxons in Winnipeg and Vancouver. If the CPC could somehow absorb these two organizations, the new party would speak in the name of practically all Canadian radicals.

The chances of Communist success seemed bright. The leaders of the underground CPC knew many of the OBU and SPC spokesmen, and were well aware that the question of affiliation of the SPC to the Comintern and of the OBU to the Profintern was causing a great deal of friction within both organizations. Both Canadian organizations possessed an unknown number of activists who were receptive to Communist arguments and initiatives. If properly handled, the activists might induce many ordinary members of the OBU and the SPC to throw in their lot with the Communists.

The CPC approached the OBU first. At OBU's third convention in September 1921, Knight described his visit to Russia and urged affiliation to the Profintern to the delegates (who included M. Popovic and J. Lakeman, a future Communist leader in Alberta). As an OBU publication put it, "his address was perhaps the most interesting part of the proceedings. A considerable number of questions were asked." The OBU leaders stalled for time by suggesting that a referendum be held on the subject of affiliation. They argued that a vote could not be taken immediately, because "so much confusion existed in the minds of workers as to the real nature of the RILU that a campaign of education should be conducted before it would be possible to get an intelligent vote."[3]

The Communists concentrated on winning over the SPC as soon as they realized that they had failed to convert the majority of delegates at the OBU convention. Under the pseudonym "T. Johnson", Custance wrote in the name of the central executive committee of the CPC to all "secretaries" of the SPC, asking them to read the text of her letter at the next meeting of their locals. Since "ample time had been taken" in the debate over affiliation, she warned:

> The time for action is here. We appeal to you to demand a Party convention at once to settle this vital question. Should this demand not be complied with, we freely instruct all militants to leave the S.P. of Canada and align themselves with the International of the World Revolution, through the Communist Party of Canada.[4]

Custance's call for action and the news that the underground CPC was planning a preliminary conference to launch a legal political party, increased the pressure within the SPC for a referendum. In a statement published in the *Western Clarion* of November 16, 1921, the Dominion executive committee of the SPC announced that a vote would be taken because "the matter had been thoroughly discussed." Although the executive stated that it had "no recommendations to make to the Party membership," it was obvious that those in control of the SPC were not in favour of close links with the Comintern.

When the votes were counted, the Communists claimed on the basis of unofficial returns that a majority of SPC members had come out in favour of the Comintern. They also pointed out that SPC branches in Edmonton and Winnipeg supported affiliation.

The impact of this "victory" was lessened by the fact that in Vancouver the opponents of affiliation had gained a small majority and that the leaders of the SPC refrained from publishing the results of the referendum until March 1, 1922. A short statement in the *Western Clarion* complained that the referendum "was completely sabotaged by the secessionists who left the party at once after recording their votes . . . counting their votes the majority for affiliation stood at 18, but since several times that number left us the Party membership obviously stands opposed to affiliation."

The "secessionists" included several veterans whose departure the SPC could ill-afford, as well as an undetermined number of those who, according to the *Western Clarion*, had joined the SPC only "a few months ago in order to vote us into" the Comintern. The remnants of the SPC fought back and remained a thorn in the side of the CPC in B.C. and Winnipeg for a year or two. They knew their Marx as well as the Communists did, they were equally effective on the soap box, and their words carried some weight among those who were involved in radical politics.

As long as there was a possibility of winning over the bulk of the SPC, Communist spokesmen were circumspect in their references to that party. As late as January 1922, Jack Kavanagh and Macdonald were paying tribute to the useful pioneering work of the SPC while deploring its "sectarianism". Speaking in Vancouver, Macdonald argued that the purist's place was in the SPC and the realist's among the Communists. He countered Pritchard's charge that the Communists were "sewer hole revolutionists" with the statement: "If a man is not prepared to become a sewer pipe Communist he is no Communist at all."[5]

The task of rallying support among radicals went hand in hand with efforts to bypass existing legislation which kept the CPC underground. A new, legal party run by Communists seemed the obvious solution. The Comintern envoy in Canada, Carl Jensen (alias Scott, alias Johnson), favoured the establishment of such an organization operating side by side with the clandestine CPC. The advice he gave during his stay in Canada (1921-1923) and in conversations with Canadian Communists in Moscow could not be ignored. Others spoke in the same vein. Among them was Max Bedacht, an American Communist leader, who visited Canada after his return from the Third Congress of the Comintern.

By December 1921, the Communists had made enough progress to convene a preliminary conference in Toronto at which they laid the foundations of the Workers' Party of Canada (WPC). The fifty-odd delegates included the leaders of the clandestine CPC, those who had joined it in recent months, and spokesmen of pro-Bolshevik organizations among Anglo-Saxons and East Europeans.

The conference approved a provisional platform of five main points.[6] These included demands for a workers' republic, for political action and participation in legislative elections "to expose the sham democracy with which we are afflicted." The program also came out in support of trade unions "to carry on the class battles caused by capitalist oppression." Point four called for a "party of action," a term that included a reference to "democratic centralism" as the "guiding principle." To drive the point home, the platform insisted that "all" members "will be required to submit to the direction of the party." Point five promised the establishment of a party press under the supervision of the party leadership.

The nine-man provisional executive elected at the end of the conference included Boychuk, Buck, Custance, A. T. Hill, Macdonald, Moriarty and Peel, the editor of the *Workers' Guard*. Its main task was to make the necessary arrangements for the founding convention of the WPC. In the meantime Macdonald toured western Canada, and Buck visited a number of towns in Ontario, to locate potential party members and explain the policies and organizational structure of the WPC.

In February 1922, the WPC was formally launched at a convention in Toronto. A wider geographical range of party organizations was represented at this convention than at those held in Guelph and Toronto. This time delegates came from as far as Montreal and Vancouver. Once again representatives of Finnish and Ukrainian Marxist organizations were in attendance. The Finnish Socialist Organization and its Ukrainian equivalent became "language federations" possessing a fair degree of autonomy within the new party. Later on, a third "language federation" was formed for party members of Jewish extraction.

One of the participants at the WPC founding convention was Earl Browder, the American Communist leader, who was to have a long and close association with the Canadian Communist movement. In the years to come, the advice he and his envoys were to give would carry a great deal of weight. By 1931 Browder could boast at a meeting of the central committee of the CPC: "I feel a sort of proprietory interest in the Canadian, as well as that of the United States Party."[7]

Among the Canadians invited to the founding convention were several radicals who did not belong to the illegal Communist party. The best-known was R. B. Russell, one of the leaders of the Winnipeg General Strike and secretary of the OBU. The possibility of winning his adherence appealed to the founders of the CPC. They realized that he was better-known in Canada than any of them. They also knew that his supporters had the reputation of being radical at a time when radical sentiments were far less prevalent than in 1919. If Russell and his friends could be induced to follow in the footsteps of Kavanagh and Knight, the CPC would have rallied practically all the prominent radical trade unionists.

Russell, for his part, was prepared to explore the possibility of joining forces with the WPC; many members and ex-members of the OBU were already active or planning to take part. Like revolutionary syndicalists in other societies, he was both attracted and repelled by Soviet Russia. The system of soviets, the emphasis on the class struggle, and Lenin's hostility to moderate trade union leaders and craft unions appealed to Russell. On the other hand, he was wary of the idea of a political party leading the political and economic struggles of the working class.

An experience Russell had had with Communist pioneers in western Canada the previous year was another stumbling block. Knight had returned from Moscow in September and had informed him that the Comintern had endorsed the OBU. This welcome news must have influenced Russell's pro-affiliation stand at the OBU convention that month. Soon after, however, disturbing evidence appeared. Scott, the Comintern envoy, did not confirm what Knight had written to Russell. Instead, Scott had spoken of a possible change in the Comintern attitude towards moderate trade union organizations in western Canada. He had tried to soften the blow by adding that Moscow was still gathering information, because there was not sufficient data available in the Soviet capital. He had asked Russell to fill in a questionnaire.[8]

In December 1921 Russell had come across more signs that the OBU was unlikely to become the channel of Soviet agitation in Canada. His chances of winning Winnipeg North as the standard bearer of the SPC in the 1921 federal election had declined when Jacob Penner, a fairly prominent member of the pre-1914 SPC and SDPC and an activist in the OBU, had also contested the seat as a candidate of the pro-Communist Workers' Alliance. In that same month the preliminary conference to launch the WPC took place in Toronto. It was attended by several members of the OBU, including Matthew Popovic. While in the east, Popovic had made statements that could be and were construed as hostile to what Russell and his closest associates stood for.

Torn by competing pressures, conscious of the rapid decline of the OBU, and aware that pro-Communist elements were gaining ground in his own organization, Russell had found it difficult to decline the invitation to attend the founding convention of the WPC as a "fraternal delegate." If nothing else, he would have a chance to make a case for the OBU to an audience he could not ignore. He had some reason to believe that his views would receive careful consideration, since many of the delegates to the convention had been associated with the OBU. The members of the newly-founded branch of the WPC in Winnipeg had actually "instructed" their representatives to "support the OBU" in Toronto.

An issue raised by Russell became the highlight of the convention. The offer of the OBU executive to form an alliance with the new party, provided the WPC accepted the OBU as its trade union component, ran counter to what Lenin had written since the spring of 1921 and to what Browder had just told the delegates. Since the decision to work in the international unions had already been taken in Moscow, the nucleus of Communist faithful had only to convert those delegates who still had doubts about the advantages of this new policy.

The Communists were so successful at the convention that Russell walked out in disgust and urged others to do the same. None, apart from OBUers, followed his lead. The most he could then do was to give his version of what had happened in Toronto and fight a losing battle against the Communists for control of what was referred to as the "left wing" in Canadian labour.

At public meetings in Winnipeg and on the editorial page of the *OBU Bulletin* the Communists were accused of propping up craft unions which the workers themselves were not eager to join. The new Communist policy involved the destruction of the OBU at the very time "when the workers are at their lowest point of resistance" to employers. The Communists were dismissed as "babblers," "adolescent revolutionists" and "potential commissars." The term "sheep" was used to describe the rank-and-file of the WPC.

The Communists fought back with several arguments. At first more than one Communist spokesman hedged when challenged to state whether the WPC was opposed to the continued existence of the OBU and really wanted workers in Winnipeg to re-enter the AFL/TLC unions. Instead, the Communists complained about the failure of the *OBU Bulletin* to inform the rank-and-file about the Profintern. They pointed out the weaknesses of the OBU. They argued that rapid progress could be made in the AFL/TLC as soon as the radicals re-entered the craft unions. They insisted, in the words of Bartholomew, that the resolution passed on trade unions at the WPC convention "was an honest attempt to carry out the instructions of the Communist International." By siding with the Comintern and the Profintern the workers in Canada would fight alongside millions of people all over the world. The alternative to affiliation to Moscow-based organizations did not appeal to Russell's opponents. As one of them put it, "by holding aloof from the Red International we become a sect like the Holy Rollers."[9]

The SPC and OBU attributed their defeat by the CPC to the unscrupulous tactics of their opponents. Indeed, examples were not lacking to show that the means used to convert radicals to Communism included a fair amount of manipulation and promises of financial assistance. And yet a case can be made that the Communists won not merely because they were more unscrupulous, but because they possessed in the eyes of many radicals two advantages over the SPC and the OBU. They supported the Bolsheviks without reservation, though their knowledge of conditions in Soviet Russia was as limited as their direct links with the Comintern. Secondly, they genuinely believed that the Bolsheviks had found a solution to all the problems that in the past had previously baffled Marxists and non-Marxists. The Communist leaders were able to transmit their enthusiasm to many ex-members of the OBU and SPC. Inflamed by the radical phraseology of the OBU, but disappointed by the organization's performance, those who joined the new party expected the WPC to offer a greater challenge to the existing order than had R. B. Russell and the *Western Clarion*. No longer would humiliating defeats follow appeals to action. Little did they anticipate that the WPC and the CPC would present in the 1920s a far smaller threat to the Establishment than had those who had founded the OBU and had fought for weeks in Winnipeg.

The program of the WPC was based on that of the Workers' Party of America formed in December 1921. In both instances the program reflected current Comintern thinking: The Communists were to win over the majority of the working class, fight for a socialist society as well as for the immediate demands of the workers, and give high priority to agitation in the existing trade unions. At the same time an effort was to be made to establish a "United Front" with the socialists.

Until 1924 the Communists carried out the bulk of their public activities through the WPC, which operated side by side with a shadowy body known to initiates as the "Z" party. This underground organization consisted of a small number of trusted Communists. They met in caucus before the WPC conventions to decide on the policies to be followed by the WPC and on the leaders that the delegates were to elect. The "Z" party owed its existence to the third Condition of Admission to the Comintern, which insisted that its sections "create an illegal party organization which at the decisive moment will help the party do its duty to the revolution."

In 1924 two important changes took place in the Canadian Communist movement. First, the WPC was renamed the Communist Party of Canada. Like the Communist Party of the United States (CPUSA), it remained a section of the Comintern until 1940. Secondly, although according to Buck, "a large number of delegates to the party convention were opposed to its 'liquidation'," the "Z" party was dissolved in line with the advice of Comintern officials to the Canadian delegates at the Fourth Congress of the Communist International in 1922.

These changes took place at a time when the Canadian Communists were trying to model their party on Bolshevik precepts. This involved, among other things, a hierarchical structure based on the principle of "democratic centralism", a term explained this way in a CPC recruitment brochure:

> Leading committees are given wide powers and responsibilities, thus ensuring the maximum unity of action of the entire party and the highest degree of party discipline.[10]

At the apex of this hierarchical structure stood the political commission, or politbureau, of the central executive committee (CEC). The members of the CEC were chosen by delegates to party conventions held every year until 1926. Most of the members of the politbureau were ex-workers who lived in Ontario and were full-time officials of the CPC or of Communist-controlled organizations in Canada.

For administrative purposes the CPC was divided first into six, and later into nine geographical districts, most of which had full-time party organizers through much of the 1920s. District 1 covered Nova Scotia. District 2 was Quebec. Ontario was divided into four districts: Toronto, Northern Ontario, Sudbury and Thunder Bay. Party organizations in Manitoba and Saskatchewan formed District 7 with headquarters in Winnipeg; Alberta was District 8, and B.C. District 9. In the 1930s District 7 was split into two, and Saskatchewan became District 10.

At party headquarters in Toronto, departments or committees chaired by a member of the politbureau supervised Communist activities regarding specific concerns. Although the number, nomenclature, and efficiency of these departments varied a great deal in the twenties, by 1929 the CPC had departments covering organizational matters, agitation and propaganda, the trade unions, women, ethnic groups, youth, and farmers.

An unending stream of circulars, directives, manifestos, queries and questionnaires flowed from party headquarters. Coping with this correspondence involved a great deal of time, energy and patience. J. M. Clarke, the leading Communist expert on agriculture in the 1920s, reflected a widespread feeling when he complained:

> Words, words, words. Oceans and oceans of empty verbosity. Millions of trollop, reams of junk, hours of scatter-brained blah that in no way indicates the slightest understanding of conditions as they actually exist out in the country and out among the rank and file of the workers.[11]

The Communist leaders found it difficult to shake off their addiction to paperwork. Decades later, contributors to the party press and delegates to party conventions were still critical of unnamed party officials for spending too much time on paperwork and too little with human beings.

To improve liaison, and to check on the performance of party organizations outside Toronto, the leaders of the CPC periodically toured parts of Canada. They spoke at district and city party conventions, addressed public meetings, and attended social functions organized under Communist auspices. Some of these tours lasted several weeks and took Communist leaders to places seldom visited by Canadian politicians except at election time. The highlights of these tours were recorded in the party press, which emphasized the size and cordiality of the audiences.

At the grass roots the party organization rested on "units" which were also known as "cells" and "nuclei" in the 1920s. The units varied considerably in size. Some consisted of just a few members, others had as many as thirty. The efficacy of a unit depended as much on the cohesion and initiative of its members and secretary as on the issues they raised and the reaction of other workers where the unit operated.

The geographical distribution of party organizations shows that between one-half and two-thirds of them were in Ontario. Thunder Bay and the Sudbury region each had as many as southern Ontario. Alberta came second to Ontario, and Manitoba & Saskatchewan third. B.C. had more organized Communists than Quebec or Nova Scotia. In New Brunswick and Prince Edward Island not a single party organization functioned in the 1920s. By and large the party was spread more widely in western than in central Canada. It existed in every urban, mining and farming community where there was a fair number of East Europeans.

In addition to building and maintaining a rudimentary network of party units, the CPC followed the example of other Communist parties in launching or taking over a series of organizations which the Bolsheviks considered "transmission belts" to the masses. These organizagions were, and remained auxiliaries to the Communist party, and are often known in non-Communist circles as "front" or "satellite" organizations. The Communists, on the other hand, use the term "mass organizations," even when membership rolls do not warrant such a description.

One of the first auxiliary organizations was the Young Communist League (YCL). Originating in a few special sections begun for young members of the WPC, the Young Workers League was formed in 1922 and renamed the Young Communist League in 1924. In that same year the YCL joined the Young Communist International, the congresses of which were attended by delegates from Canada.

Pro-Communists below the age of sixteen were enrolled in the Young Pioneers: they operated under the wing of the YCL, and had their own press. Most of them were children of party members and sympathizers. The Young Pioneers soon became a source of controversy. To some schoolteachers, newspaper editors and concerned Christians, the values inculcated by the Communists into the Young Pioneers were bound to turn these youngsters into staunch atheists and poor citizens.

The Canadian Labor Defence League (CLDL) was set up in 1925 to provide legal defence for those being prosecuted by the authorities for supporting the Communist cause or causes espoused by the Communists. Before long it became known as the legal department of the CPC. As with other organizations established or taken over by the CPC, the rank and file of the CLDL and some of its spokesmen were not party members, though leadership was mostly composed of reliable Communists. To women the Communists offered the Women's Labour Leagues (WLL), whose origins went back to the days before the First World War when such leagues existed in several Canadian cities. Led by those who came out in favour of the Comintern, the WLL formed a loose federation in 1924 and began to publish the *Woman Worker*, a monthly, in 1926.

Friendship with the Soviet Union was the main plank of the Friends of the Soviet Union founded in 1929. Until then, anyone interested in improving relations with, and learning more about the USSR enrolled in the Friends of the Soviet Union south of the border. The Workers' Sports League, formed in 1928, ran a number of sports clubs for party members and sympathizers. Other "mass organizations" catered, as we shall see, for Canadians from eastern Europe, farmers and industrial workers.

In all these organizations the members of the CPC were expected to act, as a Communist recruitment brochure explained, "through party fractions, composed of all party members in a given organization. Thus, the members of the party never cancel one another's work by conflicting policies, but rather develop the fullest possible number behind the single policy."[12]

Party fractions in turn depended on a nucleus of dedicated party members. Given the small numerical size of the WPC-CPC and its dispersal across the Dominion, much effort went into discovering potential recruits, convincing them of the need to join the party, turning them into activists, and keeping them in the CPC. The turnover of party members worried the leaders a great deal. Experience had taught them the difficulty of inducing Canadians to enter and stay in the CPC.

In the twenties the Communists encountered their most serious obstacles in Quebec, where the CPC found it almost impossible to recruit French Canadians, and so the CPC there consisted only of small pockets of East Europeans and Anglo-Saxons in Montreal. Writing in the early 1950s, Buck attributed this state of affairs to Communist sectarianism and to the failure of party members to exploit Quebecois grievances.[13] Elsewhere in Canada conditions for recruitment of Anglo-Saxons were not much better. The Maritimes remained inhospitable to the CPC after the failure of the Nova Scotia miners' strike (1925), in which the Communists had played an important role. In other parts of the Dominion, English-Canadian CPC members, most of whom were British, could be counted in dozens rather than hundreds. They remained a small minority in the CPC throughout the 1920s.

The lack of interest among Anglo-Saxons and French Canadians was counterbalanced by the relative strength of the Communists in several communities where East Europeans formed a significant portion of the population. North Winnipeg, Thunder Bay, and mining towns in Northern Ontario became, and remained, centres of party activity. This resulted in what the CPC and the Comintern were the first to admit was an uneven ethnic distribution of party membership.

Finns provided over half the members in a decade when party membership "fluctuated between a high of 5,000 and a low of 2,500. Most of the time it was not much more than 3,000."[14] The number of Finns was inflated because the Finnish Organization, "a social and cultural society" under Communist control, "compelled every member automatically to take out a card in the Party or be blacklisted or expelled." As Spector pointed out, this was "a unique basis for a Communist Party."[15]

The Ukrainians were the second largest group in the CPC. Together with the Finns and Jews, they comprised between 80 and 90 per cent of the party members. In 1929 the percentage of these East Europeans rose to 95 per cent of the total party membership.[16]

This state of affairs was partly the result of Canadian immigration policies, which enabled defeated Communists to join their relatives and friends in Canada after anti-Communist victories in the Finnish Civil War (1918) and the Russo-Polish War (1920); it was also due to the ability of Canadian Communists to absorb those East Europeans in Canada before 1918 who had held left-wing views, or who were sympathetic to Bolshevik slogans before crossing the Atlantic after the First World War; and last but not least, it was due to a lack of sufficiently attractive political and social alternatives in several East European communities in Montreal, Ontario and western Canada.

Ukrainian farmers and farmhands in the Prairies, Ukrainian and Jewish workers, artisans and others in Montreal, Toronto and Winnipeg, Finnish miners and lumberjacks in isolated Ontario and B.C. communities, Ukrainian miners in Alberta, all shared a common disappointment in Canada. Their high expectations of life and riches in the New World vanished in the face of reality: the lack of attractive opportunities in Canada for many East Europeans in the 1920s, which would decrease even more in the 1930s. Unable to speak English, and without many opportunities to learn it properly, lacking either technical skills or money to help them up the social ladder, working for employers who were eager to maximize profits, many of these semi-literate East Europeans gravitated towards the CPC at one time or another. The Communist network of consumers' co-operatives and benevolent, educational and cultural associations, the ethnic press of the CPC, and the nucleus of Communist trade union activists among woodworkers, miners and needle trades workers provided a modicum of welfare, entertainment, information and companionship for people vegetating on the fringe of an Anglo-Saxon society which seemed to need them only for menial tasks and on election day.

The ethnic composition of the CPC affected the Communist movement in several ways. First and foremost, it strengthened the impression of those Anglo-Saxons who came into contact with Communists that the CPC was an alien growth on Canadian soil, a foreign outpost of a great power, an organization with little or nothing to offer in a North American setting. This belief was and is still widely held, in spite of repeated attempts to identify the CPC with Canadian interests, traditions and aspirations. To a native Canadian a Communist was someone who spoke English with an accent, used jargon incomprehensible to most Canadians, read newspapers in what seemed to be exotic languages, and who lived in parts of the town that go-ahead Canadians were only too eager to leave.

The Communists did derive several benefits from the uneven ethnic composition of the CPC. It provided a foothold in certain communities from which the Communists could and did recruit additional party members, and from whom they obtained sorely needed funds for various Communist causes. In addition, all Communists, regardless of ethnic origin, could use the facilities of the Finnish Organization and the Ukrainian Labor-Farmer Temple Association (ULFTA) for meetings, conferences and socials. During the Depression these halls provided shelter for the unemployed who agitated under the leadership of the CPC. On other occasions, Finnish and Ukrainian choirs and orchestras performed at many a

Communist gathering where the star speaker addressed the audience in English.

However welcome such assistance was to a poor and struggling party, it was an undeniable fact that party members of East European origin were often unable or unwilling to participate in those Communist activities that the Anglo-Saxon and Celtic leaders of the CPC considered essential. A Comintern document in the late 1920s drew attention to the "Ukrainians and Finns whose peculiarity is that they hold on to their previous mode of life. They lead their own social life, do not speak English and, in general, many of them submit only very slowly to assimilation."[17]

Because of their culture, the East European rank-and-file participated in few Communist activities outside their respective ethnic community. A Communist leader of East European extraction noted, "The Finnish comrades consider themselves inferior to the working class. They say: 'We are foreigners; how can we take the leadership' . . . ."[18] In turn, the Communist ethnic press devoted more attention to events in Europe than to the struggles of the working class in Canada. Some foreign-born party members were so parochial that in 1931 a Communist official complained about "Russian members" in Montreal who "believe they live in the Soviet Union and not Canada." A number of these East Europeans actually asked party headquarters for permission to return to Russia. Requests were rarely granted, because the Soviet Union did not favour the return of unskilled and semi-skilled workers, while the party leadership in Toronto was unwilling to let members and sympathizers emigrate at a time when CPC membership was small and growing slowly.

Notwithstanding the parochial attitude of many party members of East European extraction, the leaders of the Finnish and Ukrainian language federations in the CPC were in a strong bargaining position. They could influence the execution of Comintern plans by either co-operating or dragging their feet. Their unwillingness to jeopardize the property of the Finnish Organization and the ULFTA by granting the use of halls for just any purpose approved by the party leadership, led to complaints that the leaders of the Ukrainian Communists, in particular, were less interested in the class struggle than in encouraging cultural activities in the Ukrainian community. ULFTA's reputed emphasis on mandolin orchestras provided ammunition for Communists collecting evidence of the misdirected efforts of their Ukrainian colleagues.

The question of whether a Celt or a Ukrainian should stand as the Communist candidate in the municipal elections in Winnipeg did not contribute to harmony in that local party organization.

Another, even more divisive issue was the ethnic block voting at CPC and WPC conventions. The delegates of the language federations met in special caucuses, before the party convention, to decide who would represent them on the central executive committee. This was a serious departure from the organizational principles on which a Communist party was supposed to be based.

In line with the "bolshevization" program of the Comintern after Lenin's death, in 1925 steps were taken to reorganize the CPC, and the "language federations" were abolished. No longer could Canadians of Finnish, Jewish or Ukrainian extraction become members of the WPC-CPC by joining a "language federation"; they too would have to join a factory or street unit.

As a result of these organizational changes, party members belonging to different ethnic groups suddenly found themselves in the same unit, and were often unable to speak to one another because they did not know enough English. A number of Finns and Ukrainians who were unable or unwilling to accept the new form of organization left the CPC. Moreover, the leaders of the Finnish and Ukrainian Communists were distinctly unenthusiastic in helping to reorganize the CPC. They realized the loss of their power base, and did not believe that bringing together Communists of such different backgrounds would improve the CPC.

To hasten the integration of Finns, Jews and Ukrainians within the Communist movement, special national agitprop committees for each ethnic group were established under the jurisdiction of the central executive committee of the CPC. Ethnic block voting was still in evidence in the elections to the CEC at the fifth party convention in June 1927, but in 1929 this practice ceased as part of the important changes that transformed the CPC into a Leninist-type of party.

Although the CPC succeeded in involving its East European supporters in the wider context of Canadian politics during the Depression, there were still many *de facto* ethnic units, silent reminders of the difficulties encountered by the CPC when it proceeded on the road to reorganization after Lenin's death. As a result, reorganization proceeded by fits and starts although lip service was paid to "bolshevization" and other Comintern directives. The same may be said about Communist attempts to influence farmers and organized labour.

Immersed in their daily work in industrial and mining centres, the leaders of the CPC paid little attention to what the Comintern described as the "agrarian question". During the 1920s the CPC lacked a detailed agrarian program, an omission which the Comintern was quick to note when its officials took a close look at its Canadian section in 1929.

The federal election manifestos of the CPC had little to say about the farming community in 1925 and 1926. In fact, the only major party document on the subject was a short resolution on the agrarian question passed at the second convention of the WPC in February 1923. It mentioned the extreme poverty of the mass of the farmers, criticized those who claimed to speak on behalf of the farmers, and called for the "wielding together of the various farmers' organizations into one militant nation-wide organization fighting at all times." The WPC promised to support the farmers in their struggle against "organized capital" and emphasized the need to rally the "poor and tenant farmers" on the side of the "workers in the cities."[19]

The absence of major doctrinal statements on agriculture and the farming community did not indicate a complete lack of interest in farmers, who provided the CPC with between 10 to 15 per cent of its membership during much of the interwar period. To spread the Communist viewpoint in the countryside the CPC relied at first on its own rural branches, of which, according to a Comintern publication, there were "quite a number" on the Prairies. Most members of these branches were Ukrainian farmers and farmhands. However, the ULFTA provided the outlet for most of these Ukrainians' political and social activities. In 1929 the ULFTA consisted of 185 rural and urban branches with 5,438 members.[20] It also published newspapers in Ukrainian which, like *Vapaus* in Finnish, came out more frequently and had a higher circulation than *The Worker*, the main organ of the CPC.

ULFTA's greatest success was in the Albertan countryside. A number of Ukrainians there had become acquainted with radical ideas before they had settled on the land. Some were already inclined to socialism before arriving in the New World; others were converted on railway construction sites and in mining camps where many of them had had to seek employment upon arrival in Canada. Cases of discrimination, harsh working and living conditions made them receptive to socialist slogans and ideas spread by fellow-Ukrainian or Anglo-Saxon radicals, alongside whom these future farmers had worked.

Finally, the CPC tried another method of reaching the farmer. The Progressive Farmers' Educational League (PFEL) was founded in Alberta in 1925 with the grandiose objective of

> directing the thoughts and energies of all existing labour organizations to the basic evils of the present system in order to unite their forces in a co-operative effort with the objective of establishing a co-operative system of production, distribution and exchange.[21]

In practice, however, the PFEL aimed at more modest goals. Its tiny membership, and the Comintern emphasis on the need to permeate rather than replace existing farm organizations, reduced the PFEL to the role of a pressure group in Alberta and Saskatchewan. In 1927 the group changed its name to the Canadian Farmers' Educational League.

The PFEL provided a forum for the Communist viewpoint in a *milieu* that could not be ignored for three reasons: Lenin and the Comintern had insisted that Communist parties should gain the support of peasants; in Canada only about half of the population lived in urban centres in the 1920s; on the Prairies various critics of the status quo were active and had a following of sorts. If a sizeable number of farmers could be induced to transfer their allegiances to the CPC, the party would gain a valuable foothold. Not that the Communist pioneers had any illusions of mass conversions. One of them, who farmed in Alberta, warned the readers of *The Worker* about the farmers' "deep-seated prejudices."[22]

The leaders of the PFEL were of Anglo-Saxon or Scandinavian descent; few were natives of Canada, and fewer still had much formal education. Many of the activists had been associated with pre-1918 socialist and labour organizations or had belonged to trade unions before settling on the land. What they lacked in numbers, they made up in zeal. To begin with, Carl Axelson in Alberta and Walter E. Wiggins in Saskatchewan went on speaking tours. They encouraged their listeners and hosts to buy and subscribe to *The Furrow*, the organ of the PFEL. None of these attempts to influence farmers seem to have been very successful, judging by the account John Glambeck, the secretary of the PFEL in Alberta, gave the readers of *The Worker*. Glambeck expressed his amazement that in "nine out of ten places where I have stopped over, they have said grace before meals and went to church on Sunday."[23] Nor do the irregular appearance and the financial difficulties of *The Furrow* indicate much grassroot support. Time and again its editor complained about lack of funds, so that the paper had to rely on subsidies provided in one form or another by the CPC.

The handful of party members among farmers did not confine their activities to the PFEL, just as party activists in industry and mining did not agitate only in the Trade Union Educational League. Communist farmers were also busy in the United Farmers of Alberta (UFA), United Farmers of Manitoba (UFM) and the Saskatchewan Section of the United Farmers of Canada.

At meetings of the locals of these organizations, they would try to get their resolutions passed, and to elect party members as delegates to the annual conventions of the United Farmers. To co-ordinate party work, the Communists elected as delegates would hold caucus meetings on the eve of the conventions (at which they were regular speakers).

Like many a prairie farmer, the Communists were highly critical of manufacturers of agricultural implements, and of mortgage and grain elevator companies. They sympathized with those reformers who argued that only co-operation could nullify some of the worst aspects of capitalism. Hence the Communists and the PFEL supported the existence of co-operative wheat pools and joined other farmers in calling for the establishment of a 100-per cent-membership wheat pool. The officials of the Peasant International (Krestintern) in Moscow opposed this proposal because they considered the wheat pools to be instruments of finance capital on the prairies.[24] The Krestintern view prevailed in Canada after the general line of the Communist International hardened at the turn of the decade.

By operating as part of an amorphous "left wing" critical of farm leaders who were not considered sufficiently militant in the struggle against urban eastern interests, the Communists made progress in Saskatchewan. In February 1928, two Communists were elected to the executive of the UFC (SS). The following year the delegates elected as president a man who had been associated for a time with the PFEL. Although George H. Williams had broken with the PFEL before his election to power, some of his non-Communist colleagues were so upset that they resigned in protest. The fears they expressed about a possible Communist takeover of the UFC (SS) were premature, to say the least. Before long, the Communists and the socialists led by Williams found it difficult to co-operate, and J. M. Clarke was left to lament that "numerically" the PFEL was

> comparatively weak and largely confined to Saskatchewan . . . The Left wing . . . has a number of sincere, active members willing to do the best they know how. The vast bulk of its members have studied but little and to them social theory is a closed book. . . . Practically all have but little experience in convention strategy.[25]

The limited response of the farmers to Communist overtures can be partly attributed to the lack of interest that the CPC as a whole displayed in the problems and aspirations of the agricultural community. Lack of interest, however, cannot explain the poor response the Communists often met when they wooed manual workers in the 1920s. This is surprising, because the CPC was worker-oriented, campaigned on a program of immediate demands, and might be expected to strike a sympathetic cord among politically-conscious workers.

The CPC championed the amalgamation of craft unions, the unionization of unskilled workers, the right to peaceful picketing, the organization of workers through industrial as opposed to craft unions, the introduction of social legislation of benefit to the labouring classes, and a ban on the use of troops in industrial disputes. In addition, the Communists supported those who fought against wage reductions and speed-up schemes designed to increase productivity, and opposed attempts to dismiss workers or curtail the power of trade unions.

Such a program appealed to the minority of workers who were badly dissatisfied and prepared to take militant action. The most obvious Communist successes were in industries which had a tradition of working class militancy, and which employed a high percentage of workers from eastern Europe. As in several other countries in the West, Canadian miners were fairly receptive to Communist slogans and appeals, including the demand for "nationalization of the mines, without compensation, and with workers' control." Miners in Alberta and Nova Scotia would come out with statements favouring some of the policies that the Communists advocated at home or abroad. The lumber workers and the needle trades workers displayed similar sympathies on a smaller scale. In other branches of the economy little progress was made, in spite of Communist attempts to spread their influence, or their occasional boasts in the party press and at party conventions. Buck's statement that the railwaymen were organized in fifty-six party units in 1923 did not indicate a major Communist breakthrough among transport workers.[26]

To promote Communist agitation in the unions the CPC followed the example of the American Communists, who in 1921 took over the Trade Union Educational League (TUEL) founded by W. Z. Foster in November 1920. Earl Browder had urged the extension of this organization to Canada when he addressed the founding convention of the WPC. Soon afterwards Canada became one of the four districts of the American TUEL, and sent delegates to TUEL conventions in the States. In the 1920s Buck, who knew Foster from the war years, was both industrial director of the CCP and secretary of the TUEL for Canada.[27] For organizational purposes the Dominion was divided into an Eastern and a Western section. From 1924 to 1926 the TUEL published a monthly in Toronto. Like several other organizations set up by the Canadian Communists, the TUEL received financial assistance from abroad.

The TUEL took care not follow the road that the OBU had pioneered without visible success. In 1923 it described itself as "purely an educational body" engaged in permeating the existing trade unions with the spirit of industrial unionism and the class struggle. What was known in trade union circles as "boring from within" was carried out in line with Comintern and Profintern directives to American and Canadian Communists between 1921 and 1928.

Notwithstanding the reference to the purely educational objectives of the TUEL, party members in the TLC unions agitated in line with the instructions they received from their superiors, or read in *The Worker*. In elections to union posts they stood as leftist candidates or threw their weight behind candidates considered sympathetic to their cause. They introduced motions on a variety of topics. The texts of the resolutions were often prepared by the industrial department of the CPC, or at least discussed by those in charge of Communist trade union work at the provincial, district or city level. A concentrated effort was made to get as many union locals as possible to pass the same or similar resolutions. These would be forwarded to city and district labour councils, and provincial federations of labour, in the hope that ultimately they would reach the conventions of international unions or the TLC.

By operating as a fairly compact group with a record of working class militancy, and by acting as the mouthpiece of those who, according to Buck, were critical of the "passive and reformist trade union bureaucracy," the Communists succeeded, on certain issues, in rallying the support of a fair number of delegates at the annual conventions of the TLC. Kavanagh and Buck profited from these "left-wing" sentiments as well as from Communist organizational skills when they stood for the presidency of the TLC against the incumbent, Tom Moore.

Number of Votes Cast

1923	40 Kavanagh	136 Moore
1924	44 Buck	156 Moore
1925	29 Buck	169 Moore

Prompted, no doubt, by the declining percentage of delegates eager to side with the Communists, no party member was put up for the presidency of the TLC in 1926 or 1927. Even so, the non-Communists worried about the Communists. It did not take them long to find party members obnoxious. As early as August 1922 a TLC resolution drew attention to Communist tactics in the unions. The union official responsible for the motion used the occasion to announce, "If they want their ideas, they may have them, but they must keep them out of the Congress."[28] The leaders of several international unions issued similar warnings. As these did not always have the desired effect, the moderates took other measures to prevent Communists from rallying support when they stood for election or re-election to union posts. Those who succeeded in getting elected were often not allowed to take their seats on District Trades and Labour Councils. At the annual convention of the TLC in September 1928, Macdonald's credentials as a delegate were challenged by a vote of 223 to 21. Other Communists, including Buck, were expelled from their unions on charges of "dual unionism" and of opposing the policies of the TLC.

The concerted effort to reduce Communist influence in the trade unions was most obvious in Ontario in 1927-1928. The anti-Communist campaign was so effective that in 1928 a Comintern publication lamented "the almost complete liquidation of any consolidated Left-wing representation" within the TLC, and "the continued weakening of the Communist Party strength therein."[29]

To a large extent TLC measures against the militants succeeded because in late 1926 the Communists again reversed their stand on that thorny issue of Canadian-versus-international-unionism. In 1919-1920 many pioneers of the Canadian Communist movement were so critical of the AFL/TLC that they had supported the formation of independent Canadian unions. When the Comintern "line" changed in 1921, they dutifully obeyed the Moscow directive. Then they tried hard to gain a foothold in the international unions, whose leaders they criticized for lack of fighting spirit and failure to organize the large number of workers still outside of trade unions. This criticism went hand in hand with calls for labour unity in North America, as well as warnings to those radicals in unions who, despairing of the policies of international unions, wanted to break away and form independent unions. Only in rare cases did the CPC encourage the formation of a separate Canadian union, as in the case of the coal miners.

Through much of the 1920s the slogan of "opening the doors of the Trades and Labor Congress to all unions"[30] provided an answer to those who wanted to know how the Communists envisaged the unification of various trade union centres in Canada. This slogan was coupled with demands for the loosening of ties between the TLC and the AFL headquarters in Washington. The Communists used the term "autonomy", rather than "independence", when they advocated the formation of a sovereign trade union centre in Canada. Such a policy received some backing from the Profintern, which stated in 1924 that "the inevitable sharpening of the struggle in the near future renders a great deal of autonomy for the trade union movement essential."[31]

Buck expressed similar views in American and Canadian Communist publications without, however, giving high priority to the struggle for autonomy. He realized only too well that autonomy would depend on a series of developments in the Canadian trade union movement. Too great an emphasis on autonomy would merely complicate the already difficult task the Communists faced in the unions. To avoid misunderstanding, he was careful to point out, "Canadian autonomy does not mean the secession of Canadian locals from the 'Internationals', neither does it mean weakening International bonds in any way."[32]

The Communists gained a great deal by hedging on this controversial issue. Pronouncements in favour of autonomy appealed to those unionists who were critical of the subordination of the TLC to the AFL. By refusing to support secession from the international unions the party protected itself against those union officials who were looking for more evidence of Communist "disruption".

This tightrope act by the CPC was also due to its desire to keep in step with the Comintern in Moscow, where the trade union policy of the CPC was discussed at length when Buck and Popovic attended the seventh plenary session of the executive of the Communist International in December 1926. Buck argued in favour of an independent Canadian trade union movement as part of the Communist struggle for an independent Canada.[33] It took him some time to convert Comintern officials like the East Indian M.N. Roy, J. T. Murphy of the Communist Party of Great Britain and several American Communists. Among the latter was Browder, who was "one of the most stubborn and serious opponents" of the Canadian proposal.

Buck did not report in great detail what the American actually said. He mentioned, however, Browder's remark about the inconsistency displayed by the CPC in giving different advice to miners fighting American trade-union bosses in Alberta and Nova Scotia. Browder's grudging support of the new trade union "line" of the CPC was coupled with the warning that "we must strengthen our position within" the TLC. The leaders of the CPC knew as well as Browder did that this was an almost impossible task. For several years the Communists had been losing ground in the world of labour. The CPC convention to which Buck reported on the discussions in Moscow heard him admit that "our trade union work has slackened . . . has tended to reflect the passivity of the general trade union movement."

Browder's insistence that the "slogan of Canadian independence would be valuable only if we would use it as a slogan within the Trades and Labor Congress and combine it with a consistent struggle against splits," can be explained in three ways. First, his own experiences as a Wobbly and as a TUEL leader had convinced him of the disastrous consequences of break-away unionism. Hence any attempt to bypass or even downgrade the role of Communists in the AFL/TLC unions was to be condemned. Second, throughout the years between the two world wars the American Communist leaders were perplexed and annoyed by manifestations of what they considered to be "nationalism" in the Canadian Communist movement. Buck's proposal could only impose additional strains on the TUEL, reduce the close links between the two Communist parties, and limit the ability of the larger CPUSA to influence the CPC. Third, it can be argued, Browder was a typical Comintern official whose rise to eminence was partly due to his knack for hedging when giving advice. By calling for work within the TLC, which consisted largely of affiliates to the AFL, *and* agreeing with the need for an independent trade union movement in Canada, which the AFL was bound to oppose, Browder recorded his views in a manner that made it difficult for anyone to charge him with either "sectarianism" or "social imperialism". He knew that the Canadian Communists would have to apply the new policy and that they would be the first to get the blame if something went wrong.

A favourable decision in Moscow in the wake of the failure to make progress in the international unions, led to a change in Communist policy in the trade union field. Instead of basing their main hopes on the TLC, throughout most of 1927-1928, the Communists advocated the amalgamation of the TLC with the All-Canadian Congress of Labour (ACCL), formed in March 1927 by several Canadian unions which were at loggerheads with the AFL and the TLC.

The ACCL was a heterogeneous body numerically inferior to the TLC. Its executive included men who were sympathetic to some of the Communist objectives in industry and who had fought alongside party members in the Alberta miners' strike of 1925. On the other hand, the ACCL included a bitter opponent of the CPC: the OBU. Given the weak Communist base in the unions, the CPC found it as difficult to make progress in the ACCL as it had in the TLC. Common opposition to the leadership of the international unions, a joint desire to organize unorganized workers, and united demands for an independent Canadian trade union centre, were not a strong enough combination with which to challenge the TLC successfully. In 1928 the Communists were already criticizing the leaders of the ACCL. The language and arguments used were reminiscent of what had been said and written about TLC officials a few years before.

At the end of the 1920s the Communists were very much in retreat in the unions. They found it impossible to hold out against employers who discriminated against them in various ways. The most effective forms of victimization used by employers were the dismissal of Communist militants and the "black lists" which employers drew up and sometimes exchanged with one another. These lists made it difficult for well-known activists to obtain employment in the larger factories and mines. Nor were employers the only opponents of the Communists. The authorities, the churches and the press were definitely hostile to Communist agitators, while the number of allies the CPC could find in the world of labour was limited.

Few TLC leaders had much sympathy for the Communists. What remained of the OBU "assailed" the Communists, according to Buck, "even more bitterly than" those in charge of the international unions. The OBU spokesmen could never forget that the launching of the WPC, and Comintern insistence on working within the AFL/TLC unions had cut the ground out from under OBU's feet – the very organization that had been launched as a protest against the established trade union bureaucracy. The Communist failure to make major inroads among OBU militants after 1922 considerably reduced the Communist base among the already small number of workers in Nova Scotia, the Prairies and B.C. who were hostile to the craft unions, and who saw the need for an independent Canadian trade union movement.

The remnants of the IWW in the lumber industry were also critical of Communist attempts to organize workers. No love was lost between Wobblies and the CPC, whose organ claimed that "trying to educate the IWW or their dupes, is as useless as vaccinating a policeman, they are too stupid to catch anything anyway."[34]

Even those working-class radicals who co-operated with the Communists on the picket line often turned against party members, either because they thought it expedient to do so or because they were disgusted by Communist tactics. What Communist leaders defended as "Bolshevik flexibility" in industrial disputes looked less edifying to those who had different ideas on how to fight employers, or who disapproved of sudden changes in the

Communist attitude to this or that union official or organization or group of workers. Few, for instance, would have agreed with the man in charge of Communist agitation during the 1929 strike in a steel railway car plant in Hamilton whose actions are described here by a member of the politbureau:

> [He] did not care about the hayter boys, and all the other men around the car. He thought that if we had the riveters, their skilled ability is indispensible to the boss, and he will have to capitulate. This led him to lay down the law to comrade Shelley and others, "never mind giving relief to this fellow who does not amount to much, but see to it that the other fellow gets lots."[35]

The dilemmas faced by the small Communist cadres in industrial disputes also stemmed from the difficulty of applying the party line on the factory floor or in the picket line. Directives and advice from the Comintern and CPC headquarters were supposed to take care of most eventualities and to avoid two cardinal mistakes that the Communists could make in the unions. The first of these would be to isolate themselves from the bulk of the workers by pursuing policies that were termed "sectarian". To cope with this danger, Buck warned against the "tendency to drop into the old position of negative opposition to officialdom and everybody else who is not a revolutionist or a good left-winger."[36]

The other mistake would be to follow the lead of non-Communist radicals or of moderate union officials who were more popular than the Communists among the workers. Under a policy of "tailism" the Communists would abandon the initiative to others. Non-Communists would receive the publicity and the credit if they succeeded in wresting concessions from the employers.

To prevent party members from throwing in their lot with their rivals at a time and place decided upon by non-Communists, Buck cautioned against

> lining up with centrists, twisters, fakirs and all who pay lip service to revolutionary ideals and progressive trade unionism. This is the greatest danger of all and can only be guarded against by making it impossible for any man to align himself with you without declaring definitely for a program at least as advanced as that of the TUEL.[37]

Those who heeded Buck's advice were often unable to act effectively in a rapidly changing situation on the eve, or in the course of, a strike. The result was confusion among party members on the factory floor, because they did not know whom they should support, nor to what extent. Being perplexed, their confidence in the judgement of their leaders declined. Sometimes frantic attempts would be made to reinterpret the party line to fit the emergency. As a result, the party line fluctuated considerably, while many non-Communists were confirmed in their opinion that the Communists were at best "inconsistent", and at worst "opportunists".

When post-mortems were held, the leaders had to assume part of the blame for the repeated Communist defeats in labour disputes. Not that they had much choice after an envoy of the CPUSA wrote in 1929 that "in connection with strikes the Party was always at the tail end . . . it is isolated from whole industrial areas." Occasionally, *The Worker* recorded the extent of this isolation. In Oshawa the Communists did not even know that a strike had begun because they were rehearsing a play. In the border cities, party members of East European extraction would not even join the Communist-led Auto Workers Union before Anglo-Saxon workers had done so.[38]

Confusion within the Communist ranks, and external opposition to the CPC, did not improve the party's chances of making converts to Communism in factories and mines. The workers on whose behalf party members fought, and suffered loss of employment, social ostracism and occasionally imprisonment, were seldom able to hold out for long when confrontations initiated or exploited by Communists took place. The Comintern was not far wrong when it attributed the loss of Communist influence among miners in Alberta, B.C. and Nova Scotia to the "exhaustion of the workers."[39] Unsuccessful strikes considerably weakened the Mine Workers Union of Canada in which the Communists played an important role. Nor were the Communists in a better position in the late 1920s in the two remaining centres of Communist strength: the lumberworkers and one section of the needle trades workers.

An official Profintern publication recorded the declining appeal of Communism in the unions. Only the 3,000-strong Lumber Workers Industrial Union was affiliated to the Profintern in Moscow, while an additional 10,000 organized workers belonged in 1927 to the "revolutionary minority", a term used to describe those segments of the trade union movement in which the Communists were influential.[40]

Electoral results confirmed the limited appeal of the CPC. Conscious of its weakness, the WPC-CPC rarely put up candidates under its own name in federal or provincial elections in the twenties.

Even so, members of the WPC sat for a short time in the legislatures of Alberta, Manitoba and Nova Scotia. In all three instances, they had been elected as "Labour" candidates before they joined the WPC.

The failure to contest federal and provincial elections does not mean that the CPC ignored these periods of increased political activity. On the contrary, elections provided the opportunity for Communists to recruit new party members and carry their message to as large a segment of the Canadian electorate as their limited manpower and financial resources allowed.

Public meetings, leaflets and editorials in the Communist press were used to put forward demands, some of which were in line with Canadian radical tradition, while others made it fairly obvious that the CPC was not merely another leftwing party on Canadian soil. In the federal elections of 1926, for instance, the CPC manifesto insisted that

> only the abolition of the entire capitalist system and the socialization of the means of production and distribution under a workers' and farmers' government will bring permanent relief and a full measure of life and opportunity and freedom to the masses.[41]

Like the socialists in Canada and abroad prior to 1914, the CPC put forward a number of "immediate" or "minimum" demands. These include a forty-hour work week, non-contributory unemployment insurance and a minimum wage. Furthermore, the Communists advocated major structural changes in the Canadian economy. Banks, mines and the CPR were to be nationalized without compensation and put under workers' control. Land, on the other hand, was not included among the means of production to be taken over by the state. There was to be a capital levy imposed on all holdings over $5,000 in order to "wipe out the war debt."

In the political sphere, the Communists called for the repeal of Article 98 of the Criminal Code and the abolition of the Senate and of election deposits. Links with British imperialism were to be severed, the British North America Act repealed, Canadian independence proclaimed, a "Workers' and Farmers' Government" installed, and "full recognition of and credits to the Soviet Union" granted.

The CPC realized that its own forces were far too weak to acquaint the Canadian public with these demands, let alone to carry them out. Allies had to be found. Since the French-Canadian nationalists were not eager to associate themselves with the Communists, and since the CPC considered the Liberal and Conservative parties to be "agents of vested interests," whatever their "temporary differences," the Communists were forced to seek collaborators outside the mainstream of Canadian politics. The only available ones were some trade union leaders and socialists of various hues. The latter were the more attractive, because they shared some of the Communist phraseology and basic assumptions about North American society and the superiority of socialism over free enterprise.

A similiar attitude towards certain issues was more important than differences in temperament or over tactics. Such similarity also helped the CPC to enlist the help of socialists and trade unionists in specific campaigns (for example "Hands off China", and "Save Sacco and Vanzetti" – two anarchists sentenced to death in the United States). The Communists made persistent attempts to create a broad labour party where, in addition to the CPC, there would be room – temporarily at least – for a variety of socialists and radicals. This policy was in line with Lenin's advice to British Communists to join the Labour Party. As Macdonald put it, "We cannot formulate policies from the outside, we must get inside if we are to carry weight."[42]

The instrument chosen by the CPC for this purpose was the Canadian Labour Party (CLP), formally organized by socialists and trade unionists in Winnipeg in 1921. Its program included demands for proportional representation, the abolition of the BNA Act, the nationalization of public utilities, and social legislation to improve the lot of the workers.

The WPC joined this loosely organized body as a separate entity, and urged other organizations, political or otherwise, to do the same. Delegates of the CPC attended the CLP's national and provincial conventions, sought and obtained office in the CLP, stood as CLP candidates in federal and provincial elections, and did their best to win over their non-Communist partners to the policies advocated by the Comintern and the CPC.

Communist efforts in and on behalf of the CLP yielded meagre results. A number of resolutions dealing with Canadian and international problems were passed as a result of Communist initiatives and votes. In several cases motions critical of the U.S.S.R. were rejected or amended because of Communist opposition. A good case can be made that Communist involvement in the CLP enabled the CPC to recruit or gain the sympathy of a section of the non-Communist left.

On the other hand, the CLP failed to fulfil several Communist objectives. It attracted little trade union support; locals representing a mere 9,000 members were affiliated to the Ontario CLP in 1926.[43] Under these circumstances, there was little point in turning the CLP into a Farmer-Labour Party, as the Comintern had suggested in 1924. The fourth convention of the CPC in September 1925 justified the abandonment of this project by arguing that "the partial liquidation of the agrarian crisis, together with the rapid disintegration of the national Progressive Party, makes the slogan of the Communist Party for a Farmer-Labour Party no longer practicable."[44]

Electorally, the performance of the CLP was disappointing. Most of its candidates lost their deposits in the federal elections of 1925 and 1926. According to Spector, the CLP "did not fare very well" in 1925 because "the tariff demagogy of the Conservatives is a siren song that still captivates the workers."[45] These electoral defeats were all the more galling as two future leaders of the Co-operative Commonwealth Federation (CCF), J. S. Woodsworth and William Irvine, were elected after rejecting Communist calls for a "United front".

Internal friction contributed to the uninspiring performance of the CLP. In November 1925, the Quebec wing of the CLP passed by a small majority, a motion prohibiting the affiliation of Communist organizations which were then active in that party. The Communists were disturbed by this move, and took immediate counter-measures. They condemned the attitude of the Quebec section of the CLP, and used their influence in the CLP in other parts of Canada to pass resolutions calling on the Quebec CLP to reverse its stand. Pro-Communist elements also raised the matter at the September 1926 provincial convention of the Quebec CLP, but failed to win a majority.[46]

The strength of anti-Communist feeling among socialists in Quebec was less dangerous to the Communists than the emergence of a strong anti-Communist faction in the larger Ontario CLP. Two hundred and eighteen delegates, including fifty representatives of Communist organizations, attended the Ontario provincial convention in April 1926. A motion put to the convention by the Brotherhood of Railway Car-men of America argued that the "best interests of the affiliated membership will be served by excluding the Communist Party from affiliation" to the CLP, because at conventions "the major part of the time has been taken up with useless discussion and controversy between the Communist and non-Communist delegates on matters not of vital interest to the vast majority of the affiliated membership."[47]

Although the motion was defeated, the vote showed that a substantial minority of non-Communists was no longer in favour of co-operation with the Communists. Fifty-seven votes were cast in favour of the motion, 42 abstained, and 116, including the delegates of 35 branches of the CPC, voted against, after Macdonald had argued that a federated labour party could not exclude a working-class organization.

This showdown led to a Communist reappraisal of their activities in the CLP. As in the case of Communist involvement in other non-Communist organizations, the party leaders were perturbed because a number of party members did not preserve the identity of the CPC in the CLP. Work without credit and benefit to the CPC never appealed to leading Communists. Their solution was a statement favouring the building of "the Labour party as a mass movement based on the trade unions and under the leadership of the Communist Party."[48]

Such frank declarations of intent increased tensions within the CLP. They provided ammunition for those socialists who declined to join the CLP because of the Communists. They also gave food for thought to those who had serious doubts about the advisability of the CLP following the line it had operated on since its foundation. These socialists began to follow the precedent, set by the Communists, of holding caucus meetings on the eve of CLP conventions. Their leader was James Simpson, a prominent socialist and trade unionist, who came under increasing attack in *The Worker*.

By the autumn of 1927 the lines were clearly drawn, as each side tried to limit the radius of action of its opponents. Simpson won the first round when the Toronto District Labor Council passed a motion to expel delegates who represented organizations not affiliated to the TLC. The Communists retaliated by removing Simpson's name from the slate of CLP candidates in the municipal elections in Toronto. The impact of this Communist victory within the CLP was small, because by then Simpson had had enough of both the CPC and the CLP. After accepting a key post in the Independent Labour Party of Ontario, he resigned his position as secretary-treasurer of the Dominion CLP.[49]

His departure was followed by that of other socialists who had also come to the conclusion that the CPC was not a trustworthy and worthwhile ally. The CLP lingered on, passing resolutions that the Communists sponsored. By the end of 1928 the CLP was a hollow shell, a memorial to the difficulties experienced by socialists and Communists when trying to co-operate in the political sphere. Distrust was succeeded by recriminations and then, as the Comintern veered sharply to the left in 1928, by bitter hostility during most of the Depression.

Chapter 3

"Class against Class"

In 1928 the Comintern reached several crucial decisions which affected the fortunes of all its sections, including the one in Canada. At meetings held in Moscow, leading Comintern spokesmen explained that the period of stability in the capitalist world was coming to an end and that the working class was entering another stage of revolutionary struggle similar to that of 1917-1920. Since in the coming "third period", the socialist parties would act as the "last reserve" of the old order, it was the duty of Communists to unmask the role being played in the labour movement by the socialist leaders, including left-wingers, and to win over the socialist rank-and-file. According to the Comintern, the slogan "class against class" now characterized the struggle throughout the world.

The emphasis on the struggle against the socialists stemmed to some extent from Joseph Stalin's desire to meet the criticism of those Soviet Communists who complained about the Soviet leader's lack of revolutionary zeal. It was also due to the realization that the socialists were unwilling to subordinate their policies to whatever tactic the Comintern thought was best for workers in industrial societies. Competition for the same audience in the name of a socialist society widened the gulf separating the socialists from the Communists, and led Communist speakers to denounce their rivals as "social fascists" during much of the Depression.

In Canada the full impact of the new Comintern tactics was not felt until the Sixth Congress of the Communist International (July-August 1928), at which delegates from abroad became only too aware of the differences of opinion among Bolshevik leaders like Stalin and Bukharin, two men who had previously joined forces against Trotsky. From his exile in Central Asia Leon Trotsky sent, in the summer of 1928, a lengthy memorandum criticizing the policies followed by his rivals at home and abroad. A copy of this document reached Spector, who led the CPC delegation at the Sixth Congress.

Spector was deeply impressed by what he had read; it confirmed his pro-Trotsky sentiments, which in any case went back to the early days of the struggle between Stalin and Trotsky. It was partly under Spector's influence that the CPC had declined to condemn Trotsky when it became fashionable to do so in the U.S.S.R.[1] The delay in attacking Trotsky was criticized by the Comintern, and also by Buck, whose position on this subject, however, was only shared by a minority of his colleagues in 1925. Buck's views on Trotsky did finally prevail when the Comintern applied pressure on the CPC.

At the Sixth Congress Spector "absented himself during the consideration and voting on the question of Trotskyism."[2] Instead, he exchanged views with J. P. Cannon, a prominent American Communist who was also critical of Stalin's role in the Soviet Union and the Comintern. Soon after his return to the U.S., Cannon was expelled from the CPUSA, and his apartment was rifled. Among the documents found by his former colleagues were letters from Spector, showing conslusively where his loyalties lay.

As was customary in the Communist International, Spector was invited to endorse the expulsion of Cannon and renounce his own pro-Trotsky views. He refused and was expelled from the party whose chairman he had been for several years. He also lost his seat on the executive committee of the Communist International to which he had been elected at the Sixth Congress. Spector then took a prominent part in building the North American branch of the Trotskyist movement which emerged in a number of countries. Canada was no exception. A Trotskyist organization was established here in the early 1930s, and several well-known pioneers of the Canadian Communist movement became members of it.

The Trotskyists were prone to factionalism, and were always numerically weaker than the Stalinists. In spite of denunciations in Stalinist newspapers and attacks by Stalinist goon squads in several Canadian cities, the Trotskyists drew attention to Stalin's treatment of his opponents, to the evolution of the Soviet system, and to the shifts in the CPC line. By calling for more revolutionary policies than the CPC followed in the 1930s and afterwards, and by operating as a closely-knit pressure group within the Co-operative Commonwealth Federation (CCF), the Trotskyists acted as a thorn in the flesh of the CPC in Montreal, Toronto and Vancouver. The fears of the CPC whenever there was a possibility that the Trotskyists might extend their power base in the CCF, or make many converts among workers and students, were not entirely misplaced. In spite of a high turnover in their ranks, the nucleus of Trotskyist militants possessed sufficient enthusiasm and organizational ability to cause many a headache in Stalinist and CCF circles. Even so, few Canadian radicals would have gone as far as Buck, who in the heyday of Stalinism denounced "the cynical Trotskyite adventurers" as the "most dangerous enemies of the common people of Canada."[3]

Spector's expulsion allowed another rift in the CPC to surface. Its origins go back to the days before the Sixth Congress of the Comintern, when according to Spector, "discontent was beginning to manifest itself among the younger elements with the organizational conservatism and political inertia of John Macdonald."[4] Macdonald's position in the party weakened when it became known that Comintern officials in Moscow had criticized several aspects of Communist activity in Canada. Some of the criticism Macdonald brought back from the Soviet Union was incorporated into the "draft theses" published in *The Worker* on December 22 and 29, 1928. These theses provided the basis for a major intra-party discussion as the CPC prepared for its sixth convention.

As a former trade union official who had co-operated with non-Communists in the CLP and elsewhere, Macdonald had doubts about the new Comintern "class against class" tactic. Nor was he alone. Finns and Ukrainians prominent in the councils of the CPC shared these reservations to a greater or lesser extent. Although they were careful not to oppose the new tactic in public, their lack of enthusiasm in carrying out the decisions of the Sixth Congress of the Comintern was quickly noted by Communist zealots.

The opening shots in the campaign against Macdonald were fired by Tim Buck and Stewart Smith. The latter had just returned from Moscow where he had been the first Canadian student at the Lenin School, the most prestigious Comintern educational establishment. Although still only in his mid-twenties, Smith was given a seat in the politbureau where he soon made his presence felt.

Buck and those who rallied to his side employed two methods for propagating their views. First, they spoke out at closed party meetings at which delegates to the sixth party convention were elected. Second, they wrote at length in *The Worker*, which published many contributions on the state of the Communist movement in the early months of 1929.

The criticisms of Macdonald's policies, past and present, ranged far and wide. Little seems to have escaped the attention of what became known as the "Buck-Smith faction". They complained about Macdonald's approach to organizational matters, especially the existing system of electing members to the central committee. They insisted that such members be elected from the convention floor, and that the Finnish, Jewish and Ukrainian party members no longer be allowed to select their representatives in caucuses. They drew attention to the limited numerical size of the party and the passivity of many of its members. They noted the failure of Communist policies in the trade unions and queried the need to preserve the CLP at a time when some of its non-Communist leaders were expelling Communists from the trade unions. They objected to the absence of an "agrarian program" and to the lack of interest displayed by the CPC in French Canadians.

Much of their criticism was justified, and was partly based on information which had appeared in party documents under Macdonald's signature. However, on some issues the differences of opinion were so slight that before long, each side was accusing the other of engaging in personalities instead of debating policies.

Two other issues were raised in the debate. One was the theory of "American exceptionalism" associated with Jay Lovestone, the leader of the dominant faction in the CPUSA in 1928. He argued that the strength of the American economy would enable the U.S. to avoid the kind of business slump that periodically struck other countries. Macdonald, who had no pretensions as a theoretician, nor even any interest in Marxist theory, had on occasion referred to the continued expansion of the Canadian economy. This could be interpreted as an indication that Macdonald and Lovestone held similar views. Since "American exceptionalism" clashed with the Bolshevik doctrine that economic crises were bound to occur in every capitalist economy, including the North American economies, Lovestone and Macdonald opened themselves to the charge of "revisionism", a major deviation from Marxism-Leninism as interpreted by Stalin and the Comintern officials.

Although Buck levelled the charge of "American exceptionalism" against Macdonald, more ink was spilt in the controversy over the slogan of "Canadian independence". According to Buck, this slogan was Spector's brainchild. In the 1920s Spector, then chairman of CPC, had described Canada as a British colony, and the Canadian bourgeoisie as a "suppressed colonial bourgeoisie which must be pushed forward to more aggressive action against British imperialism."[5] Under these circumstances, he is supposed to have argued that the Canadian working class, with the CPC as its vanguard, should temporarily support the Canadian bourgeoisie to throw off the shackles of British rule. At the same time the Canadian Communists attributed to Mackenzie King a "semi Chiang Kai-shek cum Mustapha Kemal role,"[6] because the Canadian Prime Minister, like the nationalist leaders in China and Turkey, opposed Britain's imperial pretensions.

Spector's views were hardly original. They were an attempt to apply in Canada the kind of policies urged by the Comintern on weak Communist parties in underdeveloped countries like China, Egypt and India in the mid-1920s. Although Buck claimed, after Spector's expulsion from the CPC, that he had misgivings about the "tailism" of the CPC, little overt opposition was expressed until 1927 when the Comintern changed its attitude towards the bourgeoisie in Asia after the Nationalist Communist alliance had broken down in China.

Spector and Macdonald became aware of the shift in Comintern policy during their stay in Moscow. In a conversation with officials of the Anglo-American Secretariat, the Canadians learned that the consensus was against dropping the Canadian Independence slogan "completely". It was felt that the slogan had its uses in the struggle against British imperialism, because it would help break "the hold of British jingoistic propaganda upon the Canadian masses," make it easier to rally the poor farmers, and aid the party in its agitation among French Canadians.[7]

Spector and Macdonald brought back to Canada the draft of a thesis which "clarified the stand considerably and corrected a certain vagueness and deviation that had characterized the propaganda for independence," and revealed a change in Communist thought on the subject:

> "With the accentuation of the antagonism of British and American Imperialism, this antagonism within the Canadian bourgeoisie will also be accentuated. The war of British and American Imperialism will bring the antagonisms within the Canadian bourgeoisie to a crisis."[8]

Neither the Liberals nor the Conservatives would be able to solve the "fundamental antagonisms". The Canadian bourgeoisie would be forced to take sides. A "revolutionary situation, and probably civil war" would follow. "The task of the proletariat is to take advantage of the contradictions within the Canadian bourgeoisie and between British and American imperialism to overthrow the bourgeoisie of Canada."

Through most of 1929 Communist spokesmen and newspapers harped on what Buck described as "the increasing inevitability of an Anglo-American war for world supremacy." To buttress this thesis, the agitprop department of the CPC produced a study entitled *Some facts on the menace of war between British and American Imperialism.*

By the time the sixth convention of the CPC met in June 1929, the "antagonisms within the Canadian bourgeoisie" were less obvious than the differences of opinion among the CPC leaders. The rift in the CPC reached such proportions that both sides held caucus meetings between formal sessions, and traded accusations when their spokesmen addressed the convention. Buck and Smith's staunchest allies were the delegates from B.C., a province known for its penchant towards radicalism, and a group of young Communists who were or had been officials in the YCL. The eagerness of young Communists to challenge the authority of their elders in the party was not confined to Canada in 1928-1929. In Britain and France, too, prominent members of the YCL were in the forefront of the struggle to adopt new and more radical policies for promoting the Communist cause. On both sides of the Atlantic the young Communists felt that these new policies would require new faces at the helm of the party, because the current leaders were incapable of shedding their "social democratic background."

The task of the young Communists in Canada was not easy, because they faced a formidable array of opponents at the beginning of the convention, including most of the prominent Communist trade unionists. The same could not be said about some of Buck's supporters, who were told that "they have not had any contact with the workers."[9] In addition, Macdonald had the backing of the Finnish and Ukrainian Communist leaders.

What Macdonald did lack was the kind of support without which no Communist leader could survive in the days of the Comintern. Envoys of the CPUSA and the YCL of the United States played an important role at the convention and threw their weight behind Buck. The more discerning delegates knew that the Americans were more attuned to Comintern thinking than the secretary-general of the CPC. Any doubts they might have had disappeared when they learned the contents of several messages that the Comintern, Profintern and Young Communist International had sent to the CPC and the YCL in recent months. These communications were "received very pessimistically by a large segment" of the delegates and contributed enormously to the strength of the group led by Buck and Smith.

Realizing this, Macdonald and his closest associates tried to limit the damage caused by the missives from Moscow by downgrading the importance of the messages from the Comintern. Mike

Buhay, who was under attack as a "rightist", found the messages "confusing", while Macdonald stated that the "CI Letter was not a very impressive document . . . the best elements of the CI have not had a hand in it." Moriarty, who had attended the fifth plenary session of the executive committee of the Comintern in the spring of 1925, added mysteriously that he knew "something of how letters are drawn up at the centre." He claimed that Buck and Leslie Morris had supplied the information on which these communications were based.[10]

These statements shocked the young zealots, and confirmed their suspicions of Macdonald as an inveterate "rightist", as a man prepared to question the very authority of the Comintern. Nevertheless, Macdonald could not be expelled without reducing the CPC to the status of a tiny sect isolated – at least temporarily – from those ethnic and labour organizations controlled by his collaborators. He, on the other hand, was not prepared to break publicly with Buck and the Comintern. At the convention he admitted that his critics had a point when they criticized this or that aspect of his leadership. He promised to do better in the future, and he co-operated with the two American envoys and his rivals in drafting a series of resolutions.

In the end an uneasy compromise was reached. The resolutions passed by the delegates reflected the current Communist line as interpreted by Buck and Smith. The elections to the highest party bodies confirmed that Macdonald's star was on the wane. Buck had a slight majority in the new politbureau. Macdonald's supporters controlled the enlarged central committee, while he himself was given the opportunity of staying on as secretary of the CPC.

On July 12, 1929, at the first meeting of the central committee Macdonald instead asked for a one year leave of absence. Before the end of that year, he was already *persona non grata* in the CPC. In May 1930 he complained about "a campaign of lies and slander" against him.[11] Expelled from the CPC in the autumn of 1930, he soon joined forces with Spector in the nascent Canadian Trotskyist movement. This was a precedent that other ex-Communist leaders (such as Max Armstrong, Malcolm Bruce) were to follow when they fell out with Buck.

Macdonald was succeeded by Buck. In a way this was an orthodox choice, prompted no doubt by the fact that during the party crisis in 1929 the telegrams sent by the Comintern to the CPC were addressed to him rather than to Macdonald. Those who chose him elected an ex-worker at a time when the Comintern was setting a premium on leaders with a working-class background. Their man had been active in the Canadian labour movement before the Bolshevik takeover in Russia. According to his own and his friends' written testimony, he had been associated at one time or another with the IWW, the SPC, the SDPC, the Socialist Party of North America, and James Simpson's *Industrial Banner*, before he had found his niche in the Communist movement. He took a prominent part in founding the CPC after his return from the States in 1919. In 1921 he became secretary of the Canadian branch of the TUEL. In the 1920s he was high in the party hierarchy, and was well-known in non-Communist labour circles through his activities in the TUEL.

After a rather shaky start as secretary-general, Buck began to display many of the attributes that would enable him to remain at the helm of the CPC until January 1962. He had great drive, knew how to listen, displayed increasing polish in his dealings with non-Communists, and succeeded in welding the leaders of the CPC into a compact group which, until 1956, displayed few public signs of discord. Potential rivals like Stewart Smith were kept on a short leash, and given tasks that were unlikely to provide them with either a power base or enough financial resources to challenge Buck successfully.

To his followers and to the public at large Buck appeared as a dedicated Communist. A fluent speaker, he was the star attraction at many a meeting organized by the CPC. He also became the author of a series of books, brochures and pamphlets on a variety of topics of interest to party members and sympathizers. As time passed, he became so identified with the Communist cause in Canada that Leslie Morris, one of his closest collaborators, wrote a short account of the CPC under the un-Marxian title of *The Story of Tim Buck's Party* (1939). With the help of the agitprop department of the CPC a Buck "cult" emerged in prose and verse. In 1945 a well-known member of the central committee mused,

> Comrade Buck, if he had pursued the arts, had the qualities which would have made him a great surgeon; he could have become a very clever lawyer; in science he would have been one of those, who have travelled the stoney road to the atomic bomb.[12]

Eight years later, Morris' wife wrote a poem, "Tim Buck's Hands" which appeared in the *Canadian Tribune*. It included this verse:

> Your hands took dreams of labouring men
> and forged them into weapons when
> they gave these dreams a consciousness
> of mission. Fanning spark to flame,

> they burned into the dream an aim
> of socialism now.

Buck's ability to retain the confidence of the Soviet officials who supervised the relations of the CPSU with Communist parties in North America was an important factor in the success of his stewardship. His periodic visits to the U.S.S.R., where he attended meetings and briefings sponsored by the Comintern and its auxiliary organizations, made him familiar with the way Comintern officials reasoned and operated from the 1930s onwards. The granting of the Order of the October Revolution on the occasion of his eightieth birthday was recognition of the gratitude felt for

> the tremendous work done by comrade Buck to foster and cultivate feelings of friendship for the peoples of the Soviet Union among the working class and broad sections of the working people in Canada.[13]

Buck's immediate problem in 1929 was to heal the split created by his decision to challenge Macdonald late in 1928. His first moves as secretary-general exasperated even further those who had opposed him in the first half of 1929. By December 1929 the Communists in the Finnish Organization were in open revolt, while those in the ULFTA overwhelmingly rejected the directives of the politbureau of the CPC in February 1930. To stamp out the opposition, Buck used methods disapproved of by the Comintern, because they reduced the already narrow popular base of the CPC. According to a Comintern publication, the struggle in the CPC was rendered more complex by the fact that "members of the politbureau, which on the whole carried out the correct line, allowed a series of mistakes on individual questions," such as the "mechanical expulsion" of Finnish and Ukrainian Communists "without preparatory explicatory work" among party members.[14]

Those who were expelled from the CPC, or merely suspended from the offices they held, included Anglo-Saxon and Celtic veterans of the Communist movement (for example, Moriarty, Peel, R. Shoesmith), well-known Finnish Communists (Ahlquist and A. Vaara), and several prominent Jewish Communists (Mike Buhay, J. Margolese and J. B. Salsberg, Secretary of the Industrial Union of Needle Trades Workers). The Comintern intervened to force Buck to re-admit a number of them after his stay in Moscow at the beginning of 1930. A commission from the Comintern came to Canada to deal with the matter. Some of the Canadian Communists were only too eager to return and resume their places in the movement they considered their own. As one of them put it, "the thought that I am expelled from the Party has paralysed me to such an extent that I don't know where I am at, and what I am doing."[15]

Factionalism in the mass organizations had barely been overcome when a new controversy over "Canadian independence cast doubts over the ability of Buck and Stewart Smith to assess the situation properly and to determine the party line on important issues. Unlike the dispute with the Finns and the Ukrainians, the discussion on Canada's role in the world "was limited to a comparatively narrow circle." Unfortunately for Buck and Smith, the narrow circle included those Communists who now counted in the Canadian party, had the ear of Comintern officials, and operated from the vantage-point of the Lenin School. Leslie Morris, John Weir, Sam Carr and several other young activists had been sent there to improve their qualifications after they had supported Buck in the struggle against Macdonald.

They were aware that the letter sent by the Comintern to the sixth party convention had indicated displeasure with the stand taken by the CPC on the subject of Canadian independence. The Comintern characterized the slogan as "false", described Canada as a "developing imperialist country" and insisted that the "main struggle . . . should be the struggle against being dragged by the Canadian bourgeoisie, or any section of it, into either of the imperialist camps in the coming war."

At the convention Buck elaborated the Comintern thesis.

It is quite easy to see how civil war is not merely a possibility, but a very earnest possibility in the event of Anglo-Saxon antagonisms sharpening to the point of declaration of war."[16]

The students at the Lenin School were dissatisfied with the way the CPC dealt with the problem. Although Buck's and Smith's formulations represented an improvement on what had been said in previous years, the students were disturbed by the fact that the party leadership concentrated on Canada as a battlefront fought over by imperialist powers. Nor did they agree with the references to the divisions within the Canadian bourgeoisie as it searched for allies in Washington and London. Instead, they argued, Canada was an imperialist power in its own right and the Canadian bourgeoisie was the chief enemy of Canadian workers.

The students in Moscow sent Smith a twenty-four page statement which angered party leaders at home. The leaders accused the students of basing their statements on "many mis-facts" and of engaging in "fractionalism". Labelled as an "oppositional program", the statement "was not actually circulated in the Party . . . very few of our comrades actually studied it."[17]

The attempt to dismiss the missive from the Lenin School failed because the students reflected the views of Comintern officials. Additional messages from the Comintern reached the CPC headquarters in Toronto. Canadians passing through or studying in Moscow were told what was required: Canada was an "imperialist country" because the "Canadian political economy contains all the characteristics enumerated by Lenin in his characterization of Imperialism, with the single exception of the possession of colonies."[18]

This lack of colonies was not considered important in view of the "vast underdeveloped area" in the Dominion. More significant were the high degree of concentration of industry in Canada and the rapidly growing export of Canadian capital.

By the autumn of 1930 the leaders of the CPC had adopted the viewpoint of their critics and Stewart Smith had confessed his errors in *The Worker*. The slogan of "Canadian independence" was condemned and the Canadian capitalist class branded as the main enemy of the workers in the Dominion. The new party line on "Canadian imperialism" was not accepted overnight. Some Communists pointed out that Canada had no armed forces worth speaking of, let alone colonies, while a well-known American Communist asked Buck at a convention of the CPUSA, "What the hell is this romanticism of Canada being an imperialist country?"[19] Since it was not desired that the latest party directive be "merely" accepted "mechanically", articles were written and evidence gathered to show that Canada was indeed "imperialist". Little seems to have escaped the notice of zealots eager to build up a good case They even discovered an "arm of Canadian imperialism" in the capital of Bolivia: a Canadian-owned company that operated "the light, power and tramways" at La Paz.

Although the difference of opinion about the attitude of the Canadian bourgeoisie towards the independence of Canada was temporarily settled, the solution never satisfied many Canadian Communists. The argument cropped up again in the early stages of the Second World War and in the succeeding decades. Not that the issue can be dismissed as an example of the scholastic hairsplitting to which Communists are occasionally prone. After all, the party's attitude to the majority of Canadians, who supported neither the Communists nor the democratic socialists, depended on the Communists' assessment of the Canadian bourgeoisie and its willingness to fight against foreign encroachment.

The delay in coming to grips with the issue of Canadian independence was not the only criticism levied against Buck and his closest collaborators. The Comintern, Profintern and Peasant International in Moscow had other grounds for complaint as they urged, prodded and attacked this or that CPC policy in the years 1929-1931. Never in its history was the CPC subjected to so much advice and criticism as during those years. Although by the beginning of 1931 the Comintern was taking a more favourable view of the CPC, the discussions and resolutions at the February 1931 plenum of the central committee of the CPC still found shortcomings in the performance of Macdonald's successors. There were complaints that the forces at the disposal of the CPC were "too limited"; that the "sectarian" and "isolated" Communist movement had "no contact with the workers in the shops"; that the "weight of our members' activity is still centred" on the organizations catering for the East Europeans; and that an unhealthy attitude, often amounting to "complete indifference", was responsible for the party's failure to win over "the young workers."[20]

Buck did not deny the validity of these and other charges. He and his colleagues promised to do better in the future, while drawing attention to the difficulties the CPC experienced in its everyday work. The members of the central committee were well aware of the state of the CPC and of the decline in party membership since 1928.

This decline had an adverse effect on party finances at the very time when the demand for organizers and propaganda was increasing tremendously. A senior CPC official attributed "the serious fall in revenue" to four factors. "Increased police intimidation" headed the list, because the "penalizing of hall-owners" made it "impossible, particularly in Toronto, to initiate social events for the raising" of funds. Second, "the inner party struggle" with the Finnish Communists caused "a great reduction in revenue." So did the "increasing demands upon the Party trade union work and mass activity."[21] Finally, there was the "unemployment of many of our members," which was as high as 50 per cent of the total membership in February 1931.[22]

The party centre in Toronto responded to demands for funds with advice and explanations. Party committees were told to make a bigger effort locally instead of waiting for money to be sent from headquarters, which was chronically short of cash. One-third of total party revenues went "out in wages for the administration for the center and Agitprop" in Toronto. A plenum of the central committee had to be postponed because a few hundred dollars were not available for travel expenses. Activists were urged to travel as inexpensively as possible. Many obeyed, but Tom Cacic, the Communist organizer among Yugoslav Canadians, "did not see why he had to ride a freight" if "certain comrades", including the member of the politbureau responsible for trade union work, "could 'ride the cushions'. . . . We tried to explain to comrade Cassic [Cacic] many reasons why this is so, but obviously it had no effect as he stayed in Toronto."[23]

Nor was Cacic the only one who refused to attend party and trade union conferences unless his fare was paid in advance. Others, such as the lawyers who defended Communists in court, kept on insisting that they be paid the sums they had been promised. To tide the CPC over, Buck obtained loans from sources he did not specify. At one stage one-third of the party's income came from loans but, as Buck lamented in February 1931, "getting loans today is a very hard proposition."[24]

The campaign to raise money took place amidst numerous indications that the CPC had lost a sizable section of its membership in 1929-1930. Those who sympathized with Macdonald, or did not like Buck's handling of the Finns and Ukrainians, left or were expelled. Others were too poor or demoralized by the Depression to pay their dues, with the result that dues-paying members declined from 2,876 in 1929 to 1,385 in 1931. This did not prevent the CPC from reporting a membership of 4,000 to the Comintern in 1931.[25] According to Sam Carr, organizational secretary of the CPC, Stewart Smith dismissed the data Carr provided with the statement, "To hell with your figures, I will give in mine."[26]

The party continued to recruit chiefly among workers, many of whom were unemployed. In Alberta miners and unskilled labourers comprised almost 80 per cent of those who joined during the recruitment drive in the summer of 1930. In Manitoba and Saskatchewan the proportion of workers was also very high. Few of these recruits were trade unionists. In B.C. barely 14 per cent were.[27]

The percentage of Anglo-Saxons in the CPC rose very slowly after 1929. The 840 new members recruited in 1930 "were almost entirely immigrant workers . . . only a small number were retained."[28] As a result, the plenum of the central committee in February 1931 was told, "only a minor percentage" of party members "are native born." In the months that followed, the percentage of East Europeans began to fall slightly. Among those recruited in B.C. in the summer of 1930, 49 were English-speaking and 56 from eastern Europe. In Manitoba and Saskatchewan the ratio was 33 to 144. In Alberta 95 per cent were foreign speaking. In Montreal two-thirds of the party members were "foreign-speaking" and "only an insignificant percentage" spoke English.

The underground *Communist Review* admitted that even in the second half of 1934, "foreign born workers are still the bulk of the membership."[29]

The continued appeal of the CPC among immigrants owed a great deal to diligent Communist work among ethnic groups in the 1920s. The Depression contributed to the radicalization of East Europeans who had fewer savings and less well-developed technical skills than Canadians of Anglo-Saxon extraction. Most of the latter had two other advantages over the East Europeans: they knew where and how to apply for relief, and they often had a better chance of receiving at least some assistance than newcomers from eastern Europe. The lack of interest displayed by many Anglo-Saxons in the Communist recruitment drives in 1930-1931 lent support to the view of Ukrainian party members that "Anglo-Saxon workers . . . are very reactionary." As a result, the CPC leaders had to fight the idea that Ukrainians should "organize Ukrainians and it is up to the English comrades to organize the English."[30]

The geographical distribution of party membership remained very uneven. Nearly all 90 members of the party organization in Quebec lived in Montreal. In that province the CPC had fewer members than in Manitoba and Saskatchewan combined (116), and only half as many as in B.C. (197). Ontario continued to supply the largest contingent of organized Communists in Canada. They were concentrated in Toronto, Thunder Bay and some of the mining towns in northern Ontario. Windsor and Hamilton had a sprinkling of party members, the majority of whom were immigrants from eastern Europe.

The February 1931 plenum of the central committee also devoted some attention to the Communist attitude towards socialists. It re-affirmed the stand taken by the CPC in 1929 in response to the Comintern claim that the socialists were the "last reserve" of capitalism. In that year the Communists ceased to campaign in favour of the CLP. Instead, they held their ex-partners responsible for the disintegration of the CLP. It was the socialists who had either expelled the Communists from the CLP or refused them the right to affiliate. Buck justified the stand taken by the CPC by arguing that a mass federated party could not be built "under revolutionary leadership" in 1929. If such a party had developed on the basis of the trade union movement, it would have been the "third party" of the bourgeoisie. Instead, he urged his colleagues to concentrate on strengthening the CPC around which the workers were bound to rally.

The new party line was accompanied by Communist attacks on

their ex-partners. Woodsworth and A. A. Heaps, the leaders of the Independent Labour Party in Manitoba, were subjected to the same treatment before the start of the Depression. Even in the midst of their dispute in 1929, Buck and Macdonald agreed in their assessment of Woodsworth, a former contributor to *The Worker*. To Macdonald, Woodsworth was "the hocus pocus of the bourgeois pacifist who plays the most damning role in the ranks of the workers today." To Buck, Woodsworth was "the most dangerous enemy we have at the present time. The eyes of our party membership must be focused upon the menace of social reformists."[31]

In view of their hostility to Woodsworth, it is not surprising the Communists tried to prevent his re-election in the 1930 federal election. While neither the Prime Minister, Mackenzie King, nor the Leader of the Opposition, R. B. Bennett, faced Communist candidates in their ridings, Woodsworth did. Nor was this a token opposition intended only to draw attention to the differences between Communism and social democracy. A top Communist urged in 1930 that the "entire" party force and finances in Manitoba be concentrated in fighting the election in Winnipeg, the "centre of parliamentary reformism."[32]

The Communist press in English and other languages reflected the party's dislike of Woodsworth and his colleagues. They were accused of paying too little or no attention to the unorganized workers and the fate of the unemployed. If they fought in and out of the House of Commons on behalf of the jobless, as Woodsworth did, their efforts were dismissed as a sham, or as an insidious attempt to divide the ranks of those already fighting under the leadership of the CPC. Communist newspapers often attacked Woodsworth and Heaps as "fakers", "labor misleaders" and "social fascists". In private correspondence the Communists were even less gracious. They referred to the two Labour MPs from Winnipeg as "bastards".[33]

In the trade unions too the party line shifted considerably after the return of the CPC delegation from the sixth congress of the Comintern. Macdonald and Spector had been told in Moscow that too great an emphasis had been placed on the slogan of amalgamating the TLC and ACCL. Instead, the Communists were to concentrate on unity from below and to turn the TUEL into an organization that would take the initiative in organizing the unorganized workers.

The decision to cease co-operation with the leaders of the ACCL enabled the party press to attack them almost as regularly as the TLC. The former were accused of engaging in verbal Canadianism, of ignoring the unorganized and unemployed workers, and of merely paying lip service to the idea of industrial unionism. The TLC and ACCL leaders were denounced as "traitors", "labour fakirs" and "misleaders", while the "workers in reformist unions" were regarded as "strike breakers".

These attacks went hand in hand with calls for militant action to defend the interests of the working class, improve its lot and rouse "proletarian class consciousness." Communist agitators did not shrink from using violent language and physical force to put their views across. Under the influence of this kind of behaviour some of their audience would get excited, act recklessly and harm the very cause the Communists had espoused.* Not that such errors of judgement appreciably dampened the ardour of many young activists. They continued to initiate strikes and advise strikers, though the party leadership was disturbed by the number of spontaneous strikes of which the local Communist organizations knew nothing and had not prepared the ground for a successful strike.

The launching of a strike in industry followed a relatively simple procedure. To begin with, contact with potential strikers had to be established. Newspapers and leaflets would be handed out at the factory gate, and workers would be invited to meetings held under Communist auspices. Those workers who appeared sympathetic, but who were unwilling to come out into the open, would be visited at home, where attempts would be made to convert them to the Communist viewpoint. Once a nucleus of sympathizers had been formed, the Communists would try to establish either a union branch or a rank-and-file committee to represent the workers.

The next step would be to exploit grievances, of which there was no shortage in the early 1930s. The hours of work were long, fear of wage cuts widespread, the threatening introduction of speed-up schemes ever present, while genuine trade unionism was seldom in evidence. Once the fear of a lockout or of mass dismissals had been overcome among the pace-setters on the factory floor, a strike became a workable proposition.

After the workers had been induced to abandon work, the Communists did their best to bring the strike to a successful conclusion. The strikers' demands would be publicized, and expressions of solidarity would pour in. The latter would take the form of telegrams and goodwill messages from pro-Communist organizations.

---

*The riot at Esteven, Saskatchewan on September 29, 1931, is a tragic example of how inflammable the situation sometimes became. A group of cornered RCMP officers killed three miners of East European extraction.

Food and small sums of money would be collected to help the strikers hold out. Everything would be done to avoid the feeling of helplessness and isolation which, according to Buck, was "one of the most demoralizing factors in our movement" in the early 1920s.

At the same time attempts would be made to spread the strike to other firms in the same industry, and party members would offer their services on the picket line to prevent anyone from crossing it. Heightened tension brought to the fore men whom the Communists described as "organizers", and their opponents called "agitators". Although few in number they were highly mobile, as police forces across Canada discovered more than once. They operated in small groups, mounted soap boxes, gave advice in private, and provided a modicum of organizational skill. Their experience in trade union organization and industrial strife was all the more welcome as these talents were not widely available. Their willingness to speak out, their tales of past achievements in other labour disputes, and their promises of aid around the corner, had, in the short run at least, a reassuring effect on those who had walked off their jobs and were beginning to wonder whether the decision to strike had been wise. In the final analysis, one can readily accept the organizers' claim that their role was often crucial. Employers, police officials and moderate trade union leaders would have been the first to admit that the presence of Communist organizers often meant the difference between a successful and an unsuccessful strike, or at least between a short and a long drawn out one.

As the Communists gained more experience, and as the Depression lengthened, their role in industrial disputes increased in importance. In 1931 they claimed responsibility for a number of strikes in small factories, in 1933 they claimed the leadership in 75 per cent of all strikes.[34] These claims, if authentic, confirm the growth of Communist influence among factory workers and miners, as well as the growing readiness of Canadian workers to go on strike.

Number of working days lost in strikes and lockouts:

1929	152,080
1930	91,797
1931	204,238
1932	255,000
1933	317,547
1934	574,519
1935	288,703

Much of the credit for this state of affairs can be attributed to the Comintern emphasis on party cells in mines and factories. Few directives were so hard to carry out in North America, and yet so useful in the long run to the Communists. The formation of factory cells, and the painful experience gained in keeping them in existence, stood the Communist militants in good stead when the trade unions began to expand rapidly in the mid-1930s. The "over one hundred shop and mine nuclei" in 1934 represented a major achievement that was all the more remarkable as the CPC had only had a few such nuclei in 1928 and none in early 1929.[35]

Strike action was one important aspect of Communist activity. Another was the unionization drive in industries where the bulk of the workers were not yet organized, or where the existing trade union hierarchy was unsympathetic to the Communists. The result was another upsurge of dual unionism in Canadian labour history. In the late 1920s and early 1930s the Communists made a determined effort to set up unions in those industries in which they were and remain keenly interested (automobile, rubber, steel, textiles, transportation).

The usual procedure was to establish a union whenever seventy-five or a hundred workers could be induced to support it. After the initial steps had been taken, a convention would be held to elect a union executive, agree on a constitution and fix the membership dues. In practice, however, the conventions were formalities at which the militants exchanged information and experiences, and listened to inspirational talk by whichever Communist leader was responsible for launching the union. The party fraction in the union being established picked the senior union officials beforehand and checked the text of the draft constitution before the delegates saw it. The available evidence indicates that a small number of party members guided the work of these unions. According to a Comintern organ, "One revolutionary union with a membership of over 2,000 had a party fraction of 25, another with a membership of 400 had a fraction of 5."[36]

A skeleton network of Communist-led unions existed by September 1933. It consisted of eleven industrial unions with branches across the Dominion, and thirty local unions that were often confined to a single city. Affiliates of these unions, and branches of some mass organizations, were attached to twelve district councils of a new trade union centre: the Workers Unity League (WUL).[37]

Few of these unions attracted a great deal of support before 1934, because the Communists operated under grave handicaps. To begin with, economic conditions were unfavourable to unions, no matter who led them. Second, the business world did not hide its hostility to Communists in industry. In labour disputes the authorities sided with management and lent the support of the state machine to end strikes as quickly as possible, or at least to prevent them from spreading to other segments of the economy. Machine gun carriers were used to intimidate striking furniture workers at Stratford, Ontario, in 1933. On other occasions less drastic methods were employed to reduce the range of Communist agitation in factories and mines. These methods had been effective in the previous decades, and seldom failed until the mid-1930s.

It would be wrong to assume that the lines of the struggle between the Communist-led unions and the employers were always clearly drawn. Many industrial conflicts were complicated by the presence and intervention of rival trade union organizations. The mere existence of Communist-controlled unions often led to friction with the more numerous non-Communists who remained loyal to the older and stronger labour organizations. Most TLC and ACCL officials were highly critical of Communist objectives and tactics, and fought any party members who stood in their way. The Communists were accused of dual unionism, of splitting the ranks of the workers, of engaging in unnecessary and ill-planned strike action, and of basing their tactics on directives from abroad. These tactics earned the Communists the nickname of "comicals" in the *OBU Bulletin*. The organ of the ACCL referred to Communists as "washroom conspirators", and contended that the activities of Communist-led unions "could not have been better devised had their purpose been the perpetuation of capitalism."[38]

The Communists could not argue that the workers were eager to join CPC-sponsored unions; still less could they prove that Canadian labour was itching for a showdown with the employers. Fear of victimization by management and trade union bosses hostile to Communism and Communists made many workers, including party members, hesitate to support militant action at a time when unemployment was widespread, and the chances of wringing concessions appeared very slim.

Worker apathy and hostility could not be easily overcome without a large number of experienced union organizers among party members. A leading member of the politbureau complained in 1931 about "tons of work, and no one to do it – most of them ignorant as hell on the question of simple tasks." To another activist he wrote, " . . . we also know, or at least think we do, the ideal type that is needed in various localities, but unfortunately, comrade Mike, we do not have such people on our shelves to send them when required."[39]

Under these circumstances, the Communist-led unions did not represent a major challenge to the TLC and ACCL except in coal mining, lumber and the needle trades – those industries in which the Communists had established a foothold in the 1920s and in which many of the workers were of East European origin. In other industries and among transport workers the Communist organizers were no more than a pinprick to the moderate trade union officials until 1934. Their attempts to rally a large number of workers were seldom successful, although their activities contributed to ill-feeling in union circles, retarded the drive towards union unity and contributed to the demise of several small unions affiliated to the ACCL.

The Workers Unity League (WUL) had replaced the moribund TUEL in January, 1930. Once again, the initiative had come from abroad. Comintern and Profintern officials had urged the formation of trade union centres based on the "class struggle" and led by Communists in Western societies. Buck was slow in grasping Comintern desires on this subject. He argued in *The Worker* as late as May 18, 1929, that abandoning the ACCL would be "contrary to all Leninist principles in trade union work."*

The launching of the WUL was justified on the ground that the leaders of the TLC and ACCL had sold themselves to the capitalists. They had failed to defend the interests of their members, organize the unorganized workers, or establish true union democracy in the unions they ran. The expulsion of Communist activists from TLC unions had shown that there was no future for militants in such unions. The WUL, on the other hand, was to do all that the TLC had failed to achieve over the years. These objectives called for a trade union centre to lead Canadian workers and replace the TUEL which had attempted to influence the TLC.

The leader of the WUL was Tom McEwen, a blacksmith who had emigrated from Scotland to Canada in 1911 and who came to the CPC via the SPC. A tireless worker who knew how to encourage, prod and criticize his collaborators, McEwen exchanged the post of industrial director of the CPC for that of national executive secretary of the WUL in 1930. Until his arrest in August 1931, he was the kingpin of the WUL, which he ran on a shoestring and with a subsidy from the CPC. This kind of assistance had its drawbacks. According to a party document seized by the police in 1931,

---

*As had happened so often to Canadian Communists, their comrades in the United States had preceded them in adopting a new Comintern and Profintern policy. The Trade Union Unity League was founded in September 1929.

> The Profintern commission, in discussing our methods of subsidy to the unions, condemned very categorically the method we have followed in the past, which only leads to lack of initiative on the Union executive (who are mainly party members), by falling back at all times on the Party whenever they get in a jam rather than putting the matter before the Union.[40]

Reliable statistics concerning the numerical size of the WUL are not readily available. The WUL headquarters seldom received reliable information from its affiliates, whose officials were overworked and harassed by the police. The data supplied by Canadian Communists to their Soviet and American comrades do not match those given to the Department of Labour in Ottawa or published in *The Worker.* What *is* certain is that there was a definite increase in WUL membership in the organization's first eighteen months and in 1933-1934. All in all, it is doubtful if the WUL organized more than 40,000 workers.

In any case, its membership rolls were padded in more ways than one. They included small groups of Communists and their sympathizers who remained in other trade union organizations (TLC, ACCL, *etc.*), where they formed what was known in Communist circles as the "trade union opposition" to the official union leadership. Furthermore, the WUL included Women's Labour Leagues. These Leagues consisted largely of housewives of East European extraction (fifty-three of the sixty Leagues were composed of Finnish women in 1929). Finally, unemployed workers provided over two-thirds of the WUL membership in 1931. Most of them were young and single, and many of them were of East European origin. In any case, only 5-6 per cent of WUL members also belonged to the CPC.

The interest shown by the Communists in the unemployed stemmed from Profintern and Comintern directives to all sections in industrial societies. The two internationals called for all Communists to give high priority to the struggle against unemployment. The Canadian Communists did so to the detriment of their activities in other fields. Before long they discovered that they had no serious competitors in the arduous struggle on behalf of the unemployed. The provincial labour parties were weak outside Winnipeg, the CCF did not exist as a viable force until well into 1933, the AFL/TLC unions concentrated on protecting the interests of their dues-paying members, and the remnants of the IWW continued to insist on the need to organize at the place of work.

The Communists took up the challenge in several ways. To begin with, in 1930 they formed special organizations for the unemployed in a number of cities. By July 1931 the Unemployed Associations were federated into the National Unemployed Workers Association (NUWA), an affiliate of the WUL. In that month McEwen estimated the former's membership at 16,000.

As unemployment spread, the Communists discovered that the Unemployed Associations were becoming unwieldy. To increase the effectiveness of their fight against unemployment, the Communists sponsored the formation of Branch and Neighbourhood Councils in several metropolitan centres. As *The Worker* put it, the Neighbourhood Councils drew "into the fighting ranks of the working class new forces, who could never be reached by the NUWA – women, youths and children."[42] These grass roots organizations succeeded in forcing the municipalities to grant relief to unemployed and destitute heads of families. In some instances these Councils also engaged in direct action to prevent the eviction of tenants who were in arrears with their rent.

Finally, the CPC sponsored the formation of Unemployed Councils, of which there were forty-five across Canada early in 1932.[43] The Councils were organizations through which the CPC hoped to co-ordinate action on behalf of the unemployed. Pro-Communist organizations, including ethnic ones, sent delegates to these councils, which were less effective than the Neighbourhood Councils. Much to the chagrin of the Communists, the socialists succeeded in gaining control of several Unemployed Councils.

Party members led these organizations, which drew attention to the plight of the unemployed by sending delegations to city halls, provincial governments and Ottawa. They complained about the inadequacies of existing relief schemes, and demanded effective action. For a time the Communists advocated relief at the rate of twenty-five dollars a week. This proposal was similar to a demand put forward by American Communists. It had to be shelved, because "in many parts" of Canada it "can only be regarded as 'leftish' as the workers don't get it when they are working."[44] Instead, the WUL and the CPC concentrated on the need for a non-contributory unemployment insurance scheme, a seven-hour working day with no reduction in pay, and public works projects on which the workers were to be paid at union rates. The cost of thse proposals was to be borne by reducing "official salaries" and defence expenditure and by introducing a "sharply graduated income tax" and a "graduated capital levy".[45]

The Communists also held mass meetings and conferences at

which the capitalist system was denounced and contrasted with the building of a socialist society in the U.S.S.R. In terms of publicity received, one of the most effective conferences was the Workers' Economic Conference, which coincided with the Imperial Economic Conference in Ottawa in August, 1932. The 502 delegates claimed to represent 216,616 workers grouped in over fifty organizations. In reality the number of people represented at this or any other Communist-sponsored conference was appreciably lower, because the publicity managers inflated the membership rolls of "mass organizations". Besides, there was a lot of overlapping of membership in these organizations.

In between conferences the WUL published mimeographed bulletins for the unemployed. Some of them had at times quite a large circulation. The most influential were the *Unemployed Worker* and the *Relief Camp Worker*.

These activities, welcome though they were to the CPC and to many of the unemployed, would not have had the same impact if they had not been combined with numerous demonstrations organized under the auspices of the CPC and its auxiliary organizations. The jobless marched with banners and placards through the streets to draw attention to their plight and their demands. They disrupted traffic in the centre of the city as they moved along to a rallying point, where they listened to speeches by their leaders and approved sending a delegation to those in power. In efforts to obtain redress of their grievances the demonstrators frequently paraded in front of the town hall, or the provincial and federal government buildings. Some of these demonstrations were known as Hunger Marches, because the unemployed marched fairly long distances before they converged on a provincial capital or Ottawa.

In the early years of the Depression the police, on orders from above, would often try to prevent the demonstration from starting, let alone from proceeding along the main streets or blocking the entrances of certain public buildings. Police officers on horseback would disperse the unemployed if baton charges on foot did not succeed. In the course of the rioting some heads and bones were broken, thought not as many as Communist accounts of "police brutality" indicated. Arrests were made and charges laid against the people held responsible by the police for organizing or taking part in a riot.

Street confrontations left a residue of bitterness that coloured the outlook of both sides. Policemen who had suffered injuries, had their hair pulled, their uniforms torn, and been greeted with shouts of "vermin", "fascists" and "Cossacks" could hardly be expected to remain dispassionate and consider the demonstrators as anything but "Communist stooges" or "savages." The rioters, for their part, were given good reason to accept the Communist version of men and events. The capitalists were heartless men, only too eager to order the use of truncheons and tear gas on people who, through no fault of their own, had no jobs and no prospects of getting any in the foreseeable future. Brute force decided the outcome of riots, while "class justice" prevailed in the courtroom where rioters were fined or sentenced to short terms of imprisonment. Canada, the argument went on, was becoming a fascist state. The Communists alone were prepared to espouse the cause of the unemployed and suffer the consequences, physical or otherwise. Only organization, planning and carefully applied pressure would ensure the granting of relief for the unemployed.

By championing the rights of the unemployed, the CPC obtained three benefits. First, it attracted a fair number of unemployed as new members. In the summer of 1935, 60 per cent of the 8,200 members were unemployed.[46] Second, the party improved its ethnic composition as unemployed Anglo-Saxons joined it. Third, the CPC won the sympathy of thousands of unemployed to whom warnings about this or that Communist move appeared simply another attempt of the rich to divide the ranks of the jobless and weaken the appeal of the CPC.

Nevertheless, the party leaders did not consider the struggle on behalf of the unemployed as an unqualified success. Party organizations, especially in Ontario, were often slow to take the initiative in rallying the unemployed. It was not unknown for organizers to disappear with funds collected for the unemployed. The granting of relief to married men tended to reduce tensions and prevented the Communists from exploiting what only the day before looked like a splendid opportunity. Although the unemployed joined the CPC in fairly large numbers, they could not easily be retained. Many recruits lost interest or moved to places where the party organization was non-existent, weak or merely unable to locate and reintegrate them into the Communist movement. More than one unemployed party member also worked for the RCMP or some other police force eager to obtain intelligence and forestall trouble.

Several episodes stand out in the campaign on behalf of the unemployed. As part of the International Day against Unemployment, organized under the auspices of the Comintern and Profintern, 122,000 leaflets were distributed and 76,150 Canadians induced to demonstrate in the streets on February 25, 1931. The turnout was higher in Toronto (13,000) and Winnipeg (12,000) than in Montreal (5,000) or Vancouver (5,000).[47]

These demonstrations attracted a great deal of publicity. They were part of a drive to collect 100,000 signatures for a petition sponsored by the WUL, which called on the federal government to introduce a Non-Contributory Unemployment Insurance bill. Over 94,000 signatures were collected after several weeks of canvassing.

According to a Comintern organ, "in Ontario and Quebec the quotas for signatures were not fulfilled," while in Western Canada they "were far exceeded."[48] The uneven performance of party organizations across the country was not unusual. Throughout much of the Depression the Communists found it easier to exploit Western radicalism and grievances than to channel discontent in Ontario, let alone in Quebec or the Maritimes.

On April 15, 1931, a twenty-four man delegation presented the petition to the Prime Minister. Obviously, there could be no meeting of minds between the Tory millionaire and a group of unemployed, many of whom were party members, and one of whom, McEwen, was a member of the politbureau of the CPC. R. B. Bennett did not reduce the tension by announcing: "Neither this government nor any other government that I am a member of will ever grant Unemployment Insurance. We will not put a premium on ideleness."[49]

Nor did he improve matters by asking his visitors whether they knew of any insurance scheme which did not include premiums. He rebuked them for insisting on public relief, and reminded them of the role of the Good Samaritan. The atmosphere became even more unpleasant when the Prime Minister suggested that those "who had a leaning towards a Communist society might be assisted to make the transition by his government." This was a particularly sore point to the delegates. Some of them were not natives of Canada, and they knew only too well that the federal government was busy deporting or trying to find ways of deporting prominent Communists.

After leaving the Prime Minister, the delegates called on Mackenzie King, the Leader of the Opposition, and on Robert Gardiner, the spokesman of the UFA caucus in the House of Commons. Although these two politicians were more sympathetic to the visitors than R. B. Bennett, the delegates were not pleased with the answers they received. The WUL newsletter used the occasion to remind the readers of King's record as Prime Minister, while Gardiner's preference for "evolution" rather than "revolution" earned him the epithet of "philistine" in the same publication.

The On-to-Ottawa Trek in 1935 marked the climax of the struggle by the Communists on behalf of the unemployed. As on other occasions during the Depression, the Communists found their most appreciative audience among those young men who had never held a decent job and had few chances of finding one. To get them off the streets and away from Communist agitators, government relief camps had been set up. Geographic isolation, spartan living conditions and a twenty cents per day allowance were not made more attractive by the fact that the Department of National Defence ran the camps for a time. The discipline which army personnel tried to enforce was unwelcome and led to friction, protests and various kinds of insubordination encouraged by the Communists. Not that much was needed to convince the young unemployed man. He knew that he was working for a pittance, and he was told that the relief camps were an attempt at the "militarization" of Canada in preparation for another war. Unrest spread rapidly. In 1934 the Communists claimed to have organized a large number of strikes in the relief camps.[50]

The situation became tense when two thousand relief workers left their camps in B.C. to join the unemployed in Vancouver in April 1935. It was the second time the Communists had organized a major walkout on the west coast. This time Arthur "Slim" Evans, one of the ablest Communist organizers, succeeded in welding the relief workers into a disciplined and articulate group of men. Their plight and bearing attracted a great deal of sympathy. Seldom were the Communists able to win such a wide range of support for a cause they had made their own. Clergymen, socialists and women's organizations expressed their solidarity with those who, in the eyes of the entire left, had vegetated in the "slave camps". The Chief Constable of Vancouver told a strikers' delegation that a system that offered young men "no other future but life in a camp" was "entirely wrong."[51] The Mayor of Vancouver and the Premier of B.C. called on R. B. Bennett to solve the problem. They hoped that somehow he would find a solution that would remove the strikers from Vancouver, where they were highly visible and a potential threat to law and order.

But politicians' words and attempts to shift the blame could not solve the strikers' immediate problem: they had to eat. Appeals and collections provided some food and money. To obtain more, the strikers paraded in the streets, occupied the Vancouver Museum and Library and marched through the Hudson's Bay Company store. None of these acts went unchallenged. Attempts to disperse the men led to disturbances and violence. On one occasion the Mayor was forced to read the Riot Act, on another to grant temporary relief.

After several weeks of public meetings, demonstrations and negotiations, the strike leaders came to the conclusion that there was little to be gained by staying on in Vancouver. The danger that the citizens of that city would be less generous in the future than they had been in the past weighed on the minds of those who were carefully planning the next move. They noted signs of lassitude among many of their followers, who were tired of marches, riots and tag days. As morale fell, there was a tendency to break ranks. Some of the strikers decided to look for work and shelter on their own. In a plebiscite others voted to return to the relief camps.

The possibility that their supporters might melt away, unless something drastic was done, provided an additional inducement to seek relief in Ottawa. However hazardous that might be, it seemed preferable to staying on in Vancouver. A trek across the country was bound to gain support and publicity for the strikers. It would also force the federal government either to grant concessions, or to reveal once again its lack of compassion for men who were no longer prepared to accept life in the relief camps as a solution.

The proposal for an On-to-Ottawa Trek did not receive the immediate approval of the Communist leaders in Toronto. Afraid that the plan was bound to fail, they vacillated for a time, and Evans and his comrades were left largely to their own devices.

Over a thousand trekkers boarded CPR freight trains which took them eastward. In several localities they stopped to rest, receive aid, and state their case. In Calgary they also used physical force to induce the authorities to grant them some relief.[52] This favourable reaction to the trekkers in Calgary made it likely that similar tactics would be used with the same reaction in other cities on the way across Canada.

The events in Calgary precipitated the decision to break up the Trek before it even reached Winnipeg, let alone Ottawa. Winnipeg had not lost the reputation it had gained in 1919. The local party organization profited from this tradition of radicalism; it was bound to do everything it could to assist the trekkers. Even more unwelcome would have been the arrival of over a thousand very politically aware young men in the capital. Even if they did not cause a riot, their very presence in Ottawa could only harm the already tarnished image of a government about to face the electorate.

The RCMP in Regina was ordered to prevent the trekkers from proceeding further eastward. Police action on a grand scale came after desultory negotiations between the trekkers and the federal government. Talks begun in Regina were continued in Ottawa, where a delegation pleaded the trekkers' case. As on other occasions when he met with delegates of Communist-controlled organizations, R. B. Bennett was flanked by members of his Cabinet. This time, however, the dialogue was more acrimonious than usual. The Prime Minister began by recording the names and birthplaces of the delegates, most of whom were not natives of Canada. He then brought up Evans' criminal record and defended once again his government's policy over the relief camps.

On July 1, 1935, the RCMP dispersed the trekkers on instructions from Ottawa. Before the day was over, one member of the Regina city police was dead, and a number of trekkers and policemen wounded. Many were arrested during or just after one of the worst riots in modern Canadian history.

The handling of the trekkers in Regina provided the unemployed with additional evidence that those in power were hostile to the jobless. The tri-weekly *Worker* had a field day denouncing R. B. Bennett. It supported the trekkers who were charged in court with incitement to riot. Non-Communists were badly divided in their assessment of the federal government's actions. Not many people in the west were prepared to defend the treatment of the trekkers. Public sympathy was with the young men who had been clubbed in Regina. The CPC profited from this wave of sympathy when it renewed its appeal for a United front. In Regina a miniature united front was actually formed with the local socialists, who for a time co-operated with the Communists in municipal affairs.

Another Trek ended in less dramatic circumstances. This time the starting point was Toronto. Of the 400 people who joined, 350 reached Ottawa after Parliament had been prorogued. The column which was supposed to come from Montreal never arrived. The trekkers camped in a field near the railway sidings, set up a committee of five to preserve discipline, and sent a delegation to R. B. Bennett.

When writing about these demonstrations, *The Worker* frequently mentioned that the unemployed enjoyed the moral and material support of "toiling farmers". The latter were, of course, a group in which the CPC remained interested. What changed in the early 1930s was the Communist line on non-Communist farm organizations. Through much of the 1920s, party members in rural communities had used the PFEL to influence the United Farmers organizations. At the height of the Depression, however, party directives insisted on the need to fight these organizations, expose their leaders, and win over to the Communist side the rank-and-file of the UFA, UFC(SS) and UFM. To carry out these objectives, something more ambitious than an Educational League was required. From its ruins emerged the Farmers Unity League(FUL) formed on the initiative of the party headquarters.*

Little was left to chance. First, party members were to do the groundwork carefully. J. M. Clarke informed those who were to organize meetings of farmers in the three Prairie provinces that they were "not to openly state that plans are under way for establishing a new farmer organization. To do so would be to warn our enemies and give them an opportunity of making a counter-move to blocking our efforts."[53]

At the same time he informed the Communists that they were free to point out the "failure of the old organizations." This, however, would not prevent members of the FUL from working "inside such bodies for the purpose of taking advantage of their disintegration and winning over poor farmers within them."

The second stage involved the holding of conferences, which over five hundred "dirt farmers" attended in December 1930. Among them was George H. Williams, who had been a member of the PFEL before he became president of the UFC(SS) and provincial leader of the CCF. At the conference in Saskatoon Williams put forward proposals, which the Communists immediately attacked.[54]

Although the conferences reflected "the rising tide of discontent on the Prairies," Clarke had few illusions about the farmers, who, in his words, "pin their faith on freak proposals. The conventions were not cluttered up with these" because the delegates were kept "busy" with "concrete proposals."[55] These proposals included calls for organized resistance against eviction, the cancellation of tax arrears, and immediate relief to distressed farmers. Medicare and free education also figured among the immediate demands. So did a guaranteed annual income of "not less than $1,000 per year for all poor farmers." At the same time the new organization advocated "unity of the oppressed farmers with the industrial workers for a revolutionary workers' and poor farmers' government."

During the next few years the FUL did its best to draw attention to the plight of the poorer farmers. It held protest meetings, and it organized marches to the capitals of the three Prairie provinces. It collected 15,000 signatures in favour of a Farm Emergency bill but

---

*Once again, the Canadian Communists followed the precedent set by their American comrades. In the spring of 1930 the United Farmers Educational League in the United States dropped "Educational" from its title.

could not raise enough money to send a delegation with the petition to Ottawa.[56] It published several pamphlets, and sent a farmers' delegation to the U.S.S.R. It joined various campaigns sponsored by the CPC between 1930 and 1935. Its members spoke at the annual conventions of the United Farmers' organizations on the prairies. Successful resistance to evictions provided welcome publicity. More was gained when additional relief was granted, partly in response to agitation organized by the FUL. The FUL also attracted attention when its members instigated "non-delivery strikes", refusing to sell grain in protest against the grain-grading practices of grain elevator companies in some parts of Alberta.

For a brief period it seemed as if the FUL was making great progress. At a time when the membership of non-Communist farm organizations fell appreciably, the FUL claimed 5,000 members, including 1,200 dues-payers, in 120 units.[57] Although the majority of FUL supporters were of East European descent, it also attracted the support of some farmers of Anglo-Saxon, Scandinavian and Teutonic extraction who had not been associated with the Communist movement in the 1920s.

Its spokesmen displayed a zeal and ingenuity worthy of their comrades in the cities. The leaders of the FUL were generally better off and had more varied backgrounds than their supporters. Several of them had been prominent in the PFEL (such as Axelson, H. E. Mills, Wiggins). The second group consisted of those who had risen to the top in the last year or so of the FUL (for example, John Bespalko, William Kardash, William Tuomi). Most of them were young, of East European extraction and destined to hold relatively high positions in the Communist movement. Finally, there were those who went over to the Communists under the impact of the Depression. They included a former member of the Alberta legislature elected on the UFA ticket, and the colourful L. McNamee, former president of the Farmers' Union of Canada, a Saskatchewan-based organization in the early 1920s. His brand of radicalism did not appeal to *The Worker*, which attacked him on several occasions before he joined the FUL in 1932.

Their efforts notwithstanding, the FUL possessed major weaknesses. It was largely confined to Alberta and Saskatchewan, in spite of attempts to turn the FUL into a Dominion-wide organization. In Manitoba and Ontario the FUL often overlapped with locals of the ULFTA and the Finnish Organization.[58] The occasional candidates sponsored by the FUL in provincial elections and federal by-elections ended up almost invariably at the bottom of the poll. The Committees of Action, on which the FUL was supposed to be based, seldom succeeded in involving prominent members of other farm associations.

This state of affairs can be attributed to factors over which Wiggins and his colleagues had no control. As loyal party members they followed the line of the CPC, trying to apply the "class against class" tactic decided in Moscow. At a time when the Communists were busy condemning the socialists and other critics of the established order, the FUL had no choice but to join in with attacks on the leaders and policies of the United Farmers' organizations. Axelson justified this policy by telling the readers of *The Worker* that "those who pretend to be friendly, who seem to be very close to what we want and need, but yet will not go all the way, are often our worst enemies."[59]

Although the leaders of the United Farmers' organizations displayed greater tolerance of Communists than had the TLC a few years earlier, they did fight back. They succeeded in defeating the motions introduced by Axelson at the annual conventions of the UFA.

The emergence of the CCF and of Social Credit increased the number of alternatives available to prairie farmers. The FUL was in no position to compete with these two protest movements, except in the communities where either the ULFTA had a strong base or where there was a fair number of Doukhobor farmers. Aberhardt and the CCF spokesmen in Saskatchewan spoke a more appealing language to many farmers than *The Furrow* with its references to "kulaks" (rich peasants), "social fascists" and "toiling farmers". The CCF program seemed radical enough to those who wanted major changes but saw no need for a "Soviet Canada" or a class struggle in the Canadian country side.

The poverty of the FUL members made it very difficult to ensure the regular publication of *The Furrow*, which had to be subsidized by the CPC. Nor was there much money to pay organizers. Local talent was slow in emerging, with the result that "hundreds of the FUL locals set up" by a few energetic activists "utterly failed from the beginning."[60] Any farmers who displayed above average initiative and organizing skill were overwhelmed by demands on their time and talents. They received very little assistance from the party headquarters, even before the arrest of the top Communist leaders in August 1931. They understood the effect of harsh living conditions, and the difficulty of making converts among farmers. A number of militants left the countryside in search of a more satisfying life in the cities.

By the autumn of 1935 the FUL was " "practically liquidated in fact without any formal decision to do so."[61] The final decision was made public in November 1935, when Stewart Smith spoke of the "necessity of working in reformist organizations instead of destroying them." Over the objections of the Communist leaders of the FUL, the CPC decided to cut its losses and called on members of the FUL to rejoin the United Farmers' organizations. The new policy was defended on two grounds. First, because the FUL was "more or less . . . an enlarged Communist Party . . . the whole atmosphere is that of Communist Party meetings rather than of a mass farmer organization."[62] Second, in 1935 the CPC could not afford to ignore the new Comintern line which emphasized the necessity for co-operating with other opponents of the status quo, the very people vilified by the Canadian Communists in the past.

The FUL, the organization that the CPC had hoped would supplant the United Farmers, left few traces when it was quietly disbanded in Alberta early in 1936. Whatever strength the Communists retained in the rural world depended on party cells and ULFTA branches. Through these they occasionally rallied sufficient support to influence the passage of a motion at a convention of farmers' organizations or to vote into office one of their members or sympathizers.

Much of the Communist agitation among farmers, the unemployed and industrial workers was carried out in the absence of the secretary-general of the CPC. Buck's arrest on August 11, 1931, his trial and imprisonment formed the climax of several years of petty persecution of Communist militants and spokesmen. Between the end of 1928 and well into 1935, activists were being arrested, taken to court and charged with a variety of offenses. Foreign-born Communists were deported or threatened with deportation. The authorities assiduously followed the activities of other party leaders before and after the top ones were arrested in August 1931. Occasionally the police raided the offices of the CPC, pro-Communist unions and mass organizations. Literature was confiscated from party offices. It became difficult to send Communist publications to Canada by sea or from the United States.

The degree of harassment and persecution across Canada depended on two factors: the amount of visible Communist activity in a given area, and the reaction of law enforcement officers to the Communist challenge in the streets, in parks, and outside factory gates. Some police forces (such as those in Toronto, Montreal, Winnipeg) were more energetic than others in curtailing the range of Communist agitation. Their zeal reflected the attitude of their employers. These, in turn, were often influenced by anti-Communist pressure groups deriving their main strength from the conservative and deeply religious segments of the population.

The result was a series of ill-coordinated attempts to stamp out the Communist movement. These were justified on the ground that the CPC was behind agitation and demonstrations, which often escalated into minor riots as the communists tried to rouse the unemployed, and encouraged working-class militancy in the belief that a revolutionary situation was fast developing in all industrial societies in the West. Evidence in support of the Establishment viewpoint could easily be found. Communist speakers did not mince words as the Depression continued. Communist newspapers and leaflets did not shy away from making statements that sounded seditious to people brought up before 1914. What appeared particularly disturbing were occasional Communist efforts to agitate among and infiltrate into the armed forces and the police. This was in line with a decision of the Sixth Congress of the Comintern. All its sections were told to pay more attention to anti-militarist propaganda, in view of the growing danger of a capitalist crusade against the U.S.S.R.

After the Sixth Congress had brought about a hardening of the Comintern line in North America, the Communists in Toronto became the object of sharper police surveillance. Detectives, acting on instructions from the Police Commission, insisted that speeches at indoor Communist meetings should be delivered in English, even if the majority of the audience consisted of unassimilated East Europeans. When speakers declined to co-operate, they were hauled from the platform. At a meeting in January 1929 tear gas was used to disperse the crowd. During the winter of 1928-1929 hall owners refused to rent their premises to the Communists, either because the municipal authorities delayed the renewal of licences for buildings used for Communist meetings, or simply because they feared damage to their property if trouble arose at meetings held under CPC auspices.

Lacking halls to meet in, groups of militants led by Stewart Smith tried to speak from street corners, only to be arrested on the spot. At first the Communists were unable to put up an effective resistance. Macdonald's critics in the CPC blamed him for this state of affairs, although he tried to encourage non-Communist union leaders to join the Free Speech Movement, set up by the CPC to draw attention to its plight.

Unwilling to give up their agitation, the Communists held meetings in Queen's Park in Toronto. Once again the police, led by Brigadier Draper, a formidable foe of the Communists at the turn of the decade, intervened. Communists were beaten up, speakers arrested, and listeners dispersed in a way Canadians were not accustomed to. The Communists led by Charles Sims fought back as best they could, although Sam Carr did not think much of their display of energy. In February 1931 he told a gathering of party officials that "Every Communist is prepared to have his head smashed in demonstrations, but is not ready to be a Communist in the [work] shop." It was left to another Communist official to acknowledge that in Toronto, because "the fight with the police was so severe and the battleground was in the open, the Party organization has been crippled."[63]

Although, temporarily at least, the Communists had lost the battle in Toronto, the various layers of government still felt insecure. The harassment of Communists and Communist-led organizations, and the increase in the number of arrests and court sentences, did not put an end to Communist agitation. On the contrary, there was plenty of evidence that the Communist movement was making a comeback. In early 1931 the membership of the CPC and many mass organizations increased, and Communist militants displayed more drive and ingenuity than in the previous year. The result was a wider range of Communist activities across the country and larger audiences ready to listen to what the Communists had to say.

Under these circumstances, the Tory Establishment in Ottawa and Queen's Park was sorely tempted to strike back at the top leaders of the CPC. They were experiencing great difficulty in coping with mass unemployment, declining agricultural prices and an appreciable reduction in industrial production. They thought the arrest and imprisonment of the best-known agitators offered a quick way of dealing with a visible centre of unrest. A jittery government at Queen's Park decided to act when rumours began spreading that the Communists were drilling the unemployed in a Toronto suburb.

On August 11, 1931, Boychuk, Bruce, Buck, Carr, Hill, McEwen, Popovic, Cacic and one other Communist were arrested. At their trial in November 1931 they were charged under Section 98 of the Criminal Code with being members of an "unlawful association", being officers of an "unlawful association" and being partners to a seditious conspiracy. Mr. Justice Wright, a Liberal and a prominent Freemason, presided at the trial, which lasted ten days.

The Tory government of Ontario took great pains to prepare the Crown's case against the accused. A well-known lawyer, Norman Sommerville, K.C., led for the prosecution. He had at his disposal a great deal of evidence, much of which had been seized by the police from the CPC headquarters in August 1931. The evidence, which included Comintern directives to the CPC, was used to show that the CPC was part of an international organization which advocated violence.

The prosecution created a minor sensation when it produced a witness that the defendants had not expected to see in RCMP uniform. Sergeant Leopold, a native of Austria-Hungary, had been an underground agent in the Communist movement; he knew many of the Communist leaders and he testified at great length about their activities, with which he was familiar from the days when he was a middle-echelon party official in the 1920s.

The accused put up a spirited defence. They proclaimed their Communist beliefs and denied that they were planning revolution. Buck, unlike his comrades, did not rely on the services of a lawyer in court. He spoke at length, without apparently making any impact on the jurymen, most of whom were Anglo-Saxons living in modest circumstances. On November 14, 1931, eight of the accused were found guilty. Buck and six of his colleagues were sentenced to five years' imprisonment; Cacic received a two-year sentence. Those who were not natives of Canada were recommended for deportation upon the completion of their sentences. All property of the CPC seized in August 1931 was forfeited to the Crown.

Appeals against conviction were entered in December 1931. The eight Communists were freed on bail of $20,000 each. This large sum of money was easily raised from several rich sympathizers. In February 1932 the Supreme Court of Ontario dismissed the appeals, except as to the third count of the indictment, that of being parties to a seditious conspiracy, and the Communists were taken to the Kingston Penitentiary.

Although the CPC was temporarily in disarray after the arrest and trial of the members of its politbureau, the Communists soon fought back. The WUL held protest meetings on the day the trial began. "An appeal for a general strike on the day of the trial" was also made but, according to a Canadian delegate to the Profintern, "this appeal met with no response in the masses."[64]

The attempt to rouse public opinion was not merely an expression of solidarity with the arrested leaders. It was also the first shot in a campaign to preserve the legal status of the CPC, which had been virtually outlawed when the Chief Justice of Ontario delivered the judgement in February 1932. In subsequent months government spokesmen emphasized that the CPC was an "unlawful association". The Communists preferred to talk about "class justice", the limitations of "bourgeois democracy", the rise of "fascism" and the "political prisoners" who languished in jail.

The campaign for Buck's release, and the demand for the repeal of Section 98 of the Criminal Code, were carried out largely under the auspices of the Canadian Labor Defence League. In 1931 it published a monthly magazine and had ten full-time officials. The number of its branches rose from about seventy in the spring of 1930 to 350 in the summer of 1933. Equally dramatic was its increase in membership: the CLDL had 25,000 members in the spring of 1932 and 43,000 early in 1934.[65] Of these fewer than half were independent members; the remainder belonged to organizations affiliated to the CLDL. Although most of these were Communist-led organizations, by 1934 some TLC and ACCL locals and a few CCF clubs had also joined the CLDL and were campaigning on its behalf.

The moving spirit behind the CLDL was the Reverend A. E. Smith, the father of Stewart Smith. An ex-member of the Manitoba Legislature, he had been active in left-wing politics before joining the CPC in 1925. At meetings and conferences across the country A. E. Smith and other spokesmen of the CLDL criticized people who would not co-operate with them in the struggle for civil liberties, and they denounced the harassment of Communists and Communist-controlled organizations as the number of arrests and court convictions rose appreciably between 1930 and 1934.

The CLDL also collected fairly large sums of money on behalf of men it defended in court. (The question of whether to pay "good workers' " money to lawyers, or to concentrate on "increased propaganda", presented a dilemma, because lawyers demanded "exorbitant fees" for services to unpopular clients.[66]) Last but not least, the CLDL and the Councils for the Defence of Foreign-Born Workers fought the threat of deportation hanging over the heads of many immigrants who were active in the CPC or its mass organizations.

The Communists were not alone in condemning the authorities. Soon they were being supported by the Trotskyists, the leaders of the newly-formed CCF, many segments of organized labour, farmers' organizations like the UFA, and newspapers in Toronto and Winnipeg. Mackenzie King, who knew where to find an issue that would help him and the Liberal Party, promised to remove Section 98 from the Criminal Code when the Liberals were returned to power. He fulfilled his promise in 1936.

R. B. Bennett and his colleagues replied to their opponents by drawing attention to the nature of the Soviet regime, the objectives and tactics of the Communist International, and the CPC's organizational ties with the Comintern. In these statements Communism and Communists were often bracketed with socialism and social-ists. In a speech to the Ontario Conservative Association, the Prime Minister urged "men and women to put the iron heel ruth-lessly on propaganda of that kind."[67]

Bennett's anti-Communism had three sources. Everything the CPC stood for was anathema to the Tory and the successful busi-nessman in him. Also, the bitter Communist attacks on him were not conducive to increasing his understanding of the Communist phenomenon. The Communists he met in the flesh, as spokesmen of this or that delegation to the federal Cabinet, made statements and asked questions which he considered provocative and imperti-nent. Finally, he received anonymous letters threatening his life because of the anti-Communist measures for which the public held him responsible or associated with him.[68] There were also rumours that the unemployed, under Communist leadership, would kidnap him and members of the Cabinet. All this strengthened his convic-tion that the Communists represented an alien and violent element in Canadian life, a force eager to destroy what he cherished most, and a stumbling block to whatever efforts he made to cope with the effects of the Depression.

The Conservative point of view received less and less support after it became known that a prison guard had fired into Buck's cell during a riot in the Kingston Penitentiary in October 1932. The clamour for Buck's release grew as the CLDL distributed over 400,000 leaflets and collected over 459,000 signatures demanding this and the repeal of Section 98. The government relented in November 1934. A crowd, which the Communists estimated at 6,000, greeted Buck in Toronto.

He found the CPC in much better shape than at the time of his arrest. Membership, which had fallen in the early stages of the Depression, had risen to 5,500 by July 1934. The influence of the CPC increased even faster during the same period. More people were prepared to co-operate with, or at least to give the benefit of the doubt to the Communists, while anti-Communism either at the popular or governmental level became more subdued. Because of this, the authorities made no attempt to deport Buck and the men sentenced with him. Instead, he went on a speaking tour that took him as far west as Vancouver.

Several factors contributed to the recovery of the CPC. First of all, after Buck's trial Stewart Smith returned from the U.S.S.R., where he had lived in semi-disgrace, to assume the leadership of the battered Communist apparatus. The CPUSA lent Jack John-stone, a native of Scotland, who had been active in the SPC before 1914. Years later, a Canadian Communist weekly pointed out that for a long period he "helped the Party in Canada to reform its ranks, strengthen the leadership and lead the campaign for the repeal of" Section 98 of the Criminal Code.[69]

The CPC was also rebuilt as an underground party. Those officials whose loyalty was suspect and whose zeal lukewarm, were expelled. They were replaced by men who often were not known to the authorities. By taking certain precautions they succeeded in eluding the police dragnet as they reorganized the CPC.

Third, necessity forced the Communists who were still at large to operate mostly through legal mass-organizations. In addition to those launched in the 1920s, the CPC formed new ones during the Depression. These included, in addition to the WUL and the FUL, the Canadian Workers' Ex-servicemen's League, the Progressive Arts Clubs and the Canadian League against War and Fascism. In a number of instances these organizations were Canadian sections of a worldwide network sponsored by the Comintern. As in other industrial societies, these organizations served the Communists well. They proved their worth as pressure groups which brought party members into contact with an increasing number of non-Communists. The conferences, meetings, demonstrations, petitions and delegations they organized, the issues they raised, and the slogans they used, attracted attention and sympathy in various circles comprising Canadians who disapproved of infringements against civil liberties, who shared the Communists' desire for change, and who were convinced that those in power had no solution to the country's pressing economic and social problems.

The Communists' ability to identify with and give expression to the feelings of many non-Communists often forced the authorities into making concessions that otherwise would not have been made. As the years passed, fewer attempts were made to restrict the right of assembly of organizations with which the Communists were associated. Moreover, the relief of the destitute and the unemployed owed something to Communist agitation. Understandably they took credit for these achievements, although they were not the only ones who had fought for the jobless.

In such a climate the authorities found it increasingly difficult to sentence Communist agitators or to deport activists. This was particularly true after March 1934 when a jury had declared A. E. Smith not guilty under Section 98. His skilful defence, and Communist agitation outside the courtroom, represent a landmark in the struggle between the CPC and the Tory Establishment.

Another landmark was the Liberal victory in the Ontario provincial election on June 19, 1934. The new Attorney-General, Arthur Roebuck, put an end to the anti-Communist measures associated with his Tory predecessor. The relatively tolerant attitude of the new Liberal administration in this key province enabled the Communists to carry out their activities almost unmolested, while still exploiting their recent martyrdom.

The expansion of the CPC in 1933-1934 would have been even faster but for a variety of factors. In the first place, the harrying of Communists, although carried out by increasingly unpopular governments in Ottawa and Toronto, produced the kind of situation the Communists have always tried hard to avoid. Bitter experience had taught them the drawbacks of illegality and persecution. In Canada a number of Communists abandoned the party forever or became politically passive, at the height of the government attack on the CPC. The fear of deportation, to countries where the authorities were much more hostile to the Communists than Canada was, made many a party member born in eastern Europe think twice before he expressed his views in public. Quite a few of those who met their obligations as members of the CPC were in and out of court, if not in jail, most of the time. They spent a great deal of their own and their comrades' time and energy in merely avoiding arrest and imprisonment.

Those who were imprisoned could not easily be replaced. It was not easy to find another Buck to lead the CPC, another McEwen to inspire the WUL, or even men to fill the void left by the one-year sentences imposed on a group of energetic YCL activists in Montreal. Those who persevered "had to adjust", as a Comintern publication put it, "to new illegal conditions."[70] This meant, among other things, that they had to learn by experience a number of lessons which could not be absorbed by consulting Comintern manuals or by seeking guidance in the memoirs of Old Bolsheviks.

Communist activists were often overwhelmed by the variety of tasks they had to tackle and the ambitious goals they were expected to reach. In the early days of the Depression the Comintern pressed the CPC to devote far more attention to the expansion of its mass organizations. Promptings and inspirational messages could not overcome the grave shortage of people with organizational skills. As a result, the activists, never mind the leaders, were badly overworked and seldom able to provide the kind of guidance and attention to problems that made all the difference in mass struggles. The more far-sighted party leaders were aware of the danger if the CPC spread itself too thinly. As Leslie Morris pointed out in 1930, "to have several campaigns at the same time is equal to having no campaign at all."[71] He and others could do little to remedy the situation. They carried on with their assigned duties, hoping that potential organizers would emerge in the course of the campaigns that the CPC sponsored or was associated with.

In some instances their hopes were fulfilled. Success, however, brought to the surface a problem that the Communists in Canada and other industrial societies had had to grapple with throughout the history of the Communist movement. According to a party resolution in 1934,

> We have one phenomenon that recurs in practically every mass organization: our comrades do splendid work in the period of establishing the organizations, but [once] the organization is established a Chinese wall is placed around it and all activity is concentrated within these limits alone.[72]

Moreover, the Communists were gravely handicapped by their "propaganda and agitation", which the February 1931 plenum of the central committee described as "too unreal and above the heads of the workers we want to reach."[73] Although Communist spokesmen periodically made similar statements in later years, no serious attempt was made to improve the situation. Party newspapers and resolutions, and to a lesser extent party leaflets, reflected the arguments and terminology used by the Comintern while the "class against class" tactic was in vogue. Calls for a "Soviet Canada"*, a "revolutionary government of workers and poor farmers", and a "dictatorship of the proletariat", seldom struck a deep chord among men facing a barrage of conflicting claims, proposals and promises before and during the federal election campaign in 1935.

Although the CPC was still an illegal organization in October 1935, Carr could boast that the federal government "did not dare to disqualify our candidates."[74] Candidates included Buck, Bruce, J. B. MacLachlan, McEwen, Popovic and A. E. Smith. The thirteen ridings contested by the Communists were selected on the amount of grass roots support the Communists thought they had in the constituency, and the attitude of CCF standard bearers towards Communist policies. Elsewhere, the CPC çalled on the voters to "elect a majority of CCF and Communist candidates."[75] In practice, however, the Communists campaigned only on behalf of a minority of CCF candidates, namely those who had come out in

---

*According to the CPC delegate to the eighth convention of the CPUSA, "soviet Canada" was to be a "section of the united soviets of North America". *The Worker*, 14 April 1934.

favour of certain planks in the Communist program and who agreed with certain Communist policies in Canada. Dislike of anti-Communist democratic socialists contributed to the decision to contest the seats of incumbent CCF members of Parliament like Angus McInnis and A. A. Heaps. R. B. Bennett and Mackenzie King, on the other hand, did not have to face Communist challengers in their respective ridings.

Much of what the Communists proposed in 1935 appeared in the election manifestos of other political parties. This was true not only of such issues as relief for the unemployed, public works, social legislation and support for the farmers, but also the demand for the repeal of Section 98. The Liberals and the CCF campaigned for its repeal, while making it clear that they were opposed to the Soviet form of government and that they had no sympathy for the CPC. The Conservative Party, however, defended the record of the Tory government, and stressed the importance of maintaining law and order, which they claimed was endangered by the Communists.

The Communists campaigned vigorously to ensure at least Buck's victory in North Winnipeg. They distributed leaflets, engaged in large scale door-to-door canvassing, held a number of public meetings, and kept on announcing that he stood an excellent chance of winning the seat. Their campaign confirmed the extent to which the CPC depended on the ethnic vote. When the election was over, Buck confessed that "for a couple of months I was overwhelmed with invitations to supper to Ukrainian and Jewish comrades to meet other Ukrainian and Jewish comrades. I have yet to meet an Englishman at one of these suppers. . . . It was the English" who elected Heaps.[76]

When the election results were announced, it became clear that Mackenzie King and not Buck was the chief beneficiary of the Depression, and of the ineptitude and "Iron Heel" reputation of R. B. Bennett. The Liberals, with their slogan "King of Chaos", did far better than the most extreme opponents of the social order. What was more galling to the Communists was their failure to corner a high percentage of the protest vote in almost every riding they contested. Three parties, none of which was four years old, won more votes than the Communist candidates, who gained 31,151 votes.

In their analysis of the election the Communists stressed the fact that the CPC did much better in 1935 than in 1930, when its eight candidates had polled a mere 6,034 votes. They also pointed out that in 1935 the "old line" parties lost ground to Social Credit, the CCF and Stevens's Reconstruction Party. This was taken as a sign that "the masses are breaking" away from the Tories and the Liberals though, Stewart Smith admitted, they " . . . are not going in a common direction. The largest part of them has been intercepted by new capitalist demagogues, Stevens and Aberhardt. These demagogues represent an incipent form of fascism."[77]

Buck and his colleagues attributed the Communist failure to make a greater impact on the electorate to "the terrific burden we carried from our sectarian past." Nor had many Communists shaken off their sectarianism in 1935, if statements like "Parliament is a pigsty" are indicative of their thinking.[78] The leaders also argued that "there was not a single Communist candidate who was not also opposed by another candidate who offered the workers an easier alternative" to the "old line" parties. How dangerous those with "an easier alternative" were, Buck explained to the central committee:

> The best elements of the CCF . . . have a good approach to the workers and are able to take daily little problems and link them up with the class struggle. There is a tendency of most of us to hesitate, a fear that we might be dealing with trifles and paltry things."[79]

What Buck and Smith did not emphasize was how far the CCF had outdistanced the CPC in the first major electoral contest between Communists and democratic socialists. The CCF never lost this initial advantage. Elections in the succeeding decades merely widened the margin, with dire results for the CPC.

Chapter 4

Towards a People's Front

Hitler's territorial ambitions and his anti-Communist stand at home and abroad brought about a new shift in Soviet foreign policy and Comintern tactics. The latter were officially proclaimed in Moscow at the Seventh Congress of the Comintern in July and August 1935, which Stewart Smith addressed as chairman of a five-man delegation of the CPC.

In the speeches and resolutions at this Congress, attention was drawn to the differences between "bourgeois democracies" and fascist dictatorships. The former, in spite of their imperfections, were preferable to the latter: hence the duty of Communist parties to fight hard for the preservation of existing civil liberties. This could be done most effectively in co-operation with non-Communists who were also worried about Hitler, Mussolini and the various fascist and semi-fascist movements in the West. As part of their anti-fascist policy the Communists were strongly advised to desist from the kind of attacks on socialists for which the Communist parties had been notorious between 1928 and 1934. Instead, they were to woo the socialists and the liberals. Every effort was to be made to involve them in joint activities against fascist propaganda, plans and aggression. Hopefully, unity among the anti-fascist elements would lead to a formal alliance of anti-fascist parties and organizations such as trade unions. The Comintern used the terms "People's Front" or "Popular Front" to describe such a broad alliance. So did the Canadian Communists until 1938, when it became fashionable to speak of a "Democratic Front".

Such an alliance of anti-fascist parties would seek power through the polls. Once elected, the People's Front government would try to strengthen the League of Nations to bar the road to aggression. At home, it would alleviate the conditions which encouraged the growth of fascism. Social legislation, public works, the removal of officials who favoured deals with Hitler and Mussolini, and more participatory democracy were the best antidotes to fascist intrigues and subversion.

The CPC delegates to the Seventh Congress of the Communist International accepted the Comintern plan for action. They, like Macdonald and Spector in 1928, criticized the performance of the CPC since the last Congress.[1] One of them referred to the "very strong sectarianism that acts like a ball and chain on the Party." As a result, the Canadian Communists had "not soberly taken into account the deep-seated bourgeois democratic illusions of the overwhelming majority, not only of the Canadian farmers and middle class people, but of the Canadian workers."

Under the influence of speeches delivered by Comintern officials, the Canadian delegates displayed a new awareness of the need for "active work in defence of the economic interests of the widest stratum of lower and lower middle class people in the towns." This represented another turnabout because, according to the same Canadian speaker, "a deep-seated sectarian attitude prevails in our Party in respect to shopkeepers, the teachers and professional people."

The call for an alliance with moderates and socialists on certain specific issues was not unusual. Even before Hitler came to power the Communists in Canada and elsewhere had tried to find allies in non-Communist circles. What was new and startling after the Nazi takeover was the Communist eagerness to seek allies across the political spectrum and the extent to which the CPC was prepared to surrender – temporarily at least – many of its previously proclaimed policies. It also abandoned some of its jargon that jarred on Canadian ears. The demand for a "Soviet Canada", which had figured prominently in Communist propaganda, was quietly dropped, and replaced by slogans designed to identify the CPC with the views of less radical opponents of the status quo.

As part of this policy, Buck presented in May 1938 a well-documented brief to the Royal Commission on Dominion-Provincial Relations.[2] The CPC wanted the federal government to become "fully responsible" for unemployment, health and crop insurance, minimal standards of education, housing, and old age pensions. It also urged a more equitable taxation system with personal income tax as the basic tax. Appeals to the Privy Council in London were to be abolished, a Bill of Rights introduced, and the "minority rights of the French Canadian people" guaranteed.

At the same time the Communists made a determined effort to

present themselves as the heirs of the 1837 rebels and the champions of "true Canadianism". On August 26, 1939, *The Clarion* assured its readers that Communism was "as Canadian as the Maple Leaf".

Communist efforts to merge into the Canadian scene involved somersaults which shocked some radicals, who charged the CPC with betraying working-class interests. The Trotskyists, for instance, disapproved of the way that the Toronto May Day Celebration Committee, on which the Stalinists were influential, "ruined the traditional proletarian character by sponsoring such proposals as pipers in kilts, the singing of the French national anthem, a church minister on the list of speakers and a generous dose of Canadian patriotism."[3]

The Communist International facilitated the Canadianization of the CPC by granting greater autonomy to all its sections in 1936. From then on Communist parties were no longer subjected to the detailed control which had forced them to refer many matters to the Comintern headquarters. Freed from the mass of paperwork involved in writing detailed reports to Moscow and the long delays until the Comintern officials there reached a decision, the Communists were able to forge ahead in a world that was favourably disposed to many of the demands they put forward or were associated with.

The Communists began by making a determined effort to establish cordial relations with the CCF, a party they had denounced since its inception. *The Worker* had criticized the Regina Manifesto and the CCF's subsequent policy statements. The Communist press in English and other languages had also denounced Woodsworth and those who shared his views.

As Woodsworth reminded Carr in 1935, the terms the Communists had used included, " 'Labour fakirs' or is it spelled 'fakers'," "yellow dogs", "traitors to the working class", "social fascists", "the third party of capitalism."[4]

The unrelenting Communist abuse of the CCF until the summer of 1934 can be attributed to three factors. To begin with, the Communists were convinced that the CCF proposals were at best utopian, if not actually harmful. "Woodsworth's policies," *The Worker* warned on February 17, 1934, "will lead to fascism, war and the continuous rule of capitalism." To prevent such a calamity, Stewart Smith insisted that "the revolutionary movement must intensify ten-fold its exposure of the capitalist theories and program of the CCF."[5]

Smith's "exposé" of the CCF was a book entitled *Socialism and the CCF* (Montreal, 1934). Writing under the pen name of G.

Pierce, he attacked CCF proposals as "panaceas for capitalism", dismissed the CCF version of socialism as "State capitalism", criticized "the fallacy of peaceful revolution" fashionable in most CCF circles, and drew attention to the "role of social reformism as the twin of Fascism."

Second, the uninspiring performance of the UFA government in Alberta in the 1930s had provided the CPC with a case against democratic socialist government, since the UFA was affiliated with the CCF. The Communists maintained that the election of CCF governments in other provinces would result in the same kind of administration as in Alberta.

Third, the Communists were appalled to discover that the CCF was making converts in the very quarters where the CPC had expected to gain additional strength in view of its fighting record in the early days of the Depression. E. Cecil-Smith was not the only Communist journalist to bemoan the fact that

> the propitious formation of the CCF just at the time when the Communist party was outlawed, has allowed them to stop the leftward shift of thousands of workers, farmers, intellectuals and others, by offering them something 'just as good' and at the same time nice and 'Canadian'.[6]

Communist interest in the CCF was not reciprocated. Nor were their attacks on the democratic socialists. By and large, CCF leaders and publications devoted little attention to the Communists, and displayed remarkable restraint in their dealings with the CPC in the period 1932-1935. As a result, Woodsworth could write with a clear conscience to Carr that the CCF had "refrained from saying anything against the Communist Party, except in so far as on occasion they have sought to defend themselves against misrepresentation. . . . We feel we are in no way responsible for the accumulated prejudices and bitterness."[7]

The Communists' adoption of Popular Front tactics was accompanied by several Communist moves to show goodwill towards the socialists. CCF leaders were no longer bitterly attacked in the Communist press unless they warned against co-operation with the CPC, as Woodsworth discovered more than once. The end of the Communist campaign of vilification preceded the decision to withdraw half a dozen Communists who had already been nominated as candidates in the 1935 federal election. In every instance the Communists announced that they were withdrawing to avoid a split in the working-class vote.

The stage was now set for a Communist attempt to transform

the CCF into a broadly-based farmer-labour party which the CPC would join as a separate entity. Such a solution would have enabled the Communists to preserve their organization (something the CPC was never prepared to give up), to influence the policies of the CCF, and to approach and make converts among the already socialistically inclined. In November 1935 the Communist proposal to join forces was reinforced by an offer to enter a "government which though unable to introduce socialism, will be prepared to carry through a revolutionary program," a phrase which Stewart Smith employed to mean:

> Control of production and the banks, the disbandment of fascist forces, the removal of the fascists from control of police forces and the armed forces, and the replacement of these forces by an armed workers' militia.[8]

The Communists knew that a Popular Front, based on the CCF and the CPC, could not be built overnight. They believed it would grow out of struggles "around the most burning issues locally, on the district scale and nationally," and that a great deal would depend on the ability of the CPC to convince the socialists of the advantages of co-operation between the two parties.

They thought that co-operation with the CCF on a national scale would stem from one of the following developments. Ideally, Woodsworth would be converted to the idea of a People's Front. This, however, was most unlikely in view of his outlook and his experiences with the Communists before 1935. Since he did not change his mind after the Comintern had changed its tactics, the Communists periodically accused him and his closest colleagues of "sectarianism", of ignoring the class struggle, of concentrating on parliamentary politics, and of letting some CCFers use "left-wing" phraseology to retain the support of CCF militants who wanted action. The unwillingness of the CCF leaders to give high priority to activities the CPC considered vital caused Stewart Smith to complain that they were "fiddling while precious opportunities burn."[9]

A somewhat less attractive alternative to the conversion of Woodsworth would have been a bitter struggle within the CCF on the very issue of co-operation with the CPC. If Woodsworth and other socialist critics of the Popular Front, whom the Communists labelled "right-wingers", were defeated, they would be replaced by what the Communists described as the "vacillating centre". The latter, the CPC believed, would be more inclined to listen to Communist proposals.

For a time the Communists placed some of their hopes on King

Gordon. His statement that the "CCF and Communists must get together" earned him an accolade from Buck, who described him in November 1935 as a representative of "some of the best tendencies in the CCF, particularly among the intellectuals."[10] The following year Buck saw a glimmer of hope in Graham Spry who, at the convention of the Ontario CCF came out in favour of carefully discussing the question of the united front.[11] Spry also expressed the view that there was merit in the objectives of the Communists, even if their methods were not conducive to unity. At the same time Buck criticized Spry, and those who shared his views, for not opposing Woodsworth's anti-CPC stand. Before the year was over Spry too fell into disfavour because he rejected Communist proposals for united action in municipal and Ontario politics.

A hostile right wing and a "vacillating centre" faced four disparate left wing groups in the CCF. Some of the left-wingers Buck considered beyond the pale, because they were Trotskyists, and hence hostile to the CPC. On many occasions Communist leaders and publications urged the CCF to expel the Trotskyists.* Other left-wingers were also unwelcome because their brand of radicalism did not meet Communist specifications. The presence of staunch opponents of the status quo in the CCF, the Communist press contended, enabled the CCF to delude a number of sincere workers who otherwise would have deserted the CCF. In the opinion of Leslie Morris, these left-wingers represented a necessary "reserve" for the Woodsworths. The third group of left-wingers met with Communist approval because they had the right attitude towards unity. Unfortunately, they failed to press their case at CCF conventions. Finally, there were left-wingers in the CCF who were nothing but camouflaged Communists. They had joined the CCF in line with these instructions given by the organizational secretary of the CPC:

> We need strong Party fractions composed of active workers, inside the trade unions, CCF clubs, Social Credit groups and incipient fascist organizations in order to possess the necessary instruments for winning the masses of Canadian people.[12]

According to an organ of the Comintern, the CPC was "willing to do all in its power to assist the pro-unity elements in the CCF."[13]

---

*The leaders of the CPC were not amused when Woodsworth suggested, "If the Communists are so keen for a united front, why not begin by having a united front of the Stalinists and the Trotskyists." *Daily Clarion* (Toronto), April 20, 1937.

Buck and his colleagues knew that a stronger and more skilfully led "left" in the CCF would increase the chances of Woodsworth's defeat and the emergence of a new leadership. Even if Woodworth's critics did not win a decisive victory in the debate over the People's Front, the ferment within the CCF was bound to speed up the process of differentiation within Canadian social democracy. Like Lenin, the Canadian Communists argued and argue to this day that no social democratic movement forms a uniform entity. Therefore, according to this argument, in periods of economic crisis, let alone a revolutionary situation, social democracy is prone to tensions, factionalism and splits. Disillusionment among socialist militants and sympathizers will increase, and induce many socialists to turn to the Communist Party. As a result, democratic socialists will lose ground to the CPC, which in turn will become a mass party.

Few CCF leaders were willing to play the role assigned to them by the CPC. Like Labour Party leaders in Britain, they were aware of the gulf separating socialists from Communists. The Communist readiness to use or condone the use of violence did not endear the CPC to a Christian pacifist like J. S. Woodsworth, nor to M. J. Coldwell, his second in command. Their role in rejecting Communist overtures cannot be overstressed. David Lewis, the national secretary of the CCF and the linchpin of its headquarters, displayed increasing distaste for the CPC in the 1930s, and in the 1940s he became one of the Communists' most formidable opponents in left-wing circles. Other democratic socialists remembered Communist manoeuvres in the CLP and the trade union movement.

Last but not least, Woodsworth and his closest collaborators knew only too well that an alliance with the Communists would hinder the socialists' chances in a society in which many people identified democratic socialism with Communism and feared that a CCF victory at the polls would lead to violence, chaos, and the end of representative government. The outcome of the 1935 federal election in a number of ridings confirmed these fears. On the eve of the election, *The Worker* listed the names of several dozen CCF candidates who had accepted either the minimum or the maximum demands that CPC local organizations had presented to them either in the form of a questionnaire or in direct negotiations. The CCF candidates specifically endorsed by the Communists included E. B. Joliffe, King Gordon, Grant McNeil and Graham Spry, as well as two members of the CCF caucus in the previous Parliament, E. J. Garland and H. E. Spencer. With the exception of McNeil, none of these CCFers was successful. Their defeats strengthened the case of those radicals who argued that Communist support was the kiss of death for democratic socialists. Moreover, Communist attacks had not prevented the re-election of Woodsworth, Heaps and McInnis.

Although the stand taken by most CCF leaders on the subject of an alliance with the CPC appeared clearcut, and was backed by the majority of their supporters, many Canadians were unimpressed. Canadians were more influenced – and the daily press reminded those whose memory was short – by other kinds of evidence. Throughout the 1930s the CCF and the CPC had often used the same jargon and taken the same or similar positions on a number of issues. More than once the two parties had looked like twin brothers to those who lacked the patience or the means to probe more deeply. Both parties had expressed their hatred of capitalism in no uncertain terms, both had demanded large scale nationalization and both were convinced of the superiority of state planning over a free market economy. Both, as Stewart Smith was eager to point out in 1935,

> have common ground on immediate issues. The CCF and the Communists are both in favour of genuine unemployment insurance, of a large scale building program, of the abolition of slave camps, of increased wages and increased relief, of a moratorium on farmers' debts, higher prices and security for the small businessman. We are both in favour of steeply graduated income tax to force the rich to pay the costs of the crisis. Second, both the CCF and the Communist Party are for the repeal of Section 98, the reform of the electoral system to provide proportional representation. . . . Thirdly, the CCF and the Communist Party meet on common ground in the fight for peace.[14]

No less disturbing to a number of Canadians was the willingness of some elements in the CCF to collaborate with the Communists and to urge other socialists to do the same. Convinced that the capitalist system had no redeeming features, that the U.S.S.R., in spite of all its imperfections, was building a socialist society, and that the time had come to mobilize all left-wing forces in Canada, these socialists were ready to make use of Communist resources, drive and organizational talents. CCF militants and groups scattered across the country pressured the National Office of the CCF to collaborate with the CPC in two ways. Some advocated close co-operation between the two parties, and looked forward to the eventual merger of the CPC with the CCF. More numerous were those who urged a "united front only on the immediate questions of the day," including "joint action" against the "evils of unemployment, in the defence of civil liberties and against the threat of war."

When their views did not influence the National Office of the CCF, they proceeded to co-operate with the Communists on their own. They worked with party members in campaigns on behalf of the unemployed, they allowed representatives of the CPC to sit on bodies planning First of May celebrations sponsored by the CCF, they graced the ranks of organizations set up by the Communists to help the Republican cause in the Spanish Civil War, and they advocated co-operation in other areas of interest to radical opponents of the status quo.

Faced with insubordination among a sizable minority of CCF activists, Woodsworth and his colleagues pursued a policy which at some cost saved the independence and distinct image of the Canadian socialist movement. The arguments they used in support of their stance revolved around two points. First, that the CCF, founded by a number of labour and farmer organizations, was a *de facto* People's or United Front: hence, they claimed, there was no need for a new organization. Second, they stressed the differences separating the democratic socialists from the Communists. Woodsworth set the tone when he told the delegates to the Regina Conference in 1933:

> The CCF advocates peaceful and orderly methods. In this we distinguish ourselves sharply from the Communist Party which envisages the new social order as being ushered in by violent upheaval and the establishment of a dictatorship . . . in Canada we believe it possible to avoid chaos and bloodshed.

The policy of non-cooperation with the Communist Party or Communist-controlled organizations was reaffirmed in subsequent CCF documents. Directives from above, however, did not end the controversy over Communists and Communism in CCF circles. Doubts were expressed about the wisdom of a policy of non-cooperation. Those who paid close attention to events in Europe argued that the left's failure to combine forces had enabled anti-Marxists in Italy, Germany and Austria to smash the socialist as well as the Communist parties; the danger of fascism was so obvious that united action alone could prevent similar defeats in other countries. Others drew up the balance sheet of CCF endeavours since 1932, and argued that more could have been achieved if the Communists and socialists had worked together. Failure to take joint action simply played into the hands of those who wanted to perpetuate the status quo.

By 1936 the pressure to collaborate with the Communists on some issues had become so strong that the CCF retreated a little from its previous stand. Not that most CCF leaders had suddenly changed their minds about the CPC and the Soviet system. What had changed was their ability to agree among themselves on how to cope with Communist overtures and those CCFers who were already cooperating with the CPC in spite of warnings and occasional expulsions. The result of these tensions was a motion passed at the national convention of the CCF by 88 votes to 7 in August 1936. It reaffirmed the decision not to collaborate with other parties. David Lewis defended the stand taken by the convention in the September 1936 issue of *The Canadian Forum*, where he warned:

> A fusion of the CCF, Communists, Social Crediters, Reconstructionists, and Left Liberals—which is what the Communists advocate—would under present Canadian conditions, create confusion, compromise the socialist objective of the CCF as a party, and might even, by way of reaction, call forth a strengthening of the right forces.

The second part of the motion was passed unanimously and could be interpreted as a concession to those who were already collaborating with the Communists. It called on all CCF units to take an active part in certain non-political activities and, whenever desirable, to co-operate with other groups. According to Lewis, "the line of demarcation between non-political and political co-operation is fairly distinct." The decision regarding non-political co-operation, he pointed out, would rest with the provincial councils concerned. Such decisions would be subject to review by the National Council of the CCF if, in its opinion, such co-operation "conflicts with the platform and constitution of the CCF."

This decision legitimized the activities of those democratic socialists who were cooperating with the Communists in organizations like the Canadian Youth Congress, the Canadian League against Fascism and War, the Committee to Aid Spanish Democracy. The CCFers who were active in some of these organizations included such well-known socialist intellectuals as Frank Underhill, and MPs like T.C. Douglas and William Irvine.

The Communists were delighted. The CCF decision represented just the sort of step the CPC wanted the socialists to take. Equally welcome was a speech Lewis delivered in October 1937. He urged his fellow-socialists to "participate with imagination, without fear, no matter who else may be participating," in a variety of organizations.[15]

Ironically, the demand for a People's Front, and for cooperation with Communists in general, lost much of its appeal soon after the motion had been passed by the CCF convention. In 1937 the national convention of the CCF devoted very little attention to the subject, and Carr was left to tell the readers of a Comintern publication that "very little advance has been achieved on the whole in the struggle for unity."[16]

Declining interest in collaboration with the CPC was due as much to events abroad as in Canada. Stalin's purge of the Old Bolsheviks, and the persecution of anarchists and Trotskyists by Spanish Communists, provided additional arguments for socialist critics of the Soviet regime and Communist parties. At home many socialists, including left-wing ones, were disturbed by Communist attempts to seek allies in the Social Credit, Liberal and Tory parties, the very parties that the CCF was fighting. Nor did the Communists endear themselves to the socialists by contesting those Ontario ridings where the CCF thought that its own candidates had a good chance of winning in the provincial election in 1937. The blow was all the greater as the CPC urged the voters to support David Croll, a Liberal, rather than his CCF opponent, while Stewart Smith dramatically withdrew in Toronto-Bellwoods to strengthen the chances of another Liberal, Arthur Roebuck. According to Smith, "Liberals and Labour are duty bound to vote together and elect proven champions of the People's Rights," and thus prevent the return of a Tory administration at Queen's Park.[17] Although the Communist daily also came out in favour of several CCF candidates, the residue of bitterness was so great that the prospect of a People's Front based on the CCF and the CPC disappeared.

Although the electoral appeal of the CPC could hardly compare with that of the CCF, Woodsworth and his colleagues had good reason to be wary of the Communists. Until well into the 1930s the CPC presented a challenge which the socialists could not ignore, for three reasons. First, the differences in the numerical size of the two parties were not all that great, even if one discounted Buck's boast that the CPC had "more active regularly dues paying members than the CCF."[18] Second, the number of experienced CCF organizers between election campaigns was not appreciably larger than that at the disposal of the CPC. What the Communists lacked in numbers they made up in mobility, cohesion and ability to carry out directives from above, without the soul-searching, the lengthy debates and the endemic hair-splitting that were notorious in CCF circles. Finally, the Communists exercised "a very considerable influence" through what Woodsworth described as "numerous subsidiaries."[19] Party members in these organizations were often in close contact with CCF militants. More than once they helped to shape the outlook of these socialists and determine the stand taken by this or that CCF club.

The attempts to prevent Communist inroads in the CCF took up valuable time which the socialists would have preferred to use in other ways. To add to the problem, action against Communists and pro-Communists often took place in public, and provided the Communists with arguments that the "right-wing leaders" of the CCF did not permit democracy within their party. This argument was used whenever members of the CCF were expelled for collaborating with the Communists. Some of those who were expelled joined the CPC, and issued statements condemning their former leaders and urging other socialists to follow them into the Communist movement.

Those who could not stomach Woodsworth's unyielding attitude towards the Communists were not the only ones to leave the CCF. Others abandoned it because they felt that the CCF was not firm enough in its opposition to the Communists. The United Farmers of Ontario (UFO) and Elmore Philpott, a prominent member of the Ontario CCF, withdrew from the CCF because they were appalled by the confusion among socialists caused by a Communist overture in 1934.[20]

In that year the Canadian Labor Defence League called on the CCF to join in the defence of A. E. Smith, the CLDL secretary, who was on trial under Section 98 of the Criminal Code. Although the leadership of the CCF was firmly opposed to this piece of legislation, and condemned the authorities for trying Communists under it, neither Woodsworth nor the Provincial Council of the Ontario CCF were prepared to join forces with the CPC in what appeared to be another Communist attempt to create a united front. They failed, however, to rally the major part of their rank-and-file. The Labor Conference component of the Ontario CCF adopted a pro-Communist stance, although probably only a minority of its spokesmen were party members. Some were ex-Communists, others Marxists, while the rest were non-conformists unwilling to accept instructions from CCF headquarters. By the time Woodsworth and Angus McInnis had reorganized the Ontario CCF organization, depriving the Communists of one of their footholds in the CCF, the UFO was no longer affiliated with the CCF. The departure of the UFO provided anti-socialists with additional proof of their argument that the CCF was incapable of coping successfully with the Communists in its midst.

Throughout the 1930s a trickle of radicals was leaving the CCF for the CPC or Communist-led organizations. They included both men and women, a sprinkling of clergymen, young university graduates and people who could not afford a higher education. Some of the former CCFers rose high in their new surroundings. Two eventually became leaders of provincial organizations of the CPC; others ran as Communist or pro-Communist candidates in municipal, provincial and federal elections; a third group found jobs in unions controlled by the CPC, while many others were on committees of organizations set up by the Communists in or after the 1930s. In nearly every instance, the Communist press emphasized that these ex-socialists had left the CCF because its leaders had acted in a way unworthy of true champions of socialism.

Rebuffed by the majority of democratic socialists, the Communists cast their net more widely. Among those they were eager to win over, the Social Crediters came second only to CCFers. Not that the Communists approved of William Aberhardt's entry into politics or of his campaign to convert Albertans to Social Credit. When the CPC saw the challenge represented by this movement of social dissent, *The Worker* analysed Social Credit at some length, and repeatedly denounced Aberhardt and his followers as "fascists" and "semi-fascists". To buttress their case against Social Credit theory, the organ of the CPC serialized a number of articles by the well-known British Marxist, John Strachey.

The fact that Social Credit had been described as a "fascist" movement at the Seventh Congress of the Comintern did not prevent the Communists from changing their attitude when they realized the implications of the new line of the Communist International, and the extent to which Social Credit represented a reaction against the Canadian Establishment. Already in the autumn of 1935, Communist spokesmen were admitting that they had been mistaken in their earlier assessment of the Social Credit movement. They also contended that the supporters of Social Credit, as opposed to their leaders, represented potential Communist allies. By voting for Social Credit, Albertans had broken away from the "old line" parties and provided additional evidence of the desire for change in western Canada. Given Social Credit opposition to finance capital, and Aberhardt's failure to introduce major reforms, the Communists expected rifts to occur within the ranks of Social Credit. The CPC maintained, from the 1930s onwards, that this process of differentiation could be speeded up if the Communists encouraged Aberhardt's disillusioned followers to join a broad movement against the status quo.

In the summer of 1937 the Communist had reason to believe that not only disgruntled Social Crediters, but the Social Credit League itself, could be drawn into a coalition with the CPC. At the height of Aberhardt's showdown with the federal government the Social Credit Board invited the local representatives of the CPC to talks in Edmonton. The Communists were urged by G. F. Powell and others to join in the campaign against Mackenzie King. The invitation to "attack the attackers" was not rejected.[21]

The reversal of the party line on Social Credit confused many activists in Alberta. As has so often happened in the Communist movement, they went from one extreme to another. From Toronto Buck accused the "Alberta comrades of simply aligning the Communist Party in a position that can be interpreted as one of unqualified support of Aberhardt."[22]

Not that the CPC was prepared to stand aside when Aberhardt challenged the federal government on certain issues. A special resolution of the eighth party convention in October 1937

> pledges to the people of Alberta that the Communist Party in every province will do all in its power to counteract the vicious campaign of misrepresentation of Alberta in the reactionary press and demand that the Federal Government stop interfering in the legislative activities of the Alberta Government.[23]

The Communists displayed the same partisanship when Social Credit fought the People's League, an organization set up by some local Tories and Liberals in an attempt to oust Aberhardt. Buck warned at the time that a change of government "would be a calamity for the people of Alberta."

To prevent such a calamity the Communists gave "very active and effective support" to the Social Credit candidate in the provincial by-election in East Edmonton in March 1938.[24] Leslie Morris, the delegate of the central committee in western Canada, led the Social Credit victory parade which followed the counting of the votes, and once appeared on the same platform as Ernest Manning, who succeeded Aberhardt as premier in 1943.

For a time the Communists thought they could form a broad progressive movement with Social Credit groups and the Alberta wing of the CCF. According to Morris, the main stumbling block to such a coalition was the "carping, put-them-on-the spot attitude of some Alberta CCF leaders to the Social Credit movement."[25] This was all the more unfortunate as Social Credit "springs from the masses and voices their needs," a view Aberhardt would have been the first to agree with.

The leaders of the Alberta CCF were not the only ones to fall foul of the CPC because of their "doctrinaire" and "sectarian" attitude towards Social Credit. George H. Williams, the spokesman of the Saskatchewan CCF, also came under fire when he proved "contemptuous" of the Communist proposal for an alliance of the opponents of the "old line" parties on the eve of the election in that province in June 1938.[26] The attack on Williams was another indication that the CCF and the CPC were drifting apart; in 1937 the *Daily Clarion* had hailed Williams's statement in favour of collaboration with the local Communists and other opponents of the Liberals in the west.

In the Saskatchewan election campaign the Communists and the socialists found little common ground. According to David Lewis, the Communists "boosted Social Credit and criticized the CCF for, in effect, not withdrawing some of its candidates in favour of Social Credit."[27] When the votes were counted, the *Daily Clarion* attributed the Liberal victory to the leaders of the Saskatchewan CCF. Their rejection of joint action with the CPC was roundly condemned; so was their tendency to regard Social Credit as a "fascist invasion" from Alberta, instead of a movement of "the people of the West against monopoly capital."[28]

When the members of the politbureau of the CPC reassessed the political situation in the Prairies after the election, they must have realized that too close an identification with Social Credit was not in the Communist party's best interests. The need for disengagement became obvious in view of the scant progress made by the CPC despite Morris's hard work to align the CPC with Social Credit. Aberhardt had paid no attention to Communist overtures; nor was there any likelihood that he would change his mind. He was firmly in control of the Social Credit League; no Communist-backed revolt of the rank-and-file could topple him or force him to change his policies to suit the CPC.

Before long, the Communists had to face the inescapable fact that the bulk of Social Crediters were and would remain hostile to the CPC, on ethical as well as on economic grounds. The opposition encountered by the Communists from this broadly based movement made the task of expanding the CPC very difficult. As a result, the Communist recruitment drive in 1938 reached only 31 per cent of the target, and the CPC continued to draw most of its support from farmers and miners of East European extraction. It had little to offer except some mild criticism of Aberhardt's failure to produce a concrete program. The only short-term solution that the Communists could think of, before September 1939, was the creation of a broad movement of opinion that would force the provincial government to carry out the reforms that the Communists thought Albertans needed and wanted.

Although the CPC had failed to secure the co-operation of Social Credit and the CCF, the Communists were not about to turn their backs on these two movements of social dissent. As late as 1939 Stewart Smith wrote, in the *Manual on Party Branch Work*, that the CPC branch should "establish the closest fraternal relations with the local CCF branches," and he added that these instructions applied "with equal force" to "Social Credit clubs."

These instructions received less publicity than Buck's search for allies in more conventional circles. Once again he followed the advice given by foreigners to the Canadian Communists. Earl Browder, who was sensitive to Comintern thinking, told the central committee of the CPC in November 1935:

> Before we have gone very far in Canada . . . we will already begin to be faced . . . with the problem of united front on a broader scale . . . . Organized political groups splitting off from the other parties and who, upon a united front basis on particular issues especially, can be brought into alliance with the basic united front.[29]

Buck drew up a list of potential allies in 1938. It included

> the trade union movement, the CCF, the progressive wing of the Social Credit movement, farmers' organizations, reform Liberals, local Labor parties . . . the broad movement led by the Civil Liberties Union and a growing progressive wing in the non-conformist church (United Church of Canada).[30]

He justified the case for an alliance of such disparate elements by drawing attention to the dangers, in his opinion, Canadians faced in those years before the Second World War. In 1936 he declared that "the main representatives of reactionary finance capital are the leaders and spokesmen of the Conservative Party, although they have important allies in the Liberal ranks and in the government."[31]

The following year he was worrying most about the "reactionary alliance" of Mitch Hepburn, the Liberal Premier of Ontario, and Maurice Duplessis, the Premier of Quebec and the leader of the Union Nationale. "This alliance", Buck argued, "is a direct result of the strivings of big capital to establish a national centre for the concentration of all reactionary forces, to stop the democratic advance of the people."[32]

To defeat the "reactionaries," in 1938, Buck urged the formation of a "democratic front" with a program

> which the people will understand and which can be carried through by dominion and provincial governments under our present government set up. Thus, it cannot be a fundamental program for the socialist re-organization of Canada, because the majority of our people are not ready to support such a program.[33]

The decision to soft-pedal socialism as a goal was part and parcel of the attempt to gain allies among non-socialists and anti-socialists. It represented another reversal of the Communist line, because as late as July 1936, Buck had claimed that "Canada is ripe for socialism."[34]

Fear of reactionary forces and the desire for a People's Front also demanded a different attitude towards certain politicians who, in the eyes of top Communist leaders, represented potential allies. The party headquarters in Toronto, for instance, urged a more flexible attitude towards Pattullo's Liberal government in B.C. than many activists on the west coast were prepared to adopt. This directive was defended on the grounds that Pattullo should not be driven into the arms of Hepburn and Duplessis.

Pattullo was not the only Liberal politician in whom the Communists were interested. For several months in 1939 the Communists considered the federal Liberals worthy of support. Quite a few eyebrows were raised in CCF circles when Norman Freed, a senior party official, declared that "there may be situations in some constituencies where it would be impossible to elect either CCF, Communist or progressive candidates. In this event, our guiding principle will be . . . to re-elect Premier King."[35]

Freed justified the new policy by arguing that "in many respects the return of a Liberal Government would be infinitely better than the election of a Conservative machine." Other Communists insisted that the Liberals were more susceptible to mass pressure than the party of Arthur Meighen, R. B. Bennett and Robert James Manion.

The readiness of the CPC to come to the aid of Mackenzie King coincided with similar overtures to some Conservatives. In 1939 Communist spokesmen expressed a great deal of sympathy for

New Democracy, a movement founded by W. D. Herridge, formerly Canada's representative in Washington and also R. B. Bennett's brother-in-law. Herridge's campaign against the leadership of the Liberal and Tory parties, and his call for action, was approved by Aberhardt and Buck. Buck argued that since neither the CCF nor Social Credit nor the CPC could win a majority of seats in western Canada, it was essential for the opponents of the "old line" parties to agree on a single candidate in each constituency. A broad movement of reform could be built through New Democracy. He also justified Communist support for Herridge by references to New Democracy gripping the imagination of the majority of people.

Against "the proposed coalition of reactionaries we must have a coalition of progressives. A temporary alliance which will unite all the progressives for us for the dominion election,"[36] were Buck's words on the matter. His call was heeded by party members in the west. In Saskatchewan they provided much of the support gained by New Democracy.

Herridge remained in the good graces of the Communist press until he suggested in August 1939 that "New Democracy ideals, if put into practice, would drive from Canada every foreign system from fascism to Communism."[37] By then the idea of a People's Front had lost its appeal everywhere. Buck blamed Canada's lack of a People's Front on the leaders of the organizations which the CPC had approached but who were "publicly antagonistic to the Communist Party."

The formation of a People's Front was not a major issue in Quebec, where the local party's survival was at stake. After the federal government had repealed Section 98 of the Criminal Code in 1936 and the Communists had distributed leaflets in the Legislative Assembly in Quebec City, the government of Premier Duplessis passed the legislation popularly known as the Padlock Act of 1937. This prohibited the distribution of Communist literature anywhere in the province, and empowered the Attorney-General of Quebec to padlock any premises where the authorities suspected that Communism was being advocated.

Duplessis used this piece of legislation widely against the Communists. He thereby aroused protests, not only from the CPC and its mass organizations, but from socialists, trade union leaders and libertarians in general. They were appalled by this restriction on civil liberties and the lack of definition of "Communism and Bolshevism" under the Padlock Act. To Duplessis's critics in the 1930s the Padlock Act appeared to be yet another example of the kind of authoritarianism not far removed from the fascism in several European countries. The existence of fascist and semi-fascist organizations in Quebec which were hostile to Communists, Jews, socialists and liberals, heightened tensions in Montreal. These the Communists exploited to strengthen their organization and win allies.

In general, French-Canadian opinion was not opposed to Duplessis's efforts to reduce Communist agitation in the thirties. The Catholic Church and most French Canadians associated the atheistic Communists with attempts to subvert the traditional Quebecois way of life. They were convinced that the Canadian Communists, if given a chance, would subject the Catholics to the same kind of treatment that the Spanish left was meting out to Catholic priests and laymen in territory held by the Republicans in the Spanish Civil War. So conservative elements in Quebec not only supported Duplessis's anti-Communist stand, but urged the federal government to ban the CPC throughout Canada.

The fact that most Communist activists in Quebec were not of French-Canadian descent made it all the easier for Duplessis and his fellow anti-Communists to depict the CPC as an alien force in the province, and to isolate the CPC from the main body of French Canadian labour. As late as 1948, the leader of the Communist Party in Quebec had to admit that Duplessis won "large majorities in working class towns and in working class constituencies of Montreal."[38]

Under these circumstances there was little that the CPC could do, although the Communists tried hard to obtain the co-operation of Catholics both in and outside French Canada. Like his comrades in France, Buck denied that the Communists were hostile to religion. He also quoted passages from papal encyclicals to show that Communists and Catholics were not poles apart. His invitations to Catholics to join a broad movement for peace, and against fascism, drew almost no response from practising Catholics. In the 1930s Catholics, to a greater extent than any other major Christian body, remained immune to the appeals of the Comintern and the CPC.

Failure to find many allies did not prevent the CPC from increasing appreciably in numbers, in the range of its propaganda, and in its influence among the young, the intellectuals, the trade unionists and the electorate.

The end of the period of persecution in English-speaking Canada, and the use of Popular Front tactics made it much easier for the CPC to enrol members. Although onerous duties, and petty-minded, pompous officials, and dreary party meetings in dingy surroundings caused many a departure of disillusioned young enthusiasts, enough remained to bring about a three-fold increase in party membership.*

Thousands of Canadians, who were disappointed by the lack-lustre performance of the two "old line parties" in the 1930s, who were unmoved by the appeal of Social Credit, and impatient at the way in which the CCF tackled its own and Canada's problems, were willing to join the CPC. To them the CPC appeared as the best champion of the victims of the Depression, the most resolute fighter against fascism and war, the only political party that had a

* CPC membership 1934-1939:

5,500 July 1934	*International Press Correspondence* (London), 21 September 1934, p. 1328.
7,000 April 1935	*The Worker* (Toronto), 13 April 1935.
8,000 June 1935	*Ibid.,* 11 June 1935.
9,000 October 1935	*Towards a Canadian People's Front* (Toronto), 1935, p. 104.
"close to" 10,000 January 1936	*The Worker,* 18 January 1936.
10,000 May 1936	*The Communist International* (London), September 1936, p. 1224.
12,500 January 1937	*Daily Clarion,* (Toronto), 1 February 1937.
15,000 October 1937	*International Press Correspondence,* 24 October 1937, p. 1390.
15,000 spring of 1938	*A Democratic Front for Canada* (Toronto), 1938, p. 47.
15,000 autumn of 1938	*The Party Builder* (Toronto), December 1938, p. 3.
16,000 early in 1939	L. Morris, *The Story of Tim Buck's Party* (Toronto), 1939, p. 30.

convincing explanation for the world's ills. The solutions offered by the CPC sounded feasible and sensible. The widespread feeling that the Communists were fighting on behalf of the poor, and that they were guiding thousands towards a better and more progressive society, of which the Soviet Union was the prototype, inspired activists to great efforts and enabled the CPC to play in the 1930s a role quite out of proportion to the size of its membership.

Its organizational structure provided opportunities for people seeking immediate action. The party saw to it that recruits were not kept idle. Party schools taught them the Stalinist version of Marxism, party publications offered them cheap inspirational reading material, and cultural organizations in which the Communists were active catered for the middle brow. The time devoted to demonstrations, meetings, picketing, the sale of party newspapers, fund-raising, the collection of signatures for petitions, and service on delegations to this or that institution, left scant leisure for soul-searching or private recreation. The campaigns organized or supported by the party were sufficiently varied, exciting and time-consuming, to absorb the energies of anybody who could keep up the pace and was eager to climb the party ladder.

An increasing number of promising recruits became *de facto* employees of the CPC. Some held positions at the party headquarters in Toronto, or worked in party offices in other cities. A few joined the staff of Communist newspapers. Others were employed in mass organizations, many of which increased their membership during this period. A large number became trade union officials in those segments of the labour movement where Communist influence was growing rapidly.

The jobs were seldom well-paid, involved long and irregular hours, and included a great deal of travel. And yet holding such a job was preferred to the monotony of factory work, or the empty life of the unemployed. Those who held or aspired to such jobs felt that the CPC alone had recognized their talents and provided them with a purpose in life.

Party officials, new or old, were occasionally criticized for their performance: for handling matters which could easily have been done by subordinates, for passing on instructions without "a regular check upon the fulfilment of decisions," for having "negligible" contact "with the masses and mass work."[39] The sending of inaccurate reports to the party headquarters was another problem, which was particularly serious when party officials overestimated the size of crowds at meetings and demonstrations.

In the long run, however, what hurt the CPC most was the unwillingness of prominent Communist trade unionists to make full use of their position and prestige to spread the Communist word. Sam Carr, the organizational secretary of the CPC, complained, in his speech to the eighth convention of the CPC in October 1937:

> Communists who are elected to important positions in the trade unions sometimes get divorced from the general stream of Party work. Under the pressure of small and large problems they face as trade union officials, some of our comrades begin to fail their duty as party officials . . . we want Communists in positions of trust to carry their positions so as to increase their own and their Party's prestige. However this will be quite impossible, if these comrades fail as they sometimes do, to participate in the general Party life, to build the Party in the unions, to strengthen the number of devoted trade unionists and to keep themselves informed of current Party life and problems. Now, more than ever, we should also combat the dangerous tendency to hide the face of the Party, we cannot permit our comrades in important positions to act as if they half agreed that our Party is an outcast.[40]

Lower down the party hierarchy, secretaries of branches (the new name for units) grappled with the high turnover of party members. This retarded the numerical growth of the CPC and made it impossible to reach the set target of 20,000 members by either October 1937 or January 1, 1939. This turnover problem was the subject of prolonged discussions at party conventions and at meetings of the central committee. The general feeling among senior party officials was that no single cause could be blamed for the fluctuation in numbers. Party membership would simultaneously rise in some parts of the country and fall in others. In some industrial centres growing Communist influence failed to produce a rise in party membership. On the west coast, where the Communists made major inroads in the trade union movement, the fluctuations reached "catastrophic" porportions, with the result that the CPC had fewer members in B.C. in May 1938 than at the beginning of 1937.[41]

Carr attributed the turnover of party members in Canada to several factors. Some left because "to attend a branch meeting is usually a tedious affair." Many branch secretaries lacked the skill to run meetings efficiently, with the result that branches spent "hours of aimless wandering in the solution of the simplest problem." Some party members raised the old complaint about the amount of work they were expected to do. An excessive workload led to the departure of some new members, once the thrill of joining the CPC had evaporated. Inactive party members and branches, on the other hand, prevented the execution of party directives at the grassroots level. Consequently, the main burden was borne by a relatively small number of enthusiasts. According to a prominent party official, not more than 10 percent of "our membership do any party recruiting."[42]

Nor were these the only complaints. The demand for financial contributions to a variety of causes sponsored by the CPC, imposed an additional strain on party members. Ironically enough, Popular Front tactics proved another source of discouragement to those who felt that the

> Party does not stand forth sufficiently as an independent organization. . . . many say so frankly, feel dissatisfied with what they call the Party 'playing the shadow', not getting the credit for the work done. . . . many new members. . . . drop out since they cannot see any special reason for belonging to the Party in addition to their activities in the labor movement as a whole.[43]

Last but not least, Carr complained that "some of our leading comrades show a strong tendency to consider the membership as something that can be moved about, commanded and instructed at will." He warned that "these practices are particularly dangerous to the growth of our Party, with the influx of native Canadians and Anglo-Saxons who are used to the democratic practices of their various organizations."[44]

The CPC leaders hoped to reduce the turnover of party members by improving "branch work", which Stewart Smith described as "the weakest link in the whole system of Party organization."[45] Party officials were told to pay more attention to the performance of branch secretaries, to attend branch meetings and guide the activities of new branches in particular.

Another device was to emphasize educational work, in the hope that the study of Marxism-Leninism would raise the political consciousness of party members, new and old. According to Leslie Morris, "If we examine the figure for literature sales in the party (which are a most perfect means of finding out how our members are studying) you will find a very bad situation."[46]

Some educational work was carried out at the branch level. The remainder was done in party schools, which ranged from evening classes and weekend schools to the Dominion Training School for party officials, "each of whom" had "at least 2 to 3 years of Party membership." They enrolled for a six-month course.

Something was also done to encourage a spirit of togetherness, because Carr felt that "only too often members of the same branch only meet formally at meetings. Recreational and social programs for the entertainment of branch members, sympathizers and friends are urgently needed."[47]

To make the branches more viable, the number of members per branch was increased to "between twenty and thirty members." As a result of this directive the total number of branches remained stationary between May 1935 and October 1937, although party membership almost doubled. The seven hundred branches were based mainly on the "territorial principle", including all party members who lived in a given area. Industrial branches were less numerous and had fewer members than area branches. In Toronto, for instance, only thirty-three of the hundred branches in 1938 were industrial.

Because of the fluctuations in party membership, a great effort was needed to recruit more members, if only to avoid stagnation. A recruitment drive in the first four months of 1938 achieved only 51 per cent of its target.[48] Successes in Montreal and southern Ontario were counterbalanced by failures in the Maritimes and rural Quebec, by the "practical stagnation of the party in the gold and nickel areas in the North West and North East"of Ontario, by the fact that the party in Manitoba was "concentrated in the city of Winnipeg, and at that in the North end," and by the "sectarianism" of the party organization in B.C., which for a time prevented the local Communists from taking "full advantage of the radical moods of the population."[49]

Carr attributed the relative failure of the recruitment drive to poor leadership and "snobbishness" among Communists, with the result that "workers, farmers, and especially working women and housewives are not recruited." He reminded his colleagues "We are not an exclusive society, we do not demand any specific level of theoretical attainment . . . . Every worker and working farmer . . . every student, professional and small business man, can join our Party. Let us open wider our gates."[50]

The ethnic composition of the CPC changed somewhat, partly thanks to repeated party directives to recruit people who, even if they were not Anglo-Saxons, were at least Canadian-born. In November 1935 Stewart Smith told the central committee that "the present leading cadres of our Party are largely foreign born cadres." He called for a "bold policy of promotion of leading forces, Canadian born leading forces into the highest posts of our Party." In practice, however, the ethnic composition of the polit-bureau did not change appreciably. Those born abroad continued to predominate until natural causes, and bitter disputes in 1956-1957, thinned their ranks, allowing an increase in the number of native Canadians at the top.

The central committee elected in October 1937 reflected the party leaders' desire to bring to the fore those who were Anglo-Saxons or had anglicized their surnames and had also distin-guished themselves in the 1930s. Only a quarter of the members of the central committee were of East European extraction. Finns, Jews and Ukrainians were as well represented as French Canadi-ans. The attrition rate among the Anglo-Saxon members of the central committee was, however, very high. The available evidence shows that only sixteen of the forty-five Anglo-Saxons elected in 1937 were considered worthy of belonging to the much larger cen-tral committee in 1943. Most of the sixteen survivors had been fairly prominent in the CPC and YCL as early as 1929.

More successful was the anglicization of the rank-and-file, although here too the proportion of immigrants remained high. In 1938 almost 1,500 of the 3,500 party members in southern Ontario were in "wards four and five in Toronto, among new Canadians, immigrants from other countries." In that same year "only 22 per cent" of the new members in Toronto were "Canadian born."[51]

What did change was the ethnic distribution among members of East European origin. The percentage of Finns in the CPC fell for several reasons. The split among Finnish Communists after Mac-donald's downfall was damaging to the membership. Some of those who were expelled from the Party or abandoned the Finnish Organization, helped to found a non-Communist newspaper which engaged in polemics with the Communist Finnish-language daily *Vapaus*. Later on, the anti-Communists profited from two events outside Canada. The disappearance of a large group of Finnish Canadian Communists who had settled during the Depression in Soviet Karelia discouraged Finns in Canada from joining or remaining in the Canadian Communist movement. In 1939 the Soviet attack on Finland led to much soul-searching among pro-Communist Finnish Canadians.

Although several prominent Ukrainian Canadian Communists disappeared in the Soviet Union in the 1930s, Communist influ-ence among Ukrainians across Canada remained strong. The ULFTA actually increased its membership from 8,080 in 1932 to 15,000 in 1938.[52] The wide range of ULFTA's cultural and social activities, the existence of a nucleus of activists whose organizational skills had been tested in a variety of ways over the years, and the failure of anti-Communist and non-Communist Ukrainian organizations to attract pro-Communist Ukrainians, all proved highly advantageous to the CPC when looking for recruits and financial support.

As the 1930s gave way to the 1940s, Communists of Ukrainian and Finnish extraction were joined in increasing numbers by members of other ethnic groups from eastern Europe. White Russians who had recently emigrated from the eastern parts of Poland, and some Doukhobors, helped to strengthen Communist influence among Russian Canadians. They filled the ranks of the Workers' and Farmers' Clubs, of which there were twenty-six in 1932, forty-seven in July 1934 and thirty-four in 1938.[53]

A sizable number of party members were Yugoslavs, prevented by American immigration restrictions from emigrating to the States via Canada. By 1939 over one-tenth of the 16,000-strong CPC consisted of Yugoslavs,[54] mainly Croats and Dalmatians. In Canada they worked in the mining, fishing and lumber industries, when not suffering long spells of unemployment. They helped to strengthen Communist influence in those industries in B.C. and were numerous among Canadian volunteers in the Spanish Civil War.

The formation of mass organizations for Russians and Yugoslavs followed similar patterns. In both ethnic communities there was a nucleus of party members from the late 1920s. Most of them lacked much formal education, were recent arrivals in Canada and had travelled a fair amount across the country in search of work. Those in charge of party work among ethnic groups put party members in touch with one another, and encouraged the formation of pro-Communist clubs in communities where Yugoslavs and Russians lived. The clubs engaged in social and cultural activities, and provided a forum for Communist speakers. When several clubs had been established, a Dominion-wide organization would be set up. The CPC would help with the technical arrangements of the founding convention, at which suitable resolutions would be passed and funds collected for Communist causes. A weekly or monthly paper would be launched. This would contain material on events in Canada and eastern Europe, and on developments in the U.S.S.R. "Workers-Correspondents" would report on what was happening in their own locality or place of work. Frequent polemics with anti-Communists would add spice to the contents, while the editorials would reflect the Communist line in North America. The newspaper editor would be a key member of the mass organization and hold a fairly responsible position in the CPC hierarchy.

The Yugoslavs and the Russians were eclipsed in the higher echelons of the CPC by party members of Jewish extraction. Hatred of Nazism, dissatisfaction with British policy in Palestine, and the Jewish tendency to take a prominent part in public affairs in democratic societies, enabled the CPC to recruit many Jews in Montreal, Toronto and Winnipeg, and, thanks to the party's opposition to anti-semitism in Canada and abroad, to gain the sympathies of many Jews who did not go so far as to join the CPC. Not that the majority of Jews with a penchant for radical change flocked to enrol in the CPC. In North Winnipeg, a Communist stronghold, Buck gained fewer Jewish votes in 1935 than did Heaps of the CCF.[55]

The Communists active in the Jewish community encouraged the formation of cultural and fraternal organizations. These appealed to hundreds of Jews interested in preserving the Jewish identity outside the framework of pro-Zionist organizations, with which the Communists had many disputes. Some Jews who took the plunge, and joined the ranks of party activists, rose very high in the CPC until the events of 1956 caused them to resign in large numbers.

The influx of Jews, Russians and Yugoslavs was overshadowed by that of Anglo-Saxons who joined the CPC in sufficient numbers to cause a change in its ethnic composition. Since many of these Anglo-Saxons were better educated, and more familiar with the Canadian scene, than the East Europeans who had joined the party in the 1920s, they became very useful as organizers, spokesmen and sometimes merely as an example of the Canadianization of the Communist movement.

The new recruits were mostly in their twenties or early thirties. Some of them came via the YCL, which had vegetated with fewer than 1,500 members in the 1920s. At that time the YCL resembled the CPC in more ways than one. The overwhelming majority of its members were of Finnish, Ukrainian and Jewish extraction. The percentage of working-class youth in the YCL was high, ranging from about 80 per cent in 1929 to 50 per cent in 1931.[56] Most of them lived in rural and mining communities. Even so, they were better educated and spoke more fluent English than their parents, and had integrated into Canadian society to a greater extent than had the average party member in the 1920s.

By and large the YCL made little impact on young Anglo-Saxon Canadians although its members took an active part in every campaign mounted by the CPC. Young Communists clashed with "reactionary teachers", fought the Boy Scouts and repeatedly called for the abolition of cadet training in high schools. Not a single French Canadian belonged to the League in 1929, while only 3 per cent were Anglo-Saxons.[57] The Communists attributed this state of affairs to anti-Communist propaganda, to the failure of the CPC to devote sufficient attention to the young Communist movement, and to the high turnover of YCL leaders (two of whom, Leslie Morris and William Kashtan, succeeded Buck as leaders of the CPC in the 1960s).[58]

In the 1930s interest in Communism, the Communist movement and its youth section increased appreciably. Thousands of young Canadians became aware of the extent to which the North American economy had broken down. Experience convinced them that massive state intervention alone could alleviate distress and reduce large-scale unemployment. This awareness went hand in hand with a growing curiosity about the Soviet system of government and the planned economy in the U.S.S.R. Young socialist intellectuals like F. R. Scott visited the Soviet Union and reported favourably on much of what they had seen. Other young Canadians were influenced by what they read on the same subject in left-wing American and British publications. Finally, the YCL – like the CPC – adopted more flexible tactics in 1935. As William Kashtan, then secretary of the YCL, explained:

> We want to make the Young Communist League an organization that will have in its ranks, not only Communists, but also young socialists and youths who are not yet Communists, even youth who may still be Christians.[59]

During the next few years the membership of the YCL rose, though not as rapidly as the CPC's. The League had 1,700 members in the spring of 1938.[60] Its strongest branches were in Montreal (with 450 members), Toronto (325), Vancouver (200) and Winnipeg (150). In Saskatchewan and Nova Scotia, however, the YCL did not exist as an organization. With the increase in membership, and the Popular Front tactics, came changes in the ethnic composition of the YCL and growing Communist influence among university students not only in western Canada, but also in Ontario and even among educated young Quebecois.

The young Communists worked hard, in Canada as in other countries, to improve relations with young socialists. Although a higher percentage of members of the Co-operative Commonwealth Youth Movement (CCYM) than of the CCF was prepared to collaborate with the Communists on certain issues, neither the CPC nor the YCL was satisfied with the progress made in converting young socialists. Some of the blame was attributed to the "poisonous anti-unity seeds" of the Trotskyist elements in the CCYM.[61] According to the Stalinists, the Trotskyists were responsible for the hostility the CCYM displayed to Communist overtures in Montreal and Vancouver, the two cities in which the Communists were most eager to strengthen their popular base.

Despite this setback, the young Communists did well in other respects. They were the leading force behind the Canadian Youth Congress against War and Fascism held in Toronto in August, 1934. Peter Hunter, who subsequently became a well-known YCL official, acted as secretary of the committee that did the spade work. Several non-Communist youth organizations, including the Student Christian Movement, took part in the Congress. Their presence, and readiness to co-operate with the YCL, laid the foundations of a new organization. Its purpose was to rally the younger generation around a program specifically designed to protect the interests of the young, who felt the impact of the Depression and worried about the possibility of another world war. The Comintern and the Young Communist International favoured the formation of such an organization in every democratic society.

These initial contacts proved invaluable in the months ahead. In May 1935 the Canadian Youth Congress (CYC) was established at a convention in Ottawa.* Buck and Woodsworth addressed the gathering, and the CPC endorsed the CYC. Six hundred delegates and observers representing two hundred religious, political and occupational organizations attended what became known as the first session of the CYC. Subsequent sessions met in Montreal (1937), Toronto (1938), Winnipeg (1939) and Montreal (1940).

The young Communists active in the CYC showed a great deal of tact and moderation in their efforts to attract, and keep in the CYC, the large non-Communist youth organizations. The YCL took great care to maintain a low profile at CYC conventions. Few representatives of the YCL attended the conventions; they preferred to operate through sympathizers and camouflaged party members in non-Communist organizations. The wisdom of this approach is understandable in the light of several attempts to brand the CYC as yet another Communist front. The young Communists and their partners immediately denied these charges, which they described as an example of "red baiting". They also stressed the non-partisan character of the CYC.

These denials carried considerable weight, first among the youth

---

*Once again Canada followed the example of the United States. The American Youth Congress was launched in August 1934.

and then among the Canadian Establishment. The CYC included the YCL, the CCYM, some Liberals, an occasional Conservative, the youth sections of several farm organizations in western Canada and a broad but shifting conglomerate of Protestant youth groups. French-Canadian youth was under-represented, and those who did participate reflected to some extent their elders' suspicion of Communism and Communists. Even so, the CYC was the first organization in Canada to embrace, however briefly, a broad range of opinion among the young.

The Canadian delegates who went to the International Congress against War, held in Geneva in 1936, represented a fair cross-section of the CYC. They included William Kashtan and three young MPS: T. C. Douglas, the future CCF Premier of Saskatchewan, Paul Martin, a future member of the Liberal Cabinet in Ottawa, and Denton Massey, a Conservative backbencher. The Congress they attended was sponsored by the Young Communist International, prominent pacifists, and well-known liberals desirous of mobilizing public opinion against Hitler and Mussolini.

Before long the Canadian Establishment accepted the CYC as a respectable and responsible organization worthy of support. As a result, CYC conventions received goodwill messages from the Governor-General, the Lieutenant-General of Saskatchewan, the Primate of the Anglican Church in Canada, the president of the Canadian Legion, Premier Hepburn of Ontario, Mackenzie King, and the leader of the Social Credit group in the federal Parliament, among others.

The ability of the CYC to blend into the Canadian scene was partly due to its chief spokesman, and partly to the demands the organization put forward. Kenneth Woodsworth was a graduate of McGill and had been active in the Student Christian Movement. Unlike his more famous relative, he did not find it difficult to collaborate with the Communists either before or after the outbreak of the Second World War.

The CYC called for funds to be allocated for the training and rehabilitation of youth, demanded improved health standards, better educational and recreational facilities, and urged that a more determined effort be made to counter unemployment among the young. It attacked the Padlock Act, expressed sympathy with workers' attempts to form trade unions, and opposed "expenditure on defence when the people are suffering from unemployment."[62] CYC spokesmen condemned the appeasement of Hitler, Mussolini and Japan, upheld the principle of collective security in international affairs, and expressed sympathy with China, a victim of Japanese aggression, and with Republicans in Spain.

The magazine *New Advance* reflected the Canadian Communists' attitude towards youth in the late 1930s. In some respects, their approach was highly conventional. Although the Communists have often been accused of advocating immoral behaviour, and although there is plenty of evidence that some of the top leaders of the CPC were involved in extra-marital affairs, the advice given in *New Advance* would have gladdened many a mother's heart. In March 1938, for instance, the magazine argued that "if youth cannot find fulfilment within marriage, neither can it do without marriage." It warned that "'petting' which is not so generally frowned upon [as abortion], merely stimulates the sex drive and results in a feeling of incompleteness and dissatisfaction."

The efforts made to rally the young were paralleled by attempts to induce prominent Canadian intellectuals to lend the prestige of their names to the worldwide campaign against fascism which the Comintern sponsored until September 1939. The task in Canada was made more difficult by the fact that few intellectuals were members of the party. The founders of the CPC, unlike those of the CPUSA, included very few intellectuals. The leaders in the 1920s enrolled hardly any, partly because they gave very low priority to the recruitment of intellectuals and university graduates. Those who threw in their lot with the CPC were a diverse crowd. A. E. Smith was a former Methodist minister, and J. S. Wallace the head of an advertising agency and a prominent Liberal in Nova Scotia before he placed his gifts at the service of Communism.

In the early 1930s the impact of the CPC among intellectuals increased in two ways. To begin with, there emerged a nucleus of young intellectuals who identified themselves publicly with the CPC. One of them, S. B. Ryerson, came to the Communist movement via Upper Canada College and the Sorbonne. Others lacked his academic qualifications but were equally dedicated. Some were Anglo-Saxons, others anglicized Canadians of East European origin. Those intellectuals who were not wholly involved in the party apparatus or the Communist-led trade unions were active in the Progressive Arts Clubs which existed in a number of cities. The first Progressive Arts Club (PAC) was formed in December 1931. It organized readings, symposia and exhibitions, published a small anthology of working-class songs, and sponsored the Workers' Theatre, which produced short plays and sketches by Canadian and foreign playwrights. Its repertoire included a "one act satire of the CCF," and "Eight Men Speak," which dealt with the Communists sentenced in November 1931. This play achieved some notoriety in left-wing and libertarian circles, because the authorities in Toronto tried to ban its performance in 1934. In addition, the PAC published a literary review. *Masses* was the Communist answer to socialistically inclined *Canadian Forum*. Published irregularly between April 1932 and April 1934, at one stage it claimed a higher circulation than its better-known rival.[63]

Two years later, the Communists launched *New Frontier*. The editors of both these pro-Communist periodicals tried to apply, in Canada, those cannons of "socialist realism" that were, and are, fashionable in the U.S.S.R. Short stories and poems described the plight of the poor, and the resistance of workers and farmers to the authorities and the capitalists. Extracts from plays performed at the Workers' Theatre – renamed the Theatre of Action after the change in the Comintern line – dealt with the same topics. Articles on Canadian politics and international affairs discussed the issues of the day from an anti-fascist and pro-Communist angle. Editorials called for art and literature to be at the service of the working class, bemoaned the federal government's lack of interest in cultural matters, and called on intellectuals to join the struggle for peace and socialism.

The contributors included supporters of the CPC as well as those who sympathized with the CCF in the second half of the 1930s. Leo Kennedy, C. Day Lewis, Dorothy Livesay and E. J. Pratt contributed poems, A. M. Klein and Jack Parr wrote short stories, and Avrom and Laurence Hyde supplied drawings. Two young Canadians who were to gain fame, in political theory and linguistics respectively, C. B. Macpherson and S. I. Hayakawa, reviewed books. The high quality of many contributions and the technical layout, which resembled that of the *Canadian Forum*, did not ensure the survival of *New Frontier*. In November 1937 it folded "owing to financial and circulation difficulties." A note told subscribers that "our subscription list has been taken over" by *New Masses*, a well-known pro-Communist review in New York.

Communist influence among intellectuals also increased when the CPC made a determined effort to gain the sympathy of a broad spectrum of non-Communists who were disturbed by certain developments at home and abroad. Attempts to curtail the civil rights of Communists in Toronto, long before Buck's arrest in 1931, had brought party members into contact with Protestant clergymen, professors at the University of Toronto and pacifists grouped around the Fellowship of Reconciliation. These people provided a nucleus of intellectuals who were prepared to join forces, or sympathize with, the Communists when party members organized a Canadian Congress against War and Fascism in Toronto in October, 1934.

The delegates to the Congress included socialists who had failed to find a niche in the CCF after the expulsion of the Labor Conference from the Ontario CCF (for example, E. A. Beder, Elizabeth Morton). They were joined by Protestant clergymen like Dr. Salem Bland, who was associated with several mass organizations.

The Canadian Congress against War and Fascism called for the formation of a new organization, the Canadian League against War and Fascism. A similar organization had existed in the United States since September 1933. In 1937 the Canadian Communists followed once again the example of their American comrades, "to bring the name of our organization more into line with our program."[64] It became the Canadian League for Peace and Democracy.

Like other mass organizations, the League was the Canadian branch of a worldwide movement, launched by the Comintern in western Europe in the early 1930s. It represented an attempt to mobilize intellectuals prepared to combine opposition to war and fascism with support of Soviet foreign policy. In Europe and North America this platform attracted many well-known intellectuals, who signed manifestos and delivered speeches at anti-fascist congresses and conferences until the outbreak of the Second World War.

In Canada the Communists did their best to reassure sceptical liberals and socialists. McEwen and Stewart Smith were the only well-known Communists on the League executive in 1935. They were overshadowed by prominent CCF MPs (such as T. C. Douglas, William Irvine), a Social Credit MP and several clergymen. For a time T. C. Douglas and Frank Underhill, one of the best-known socialist intellectuals in Canada, were vice-presidents of the League. Its moving spirit was A. A. MacLeod, a very able Communist, who held the position of president from 1935 to 1939.

The Communists worked hard for the League and gave it a great deal of publicity. At home the League denounced fascist and pro-fascist groups, and campaigned vigorously against the Padlock Act. It urged the Prime Minister to ban the export of war materials to Japan, and called on Canadians to boycott Japanese goods after Japan had attacked China in 1937. At the same time the League defended the foreign policy of the Soviet Union, deplored the failure of the western powers to aid the Republicans in the Spanish Civil War, and warned Canadians against the machinations of Hitler and Mussolini. The League of Nations was held up as the best instrument for world peace.

The international situation, coupled with Communist organizational skill, enabled the League to rally a fairly large number of organizations. Some locals of the TLC, a dozen CCF clubs, and non-Communist as well as pro-Communist youth organizations were affiliated to the League and sent delegates to conferences periodically organized by the League. Statements endorsing the work of the League came from people as diverse as General Chiang Kai-shek and the president of the Native Sons of Canada. As late as January 1938 J. M. Coldwell spoke under the auspices of the League. The association with such an imposing array of personalities enabled the League to claim the support of organizaions representing 337,000 Canadians in October 1934, 350,000 in 1935, and over 250,000 in November 1937.[65]

A closer look at these figures reveals a less impressive picture. They include members of organizations that merely sent observers to some League conventions. They also include Communist mass organizations whose memberships overlapped considerably. In any case, the appeal of the League declined when well-known socialists like T. C. Douglas left it in 1938.

While intellectuals in the Canadian League for Peace and Democracy expressed, on Canadian soil, their hostility to fascism, nine hundred party members and over three hundred sympathizers went to Spain in an attempt to prevent General Franco from winning the Civil War with the aid of Nazi Germany and Fascist Italy. The volunteers represented a fair cross-section of the party membership at home. The majority of them were under forty, of Finnish or Slavic extraction, and few of them had held a steady job during the Depression.

The CPC established a special network to recruit and transport the volunteers, who reached Spain by devious routes. The first group left Canada in December 1936, and upon arriving in Spain joined the International Brigades set up under the auspices of the Comintern and the Communist Party of Spain. Attached first to American anti-fascists, the Canadians soon expressed their desire for a separate Canadian unit. Their wish was granted and in June 1937 the Mackenzie-Papineau Battalion was formed as part of the Abraham Lincoln Brigade in which Americans predominated. Led by brigade commanders and brigade commissars who were not Canadians, the Mackenzie-Papineau Battalion shared the tribulations of other units in the International Brigades. About half of the 1280 volunteers from Canada lost their lives near Madrid, Teruel, and on the banks of the Ebro, before the survivors were evacuated to France on the eve of Franco's final victory.[66]

The exploits of these Canadian anti-fascists received scant publicity at home, except in Communist publications and through the efforts of two organizations backed by the CPC: the Committee to Aid Spanish Democracy, and the Friends of the Mackenzie-Papineau Battalion. Although public opinion outside Quebec was unsympathetic to Franco, it shared Mackenzie King's opposition to Canadian involvement in European affairs. The Foreign Enlistment Act of 1937 was an expression of this policy. Section Three of the Act stated:

> Any person who, being a Canadian national whether within or without Canada, voluntarily accepts or agrees to accept any commission or engagement in the armed forces of any foreign state at war with any friendly foreign state . . . is guilty of an offense under this Act.

The Communist press, which chronicled the struggle of Franco's opponents, was in much better shape than Communist publications in the 1920s. On May 1, 1936, the *Daily Clarion*, subtitled "a champion of peace, progress and democracy", replaced the tri-weekly *Worker* first published in March 1922. The new daily had better coverage of world affairs, and was more readable, than its predecessor. By 1939 news about party organization and problems was very brief and sandwiched between a sports page, reports of labour unrest in Canada and Nazi spies in North America, reviews of books written by anti-fascists, and photographs of King George IV, crooners such as Bing Crosby and actresses such as Sally Rand, the "promoter of the 'nude' ranch at the San Francisco World Fair."

Despite these attempts to cater for popular tastes the paper did not pay. Each year the *Daily Clarion* asked its readers to donate approximately $40,000 to the sustaining fund, because circulation and revenue from advertisements remained lower than the party leaders had expected. Detailed information on these matters was not given; all we know is that in June 1936 the central committee "decided to achieve the increase of the circulation to 25,000."[67]

In 1939 the paper ceased publication to avoid "undue and unfair sacrifices." It was replaced by a tabloid weekly, *Clarion*, which was published in Toronto and Winnipeg, where the Communist *Voice of Labour* had folded after an eight-month existence in 1934. In Vancouver in 1935 the CPC launched the weekly *B.C. Workers' News*. It soon had a circulation of 3,000, and still appears today, though under a different title. In Montreal *Clarté*, billed as "an organ of popular opinion", spread the Communist viewpoint in French from 1935 to 1939. Dailies in Finnish and Ukrainian catered for a sizable proportion of party members and sympathizers. The number of monthlies, bi-monthlies, weeklies and bi-weeklies in other East European languages rose appreciably in the 1930s. In addition, there were publications in German, Italian and Japanese, while mimeographed factory bulletins in English reflected continued Communist interest and growing strength in the trade union movement.*

The long years of patient work in the trade unions and among the unemployed bore fruit at last. By the summer of 1935, 120 units existed in factories, mines, workshops and relief camps. Of the 8,200 party members 2,600 were trade unionists. Of these, 1,600 were enrolled in "revolutionary and independent unions", and the remainder in "reformist" ones (that is, TLC, ACCL).[68] Among them was a fair number of militants who, through trial and error, with or without encouragement from their superiors, had gained useful experience as organizers and public speakers. They were valuable representatives of a party known for its readiness to fight the established order on a number of issues of everyday concern to thousands of Canadians.

The Comintern change of tactics in 1935 made it much easier for American and Canadian Communists to operate in the unions. Once the leaders of the CPC had realized that the WUL had no future except as a splinter group, and that its continued existence would make it much more difficult for the Communists to collaborate with the non-Communist union bosses, steps were taken to integrate the WUL unions into one of the two major Canadian trade union centres. At first the CPC toyed with the idea of inviting the Communist-led unions to join the ACCL. This trade union centre had suffered badly during the Depression. Some of its losses can be attributed to the "boring from within" activities of Communist opposition groups within the ACCL affiliates in 1934-1935.

Ill-feeling between the two organizations did not prevent the WUL and the ACCL from inviting all other trade union centres in Canada to discuss co-operation between the various segments of the fissiparous trade union movement. Camouflaged Communists in the ACCL unions supported the demand for "unity of action". Although pressure from below was not strong enough to bring about an alliance of the ACCL and WUL, it was widely based enough to force A. R. Mosher to make concessions. He told the ACCL convention in May 1935 that the ACCL executive would not

---

*The CPC also bought radio time to disseminate its policies. In 1939 Leslie Morris could write that "particularly in our Western districts, our provincial committees are regularly on the air," *A Handbook of Party Education* (Toronto), p. 15.

interfere in cases where ACCL locals wished to collaborate with the WUL or AFL/TLC unions.[69]

According to Salsberg, the "orientation" towards the All-Canadian Congress of Labour was "reversed at a moment's notice, actually without prior discussion by us, because of the thinking" of the Comintern.[70] Actually, the Canadian Communists followed once again the example of their American comrades, who were busy rejoining the international unions from which they had been expelled in the late 1920s, or which they had abandoned in favour of the Trade Union Unity League. At first, the CPC thought that the WUL would be able to negotiate terms of entry into the TLC. However, a lack of sufficient bargaining power and their eagerness to apply Popular Front tactics in the trade union field, forced the Communists to disband the WUL early in 1936. By then the genuine components of the WUL had amalgamated, or were seeking amalgamation, with the TLC unions, "industry by industry", while Stewart Smith was urging party members "everywhere" to "stand forward as the main builders of the A.F. of L."[71]

The Communists justified their new policy on several grounds. The size and strength of the AFL/TLC unions made them more attractive than the ACCL. Moreover, the TLC was less hostile to the Communists than before; most Canadian locals of international unions and district trades and labour councils did not act upon an anti-Communist circular issued over the signature of the president of the AFL. Third, the founding of the WUL was attributed to the expulsion of Communist militants from the AFL/TLC in the late 1920s and to the failure of the TLC to organize the unorganized workers. The very existence of the WUL, the Communists claimed, "made it possible for us to adopt broader and bolder united front policies."

As in other countries, the prospect of going cap in hand to the very trade union leaders denounced by Communist publications as "labour fakers" and "traitors" did not appeal to many party veterans. Among them was J. B. MacLachlan, the most prominent Communist in the Maritimes in the 1920s, and the president of the WUL in the 1930s. A rebel who had been critical of Communist tactics on several issues, MacLachlan left the CPC over the question of the dissolution of the WUL. His opposition to the merger with international unions made it more difficult for the party leaders to induce the members of the Mine Workers Union of Canada to rejoin the United Mine Workers of America.

The CPC eagerly availed itself of the opportunities offered by amalgamation. The request for amalgamation came at a time when moderate trade union leaders were less antagonistic to Communism and Communists than ever before. Their change of attitude can be attributed to the impact of the Depression, which reduced the number of dues-paying members, and to the victories of fascism, which many attributed to disunity in the ranks of organized labour. As a result, the Communists, while not welcomed with open arms, were acceptable to their rivals.

In the years 1936-1939, dual unionism was a far less divisive issue in the labour movement than it had been in the days of the WUL, while the workers showed a greater readiness to join unions than at any time since the late 1910s. Attempts by employers and the authorities to deflect the unionization drive had only a limited success. The use of the police and court injunctions, the reliance on workers who were prepared to cross the picket line, anti-union editorials and headlines in the popular press, and attacks by politicians such as Mitch Hepburn heightened tension, frightened the lukewarm, but only prevented the unions from expanding faster. Major breakthroughs were achieved anyway: the percentage of unionized workers rose appreciably, and genuine unions were established where none had existed before. Dramatic episodes, such as the strike at the Oshawa General Motors plant in 1937, drew attention to the problems faced by the unions, to the violence engendered by labour disputes, and to the obtuse way in which employers and provincial governments often behaved.

The Communists did their best to highlight the incidents, slogans and demands that helped the unionization drive. Communist newspapers and leaflets denounced anyone who represented an obstacle to the CPC in the world of labour: the Trotskyists were just as villainous as big business. News of riots, wage increases won, fringe benefits gained and collective bargaining agreements signed, accounts of how success was achieved, and photographs of prominent fighters for trade union rights, filled the pages of the *Daily Clarion*. The victories won by the Communists depended, of course, on more than favourable publicity and hard-hitting propaganda. A great deal of unglamorous work was required of party members as well; this a number of party members were prepared to do just as they were ready to face the police in demonstrations, and to spend long hours in picket lines. Sometimes they also engaged in physical violence, especially against those workers whose desire for a job made them willing to cross the picket line. All in all, violence in labour disputes was more prevalent in the mid-1930s than on the eve of the Second World War.

The CPC made rapid progress in the ranks of organized labour, by making use of existing factory cells and creating new ones, by giving much higher priority to employed rather than to unemployed workers, by directing activists into selected unions, and by providing temporary financial assistance to party members and sympathizers engaged in unionization drives. This was true particularly in those industries where no genuine unions had existed before the mid-1930s (automobile, merchant navy, rubber, steel, textiles) or where the Communists had had a foothold in the 1920s (coal mining, lumber, needle trades). The unionization drive on both sides of the border was spearheaded by the Committee for Industrial Organization (CIO), composed of twelve international unions which were part of the AFL until their suspension in August 1936. In Canada these unions remained part of the TLC until the outbreak of the Second World War.

Of all the provinces the Communists were most successful in B.C., although even there their greatest victories were won in the early 1940s. Harsh living and working conditions, employers to whom the idea of genuine unionism was anathema, and a labour force exposed to frequent loss of employment (as the demand for B.C. exports suddenly declined), created a milieu in which working-class militancy and left-wing radicalism had thrived long before the formation of the CPC. By the end of the 1930s the Communists had partly merged into the local labour scene, though they had not been able to overcome their sectarianism, the bane of many radical movements in B.C.

The full extent of their inroads on the west coast and in other parts of Canada, could not easily be assessed because the Communists advocated policies in line with those of the moderates in the trade unions. Few, for instance, could accuse McEwen of extremism when he told the third WUL convention in November, 1935, that the "employer should be given all possible chances to make an amicable settlement prior to the strike."[72]

The Communists were considered an integral part of the labour movement; they carried out popular policies, and the unions in which they were prominent often won concessions which those who bore the scars of the Depression appreciated. Not that many were eager to question, let alone challenge, the role the Communists were playing in the unions. To oppose the Communists would have meant arousing their wrath and facing a showdown that could not have been won in view of the spirit of the times, and the existence of a tiny, but close-knit, group of Communists who were prepared to eliminate anyone who stood in their way. Few TLC unionists, apart from a few devout Catholics and staunch democratic socialists, worried a great deal about the implications of these Communist successes. Fewer still were prepared to take counter-measures, at least before the Hitler-Stalin non-aggression pact of August 1939.*

The fact that many workers were prepared to vote for, or at least to abstain from opposing, Communists in the unions did not mean that they supported Communist candidates in municipal and provincial elections. Then, as later, the more important the office, the less inclined were the workers to trust CPC-promoted candidates.

In the municipal field Communist inroads were the result of the interplay of several factors. In the first place, the Communists had to overcome their own disinclination to participate in municipal politics. Like other radicals in North America, many party members considered involvement in local government to be a waste of time, as something unworthy of revolutionaries engaged in the more important task of overthrowing the capitalist system and building a socialist society. Once the predisposition to ignore or downgrade municipal politics had been overcome, the CPC had to produce a program that would attract the poorer sections of the electorate. In the days of the Popular Front the Communists advocated slum clearance, better recreational facilities, improved unemployment relief, reduced mortgage interest rates, public protection against the "profiteering" of fuel and food combines, and a system of "just and democratic taxation."[73]

Last but not least, the Communists had to take into account the likely reaction of those whose votes they solicited to the party label. In view of the distrust which the CPC aroused in many quarters, and the tendency of most Canadian political parties not to enter municipal politics under their own label, the CPC, too, found it advisable to create separate organizations to contest aldermanic and school board seats. These organizations, which still exist under different names in many Canadian cities and towns, operate on the assumption that "politically conscious voters know that a certain electoral alliance, a certain spokesman, a certain program reflects the point of view of the Communists."[74]

---

*Only two trade union organizations did not hide their dislike of Communism and Communists. The Quebec-based Confederation of Catholic Unions called for a ban on the CPC in 1936 and 1938. The Canadian Federation of Labour (CFL) was also hostile to the Communists. Its leaders broke away from the ACCL in October 1936, partly because A.R. Mosher did not share their desire to condemn the "anarcho-communists" in the Executive Board's report. The CFL attracted little support, although for a time its spokesmen included several well-known personalities (e.g. W. T. Burford, R. B. Russell).

In and after the 1930s, the leaders in these organizations were trade union officials, members of the CCF sympathetic to the Communists, and individuals active in community affairs. Thus, many voters gained the impression that the candidate in question was backed by a wide range of public-spirited citizens. In some instances, district councils of the TLC endorsed Communist candidates.

The first Communist victory at the municipal level preceded the application of Popular Front tactics. In 1926 Bill Kolisnyk, a small business man of Ukrainian extraction, won an aldermanic seat in Winnipeg. He was the first Communist to gain public office in North America, and the first of several party members to grace the Winnipeg City Council. Other Communist successes before 1935 attracted less attention. Several months before Buck left the Kingston Penitentiary, *The Worker* could boast that "twenty-five revolutionary workers sit upon capitalist councils and school boards."[75] At Blairmore, Alberta, a pro-Communist slate won, by a small majority, control of that municipality in January 1933 and promptly renamed the main street "Tim Buck Boulevard".

Buck's popularity was greater in Blairmore than among Torontonians. Although the number of votes cast for Buck in municipal elections rose dramatically from 5,974 in 1932 to 45,112 in 1939, it was his colleagues (Norman Freed, John Weir, among others) and his future opponents (Salsberg, Stewart Smith) who profited from the party's appeal and ability to mobilize support. This was particularly true of Wards Four and Five, where the Communists did far better in the late 1930s than at the height of the Depression. Once again the ethnic vote contributed a great deal to Communist successes. So did the Communist organizational work. The CPC saw to it that there was a full-time organizer in both wards, which, by October 1938 possessed some of the heaviest concentrations of party members in any metropolitan centre in Canada. There was one party member for every eighty-one persons in Ward Four, while in Ward Five the ratio was one member out of every 128 residents.[76]

Election campaigns and successes, and the performance of Communist aldermen and school trustees, had several results. These wins boosted the morale of party members who had battled against heavy odds for years, and who needed an occasional victory to reassure themselves that they were not an isolated group ignored and distrusted by their compatriots. Even when victory eluded them by a few hundred votes – as was the case more than once –

their leaders could always argue that a little extra effort next time was bound to produce a different result. The vote garnered by Communists also allowed Communist spokesmen to make a good case that the elected party members were not wild men, bent on destruction, but men and women who put forward proposals that many Canadians supported whatever their party affiliation. Moreover, electoral successes enabled the CPC to enlarge its membership. As an organ of the Comintern pointed out, "the most significant gains are being made in and nearby those cities where Communists have already gained seats."[77]

In provincial elections the CPC put up few candidates under its own label in the 1930s. Instead, party members stood as candidates or supported those who presented themselves as the United Front in Saskatchewan (1934), the United Front of Workers and Farmers in B.C. (1934), and as Labor, Labor Farmer or Labor Progressives in Ontario (1937). By these means some of the controversy associated with the CPC was diverted on election day, while Comintern slogans were still publicized. Not that Woodsworth and his colleagues were pleased with this camouflage, especially when "Labor" candidates opposed CCF nominees in some Ontario ridings in 1937.

The Communist candidates in provincial elections, as in municipal ones, did their best to show that they were supported by as many organizations as possible. Union locals and branches of mass organizations figured among the sponsors of prominent Communist candidates. In one case at least, it was not only the man in the street who was awed by the backing given to a party leader. David Lewis was also taken in by the galaxy of union organizers who endorsed Salsberg in 1937. He urged that the CCF candidate should be withdrawn to avoid a split in the labour vote. Woodsworth's reply was short but predictable. He disputed the view that Salsberg and those who sponsored him represented labour. Since the Conservative candidate was also pro-labour, Woodsworth asked whether Lewis wanted the CCF to refrain from opposing the Tory as well.[78]

Only one of the candidates put up or strongly supported by the CPC was successful: J. Litterick, secretary of the CPC in Manitoba. A native of the United Kingdom, he had been active in several parts of Canada before the party leadership selected him as a candidate, without, however, first obtaining the support of the local Communists.[79] An electoral law that did not discriminate against smaller parties and years of patient work among ethnic groups in

North Winnipeg, enabled Litterick to become the first of two Communist MLAS in Manitoba in 1936. The Legislative Assembly provided them with a useful form in which to display their debating skill and raise issues of interest to the CPC and their constituents. This foothold the Communists lost in the 1950s under the impact of the Cold War, Khrushchev's denunciation of Stalin, and changes in the provincial electoral law.

Chapter 5

From an "Imperialist" to a "Just" War

In the years preceding the Second World War the CPC approach to Canadian foreign policy displayed a certain dichotomy. On the one hand, the Communists were loud in their denunciations of Hitler and Mussolini and had few illusions about the ambitions of the two dictators and the rulers of Japan. Time and again they insisted that only a coalition of states, dedicated to collective security through the League of Nations, could prevent aggression. The U.S.S.R., they argued, was the cornerstone of this security system which they urged Canada to join.

Until 1938 these proposals were coupled with bitter attacks on whatever attempts the Canadian government made to strengthen the weak Canadian armed forces and to co-ordinate the Canadian and British defence schemes. The Communists were convinced that the co-ordination of British and Canadian military and naval policies would increase the risk of war and promote militaristic tendencies in Canada. The Communists, however, were not alone in thinking and arguing along these lines. Many other Canadians shared these sentiments to a greater or lesser extent. The prevalence of these views contributed to the lack of drive displayed by the Liberals in re-arming Canada.

The signing of the Soviet-German Treaty of Non-Aggression and Friendship caught the Canadian Communists by surprise. Like Communists elsewhere in the world, they had not been informed of the secret negotiations that preceded the treaty, let alone the decision to partition Poland. Nor did they at first realize the extent to which the Treaty would affect the international situation and their own role in Canadian politics.

Their first task was to explain and justify the treaty to those who had taken Communist anti-Nazism at face value. *The Clarion* insisted that the pact did "not make the slightest change in Soviet foreign policy" and that it "is seriously weakening Hitler's hold upon the German people."[1] The Communists also claimed that the pact had actually strengthened the cause of peace in Europe and had saved the U.S.S.R. from getting involved in a war with Germany, into which anti-Communist politicians in London and Paris were trying to divert the Führer.

When Hitler started the Second World War by invading Poland, Buck urged "full support to the Polish people" in a telegram to Mackenzie King.[2] He also called on Canadians to prevent a last minute compromise between Britain and Germany. The decision to fight on "two fronts", against Hitler and against the appeasers in Britain, was similar to the decision adopted by the British Communists at the same time. No sooner had this stand been taken, however, than the British and Canadian Communist parties reversed their policy in favour of one that was fully in line with the latest Soviet moves. By joining in the attack on Poland on September 17, 1939, the U.S.S.R. drew even closer to Nazi Germany and sealed the alliance which lasted until Hitler attacked the Soviet Union in 1941.

The dramatic shift in Soviet foreign policy had enormous repercussions in all sections of the Communist International. The Canadian section was no exception, once the Comintern had declared in October 1939 that "the war has basically altered all international relationships and is profoundly changing the class and political alignments within each capitalist nation."

As soon as the Comintern limited its attacks to the "warmongers" in London and Paris, the Canadian Communists followed suit. They began by admitting publicly that they had been wrong in September 1939 in describing the war as "anti-fascist". Instead, the CPC now denounced the war as an "imperialist one", campaigned under the slogan of "Withdraw Canada from the Imperialist War" and called on Canadians, "to make it abundantly clear to the King Government that the Canadian people are more interested in an early peace than in the prosecution of the war."[3]

When the federal government did not get the Communist message, one of the clandestine organs of the CPC announced: "For us in Canada the principal danger of fascism comes not from Nazi Germany but from the war policies of the King Government."[4]

Because of this stand on the crucial issue of the day, legal Communist publications in Canada, and Canadian Communists contributing to Communist publications abroad, did not pay much attention to Hitler. Little was said about his reign of terror in Poland or the Nazi treatment of Jews in German-held territories. The western Allies were treated more harshly. They were blamed for their failure to sign an alliance with the U.S.S.R. and reluctance to stop Hitler before September 1939. They were also accused of planning to attack the U.S.S.R. during the Soviet-Finnish War of 1939-1940. Critics of British war aims and advocates of American neutrality received a great deal of favourable publicity in the Communist press. So did those British left-wingers who preferred an immediate peace to a war against Nazism. Articles hostile to British imperialism in India and elsewhere were frequently published, while little space was devoted to the loss of independence of a growing number of European states conquered by Hitler's armies.

On the other hand, at least one clandestine organ of the CPC did periodically condemn "German imperialism" and "German capitalism". These attacks, however, were less numerous than those on the British government. More than once, denunciations of the belligerents were accompanied by statements that "the Communist Party is opposed to a victory of either side in this imperialist war."[5]

As far as domestic affairs were concerned, the Communists used existing shortages and government interference in industrial relations and the economic life of the country as evidence of the nefarious role of big business. The Communists warned that the continuation of the war would be at the workers' expense. Pegged wages, industrial and military conscription, and an end to what remained of civil liberties were in store for them. The capitalists were bound to use the war and the machinery of government to increase their profits. The leaders of the CCF were held responsible for much of what had happened. As an underground Communist paper put it, "theirs is the most despicable role of all – that of trying to chloroform the people with pseudo-socialist phrases and to herd them into the imperialist slaughter."[6]

Newspapers and leaflets were the main vehicles of written Communist propaganda. On Armistice Day in 1939, "hundreds of thousands of folders entitled 'The People want Peace' " were distributed over the signature of the "Dominion Executive Committee" of the CPC.[7] On other occasions, leaflets were issued by local party bodies.

Apart from propaganda, the CPC gave "a lead to the workers and farmers of Canada by carrying forward the struggle against the imperialists, against profiteering and for higher wages, into a struggle for peace."[8] Communist attempts to exploit discontent involved party members in strike action and agitation in the Canadian armed forces. In some branches of industry and transportation these Communist initiatives bore fruit and damaged the Canadian war effort. At the very time when Hitler was conquering Norway, the Communist-led Canadian Seamen's Union organized a strike on the Great Lakes that tied up shipping for six days.[9]

The anti-war activities of the CPC attracted the attention of the authorities. Distributors of Communist publications were arrested and sentenced to short terms of imprisonment. So was the Communist who for a time operated a secret radio broadcasting station, using scripts prepared by the underground CPC. Communist speakers found it increasingly difficult to rent halls for meetings. *The Clarion* and the *Clarté* were banned in the autumn of 1939. The former reappeared on a more modest scale as the *Canadian Tribune* in January 1940. It had several non-Communists on its editorial board.

Government pressure against those who wanted to withdraw Canada from the war against Nazi Germany increased in proportion to Hitler's conquests. On the eve of the entry of German troops into Paris in June 1940, the Federal Government issued under the War Measures Act an Order-in-Council which banned, not only all pro-Nazi organizations, but also the CPC, the YCL and several mass organizations. Several Communist newspapers in English and other languages, mainly East European ones, were banned, seals were placed on the property of the ULFTA, and a number of Communist activists and leaders, including the majority of the central committee, were arrested. Those who did not escape the police net were sent to internment camps, which the Communists immediately dubbed "concentration camps". The 110 interned Communists were not the only inmates of these camps. They shared the premises with Germans, Italians, small groups of fascists, and some Quebecois who were opposed to Canada's participation in the war against Hitler.

Government repression placed the CPC in a very difficult position. Although some of the top Communist leaders, including Buck and Carr, escaped arrest, the return to the days of illegality was very unpleasant. Much time and effort went into ensuring the safety of those who remained in Canada. It was not easy to maintain contact with those, such as Buck, who retired to the U.S.A. without giving up the posts they held in the CPC. Geographical distance, and the understandable fear that ambitious party leaders in Canada might try to supplant those who had taken refuge elsewhere, increased friction among members of the politbureau.

Furthermore, the politbureau disagreed on the application of the anti-war tactics of the CPC.[10] Stewart Smith, who remained in Canada and played a key role in guiding the underground party organization, was accused by his rivals of mechanically applying the anti-war policy of the Comintern with the result that CPC propaganda provided ammunition to those who bracketed the Communists with the fascists.

There is plenty of evidence to the charge that the Communists did engage in what is sometimes referred to as "revolutionary defeatism". At a time when Hitler was master of Europe, the clandestine organ of the Toronto district of the CPC informed its readers that "Canadian capitalism, not German capitalism, is our main enemy."[11] To drive the point home, the same issue contained the statement, "Our main enemy is not German imperialism." On another occasion, the publication declared: "As Canadian Communists their sacred duty is to work night and day for the defeat of their 'own' bourgeoisie, and that they are doing and will do."[12]

The members of the politbureau were also divided over Canadian independence.[13] Like John Macdonald in the 1920s, the politbureau argued in May 1940 that Canada was still a semi-colony, because the federal government lacked the freedom to decide on such vital issues as war and peace. A majority of the politbureau maintained that Canada was bound to be involved in a forthcoming imperialist war between the U.S. and Britain, called for Canadian withdrawal from the British Empire, and insisted that the task of progressive forces was to complete the bourgeois democratic revolution which had been defeated in 1837.

The minority in the politbureau opposed these views with Buck's support. It insisted that the main dividing line in Canada was between the supporters of monopoly capitalism, including the French-Canadian bourgeoisie, and their opponents. Therefore it was the duty of the Communists to lead a broad movement against the monopolists. The struggle for self-determination in Quebec would be led by the working class, not by the local bourgeoisie.

The difference of opinion in the politbureau was not resolved until Buck resumed effective control of the party apparatus, and the political situation had changed drastically with Hitler's invasion of the U.S.S.R. In February 1942, a meeting of Communist officials reaffirmed the stand taken by the CPC in the early thirties on the subject of Canada's status. Once again the Communists insisted that Canada was an independent state. The Canadian bourgeoisie had full power because the Canadian "bourgeois democratic" revolution had essentially been completed.

Friction among the leaders of the CPC was not the only source of Communist weakness in 1940-1941. The illegal status of the CPC led to "a tendency of fatalism on the one hand and fear due to lack of perspective on the other."[14] A third disadvantage stemmed from policies espoused by the CPC in the early part of the war. Party members unable and unwilling to stand the strain, left the CPC in droves. These deserters tended to be those who joined or associated with the CPC in the Popular Front days, rather than the seasoned veterans; but even among the latter there were some who had privately questioned the wisdom of the drastic change in the party line in September 1939. Their anxieties were not shared by party members of Ukrainian extraction. The destruction of the Polish state they hated, and the entry of the Red Army into Lvov, seemed a fulfilment of their dreams.

The public showed little sympathy for the stand taken by the CPC, although the Communists did their best to exploit the discontent that arose as the ramifications of the war increasingly affected life in Canada. In 1940 Buck was forced to write, "It would be an exaggeration to say that the slogan of the Communist Party of Canada 'Withdraw Canada from the Imperialist War' has become the slogan of the masses."[15]

The extent of the Communists' isolation was shown in the federal election of March 26, 1940, which the CPC election manifesto described as "no better than one of Hitler's plebiscites."[16] Police harassment contributed to the decision to contest only ten ridings. "Where there are no Communists running, mark your ballot Peace," advised an illegal organ of the CPC. The candidates included Buck, McEwen, Morris and Wiggins. None of their election campaigns compared with those fought by the Communists in 1935. It was as if the leaders knew that few would be converted to what the Communists advocated. Crudely duplicated brochures advocated "No conscription. Bring our boys back to Canada." The Communists also demanded the repeal of the War Measures Act, high wages, "parity prices for farmers," "jail the war profiteers." They called on workers to "unite to defeat the imperialists on both sides of the imperialist war." "Wives, mothers, sisters" were urged to "wipe the tears from your eyes and demand – for all to hear – that your husbands, sons and brothers are returned to you from the carnage in Europe!"[17]

The Communist candidates won 14,616 votes, while the CCF polled 393,230. The only consolation that the Communists could derive from the federal election was Mrs. Dorise Nielsen's victory as a "Unity" candidate in North Battleford, "an almost completely" rural riding in Saskatchewan. An ex-teacher born in England, and the wife of a farmer, she had been prominent in the local CCF organization, which had been dissolved because of its sup-

port for "unity". Those who voted for her included Social Crediters, CCFers, as well as those who had sympathized with the CPC
since the days of the FUL.

As an MP Mrs. Nielsen concentrated on three issues. To begin
with, she opposed conscription. Second, she was a staunch critic of
restrictions on civil liberties: more than once she called for the
freeing of Communists, or, as she put it, "anti-fascists" and
"labour leaders". Third, she advocated a new political organization which would defend the interests of the Canadian people. It
was launched after the British Communists had initiated the British People's Convention.

The embryonic Canadian People's Movement put forward a
number of demands couched in such terms that the authorities
could not easily interpret them as an excuse to ban the organization.[18] "The establishment of the government of the people, by the
people, and for the people" preceded "adequate relief for the
unemployed" and the fight for collective bargaining. The call for
"the release of all trade unionists and other anti-fascists now
interned" revealed some of the objectives of the sponsors. So did
Point Ten: "Friendship and collaboration with the common people of all countries to end exploitation and war." This was one way
of saying that the Communists were for peace. The call to defeat
Hitler and Mussolini did not figure in this document, which
received a great deal of publicity in Communist publications at
home and abroad.

The Canadian People's Movement organized a number of
meetings at which Mrs. Nielsen was the star speaker, when she
was not campaigning on behalf of Communist candidates in
by-elections. She attracted the support of unions in which Communist influence was strong, and of an occasional academic or
clergyman. Among scholars and men of the cloth who chaired
Mrs. Nielsen's meetings were some people who had not been
closely associated with Communist causes before September 1939.
Most of them were either pacifists, or men who felt strongly about
restrictions on civil liberties in wartime.

The new Comintern line also affected Communist agitation
among the young. Gone were the days when Communists, young
or old, daily denounced Hitler and his sympathizers, and repeatedly called for a broad movement to bar the road to Fascism and
Nazism. Now the young Communists and their allies repeated the
anti-war arguments of the CPC. Special attention was paid to the
struggle against conscription. The Communist monthly for the
young fired the first shot by urging "an immediate campaign to
mobilize public opinion of all the country against conscription."[19]

David Kashtan, secretary of the CPC, followed suit by declaring: "As an organization we are against conscription because of the nature of this war which we consider unjust and not a war of freedom."[20] The third stage was reached when the Communists tried to steer the CYC in a direction favourable to the party without too blatant a display of anti-war sentiments, which might alienate those who previously were prepared to support the CYC.

In February 1940 the CYC sent out half-a-million copies of a Conscription Questionnaire. In June 1940 the *Canadian Tribune* published a statement of the pro-Communist Montreal Youth Council, a statement which included the sentence: "Conscription today is the greatest threat to the lives and security of Canadian youth." The following month, the fifth session of the CYC countered growing criticism of its anti-war policy with arguments about the need to defeat the "forces of totalitarianism", "fascist forces" and "fascist governments". The impact of these anti-fascist sentiments was weakened by the qualification:

> While recognizing that our Canadian democracy was subject to attacks from abroad, it was nevertheless felt that some of the most real threats to our democratic institutions and liberties were inherent in recent legislation passed by the Mackenzie King government.[21]

By the time *The Canadian Tribune* printed these words, the CYC had lost much of its former appeal. The number of delegates to the fifth session of the CYC was appreciably smaller than at earlier ones. Some youth organizations (for example, the YMHA and YMCA) withdrew from the CYC before the meeting in Montreal; others (including the YWCA and the Greater Winnipeg Young Men's Liberal Association) severed their connections with the CYC at the end of the fifth session; the CCYM stated that the young socialists would reconsider their attitude towards the CYC. Among the CCYM spokesmen at the session were David Lewis and Grace McInnis, the daughter of J. S. Woodsworth.

Abandoned by its largest components, the CYC lingered on for another year and a half. Aware of the blow they had suffered, the Communists made no effort to revive the CYC when the political climate changed in the later stages of the Second World War.

In the trade unions, however, the Communists could not be neutralized as easily as among the educated youth. The positions they held in the unions, and the struggle they fought against wartime labour legislations, placed them in a strong position. The opposition they encountered was disparate and unable to agree on the best way of countering the Communist challenge. Some advocated the expulsion of prominent Communists from labour bodies, and in several instances they succeeded. Others, for a variety of reasons, opposed this drastic step and continued to work alongside party members on union executives. Although the spirit of toleration and co-operation of the Popular Front days was replaced by distrust, in many industrial unions neither side was strong enough to dislodge the other. The fear that in-fighting in the unions would considerably weaken the labour movement played into the hands of the Communists, who wanted to avoid any move that might imperil their grip on several unions.

Even so, they lost ground for several reasons.[22] Arrests and internment deprived the CPC of many of its most experienced and popular union officials. Others were too busy dodging the RCMP to give their undivided attention to union affairs.

Another blow to the Communists was the decision of the TLC to expel the Canadian locals of the CIO in September, 1939. The expulsion was the result of heavy pressure from the AFL. It was strongly opposed by Communists and non-Communists who had resisted the move for several years. The expelled unions included influential Communists as well as a nucleus of staunch anti-Communist democratic socialists led by C.E. Millard. This nucleus was considerably strengthened when Silby Barrett, the best-known CIO leader in Canada, joined forces with Millard.

The third Communist defeat occurred when the expelled CIO unions combined with the ACCL to form a new Canadian trade union centre, the Canadian Congress of Labour (CCL), in September 1940. The president of the new organization was A. R. Mosher. He had had unpleasant experiences with the Communists in the ACCL in the late 1920s, and he had been the object of bitter Communist attacks at the height of the Depression. The passing of the years had done little to temper his dislike of Communists. He combined these anti-Communist sentiments with the belief that Canada needed a labour party. He felt that only the CCF, with the organization and financial backing of the unions, could fulfil this role.

The marriage of convenience between Communists and anti-Communists was subject to many strains as the two sides jockeyed for position in the new organization. Unanimity could only be reached on such matters as opposition to the AFL, the need to organize unorganized workers, and protection of the rights of labour in wartime. On other issues there was little agreement. Differences of opinion delayed the merger of the ACCL and the expelled CIO unions, and led to prolonged debates at the founding convention of the CCL. The Communists and their friends opposed a resolution urging the affiliated unions "to refuse membership to any person known to be a member of subversive groups."[23] The same resolution condemned Fascism, Nazism and Communism. The Communists also criticized Mosher for insisting in his presidential address that first priority should be given to the struggle against Hitler.

On these issues the Communists rallied a substantial number of delegates. However, the Communists could not prevent the election of Mosher. A young member of the executive of the International Woodworkers of America (IWA), Nigel Morgan, won 74 votes as against 148 for the veteran union leader.[24] Morgan's performance was all the more remarkable as party members represented a small minority among his supporters. More decisive, however, were the results of the elections for the executive committee of the CCL. All of its six members were identified with or favourable to the CCF.

This nucleus of non-Communists acted immediately to consolidate its victory.[25] The measures taken by Mosher and Millard exasperated the officials of the Communist-controlled unions. They complained about lack of union democracy, a charge the Communists often made when they were out-voted and out-manoeuvred. Pat Conroy, a key member of the CCL executive, dismissed the charge in March 1941. He referred to the "talk of democracy by certain people, who had never practised it, and would not practise it, their chief method of determining policy being in a caucus."[26]

Since the union officials associated with the CPC did not merely complain, but also engaged in counteraction to rally support, C. S. Jackson, president of the United Electrical, Radio and Machine Workers of America (UE) in Canada, was suspended from the executive council in May 1941.

Hitler's invasion of the U.S.S.R. released the CPC from the doldrums. It did not take the leaders long to realize that the party line had to change. What had been described as an "imperialist" war became, according to Leslie Morris, "a just war, a people's war of national freedom and liberation."[27] In these circumstances the Canadian People's Movement was no longer needed, and it disappeared from sight. No longer was Mrs. Nielsen the main spokesman of the Communist cause in Canada. Now the CPC moved back into the limelight with statements issued in its own name, while Buck elaborated the party's stand in articles, brochures, speeches, and letters to the federal Cabinet and MPs.

For the next four years every major Communist pronouncement gave priority to victory over Hitler and his allies. Time and again Canadians were told to contribute their share to the struggle of the United Nations. They were also warned that Hitler could not be defeated without a high degree of "unity" among his opponents The CPC applied the term "unity" in three ways. First, the Communists wanted Canada to establish the closest of relations with her allies, in order to win the war and lay the foundations of the postwar world. Second, they used the term "unity" when insisting on the need for cordial relations between English and French-speaking Canadians. Finally, "unity" meant identity of purpose among the various classes in Canadian society.

According to the Communists, the Canadian people believed in and desired unity. Nevertheless, there were groups and individuals who were opposed to it for a variety of reasons. These elements had to be unmasked and fought as part of the drive for unity in the struggle against Hitler. Readers of Communist publications were shown three kinds of opponents of unity. The first group included those who were lukewarm towards the prosecution of the war. The second category consisted of those who wanted to win the war, but failed to realize the need for concessions to labour and French Canadians, so that the energies of these two segments of the population could be properly channelled. Last, but not least, were radicals who advocated major reforms in wartime, refused to give up the right to strike during the duration of hostilities, and were sceptical of the professed objectives of the U.S.S.R. and Canadian Communists. The CPC considered the views and activities of these radicals very harmful, because they diverted attention and energy from the common struggle and needlessly divided public opinion.

Not content to condemn and denounce those who failed to promote the cause of unity at home and abroad, the Communists put forward a number of specific proposals. These included calls for sacrifice, and frequent demands for a more efficient prosecution of the war. After the invasion of the U.S.S.R. the Communists were prepared to do almost anything to hasten the defeat of Hitler and his allies.

They volunteered for military service overseas, where some of them were killed. In fact far fewer party members lost their lives in the Canadian armed forces during the Second World War (43), than in the International Brigades during the Spanish Civil War (600).[28] Party newspapers and spokesman invited Canadians to join the armed forces or at least to vote in favour of sending conscripts abroad. "If you are not engaged in vital war production, get into uniform," recommended the Toronto committees of the CPC and YCL in a pamphlet that began with the words "Canada is in mortal danger," and included the call to "build a powerful Canadian army." What the Communists meant by a "powerful" army was explained by Buck when he wrote: "Canada has adequate manpower resources to maintain half a million men overseas."[29]

At the same time the leaders of the CPC, the mass organizations and the unions controlled by the Communists became enthusiastic supporters of various drives to increase production, reduce waste, subscribe to war loans and collect funds for the Red Cross. As Buck promised in 1942, "Communists will not play into the hands of the enemies by making satisfaction of the workers' needs a condition for working class support to the war effort." What was even more gratifying to the authorities and the employers was the Communist stand on the subject of strikes in wartime. More than once they came out against strike action, and urged others to do likewise. They criticized union leaders like Millard for refusing to support the "No Strike Pledge". When strikes did take place, the Communists welcomed moves to end them as quickly as possible, and urged the resumption of "full production".

In the campaign to boost Canadian morale and to get rid of what Buck described as "complacency", Communist newspapers diligently recorded a whole variety of contributions to the Canadian war effort. Nothing was too insignificant to escape their notice. When good news was scarce, *New Advance* published an interview with an anti-fascist bride who declared: "We felt that getting married then was a smack in the face of fascism."[30]

Patriotic sentiments and activities soon brought their reward, as Communists established contact with Canadians who had either ignored or fought them in the past. Party leaders now appeared on the same platform as Liberal and Tory politicians, clergymen of several denominations, newspaper editors critical of the CCF, and leaders of ethnic groups who had formerly fought the Communists. What took place in Canada was, of course, similar to what was happening on a larger scale in London and New York.

The policy of collaboration eagerly pursued by the Communists was severely handicapped by the fact that the CPC remained an illegal organization even after Hitler's attack on the Soviet Union. Many of the CPC's experienced officials and trade unionists were under arrest or in hiding in this country, while some of the top leaders of the Canadian party were cooling their heels in the United States. To enable the CPC to regain its freedom of action and its former influence, the Communists repeatedly called for the release of interned Communists, for the removal of the ban on the CPC, and for the return of the ULFTA property seized in 1940.

To that end a number of avenues were explored. The CLDL was transformed, after Hitler's attack on the Soviet Union, into the National Council for Democratic Rights. Its secretary, A. E. Smith, became the hard-working head of the civil liberties bureau of the *Canadian Tribune*, which attempted to rally the support of individuals and organizations in the campaign. The *Canadian Tribune* gave a great deal of publicity to statements, appeals and advertisements by those in favour of lifting the ban. Those who lent their names included individuals who had sided with the Communists in the past, as well as a fairly large number of educators, lawyers, clergymen and trade union leaders who felt that the federal government was being obstinate, petty-minded and unreasonable. A joint letter to the press by personalities as far apart politically as Morley Callaghan, the novelist, Clifford Sifton, the newspaper owner, F. A. Brewin, a well-known CCFer, and Watson Kirkconnell, a professor whom the *Canadian Tribune* attacked time and again because of his staunch opposition to Communism and the CPC, argued that the ban on the CPC was a "bad law that is imperfectly enforced" and "a symbol of repression of opinion."[31]

Given the record of the Red Army on the battlefield and of Communists in Canadian factories, the campaign rapidly gained ground in non-Communist circles. Editorials favouring the release of interned Communists and the lifting of the ban on the CPC appeared in many newspapers. The TLC, the CCL, and Mitch Hepburn, the Liberal Premier of Ontario, put forward similar demands. The members of the House of Commons reflected the views of the articulate segment of public opinion. On two occasions the Parliamentary Defence of Canada Regulations Committee urged the government to remove the ban. Louis Saint-Laurent, the Minister of Justice, however, remained unconvinced. The most he was prepared to do was to free the interned Communists.

To force the hand of the authorities, fourteen senior Communist officials living underground surrendered of their own volition to the RCMP on September 25, 1942. During their short stay in jail Premier Hepburn sent them cigarettes and candy. Public pressure mounted; Coldwell, David Lewis and Professor F. R. Scott visited the Department of Justice in Ottawa to urge the release of Buck and his comrades. Set free in October 1942, the Communist leaders immediately resumed the kind of work they had done in the 1930s, although before their release they had signed a declaration promising to refrain from political activity.[32]

For a time the Communists operated under the guise of the Dominion Communist-Labour Total War Committee, which was launched at a conference at the Royal York Hotel, Toronto, in August 1942. This arrangement was at best temporary. To play a role in Canadian politics the Communists needed a legal party organization, not a makeshift Total War Committee. Since the federal government was not prepared to co-operate by lifting the ban on the CPC, the Communists decided to regroup their forces by forming a new party.

The founding convention of the Labor Progressive Party (LPP) was held in Toronto on August 21-22, 1943. It was attended by five hundred delegates representing LPP clubs established in the weeks before the convention and run by CPC members.

The debate over the name of the party was heated. Twelve delegates from B.C. voted in favour of retaining the old one. The bulk of the delegates, however, accepted the one proposed by the party leaders in Toronto. It was felt at the time that the "name Labor Progressive would appeal to broader circles, that it would bring us votes in the parliamentary field, that it would re-assure those liberals 'frightened' by the term Communist."[33]

The convention elected Buck as national leader, and a national committee (NC) of sixty-two men and thirteen women. Thirty-six of its members came from Ontario, twenty from Quebec, sixteen from western Canada and three from the Maritimes. Their names were made public at the time, a procedure the LPP did not follow after 1946. The national committee in turn elected a national executive committee (NEC) of seventeen members. Mrs. Nielsen was one of the three female members on the executive. Anglo-Saxons predominated in the highest party forum: there were only two Quebecois and four Canadians of Jewish extraction. In addition to Buck, the key members of the NEC were Sam Carr, organizational secretary, Charles Sims, executive secretary, J. B. Salsberg, who was put in charge of work in the trade unions, and S. B. Ryerson, who became responsible for "education and publicity", a term that replaced Agitprop.

The election of members to the national and national executive committees followed the adoption of the party program and party statutes.[34] The LPP program resembled that of Communist parties in other democratic societies. The LPP asserted its opposition to "violence, conspiracy and secrecy," and insisted that it was not going to use force "as a means of imposing any form of government or economic reform on the Canadian people." Instead, the LPP dedicated itself to the task of "educating and organizing the Canadian workers, farmers and middle-class in the cause of a consistent struggle for democracy, to the end that the majority of the Canadian people shall, by its own decision, achieve the great aim of socialism."

This could be done by a "movement for independent labour, farmer political action," and by "electing majorities to the governments of Canada, municipal, provincial and federal, so as to establish labour-farmer governments which can lead the nation in effecting profound reforms in the economy and law of Canada." The reforms the LPP had in mind at the time included many of those favoured by the CPC during the Popular Front period: medicare, full employment, slum clearance, old-age pensions at age sixty, reform of the taxation system, raising "sub-standard wages", and the creation of a "democratic national labour code." The program called for the protection of the "family farm", and the "interests and rights of small business people." It demanded the nationalization of monopolies "that flaunt the national interest and interfere with democratic reconstruction." The LPP also advocated the abolition of the Senate, the extension of the franchise to "all who reach the age of 18," bringing "Canada's Constitution up to date" by amending the Statute of Westminster and the BNA Act, making anti-Semitism a punishable offence, and adopting "a distinctive national flag for Canada and an official national anthem."

Two other demands reflected issues about which the Communist leaders felt and still feel very strongly. A change in the electoral law allowing the introduction of proportional representation would make it easier for a small party like the LPP to gain a foothold in the federal Parliament. "Full rights of citizenship to all Canadians" would put an end to what the Communists have long argued is a serious form of discrimination against immigrants who play a prominent role in the Communist movement. In a number of instances the authorities have declined to grant citizenship papers, on the ground that applicants who were deeply involved in Communist agitation were unlikely to display the kind of loyalty and dedication to Canada expected from her naturalized citizens.

The party statutes adopted in 1943, and revised in 1946, 1957 and 1962, established a network of party organizations which still exists today. The branch or club became the basic organization of the LPP. For a fee of one dollar, five persons or more could apply to the provincial committee for a club charter, which the national committee alone could grant. Every club elected an executive consisting of a chairman, secretary, treasurer, and education and literature directors. All were elected for a one-year term.

"In its own community," the club was expected to become "the rallying centre for public work on the broadest basis and the standard bearer of the Party, not only in election campaigns, but at all times and in all democratic community activities."[35]

One of the main tasks of each club was to recruit additional members. Its members were empowered to decide by a majority vote whether or not to accept any applicant. Expulsion from the LPP, however, was "subject to final approval by the Provincial Committee of the Party." The expelled member could complain "to the higher Party body, up to and including the National Convention of the Party."

As in the case of the CPC branches or units, the LPP clubs were either industrially or residentially based. A fair number of the residentially-based clubs were in fact ethnic groupings, and some other "residential" clubs were in fact youth clubs, which were formed in an attempt to attract and channel the zeal of younger party members. To encourage housewives to join and stay in the LPP, clubs limited to women members were also formed.

Party members who could not be attached to a club, because none existed in their neighbourhood, had the status of "members at large", under the direct supervision of the provincial committees of the LPP. An analogous status was granted to those party members who could not afford the luxury of disclosing their membership in the LPP, except to a tiny number of party officials who knew how to respect these valuable members' desire for anonymity. Among them were individuals who belonged to other political parties (especially the CCF), civil servants, and professional people whose standing in society neither they nor the party leaders were eager to jeopardize. In some instances, these professional people were sufficiently numerous to form party clubs separate from the general run of party clubs. These special clubs seldom received mention, let alone publicity, in the party press or at party conventions.

To co-ordinate the work of the clubs, the statutes provided for a delegates' council of club representatives in a given area. All the LPP clubs in a given city formed the city party organization. Its secretary acted as the party leader in that locality. In larger conglomerations he was a paid official who had been a member of the CPC for some time. A provincial party organization existed in most provinces. Each held a convention every two years to review the work done in the preceding period, to discuss future problems, and to elect or re-elect the provincial leader and the provincial party committee. This committee in turn elected a smaller executive.

The statutes called for national conventions every two years.

These conventions were held in Toronto and were attended by delegates selected beforehand by provincial party organizations. In Ontario they were chosen by the four regions, or districts as they were known in the 1920s and 1930s. At the end of the national convention the delegates elected the national committee. The several dozen members of the NC met at least twice a year after 1950. Day-to-day activities were carried out by the national executive committee or politbureau. In the 1960s, the NC became the central committee and the NEC resumed the old name of central executive committee (CEC). It was composed of top party leaders, most of whom lived in Toronto or Montreal. It met frequently.

The organizational structure of the LPP was based on that of the CPC, and modelled on that of the Bolshevik party. The term "democratic centralism" was not inserted into the party statutes until 1957. On the surface, the LPP provided channels through which the rank-and-file could contribute to pre-convention discussions, take part in the decision-making process and elect the leaders. In practice, however, the LPP was hierarchical in structure and highly authoritarian in outlook, as many party members would complain in 1956-1957.

The existence of a group of experienced leaders working full-time in the national and provincial headquarters of the LPP, the absence of a truly democratic tradition in the Communist movement, the feeling that ranks had to be closed in the face of a hostile world, all made it very difficult for militants or even coteries of party officials to challenge the politbureau successfully. With one or two exceptions, whatever debate there was took place behind locked doors, with the result that between 1946 and 1956 the rank-and-file learned little about differences of opinion at the top.

Nor were party members encouraged to turn the LPP into a debating club. Instead, they were given tasks that kept them busy, tested their aptitudes, endurance and loyalty, and gave the ambitious an opportunity to attract the attention of party leaders. Carried along by the belief that they were engaged in a worthwhile cause, and that the Communist movement in North America, Asia and Europe was advancing rapidly, party members devoted their energies to reaching the goals set by the LPP leadership.

The network of LPP clubs spread rapidly as party membership increased dramatically. By the end of the Second World War, LPP clubs existed in parts of Canada that the CPC had never reached. On the whole clubs were more numerous in urban and mining centres than in rural areas. Among prairie farmers the LPP relied primarily on those of East European extraction and on ex-members of the FUL.

In urban centres, too, the LPP depended to a large extent on immigrants from eastern Europe. In the federal constituency of Cartier-Montreal an effective party machine, trade union support and the voters' hatred of the European and Quebecois varieties of fascism, got Fred Rose elected to the House of Commons. In a by-election on August 9, 1943, he defeated David Lewis, the powerful secretary of the CCF, by a majority of 2476 votes. Both men were of Jewish extraction and both were staunch opponents of fascism. In the Ontario provincial election in August 1943 Salsberg and MacLeod were successful. They, like Rose, profited from the pro-Soviet euphoria after the battle of Stalingrad, and received the bulk of their support from voters of East European descent.

These successes provided the LPP with useful forums, which the Communists used to explain the party's stand on major issues or to raise matters of interest to their constituents. Salsberg's and MacLeod's talents were so obvious that they soon gained the grudging respect of their fellow-legislators.

In municipal elections the Communists surged forward. Almost every major city west of Montreal had at least one alderman either belonging to the LPP or closely associated with it. The Communist aldermen and school trustees owed their victories to the votes of non-Communists who were as impressed by the record of the Red Army as by the LPP candidates. The views expressed by the Communists, and the proposals they put forward, sounded sensible and progressive to those voters who felt that municipal councils could do with new faces and that powerful business interests had to be checked.

However gratifying these electoral victories were, the Communists did even better in the trade unions.[36] The expansion of the labour force, the introduction of collective bargaining, which provided a strong impetus to the unionization of manual workers, and the federal government's eagerness to avoid social strife and maintain a high level of industrial production, made it easier for the Communists to recoup the losses suffered as a result of their previous anti-war stand and the arrest of Communist union leaders.

By championing, within strict limits, the rights of organized labour, by concentrating their experienced activists in the industries they considered vital, by displaying the drive and organizational skill for which they were well-known, the Communists made rapid progress. So did CCFers. Although the Communists and democratic socialists worked side by side in the unions, distrust and recriminations characterized their relations, tempered by the awareness that neither side was strong enough to drive the other into the wilderness.

In the TLC, Communists achieved a major success when J. A. (Pat) Sullivan, president of the Canadian Seamen's Union, was elected one of the three vice-presidents in 1942. The following year he was elected, by almost two-thirds of the delegates to the annual convention, as secretary-treasurer of the TLC. In the CCL the Communists could not boast of a similar triumph. On the other hand, they consolidated their grip over the unions in which they had been active in the late 1930s. At the end of the Second World War the Communists and their friends controlled, or were very influential, in unions comprising "more than a third" of the CCL membership.[37] Among these unions were the International Fur and Leather Workers Union, the International Union of Mine, Mill and Smelter Workers of America, the United Automobile Workers (UAW), the IWA and the UE.

The LPP headquarters could depend on the leaders of the Canadian districts of these unions to defend the line taken by the LPP on all major issues. They could also be relied upon to channel union funds to various Communist causes and to subsidize, among other things, the *Canadian Tribune*. The Canadian districts of these unions provided jobs for party members and sympathizers with legal training or a journalistic background. Time could always be found for non-union activities during office hours. Some of the pro-Communist and Communist union officials and union staff stood as LPP candidates in provincial and federal elections. At the polls they benefited from their association with these unions.

Communist activities in the political arena were based on the premise that the Tories represented, and would continue to represent after the end of the war, the main enemy of the working class. Hostility towards the Conservatives was based to some extent on bitter memories of the measures the Tories had taken against radicals during and immediately after the First World War, and of R. B. Bennett's persecution of the CPC during the Depression. Statements by prominent Tory opponents of Mackenzie King strengthened the Communists' suspicions that a new round of persecution would begin if ever the Conservatives returned to power.

Given the Communist fear of a Tory comeback, and their awareness that they could not prevent it unaided, party spokesmen advocated the formation of a broad alliance to bar the road to the representatives of "high capital". The allies whom the Communists had in mind were the trade union movement, farm organizations, the CCF and at least some segments of the Liberal Party. The inclusion of Liberals was defended on the ground that there were progressive elements in that party, and that nothing should be done to drive the majority of the Liberals into the arms of the

Tories. A coalition of Conservatives and Liberals would produce a government that would be far less responsive to the needs of the people than Mackenzie King's after Hitler's attack on the Soviet Union.

The formation of an anti-Tory alliance presupposed close relations with the CCF. The Communists therefore took a few tentative steps to improve relations with democratic socialists in 1941. A Communist candidate withdrew from the B.C. provincial election after urging the voters to support the CCF. For a time the *Canadian Tribune* toned down its criticism of CCF leaders. These moves were followed by attempts to affiliate the LPP to the CCF. Just after the founding convention of the LPP, Buck addressed a formal request to the national council of the CCF. He promised that "the Labor Progressive Party, as an affiliate of the CCF, will accept . . . the CCF program and constitution."[38]

The National Council of the CCF voted overwhelmingly in favour of rejecting the application for affiliation in September 1943. In a public statement above David Lewis's signature, the CCF drew attention to Communist opposition to the war in 1939-1941, referred to the collaboration between Communists and Hepburn in Ontario after Hitler's attack on the Soviet Union, pointed out that the doors of the CCF were open to all those who wanted to join it, and appealed to "all Canadians to reject this latest attempt to split and disrupt the forces of progress in Canada, which are solidly uniting within the CCF."[39]

The CCF's refusal to co-operate with the LPP had two consequences. The LPP abandoned its slogan of a "CCF-Labor Coalition", which the Communists had been advocating for a short time as part of their campaign for close relations between the two parties. Also, socialist opponents of LPP affiliation to the CCF came under heavy fire. Fred Rose described what the Communist leaders thought of their rivals, when he wrote in the July 1944 issue of the *National Affairs Monthly* "CCF policies are a mixture of morbid defeatism and featherbrained utopianism."

The complaint about morbid defeatism referred to the lack of enthusiasm shown by many socialist intellectuals when they heard of the agreement between Churchill, Roosevelt and Stalin in Teheran in December 1943. While most students of international affairs saw in the Big Three meeting a harbinger of a peaceful postwar world, a writer in the *Canadian Forum* had the prescience to write that "a melancholy prospect awaits us."[40]

More ink was spilt when the Communists had scrutinized the proposals put forward by the CCF to cope with Canada's wartime and postwar problems. Coldwell's call for the conscription of wealth encountered strong Communist opposition. Leslie Morris expressed "deep concern" that the CCF leadership should advocate this policy, one which was "patently unrealizable as a practical measure of total war policy."

[It] "would bring about violent social conflict . . . to advance narrow party considerations ahead of the national interest as the CCF appears to do, weakens the war effort and confuses the workers and farmers,"[41] Morris warned.

Similar objections were raised when the CCF argued that mass unemployment would follow the end of the hostilities, and when socialists claimed that the majority of Canadians supported socialism. The CCF's emphasis on socialism as an immediate goal drew the ire of the LPP down on them. In public the Communists declared that unemployment under capitalism need not take place, provided those in power adopted the proposals put forward by the Communists in the LPP program and manifesto for the 1945 federal election. At the same time they insisted that Canadians did not favour a socialist society. They used public opinion poll findings to buttress their case against CCF demands for nationalization. They warned that talk about socialism would endanger national unity during the war, and would simply strengthen reactionary tendencies among Liberals, many of whom might be tempted to form a coalition with the Tories with dire results for Canadian workers and farmers.

Differing interpretations of trends at home and abroad went hand in hand with disagreements over the role of the CCF in Canadian politics. The democratic socialists considered the CCF as the party of social and economic change, as a movement that had the backing of workers and prairie farmers. The Communists challenged the claim that labour stood behind the CCF. Once again, Gallup Poll data were used as evidence for the Communist case.

The Communists did not confine their arguments to brochures, newspapers and the hustings. They fought hard to prevent unions from affiliating to the CCF and contributing to CCF election coffers. Although they spoke of the need for trade union involvement in politics, and of an independent labour stance in public affairs, they insisted time and again that the CCF did not deserve the support of organized labour. In trade union circles their arguments against the CCF centered around the policies that the CCF favoured and the refusal of the CCF leaders to allow the affiliation of the LPP. Repeatedly, the Communists complained about the CCF demand for "socialism now", its unwillingness to support the "No Strike" pledge, and the socialists' hostility to Communists. The highly critical attitude adopted by the CCF towards Mackenzie King, the

Liberals in Quebec, and Social Credit in Alberta, also came under fire. The stand taken by the CCF on all these issues, the Communists insisted, hurt the working class and materially reduced the chances of building a broad labour-farmer coalition capable of influencing the course of Canadian politics.

The Communist critique of the CCF carried considerable weight in the world of labour. Few union locals took the plunge and aligned themselves with the CCF, in spite of proddings by CCF leaders like Lewis and trade union officials like Millard. There are several reasons for the failure of the CCF to win widespread union support. To begin with, the Communists were well-entrenched in several major CCL unions and used the weight of their union position to promote the party's line on the CCF. On the CCL executive, party members and their allies represented a powerful block which, as Mosher frequently discovered, could not be easily by-passed, let alone dislodged. At the annual conventions of the CCL, Communist-inspired resolutions and Communist-supported candidates rallied a considerable number of delegates. At the CCL convention in September 1941 Nigel Morgan once again challenged Mosher for the presidency. The election returns show that a higher percentage of delegates supported Morgan in 1941 than in 1940.

The anti-Communists in the CCL did not improve their image when they took administrative measures to reduce Communist influence in certain CCL unions. They were accused of ignoring union rules, stifling union democracy, and engaging in partisan politics to further the interests of the CCF. The most notorious case of intervention took place on the west coast where Mosher failed to impose his will on the Boilermakers and Iron Shipbuilders Union.[42]

Opposition to the CCF brought together those trade union leaders who were party members or sympathizers and those who were sympathetic to Mackenzie King and his brand of liberalism. The latter were opposed to any further strengthening of the CCF, in which they saw a powerful challenge to the Liberal Party after public opinion polls and the provincial elections in Ontario (1943) and Saskatchewan (1944) revealed the growing appeal of the CCF. Under these circumstances, the Communists both inside and outside the unions found it easier to get along with most of the Liberals in the TLC than with the anti-Communist democratic socialists in the CCL or the CCF leadership.

In September 1943 the members of the national council of the CCF were almost unanimous, and in January 1944 wholly so, in rejecting Buck's proposals for affiliating the LPP to the CCF. They were equally hostile to a Communist proposal that the CCF not put up candidates in a certain number of federal ridings where Buck thought the LPP had a fair chance of success. In return, the LPP was prepared to not compete with the CCF in other constituencies in the forthcoming federal election. Such an electoral arrangement would have enhanced the chances of several Communist candidates and made it easier for the LPP to gain a bigger foothold in the legislative arena.

The stand adopted by the CCF leaders was backed by the majority of democratic socialists. In Ontario, where the socialists had plenty of evidence of collusion between Liberals and Communists, the provincial CCF convention in April 1944 voted by 470 votes to 2 against co-operation with the LPP.[43] Here and there, however, voices were raised in favour of collaboration. Two CCF members of the Manitoba Legislature were suspended for coming out in favour of Communist proposals. (One of them was a member of the CPC when he died in 1972.) One CCF member of the Ontario legislature resigned over the issue and another was expelled from the CCF. At the convention of the B.C. CCF in May 1944 the motion for co-operation between the two parties was defeated by sixty-eight votes to forty-two. Nathan Cohen left the CCF and resigned as editor of the pro-CCF *Glace Bay Gazette* in order to join the LPP and the editorial staff of the *Canadian Tribune*, only to abandon both, before he became well-known as a critic.

Rejection of Communist offers was partly due to the belief that democratic socialism and Soviet Communism were incompatible, no matter what Buck might say. It was also a reaction against Communist behaviour in the electoral field* and elsewhere. In spite of the Communists' often expressed desire for "labour unity" and co-operation with the CCF, they had put up Fred Rose as their candidate in the federal riding of Cartier-Montreal after David

---

*On several occasions before and after 1944, CCF spokesmen and papers accused the Communists of making deals with the "old line" parties to prevent the election of this or that CCF candidate. By putting up a Communist candidate, the Communists could and did split the vote that normally went to the democratic socialists and thus ensure the return of a Liberal or Tory in a close contest.

At his trial in 1949, Carr mentioned in passing that he visited Ottawa a number of times to discuss the 1945 elections with two prominent Liberals, whose names he gave. (*The Globe and Mail*, April 8, 1949, p. 2.) Neither the member of King's government nor the Liberal organizer mentioned by Carr denied the charge.

Lewis had entered the field.* Subsequent Communist attempts to "by-pass the CCF" by advocating a "Liberal Labor Coalition" turned dislike into contempt. By September 1944 the theoretical organ of the LPP had to admit that the CCF leaders had "denounced" the Communists as "Liberal stooges".

The Communists laid themselves open to this description by campaigning vigorously for a "Liberal Labor Coalition" in the last stages of the Second World War. Because of their dislike of the Tories, and the refusal of the CCF to join forces with Buck and Mackenzie King, only the Liberals were left as prospective partners of an LPP eager to carve a place for itself in the mainstream of Canadian politics.

In the eyes of the Communists, the coalition proposals revealed in May 1944 had two major advantages. They conclusively showed that the Communists were not violent men or doctrinaires, but men and women prepared to co-operate with those in power to win the war and to deal with the important problems that the Canadian economy was bound to face at the end of hostilities. For those reasons no reader of the Communist press in late 1944 or early 1945 could come across much criticism of the Prime Minister. On the contrary, the politbureau of the LPP praised the federal Cabinet, "as the government which despite its shortcomings, maintains Canadian unity behind the war effort and is projecting policies of international co-operation and social reform along Teheran lines after the war."†

In provincial elections the Communists also found it easier to support the Liberals than to co-operate with CCFers. In Quebec the Communists advocated the formation of a Liberal-Labor Coalition against Duplessis, and they supported the Liberals in several ridings in the provincial election of 1944.[44]

---

*Some of the Communist hostility to Lewis was due to the sympathy he showed for V. Alter and H. Erlich, two prominent Jewish Polish socialists shot by the Soviet secret police after Hitler's attack on the U.S.S.R. (Walter D. Young, *The Anatomy of a Party: The National CCF, 1932-1961* (Toronto, 1969), pp. 270-272.) To the Canadian Communists Lewis's interest in the fate of these two victims of Stalin's terror was yet another example of CCF mischief-making and readiness to sow discord among Hitler's opponents.

† *Canadian Tribune*, June 3, 1944. Two months later, a well-known CCF publication quoted Buck as saying that the philosophy of Mackenzie King's Liberal Party most closely approximated what "used to be known as Communism." (Gerald Caplan, *The Dilemma of Canadian Socialism. The CCF in Ontario* (Toronto, 1973), p. 135.)

The second advantage to the LPP of a Liberal-Labor Coalition was the possibility of bypassing the CCF in the electoral arena and the trade unions. Hemmed in between reform Liberals and the expanding LPP, the standard bearer of "Labor" and a partner in the postwar federal Cabinet, the CCF would wither away and its rank-and-file go over to the Communists. However unrealistic the proposal may have appeared to Canadians, it must be remembered that access to power was of immeasurable assistance to half-a-dozen Communist parties in western Europe, as well as those in Chile and Cuba, which joined coalition governments.

To speed up the disintegration of the CCF, the Communists kept up a steady barrage against socialist leaders hostile to the LPP. They were branded as "irresponsible", their tactics were called "restless" and their policies "partisan", demoralizing" and "dangerous" to Canadian and working-class unity. At the same time the rank-and-file of the CCF was urged to force the Coldwells and David Lewises to change their attitude towards the LPP and Mackenzie King. This campaign reached its climax at the national convention of the CCF in December 1944, to which Buck sent a message, "appealing to CCF members . . . to reject the false and partisan policy of Coldwell and the CCF leadership."[45]

Similar appeals were made at election time. The *Canadian Tribune* described the decision of the CCF to contest the Grey North federal by-election (held February 5, 1945) as "the crassest expression of the blind partisanship of the CCF leaders." Instead, the LPP supported the Minister of National Defence, General McNaughton, urged the voters to elect him "for victory's sake", and called on "all workers and all members of trade unions to reject and defeat the most harmful and reckless policy of the CCF."[46]

Because of the Communists' strong dislike of the CCF, only the most credulous could have been surprised when a prominent member of the national committee of the LPP wrote in the *Canadian Tribune* on December 16, 1944, that the LPP favoured the CCF's "resounding defeat at the polls." The Communists carried out their promise in the Ontario provincial election and the federal election, both held in June, 1945. By contesting a large number of constituencies, the Communists split the vote that would have gone to the CCF if the Communists had abstained from putting up candidates. In the Ontario provincial election twenty-one of the thirty LPP candidates contested ridings won by the CCF two years earlier. When the votes were counted, a case could be made that Communist intervention had cost the CCF five seats in the Ontario election and ten in the federal.[47]

The pro-Liberal stance of the LPP was so pronounced that Buck came under fire when the world Communist movement changed its line. The first signal that something different was required from Communists in North America came in an attack on Earl Browder. Jacques Duclos, a French Communist leader well-known for his loyalty to Moscow, accused the American of reducing the CPUSA to an adjunct of Roosevelt's Democratic Party, and blamed him for replacing the CPUSA with a Communist Political Association in 1944.[48]

Since the American Communists well knew that Duclos reflected Soviet thinking on the subject, Browder's days as party leader were clearly numbered. Before long he was replaced as leader and expelled from the party. A new party line was proclaimed; its chief exponent was W. Z. Foster who was familiar with the Canadian labour scene before and after 1914.

In view of the close relations between the Canadian and American Communist parties, and the policies pursued by the LPP, Buck realized that some of Duclos' criticism of Browder could easily be extended to his own stewardship. He complained in August 1945 that "different comrades in different parts of the country put their finger on revisionism in our own party work, by picking out, in different places and in different times, almost everything that we have ever done."[49]

The most prominent critic was the leader of the LPP in B.C., a province that had always harboured more than the Canadian average of radicals whom their opponents like to describe as "sectarians" and "dogmatists". Fergus McKean, an ex-worker who had been interned for a time during the Second World War, addressed for two hours a session of the national committee of the LPP in August 1945. What he actually said is unknown, since the Communist press never published the text of his speech. All that the rank-and-file of the LPP could learn about him in Communist publications is what his opponents claim he said and did.[50]

McKean criticized Buck's policies, with the help of quotations from the writings of Marx, Lenin, Stalin and Buck. He objected to the support given by the CPC to New Democracy in 1939, and by the LPP to the Liberals after 1941. He maintained that the "No-Strike Pledge", which had full Communist backing, "could not but produce the abdication" of the independent role of the trade unions. Through the "abolition" of the CPC, and the formation of the LPP, Buck and his closest collaborators had set up "a bourgeois parliamentary party". This claim drew the retort that McKean's objection to "parliamentary work" stemmed from "his desire to capitulate and leave alone the parliamentary field as a monopoly of Social Democratism."

Carr, Morris and Stewart Smith refuted McKean. They accused him of ignoring the classics of Marxism-Leninism and of misquoting Lenin, Stalin and Buck. With the help of suitable quotations from the works of these authors they defended the policies followed by the LPP. They focused on those aspects of the party record that showed that the Canadian Communists had been less closely identified with the Liberals in Ottawa than Browder had been with Roosevelt's New Dealers. At the same time, they admitted in passing that the LPP had committed three sorts of errors in recent years. To begin with, the slogan of "Liberal-Labor Coalition" had been liable to misrepresentation. Second, they had erred in making statements that seemed to indicate that business cycles could be avoided and full employment achieved under capitalism. Third, they claimed that their gravest mistake had been in not criticizing Browder's views in public. Buck spoke along the same lines without dealing with McKean at any length.

It was obvious before the end of the meeting that McKean was isolated in the party hierarchy. None of his colleagues was prepared to support his view that "revisionism was rampant" in the Canadian Communist movement. His own style of leadership had been under attack for some time. Any chances he might have had of rallying the party organization in B.C. disappeared a fortnight before the NC meeting. As the initiator of "a campaign of slander", he was suspended from the post of provincial leader.

At the meeting of the national committee in August 1945, McKean uttered one of the gravest charges that can be levelled against Communists. According to Buck, McKean "deliberately" chose to "propagate a monstrous lie against the tried and trusted leaders" of the LPP. In conversation with William Kardash, a LPP member of the Manitoba legislature, McKean asserted that Buck and several of his closest collaborators in the early 1930s "had become '*agents provocateurs*' as the price of their release from the Kingston Penitentiary" in 1934. Unable to substantiate his charge to the satisfaction of a specially appointed Review Committee, McKean was promptly expelled. A communique of the national committee described McKean "as an unprincipled traitor and disruptionist," and reassured party members that his expulsion "uprooted at the source a brazen attempt of a conspiracy aimed at beheading and ultimately destroying the Marxist party of the Canadian working class."

The members of the national committee dispersed, after passing a resolution admitting that revisionist tendencies did exist in the LPP. They called on party members to combat both "Browderism" and the "sectarianism" associated with McKean.

McKean's wife and several other party members in B.C. were shortly afterwards expelled from the LPP. Several months later, McKean was briefly in the news again. The national Committee of the LPP denounced his attempt to form a "Communist Party of Canada", and attacked him as "an enemy of the working class."[51] Nothing came of his project to create a rival Communist party, except a rambling polemical work which he wrote against his former colleagues.

Chapter 6

Spies and Others

The end of the war with Germany precipitated a federal election. How many candidates the LPP should put up had already been discussed at several meetings of its national and national executive committees. As long as there was some hope of accommodation with democratic socialists, the LPP intimated that the Communists would not contest the constituencies already represented by CCFers in Parliament: all the LPP would do would be to "select a limited number of constituencies which offer good prospects . . . and concentrate the party's strength and resources . . . in those constituencies."[1]

The decision to challenge the CCF in other ridings as well was taken early in 1945. It was defended on the ground that it would be "unrealistic" to expect the CCF to change "its partisan policy of placing party considerations above all others." The way was now open for the LPP to contest a number of ridings in which the CCF would have a good chance of winning but for the intervention of Communist candidates, who diverted votes which would normally have gone to the CCF.

In the end the LPP contested under its own label sixty-seven of the 245 federal constituencies. In three other ridings the *Canadian Tribune* urged Canadians to vote for "independent labor"; these three candidates were McEwen, a veteran Communist, a member of the national committee of the LPP who ran in Nova Scotia, and Nigel Morgan who in 1945 succeeded McKean as leader of the party in B.C.

The large number of candidates was justified with references to the amount of LPP grassroots support in the constituencies contested by the Communists. Buck also argued that the "Liberals alone, as they stand, cannot be trusted to carry through progressive reform policies in the postwar period." It was left to a party activist to point out after the election that "the only reason given for running so many candidates was that it gave us the standing of a National Party and therefore entitled us to free radio time on a national scale."[2]

The issues on which the Communist candidates campaigned had also been decided long before Mackenzie King had announced the date of the election. The electoral program of the LPP was set out in an attractively produced brochure *A Better Canada – To Fight For – To Work For – To Vote For*. It included statements such as:

> The conditions for achieving in Canada a real People's Peace are ready in our hands provided we learn the lesson that the price of national greatness is national unity.

After explaining that the LPP was dedicated to the "establishment of Socialism", the brochure warned that the real issue in the election was not socialism versus free enterprise, but "to decide whether we can organize government policy in such a way as to maintain a high level of production and purchasing power in accordance with the people's needs and economic interests."

The success of such a policy would depend on the election of representatives of labour, trade union and farm organizations, of the CCF and "progressive Liberals in town and rural districts." The brochure called on Canadians to elect LPP candidates, but had no advice to give to people who lived in constituencies where no Communist was standing.

The LPP's election platform was very similar to the program adopted and the resolutions passed at the founding convention of the LPP in August 1943. There was emphasis on full employment, public works and social legislation. Public ownership was urged only in the cases of the electrical and coal-mining industries. The Dominion government was to have responsibility for social legislation and labour standards, and for the regulation of corporations, trade and commerce.

The LPP made an all-out effort in the election campaign. Buck and other leaders criss-crossed the Dominion, addressing quite large crowds and speaking on the radio. Activists canvassed patiently, and distributed leaflets and party newspapers. Trade union officials, who either belonged to, or were associated with the LPP, issued statements urging the election of this or that Communist candidate. Encouraged by the optimistic forecasts periodically issued by the LPP leaders to raise the morale of their followers, many party members believed that the LPP had a good chance of winning between twelve and thirty seats and of holding the balance of power in the postwar years.

Although the LPP won more votes (109,778) in the 1945 election than it ever had, or ever would, the results were a major disappointment to the leaders and the rank-and-file. They could not ignore the fact that they had gained the support of fewer than 2 per cent of the electorate, and that they were demonstrably weaker than the CCF, which had polled 816,254 votes. The Communists did better than the socialists in only four of the sixty-one constituencies contested by both parties. One of these was the Yukon riding, and the other three had an appreciable number of voters of East European extraction. What was even more galling to the Communists was their failure to elect more than one MP.

The election results were discussed briefly in the Letters-to-the-Editor column of the *Canadian Tribune*, and at the meeting of the national committee of the LPP in August, 1945.[3] As in 1935, the leaders derived some consolation and saw some significance in the fact that third parties had the support of so many voters. The absence of a "progressive majority" in the House of Commons was attributed to the "narrow, partisan" policies of the CCF leaders. They had refused to co-operate with the LPP and had campaigned on a platform emphasizing socialism, something the majority of voters did not want. This analysis did not silence criticism of the performance of the LPP at the polls. Some members expressed the view that the party had made a major mistake in spreading its resources too thinly by sponsoring so many candidates. They would have preferred the LPP to concentrate on those ridings where the Communists had had a reasonable chance of sneaking in past the divided ranks of the anti-Communist candidates. It was argued that the election of Buck would have represented a major breakthrough, because it would have given him a highly valuable forum.

Other critics claimed that the slogans "Liberal Labor Coalition" and "Make Labor a Partner in Government" had harmed the LPP. Carr referred to "many comrades" who thought that the coalition slogan "cost us votes and may have cost us some seats." Party members did not understand "the main substance" of the slogan. Instead of defending it in discussions with democratic socialists, Communists in "many places . . . capitulated to CCF pressures and in fact did little to explain the policy correctly."

After blaming some of the rank-and-file for having failed to grasp the latest example of what used to be termed "Bolshevik flexibility", Carr admitted that "very poor" work had been done to explain the slogan in question. Leslie Morris, on the other hand, reminded his colleagues that the two slogans were "specific expressions of the policy of compromise between the classes for specific aims," a view shared by the leaders of the CCF. At the same time he warned that "if a comrade rejects the conception of a national democratic front, he is against the party line."[4]

When the votes were counted, the LPP learned that Mrs. Nielsen had lost her seat in the House of Commons. Fred Rose, on the other hand, was re-elected by an increased majority*; however, his brief parliamentary career would soon come to a sorry end.

Several branches of the Soviet secret service had operated on Canadian soil since the early 1920s. Their task was to collect material on Canada and Canadians, as well as help with the transmission of data, couriers and others to and from the United States. The work of these Soviet agents, some of whom operated as a branch of the Comintern apparatus, was facilitated by several factors.

To begin with, immigration control in Montreal had the well-deserved reputation of being very lax; agents could enter or leave Canada here without much risk. Moreover, Canadian passports could be obtained and forged without difficulty. Canada's good name in the world made them all the more valuable to Soviet and Comintern agents. Tito had one before the war; Trotsky's murderer carried one in 1940. So did a number of Soviet intelligence officers caught by Western security services in various parts of the world after the Second World War. Last but not least, the presence of a Soviet trade mission in Montreal (1924-1927) and of a Soviet embassy in Ottawa (after Canada and the U.S.S.R. had established diplomatic relations in 1942), made it easier for Soviet intelligence to recruit agents among pro-Soviet Canadians.

Because of Canada's geographical position, growing industrial capacity, nuclear research facilities and close contact with the United States and the United Kingdom, it was an obvious target for the Soviet government, which was eager to collect data on a great variety of topics. The gathering of information proceeded along classical lines. Overtures were made to people who were already sympathetic to the Soviet Union, or who admired the record of the Red Army in the Second World War. Hard cash was paid out in small quantities and more was promised. Before long Soviet military intelligence was making use of the services of at least a dozen Canadians who represented a fair cross-section of the

*The LPP had 900 members in the riding. (*Club Life*, Toronto, August 1945, p. 4.)

Canadian middle-class. Some were French Canadians, while others were of Anglo-Saxon or East European origin. Most of them held positions that gave them access to valuable information in the civil service, armed forces or defence industries. At a time when pro-Soviet sentiment was widespread in Ottawa, some of them were known for their pro-Soviet views.

The spy ring was brought to light only when Igor Guzenko, a young cipher clerk who worked for the Soviet military attaché, sought political asylum in Canada on September 5, 1945. He took from one of the embassy safes a number of confidential documents which gave the Canadian authorities a great deal of valuable evidence. Ironically, they did not at first welcome Guzenko. He spent several agonizing hours trying to convince journalists on the *Ottawa Journal*, and officials in the Department of Justice, that he was carrying important material. They not only rebuffed him but urged him to return to the Soviet embassy.

The unwillingness of Canadian officials to accept the man and the documents indicates the extent to which those who ought to have known better were unwilling to accept the proposition that a Soviet spy ring was operating in Canada. Their initial treatment of the defector stemmed to some extent from their desire not to antagonize the U.S.S.R. at a time when the Soviet Union was an ally. Some at least were also worried that Guzenko might have been planted by those who had a vested interest in poisoning relations between Moscow and the West. Guzenko's credentials were only established when the RCMP noted that Soviet diplomats had broken into his apartment in the hope of finding him there and bringing him back to the embassy. They were too late, however, to prevent the discovery of the spy ring; the news was all the more sensational because this was the first of the spy rings unmasked in the West after the war.

There was a delay of several months before the authorities proceeded with arrests. Among those subpoenaed were two well-known leaders of the LPP, MP Fred Rose and Sam Carr, who as organizational secretary ranked second only to Buck in the Communist hierarchy. Both men came from eastern Europe and had, like many other immigrants, anglicized their surnames in Canada. Both had been active in the Communist movement in the 1920s, and had spent some time in the Soviet Union. They had also caught the eye of the Canadian authorities on several occasions as they rose in the CPP in the intervals between terms of imprisonment.

The exact day when they began their association with Soviet

military intelligence is not known. The documents Guzenko brought from the embassy safe showed that Carr and Rose were working for the Soviet military attaché during the Second World War. Carr's file included a reference to "financially secure, but takes money. It is necessary occasionally to help."[5]

Buck and his colleagues took several measures to limit the damage caused to the Communist movement by these disclosures. Readers of the Communist press were assured that the LPP "does not and will not condone acts of espionage." They were also told that "Canada's national security lies in friendship with all peace-loving countries and especially with the U.S.S.R."[6] A special communique from party headquarters announced the removal of Carr "from official positions in the party" because nothing had been heard from him since he had received a leave of absence and gone south early in 1946. At the same time the NEC declared that it was not prepared to countenance his failure to appear when subpoenaed by the authorities.*

The LPP rushed to the aid of Rose, who was tried under the Official Secrets Act in the spring of 1946 and sentenced to six years' imprisonment. The Communist press gave publicity to his plea of innocence, and to the activities of those who subscribed to his defence fund. It also deplored the way he had been treated in court and in prison.

For several months much ink was spilt in an effort to refute at least some of the charges levelled by the popular press, some politicians, and the Royal Commission of enquiry into espionage in Canada, against the arrested men and the Communist movement in general. The government was charged, for example, with keeping suspects incommunicado, although the evidence against half of them was insufficient to secure their conviction.

The main line of Communist defence in the press was fairly simple. On some occasions an attempt was made to dismiss the charges out of hand. On other occasions the LPP downplayed the

---

* From the *Canadian Tribune*, April 20, 1946. The FBI discovered Carr in New York and deported him to Canada in February 1949. Tried under the Official Secrets Act, he received a six-year sentence for conspiring with Soviet embassy officials to "utter a forged Canadian passport" for a Soviet secret agent in the United States. (*The Globe and Mail*, Toronto, April 9, 1949, p. 2.) Unlike Rose, Carr stayed in Canada after the completion of his sentence. On January 2, 1974, *Canadian Tribune* informed its readers that Carr was "national secretary" of the United Jewish People's Order, a pro-Communist organization in Canada.

charges. After all, it was difficult to ignore them altogether when the *Canadian Tribune* published a Soviet diplomatic note in which the Soviet Government admitted that "the Soviet Military Attaché in Canada received . . . certain information of a secret character" and announced that he had been recalled.[7] By and large, the Communists preferred to argue that what had happened in Ottawa was part of a worldwide anti-Soviet plot.

Quite understandably, the Communists wanted to ignore the whole sordid subject of Soviet spying in Canada and hoped that all Canadians would forget it as quickly as possible. Their opponents saw to it that the connection between leading Communists and illegal operations on behalf of a foreign power were brought up when party leaders insisted that they were loyal Canadians and that the LPP was independent of Moscow. What anti-Communists had always claimed that the Communists were doing and getting paid for, had actually taken place. Nothing more damaging than the spy case could have hit an organization already suspected in most Canadian minds of being identified with a great foreign power.

The immediate impact of the spy case on the members of the LPP cannot easily be assessed. The rank-and-file and many leaders could plead ignorance of what had happened in wartime Ottawa. The more discerning leaders might have suspected something if they had had the opportunity of watching some of the accused in action. However, they had neither the inclination nor the means to investigate their colleagues. They had been too busy doing the work allotted to them. In any case, they believed that no information should be withheld from the Soviet Union, the first socialist state in the world and a leading opponent of Nazi Germany. Many party members reacted similarly, although the disclosures raised a number of disturbing questions for those who were politically more sophisticated or who already had other doubts about the LPP.

It was partly to divert the attention of party members from the seamier aspects of Communist activities that the leaders of the LPP launched a campaign to mobilize the rank-and-file for what appeared to be an exciting project: the launching of a Communist daily. In line with Lenin's dictate on the need for a strong party press, the Canadian Communists had always devoted a great deal of attention to their newspapers. For three years they published the *Daily Clarion*, no mean achievement when one bears in mind that the more popular CCF could not boast of a similar success.

The *Daily Tribune* was expected to be a viable undertaking. Communists searching eagerly for signs of industrial strife noted "the growing militancy of the labor movement." Evidence in support of this statement did exist: the Ford strike at Windsor in 1945, and the strikes of steelworkers at Hamilton, of seamen on the Great Lakes, textile workers in Quebec, and woodworkers and hard-rock miners in B.C. in 1946. Ironically, the leading Communist expert had not foreseen the extent of the strike movement. In a pamphlet he suggested that 1946 would be the year in which the unions would be well advised to concentrate their efforts on the legislative bodies.[8]

The Communists had played an important role in these and other strikes, and could be expected to influence developments in the world of labour if prices rose faster than wages and employers remained stubborn in the face of moderate demands. In the past, labour strife had helped to increase the circulation of Communist publications and the number of subscribers to Communist newspapers. Hence there was ground for hope that the *Daily Tribune* would gain new readers if labour disputes involved more workers than in 1946.

The January 1947 issue of the theoretical organ of the LPP noted:

> The labor movement in Canada has grown to a degree of maturity when it possesses the writers, reporters, artists, printers, and editors, who can, with solid financial backing, put out a paper for working class and progressive families sufficiently varied to meet their thirst for news and views.

Such a paper, the *National Affairs Monthly* promised, "will possess the indispensible quality that it will tell the truth – not in some hypocritically 'objective' way, but in a frankly partisan manner, as a fighter for the people's rights."

The LPP leaders assumed that many of the paper's expenses would be covered through advertisements inserted by labour and mass organizations as well as by small business men sympathetic to the Communist cause, or eager to have Communists and pro-Communists among their customers. Finally, a daily was considered a symbol of maturity or, as the Communist monthly put it: "The Canadian labor movement and its left-wing does not deserve to be called fullgrown until it possesses such a daily paper."

Presented with these arguments, party members and sympathizers were invited to make the appropriate financial sacrifices. The pressure was greatest on members of LPP clubs, although pro-

Communist unions and associations were also expected to contribute substantially.

Appeals and dedication, however, could not meet the targets of the fund-raising campaign: $150,000 by February 15, 1947, and $250,000 by May 1, 1947. The first issue of the daily came out on May Day although only $131,018 had been raised by April 14. The sum of $250,000 proved to be too ambitious and was never reached. The daily folded in early November 1947.

The cost of publishing the paper was high, even after cuts in the editorial staff. A stable circulation of 15,000, a figure deemed necessary for its survival, could not be guaranteed. Paid circulation hovered around 7,000.[9] Advertisements, sales and subscriptions covered about 20 per cent of the publication costs. The rest had to be met by dipping into the Foundation Fund. Over half the money raised came from Ontario. The other provinces contributed far less; some failed badly in meeting their quotas because they were in the midst of campaigns to raise money for Communist weeklies in Montreal and Vancouver, as well as the Communist press in East European languages.

The return to a weekly *Canadian Tribune* was described as a "temporary retreat". Few party members were fooled. Hundreds decided to cut their losses by leaving the LPP with its unending appeals for money. Many of those who remained in the party displayed "cynicism" and "disillusionment" because of what had happened. Morris, as editor, had to take some of the blame. Stewart Smith's popularity also suffered because of the way he had handled party members during the fund-raising campaign in Ontario.

The collapse of the *Daily Tribune* reflected the limits of Communist influence. So did the results of several recruitment campaigns. In 1943-1944 party membership went up, and the social and ethnic composition of the LPP became less lopsided than the CPC had been in the years between the two world wars. Nevertheless, those responsible for the numerical expansion of the LPP were only too well aware of problems. First, a number of party members, including manual workers, left the LPP because they were highly critical of the "Liberal Labor Coalition" slogan. Second, a number of party members who had served abroad did not resume party membership after demobilization, in spite of efforts to locate and reintegrate them into the Communist movement. Third, "the turnover in membership" gave the leaders "cause for serious reflection."[10] As a result, the target of 25,000 members by January 1,

1944 was not reached either then or later. (The LPP had fewer than 20,000 members in January 1946.) Under these circumstances, the LPP did not announce the size of its membership, a sure sign that the party was not doing well.*

This state of affairs made large-scale recruitment all the more desirable. The second LPP convention in June 1946 set the target of 10,000 new members. By May 1947, "close" to 2,000 had been enrolled, and William Kashtan had to warn his colleagues: "There is no doubt that reaction was able to achieve a limited and partial success with its red-baiting attack upon the Party."[11] Only in Saskatchewan was the LPP in better shape at the end of 1946 than in the wartime years. Its provincial leader could write in the October 1946 issue of *Club Life* that the LPP "is beginning to recover from the low point in organizational strength following upon the CCF victory, and the widespread social democratic illusions which were current in that period."

Recruitment drives did not take place in a vacuum, since the recruiters operated in a milieu largely dominated by other political forces. These could not be ignored, even when the LPP was not making a major effort to form an alliance with other parties, as had been the case in the last stages of the Second World War. It was obvious by July 1945 that the attempt to "by-pass" the CCF through a "Liberal-Labor Coalition" had failed dismally. Similar tactics could not be tried again in the near future, because that would expose the Communists to another defeat and more ridicule in left-wing circles. In addition, the international situation and the close relations between Ottawa and Washington precluded advocating a Liberal-Communist alignment in Canadian politics.

Now the LPP criticized the postwar policies at home and abroad of the Liberal government. Periodically, the LPP put forward proposals to deal with this or that problem, and saw to it that they were publicized. Some of the proposals were fairly detailed; few were revolutionary by post-1945 standards. Subsidies, public works, welfare legislation, controls over this or that branch of the economy, and a modicum of nationalization, were suggested as solutions to unemployment, underconsumption and minimal health standards.

Although the LPP saw itself as the most resolute champion of the people's needs and rights, Communist spokesmen insisted that a

---

*The Communist *World News and Views* (London) announced on March 22, 1947, that the LPP had 23,000 members. It is highly debatable whether the bulk of them were dues-paying members.

People's Coalition was required to rouse public opinion in favour of the reforms envisaged by the LPP. The components of the People's Coalition resembled those of the Popular Front of the 1930s: Communists, trade unions, farm organizations, disgruntled Social Crediters and the CCF.

Socialists were invited to co-operate with the LPP against Tory Premier George Drew in Ontario, Duplessis in Quebec, and the Liberals in Ottawa. Unity was advocated as a means of defeating employers, anti-Communist trade union leaders, and governments that were under the sway of big business. These calls to unity attracted less attention than the periodic attacks on the CCF program, proposals and leaders in the federal Parliament. Much of what was written in LPP publications about the CCF in 1945-1947 was a rehash of Comintern and Soviet interpretations of social democratic movements and ideas: the socialists are closer in their outlook to non-socialists than to Communists; they merely want to reform capitalism instead of destroying it; the Communists alone are able and willing to show the way to a socialist society. Moreover, the socialists are responsible for the lack of unity among the opponents of the "old line" parties in Canada; they have sowed "reformist illusions" among workers and prairie farmers; these "illusions" have prevented the people of Canada from fighting big business more effectively; it is the duty of Communists to go on patiently exposing the views and records of socialist leaders and intellectuals like Coldwell and Lewis.

At a meeting of the national committee in January 1948, Buck presented a lengthy report in which he condemned the foreign and domestic policies of the Liberal government in Ottawa and President Truman's attitude towards the U.S.S.R. and her allies. To meet Mackenzie King's challenge, Buck urged that the LPP support the CCF in the forthcoming federal and provincial elections by using the slogan "Unite at the Polls – Elect a CCF government".[12]

This dramatic change in the party line was defended on the ground that the CCF had the backing of a large number of workers and farmers who had already broken away from the old-line parties. At the same time Buck called for more vigorous action against "right wing" CCF leaders who were hostile to the Communists.

The new directive met with some resistance, even though Buck had qualified his support for the CCF, and had buttressed his case by reminding his colleagues that Lenin had urged the British Communists to co-operate with the Labour Party. Some of the members of the NC asked whether this was the right time to support the socialists. The question was very relevant, because relations between socialists and Communists in western Europe were worsening under the impact of the Cold War. Buck was leading the LPP in a direction that Communist leaders well-attuned to Moscow would have avoided in the light of authoritative Soviet pronouncements in the second half of 1947. It seems that Buck had misread the signals from eastern Europe in his eagerness to improve the position of the LPP.

In reply to his questioners, Buck admitted that it would have been better if the NC had come out earlier in support of the new policy. He mentioned June 1947 as a better date. To a comrade who asked whether the LPP should support affiliation to the CCF as part of the new line, Buck pointed out two reasons that such a proposal was hardly realistic: because of the constitution of the CCF and because it would divide the socialists on the issue of the LPP at the very time when unity was needed to elect a CCF government. To strengthen support for the new line, Buck announced that the politbureau was unanimously in favour of it.[13]

As soon as the new policy had been proclaimed the leaders of the LPP worked hard to put it into effect. Attacks on CCF spokesmen were toned down, and the number of candidates that the LPP put up in the provincial elections in Alberta, Ontario and Saskatchewan was appreciably lower in 1948 than in 1944-1945. Instead, the Communists campaigned for a number of CCF candidates.

The results achieved were poor. The CCF, eager to avoid any identification with the increasingly unpopular Communists, dissociated itself publicly from the LPP in the course of the provincial elections, and denounced Communism and Communists. Once again it put up its own candidates in the two Ontario ridings held by the Communists since 1943, and refused to sanction joint CCF-LPP candidates elsewhere. To the Communists this was another indication that the Ontario CCF in particular was playing the game of the Conservatives, and that the socialists were not really eager to bring about the defeat of Premier Drew.

It was left to R. M. Laxer, secretary of the Ontario LPP, to explain why the Communists in the first place supported the CCF.

> We have much in common with the CCF provincial program in Ontario and Saskatchewan. It is therefore much more difficult for a CCF government to introduce reactionary measures because of the pressure of the masses upon which it bases itself for support. . . . Even though Coldwell, Scott, Millard and Conroy are in the same war camp, they lead a party which is different from the old line parties because its following is made of workers and farmers who are progressive and

against war – the most progressive section of the people next to the followers of the LPP.[14]

The call for party members to support the CCF at the polls produced an unwelcome situation for the leaders of the LPP. Although Buck had insisted on the need to differentiate between the right-wing CCF leaders and the remainder of the CCF, LPP organizers at the grassroots level did not make such fine distinctions. Party headquarters blamed them for giving unqualified support to the CCF especially in Ontario. This was held against them when the line of the international Communist movement changed under the impact of growing American-Soviet antagonism.

The LPP followed suit by announcing in December 1948 that the adoption of the slogan "Elect a CCF Government" had been an error. Once the party leaders had spoken, their followers could express similar sentiments in print. Before long the *Canadian Tribune* was printing some criticism of the slogan. Several Communists argued that the slogan had complicated the struggle against the CCF, because LPP spokesmen had toned down their criticism of social democracy. Many party members were confused by the new line, while "our association with the CCF is considered by many people as a (typically opportunistic) bid for numerical support."[15] Some of the bolder spirits asked how the leadership could have adopted the slogan in the first place. Ryerson, the organizational secretary, explained to them that "the main reason for surrendering to the pressure of opportunism was ideological political weakness."[16]

After the party convention in February 1949, Buck succeeded in burying the subject, which by then he was finding very distasteful. His opponents, however, brought it up again, during the party crisis in 1956-1957 as part of the indictment against him.

Chapter 7

The Cold War

The worsening of relations between the U.S.S.R. and the United States affected the Communist movement in every Western country. The LPP, reeling under the blow of Guzenko's disclosures and the trial of members of the spy ring, was among the first Communist parties to experience the drawbacks of isolation and stagnation after the heady progress of the latter stages of the Second World War.

Although the LPP put on a brave front and tried to keep up its activities on the scale the Communists had maintained in 1943-1945, the LPP began to lose ground after 1946. The process was slow at first, but then gathered speed until by 1956 the LPP had almost disintegrated. However hard the Communists tried to hide the extent of their losses in the late 1940s and throughout the 1950s, they were unable to conceal them whenever Communists and non-Communists confronted one another and their respective support could be easily verified. By the end of the 1950s the LPP had lost so much of its former influence as to possess but a shadow of its former strength and self-confidence.

Many factors contributed to the erosion of Communist strength. To begin with, a high level of employment and a rising standard of living made it much more difficult for Communists to find issues that could be exploited as evidence that capitalism meant large-scale misery. LPP spokesmen, however, believed and insisted that the boom would soon end. When this prophesy proved false, the Communists did not re-examine their assumptions but kept on arguing along the same lines. This did not enhance their reputation as reliable forecasters. Fewer and fewer Canadians paid attention to doleful complaints couched in Marxist-Leninist jargon. Many people thought at the time that the Communists were utterly wrong but that they had some vested interest in harping on misery and business slumps.

The expansion of the Canadian economy and the rising standard of living affected party members also. According to the theoretical organ of the LPP:

> Many of our comrades' and friends' economic status changed. Many became small businessmen, landlords and a good many enjoyed high incomes. . . . A lot of comrades who have had a long and honourable record in its CPC-LPP activities, begin to find it more convenient to become less active, less outspoken and spend more time enjoying their new economic position.[1]

No less damaging to the Communist cause were the mass media which, regardless of whether they operated at a sophisticated or propagandist level, provided a picture of the Soviet Union, Soviet ambitions and occasionally of Communists in Canada, that was distinctly unfavourable to the LPP. Publicity of this sort was bound to affect anyone toying with the idea of voting for the LPP or joining the party, as well as many existing party members. This critique of Communism and Communists was all the more effective because it was based on fact, was frequently the work of people who were associated with the non-Communist left, and was confirmed by Canadian opinion-makers during their visits to Europe or through their contacts with American and British experts on Communism and Soviet foreign policy. As Buck's successor admitted in 1964: "The charge that Communism is alien to our way of life received wide endorsement, and this charge too was assisted by the tragic errors of the Stalin period."[2]

The LPP lacked the arguments and the financial resources to make an appreciable dent in Canadian public opinion. What the Communists said and wrote did not strengthen their case. Time and again they repeated crude Stalinist slogans and adopted what seemed to be an obtuse view of world events which few non-Communists would accept, and much of which the Communists in Europe and North America had substantially abandoned after Stalin's death. The Communists' glorification of Stalin during his lifetime, their zealous defence of every Soviet move and proposal, and their bitter attacks on anyone who did not toe the Soviet line, did not increase the appeal of the LPP and the U.S.S.R. in Canada. Sometimes, however, the Communists just could not fight back. Their inability to answer the questions raised in a leaflet distributed at every door in Wards Four and Five in the Toronto municipal election in 1950 contributed to the defeat of their candidates. Not that it was easy for them to say anything when asked:

> Telephone rates? Water rates? Gas rates? Living standards? Who are you trying to kid, comrade? Tell us about the death rates in the concentration camps of Siberia.[3]

The LPP carried on its activities within the narrow limits imposed by the general line of the international Communist movement. Not that the Canadian Communist leaders were always able to grasp the changes in the line, which had to be followed by perusing the pages of *For a Lasting Peace, For a People's Democracy*, organ of the Information Bureau of Communist and Workers' Parties, better known as the Cominform. Although the LPP was not a member of this organization, founded in August 1947, Buck and other Canadian Communists contributed articles to the Cominform publication, reprinted in the Canadian Communist press resolutions passed by the Cominform, and – publicly at least – shared the sentiments expressed by Soviet and Cominform leaders.

The policies advocated by the LPP during the Cold War were a mixture of the old and the new. The LPP continued to campaign for the sort of economic reforms, social legislation and concessions to farmers that had figured in Communist documents in the Popular Front days and in 1943-1945. Party orators and publications also stressed the need for secondary industries, and condemned the takeover of resource industries by American interests. They asked for legislation to curb the power of big corporations regardless of the nationality of their owners.

In the political sphere the Communists demanded a new constitution, a strengthening of the legal position of trade unions, a Bill of Rights, and an end to anti-Communist legislation. The Communist leaders feared another wave of persecution. They knew that in this period of growing international tension there were organizations and politicians who were eager to deprive the LPP of its legal status. They suspected the American government of encouraging anti-Communist measures as part of a worldwide capitalist drive against the Soviet Union. The harassment of the CPUSA appeared as a portent of things to come in Canada, and induced the LPP to establish a rudimentary underground network in case it was banned by the Canadian authorities.

The Communists accepted the Soviet view that the rulers of the U.S. had replaced Hitler as the most dangerous enemy of the Soviet Union, its allies and supporters. This enemy of theirs was powerful, ruthless and highly skilful. It would use any means from propaganda to terror, to disrupt Communist opposition parties and to subvert governments which were building socialism under the leadership of the U.S.S.R. In the under-developed and industrial societies the Americans were bound to side with those who wanted to preserve the status quo and would allow American business to increase its profits.

Canada, the Communists maintained, was particularly vulnerable to economic and other penetration. Geographical proximity, military ties, American investment in Canada, the impact of American mass culture, the high level of trade between the two countries and the servile attitude towards the U.S. of Canadian political parties, including Social Credit and the CCF, made the task of defending Canadian independence exceedingly difficult.

Given this interpretation of world affairs and of the dynamics of American-Canadian relations, the Canadian Communists had to relegate to the background some of their previously advertised views. References to "Canadian Imperialism" seldom appeared after 1946, when Buck had declared "Canada is an imperialist state. The Canadian bourgeoisie is an imperialist bourgeoisie."[4]

From 1948 on the Communists insisted with increasing shrillness that the U.S. had taken over Canada. The Liberals in Ottawa were held primarily responsible for the American takeover; their chief accomplices were the right-wing leaders of the CCF. Coldwell, Lewis and others had used the prestige enjoyed by the CCF in many quarters to mislead the workers in several ways. By drawing attention to "Communist totalitarianism" the CCF leaders had slandered the U.S.S.R. Their criticism of Soviet policies in Eastern Europe, the United Nations, among others, had provided ammunition for anti-Communists bent on unleashing a Third World War. To compound their crimes, CCF spokesmen in Parliament approved of such American economic and military initiatives in Europe as the Marshall Plan and the North Atlantic Treaty Organization (NATO), and supported the United Nations forces in Korea.

The struggle for peace, the Communists insisted, had to be given the highest priority. The U.S.S.R. needed and wanted peace, while American leaders were prepared to risk a nuclear showdown with either the Soviet Union or China or both. To a large extent peace would depend on the readiness of men and women all over the world to express convincingly their hatred of war and to force governments to act peacefully. The pressure had to be applied in the West, because the Soviet government had already indicated its support for peace. In any case, it was capitalism that bred war. Socialist societies were intrinsically incapable of planning, let alone of starting a war.

The formation of a pro-Communist peace movement in Canada followed in the wake of a World Peace Congress in Paris (April 1949), at which an executive was elected. The following month, in Toronto, Dr. James G. Endicott, the Canadian member of that body, addressed the All-Canada Congress in Defence of Peace.[5] He helped establish the Canadian Peace Congress and was active in the campaign to rouse Canadian public opinion against the threat of war. It was hoped that the force of public opinion would make the federal government cut the defence budget and renounce its NATO commitments.

In 1949 and the early 1950s the Communists, and their supporters on the subject of peace, collected signatures for two petitions. The first one, known as the Stockholm Peace Petition or Ban the Bomb Petition, called (among other things), for the "unconditional prohibition of the atomic weapon as a weapon of intimidation and mass extermination of people." A second petition followed in 1951. It called for a Five-Power Conference to settle international disputes and to bring the conflict in Korea to an end. The Canadian Communists saw nothing incongruous about praising the successes of the North Korean Army and Chinese volunteers against the United Nations forces, which included Canadian troops, while insisting in the same breath on the need for peace.

The president of the Canadian Peace Council, Dr. James G. Endicott, belonged to that group of missionaries and their children who, after returning from the Far East, associated themselves with causes dear to the LPP. As he said in 1960, "I believe that our movement fulfils the righteous purposes of God in history and that God uses Communists for the establishment of peace whether they know it or not."[6]

This was not the first controversial statement he had made in Canada or abroad. A tireless speaker who often braved hostile audiences on his extensive lecture tours, Endicott was very critical of American policies and designs. The U.S.S.R. and Mao's China he treated with much sympathy, although occasionally he would deplore some of their moves. This did not prevent him from winning an International Stalin Peace Prize in 1952. The prize included the award of 100,000 rubles, a sum that the *Canadian Tribune* explained was the equivalent of $25,000.[7] Soviet recognition of his efforts at the height of the Cold War did not enhance his popularity in Canada. The idea of a clergyman siding with the Soviet Union was anathema to many people. Others were annoyed when the Soviet press published his complaint about restrictions on civil liberties in Canada.

Lester Pearson reflected widespread sentiment when he argued that "a man who, professing honest motives and high ideals, goes among strangers and maligns his country with this kind of falsehood is beneath contempt. In a Communist society he would be beneath the ground."[8]

The LPP was the main driving force behind the Canadian Peace Congress and the Peace Councils established in a number of cities. Its national committee "directed", in February 1950, "the entire energy and activity of the Party into the fight for peace." As in every other Communist campaign, a great deal depended on the degree of rank-and-file involvement. The contribution of party members across the Dominion varied enormously. The best performers were six young Communists, each of whom collected a thousand signatures for the Ban the Bomb Petition. At the other end of the scale were the Communists and their sympathizers with "less than 7,000" signatures in Winnipeg, a figure that compared unfavourably with 3,500 in Glace Bay and 5,000 in Regina. Toronto provided the most signatories with 57,000 names, while Vancouver came second with 24,000.[9]

The Communists were, of course, particularly anxious to enlist the support of people influential in public life. Here and there they succeeded. Among the 448,000 signatures the Canadian Peace Congress claims to have collected on the two petitions, one comes across the names of over sixty Protestant ministers, as well as trade union leaders who were known for their pro-Communist sympathies. In Quebec the mayors and councillors of more than seventy municipalities endorsed the Stockholm Appeal. They were, no doubt, influenced by the Communist argument that the federal government was about to reintroduce conscription.

The CCF remained largely unmoved by the peace campaign, in spite of a certain amount of soul-searching and determined Communist efforts to use peace as a bridge to other forms of co-operation with the democratic socialists. The Communists obtained the signatures of several socialists who had been more prominent in the CCF in the 1930s than in the 1940s. The signatories included L. St. George Stubbs and four former CCF MLAS. They were joined by two obscure CCF members of the Ontario and Saskatchewan legislatures.

More disturbing to the leaders of the CCF was the reaction of their inchoate left-wing, which, as in the 1930s, found it difficult to resist some Communist proposals. A few CCF clubs, mainly on the west coast, supported the Stockholm Petition, which M. J. Cold-well, the National Leader of the CCF, described as a "cruel deception".[10] Three CCF members of the B.C. Legislature could not resist adding their signatures. When reminded that the national convention of the CCF had unanimously condemned the Stockholm Petition in 1950, the executive of the provincial CCF organization in B.C. argued that the three MLAs had "simply forgotten about the convention resolution."[11] Some spokesmen of the old line parties had better memories. These Liberals and Tories used socialist signatures on the Peace Petition as additional evidence in support of their oft-proclaimed contention that Communists, crypto-Communists and Communist sympathizers had infiltrated the CCF, and that the CCF was therefore unworthy of popular support at the time when Canada was making great sacrifices in the defence of western Europe and Korea against the Communists.

All in all, the peace campaign was not a great success, although a case can be made out that the emphasis on the struggle for peace enabled the LPP to influence the attitude of people who otherwise would have remained impervious to other Communist initiatives. In 1956-1957, however, anti-Buck Communists thought differently. They maintained that by concentrating on peace and electioneering the LPP distracted Communists from the "class struggle". Instead of organizing and leading the workers, the LPP courted pacifists and a segment of the middle class critical of American and Canadian foreign policies.

Buck and his closest associates were disappointed with the peace campaign. It was left to Leslie Morris to explain to his fellow Communists the reasons for their lack of success: the "main weakness" of the peace campaign was the "failure to win over" the "organized labour movement" for "the fight for peace." He placed the blame for this state of affairs "in the first place on the most conscious peace fighters, the Communists and left wingers, who still tend to look at peace as a 'private monopoly'."[12] Few critics of the LPP could have said more.

After 1947 the decline of the LPP was particularly noticeable among organized labour. The positions held by party members and sympathizers in the AFL-TLC and CIO-CCL unions at the beginning of the Cold War gave the LPP several strong levers in the world of labour. Communists on the executive of union or city labour councils could raise issues of importance to the LPP, introduce or defeat motions, and influence the selection of delegates to the annual conventions of the CCL and TLC, and of union representatives on government boards. Party members and sympathizers edited union papers, acted as union lawyers, and had a great deal of say in the recruitment of organizers in the field and of staff at union headquarters. Access to union funds enabled them to channel fairly large sums of money to causes sponsored or supported by the LPP at home and abroad. All in all, the positions acquired by the Communists in the unions strengthened the LPP enormously, while at the same time depriving the anti-Communists of positions from which to mount an effective counter-attack in the unions.

Although the Communists held a number of key union posts, they had to contend with a rank-and-file which, even after years of Communist domination in some instances and of infiltration in many others, was not immune to the appeal of other forces in the trade union movement. These forces included certain officials and activists associated with the CCF, and others who were pro-Liberal. In alliance with American trade union leaders in Washington, Detroit, New York, Philadelphia, Portland, and other cities, they presented a formidable alternative when the political climate in North America and Europe altered.

The start of the Cold War, and the association of Communist union officials in Canada with unpopular Soviet moves, placed party members at a disadvantage when the anti-Communists made a concerted effort to dislodge those members of the LPP and their friends who had played a prominent role in the unions. In a series of skirmishes and battles, culminating on the floor of the annual conventions of the TLC and CCL, the Communists were outmanoeuvred and outvoted. Their claim that the campaign against the Communists was part of a capitalist plot against the working class commanded less and less support. Anti-Communists could always point out an accusing finger at the Communists' collaboration with the authorities and the employers in the later stages of the Second World War, and sometimes even after the war.[13] Communist attacks on anti-Communist trade union leaders made party members vulnerable to the charge of slandering fellow unionists. Their praise of the way that "progressives" ran unions like the UE in Canada drew the retort that the UE was "wearing a halo of virtue round its head while all other unions are black with sin."[14] Their association with the U.S.S.R. met with widespread disapproval, and could be used as evidence that their prime loyalty was not to the Canadian working class but to a superpower. The failure to create a broad base of support among manual workers deprived them of enough grassroots support to withstand the onslaught of their opponents.

The struggle began in earnest at the annual convention of the TLC in October 1947.[15] A number of locals across the country introduced a motion that described the LPP as "totalitarian in its methods," insisted that "many trade unionists have suffered through the actions of individual Communists who placed party loyalty ahead of the welfare of the trade union movement," and demanded that "members of the Communist Party be barred from holding office in the Congress."

The attempt to exclude Communists from trade union office led to a prolonged debate. The opponents of the resolution, who included several Communists, argued that a trade unionist's political beliefs were his own business, so long as his activities did not harm the trade union movement. Supporters of the resolution drew attention to the role the Communists were playing in eastern Europe, and warned that the Communists, unless checked, would take over the TLC in ten years' time. The president of the TLC, Percy R. Bengough, threw the weight of his office behind the opponents of the resolution. The following day a different and more innocuous resolution was debated and passed. It made no reference to the role of the Communists and merely condemned "the actions of any party or individuals which seek to use this Congress or its affiliated Organizations for their own particular advantage."

The following year the same issue was raised again. By then the Communists were in a much weaker position. The Communist takeover in Prague in February 1948 and the Berlin Blockade provided additional arguments for the anti-Communists, who were already fighting the Communists and their allies in trade unions throughout North America. Although the president of the TLC continued to display a marked distaste for strong action against the Communists, the convention passed a resolution critical of Communism and Communists.[16]

The TLC debate over Communist objectives at home and abroad was intertwined with a highly explosive issue: the future of the Canadian Seamen's Union (CSU), an affiliate of the TLC. Its Communist leaders could take legitimate pride in having improved working conditions on ships. They – and the LPP – also knew that they held a stranglehold over important segments of the Canadian economy, they could tie up shipping on the Great Lakes and the Atlantic. In March 1947, J. A. (Pat) Sullivan, one of the founders of the CSU, broke with the LPP and began a rival union: the Canadian Lake Seamen's Union. Before long he joined forces with the Seafarers' International Union (SIU), an affiliate of the AFL. Sullivan's turnabout aroused the wrath of the Communists, who fought their rivals in what became one of the most bitter inter-jurisdictional disputes in Canadian labour history. The opponents of the CSU had the backing of employers and of anti-Communist leaders of the Canadian districts of several international unions affiliated with the AFL/TLC. Their spokesman was Frank Hall, vice-president of the Brotherhood of Railway and Steamship Clerks.

Raiding for members in the name of "anti-Communism" led to the charge of dual unionism and the temporary suspension of both Hall and his union from the TLC. The annual convention of the TLC in October 1948 endorsed the stand of the executive council, by 545 to 198 votes, with 181 abstentions. It also declared that the CSU alone could represent sailors in the TLC.[17]

The attempt to muzzle prominent anti-Communists and defend a controversial union was challenged by the AFL. Its bosses were already engaged in a campaign to rid unions in the United States of Communist officials. In February 1949 the executive council of the AFL reached the conclusion that the "Communists exercise influence" in the TLC "far in excess of their proportional strength."[18] Few observers of the labour scene would have questioned the accuracy of this statement; many, however, were disturbed when the AFL called on the TLC to take "vigorous action to eliminate completely every vestige of Communist influence and control in the affairs" of the TLC.

The immediate reaction to the AFL call was highly unfavourable. Bengough complained that the AFL had acted without giving the TLC executive an adequate hearing. He also declared that the TLC was not prepared "to substitute the methods of dictatorship" or "advocate the curtailment of freedom of others."[19]

Increasing tension between the Soviet Union and the United States contributed to growing friction between Communists and non-Communists in every western society. It also brought about a change in the attitude of the TLC leaders towards Communists in general and the CSU in particular. The CSU engaged in a long strike on the east coast in the spring of 1949, while pro-Communist labour organizations halted Canadian shipping in other parts of the world as part of a concerted drive to prevent the economic recovery of western Europe under the American-sponsored Marshall Plan. According to the evidence provided by a top leader of the CSU after he had broken with the LPP, the strike was called "at the secret request of the British Communist Party to create an artificial strike issue for the dock workers in London."[20]

The executive council of the TLC could not afford to ignore the strike, because its ramifications were felt by members of the

AFL-TLC unions in a number of industries. Before the strike actually began the TLC had urged the CSU to accept the award of the Board of Conciliation. After the strike had begun, the TLC tried to secure a compromise settlement. Bengough also suggested that some of the members of the CSU executive should resign. He actually induced the CSU to call off the strike on May 31. The following day, however, the CSU leaders reversed their earlier decision, and decided to continue what increasingly resembled a "political strike". The CSU's failure to follow Bengough's advice led to its suspension from the TLC on June 3, 1949.[21] The decision to act against the CSU was prompted by a statement by representatives of fourteen international unions. They announced that they were no longer prepared to sit with the CSU delegates in the TLC.[22]

The TLC's convention in September 1949 expelled the CSU by 702 votes to 77, with about 200 abstentions. Delegates from B.C. provided more than half of the votes in favour of the CSU. Resolutions critical of several aspects of Canadian foreign policy were also rejected by large majorities. Among the defeats that the Communists and their friends suffered at this convention, one of the most stinging was passage of a motion that called on all affiliated organizations to remove Communists from their posts. The convention also insisted that "nominees, allowing their names to go forward for the offices of President, Vice-Presidents and Secretary Treasurer . . . shall clearly and audibly speak the following words to the assembled delegates:

> . . . I am not associated in any manner whatsoever with any group which expounds or promotes or encourages any doctrine or philosophy inimical to or subversive of the fundamental principles and institutions of the Government of the Dominion of Canada, and, further I make oath and say that I will be faithful and bear true allegiance to His Majesty, King George the Sixth, his heirs and successors, according to the law, so help me God.[23]

The call for an oath received overwhelming support, though there were sceptics who warned that the "Communists would take any sort of oath, and it means nothing." Their scepticism was understandable. In 1931 a leading member of the politbureau of the CPC had advised: "It is quite permissible for our comrades to lie like hell on the question of membership in the C.P. and to govern their activities accordingly."[24]

Additional anti-Communist measures were taken at the TLC convention held after the outbreak of the Korean War in 1950.

The credentials of a number of Communist and pro-Communist delegates were successfully challenged. Also, the TLC unions were told that they would face suspension unless they got rid of union officials who belonged to the LPP. Finally, the constitution of the TLC was amended to enable the TLC executive to bar Communists from attending the annual convention as delegates.[25]

Resolutions proposed by the Communists and their friends were easily defeated. The proposal to repeal the anti-Communist measures passed at previous TLC conventions met a similar fate, though the debate indicated soul-searching in some quarters. Several delegates did not like the prospect of the executive deciding who could and who could not represent a union local or labour district. The view that a union official's opinions need bar him from holding a union post was again raised. The anti-Communist answer was simple: a Communist's first loyalty is to his party, an organization that follows the orders of "Russian imperialism".

Similar developments took place in the CCL, where even before the Cold War the lines between Communists and anti-Communists were more clearly drawn than in the TLC. Mosher and Millard had tried hard to reduce Communist influence in the CCL during the Second World War, when conditions for an anti-Communist drive had been far less favourable than later on. Being staunch socialists they were critical of Soviet Communism. In addition, they held the LPP responsible for the unwillingness of many CCL locals to support the CCF as the political arm of organized labour.

Their attempts to align CCL locals with the CCF in the early postwar years met with considerable opposition. Although members of the LPP formed a tiny minority of the rank-and-file of the CCL, they were well-entrenched in at least half a dozen CCL unions and on many issues could rally a substantial number of delegates at the annual conventions, where the issue of Communism and Communists invariably cropped up in one form or another. Acrimonious debates ensued before votes were counted and the ratio of forces was established.

At the annual convention in October 1947 the debate on a motion condemning "rampant and militant Russian communist imperialism" and "monopoly capitalist imperialism" and advocating in their place a third, democratic socialist way of life, showed that the Communists would oppose any attempt to bracket the U.S.S.R. and the U.S., just as on other occasions they took exception to those who bracketed Communists and fascists as men unworthy of holding trade union posts. The outcome of the debate revealed that the Communists and their supporters in the CCL formed a distinct minority. The motion was carried by 546 votes to 165.[26]

A year later the delegates to the CCL convention debated motions on international affairs and the role of Communists in the unions. Mosher used the occasion to warn his opponents that "unless you change your tactics and change them soon you will be thrown out." Pat Conroy, the secretary-treasurer of the CCL, challenged the audience with the question: "Are the delegates here Canadians or Russians, I should like to know?"[27] The vote showed that the majority of delegates had reacted in the way Conroy wanted.

Mosher's threat was delivered in the course of a debate in which the Communists tried once again to prevent too close an identification of the CCL with the CCF. One of their spokesmen claimed that to "endorse the CCF only" as the political arm of the CCL "was a narrow approach, and that a wider appeal to the electorate could be made by endorsing independent labour candidates in certain constituencies." This proposal received little support, partly because the delegates were reminded that "independent" labour candidates in certain instances turned out to be "stooges of the LPP."[28]

In 1949 the delegates to the CCL convention discussed the unflattering references to the leaders of the CCL in an editorial published in the organ of the International Union of Mine, Mill and Smelter Workers. C. S. Jackson, president of the UE and spokesman of the pro-Communist forces at several CCL conventions, tried to explain the editorial by arguing that "the language of the working people is replete with forceful expressions arising out of the need for constant struggle and fight on the part of the workers."[29] Ironically, he was defending the kind of language the Communists always complained about when their opponents attacked them in union debates and publications. Then the anti-Communists were accused of using "vicious" and "hysterical" language.

A fair amount of canvassing, organizing and manoeuvring preceded the debates and the voting at the annual conventions. Maximum support for either faction at the conventions depended on the ratio of forces in various unions, city labour councils, labour federations, among others. In most instances delegates sent to the convention reflected the result of local debates on such issues as the East-West conflict, Canada's place in the world, the role of Communists in the trade unions, and the attitude towards the TLC, employers' organizations, and federal and provincial labour legislation.

The wirepulling that went on before and during the annual conventions has been graphically described by Irving M. Abella. His *Nationalism, Communism and Canadian Labour* deals mainly with the activities of anti-Communist union officials whose archives he had the opportunity of inspecting. The LPP, on the other hand, did not open its records. As a result of Communist secrecy, any account of what the LPP was doing in the unions has to depend on scattered data provided by the party press, enterprising non-Communist journalists and disillusioned union leaders who broke with the LPP at this time.

In theory, and sometimes in practice, the delegates to the union and CCL conventions represented the views of the rank-and-file. The average trade unionist, however, was fairly apathetic and was seldom prepared to take prolonged interest in union affairs. Union meetings were ill-attended; the longer they lasted, the smaller the audience of non-Communists. The Communists, on the other hand, displayed greater staying power. Often their opponents accused party members of waiting until the hall was half-empty before introducing an important motion or calling for a key vote.

The unionist who regularly attended the meetings of his local was aware that two small minorities were competing for his vote. One was a scattering of party members and their sympathizers, some of whom were CCFers. The other was the majority of CCFers who were active in the unions. They were often backed by Catholic Action groups, the formation of which the Catholic hierarchy encouraged on both sides of the Atlantic for the specific purpose of dislodging the Communists from the unions.

The struggle was particularly bitter on the west coast, where the Communists were well entrenched as late as 1948.[30] They controlled the B.C. Federation of Labour and the Vancouver Labour Council through such powerful unions as the IWA and the International Union of Mine, Mill and Smelter Workers (IUMMSW).

Their grip was decisively broken only when Mosher sent William Mahoney of the United Steelworkers of America to reduce the role of Communists in B.C. unions. Mahoney succeeded in rallying sufficient support to inflict serious defeats on the Communists. His task was considerably eased by two mistakes the Communists made when they were seriously challenged. Harvey Murphy added to his reputation as a controversial figure in the Canadian labour movement by making intemperate remarks about fellow CCL leaders at a banquet given by the B.C. Federation of

Labour at the Empress Hotel, Victoria, in April 1948. He thereby provided the anti-Communists with another argument against the IUMMSW, which was suspended from the CCL in August 1948.

Soon afterwards, growing pressure on the Canadian Communist leaders in the IWA induced them to take drastic action. They made secret arrangements to break away from the IWA and form a new Canadian union of lumberworkers. The move was carefully planned. Furniture in the offices of the IWA was removed, and union funds salted away, before the rank-and-file and the public were informed of what the Communists were actually planning.

The Woodworkers' Industrial Union of Canada failed almost from the beginning. The Communists lost more ground among woodworkers than they would have done if they had decided to fight it out in the IWA. It did not take them long to realize that the breakaway had played into the hands of their enemies. Once the mistake had been acknowledged in 1950, the party leaders did their utmost to induce the militants to return to the IWA. The threat of court action secured the return of the IWA funds the Communists had diverted prior to launching the new union.

The story of the struggle between the Communists and anti-Communists during the Cold War would be incomplete without a reference to the unaligned unionists who were courted by both sides in the CCL. Among them were people who had been unwilling to throw in their lot with Millard at the beginning of the Cold War. Several were prominent trade unionists who had collaborated very closely with party members in industry and mining, who disapproved of Millard's policies in several areas[31], and who carried considerable weight in union circles. This was particularly true of Pat Conroy, secretary-treasurer of the CCL, and of George Burt, director of the Canadian district of the UAW.[32] For a time they held the balance of power in the struggle between Communists and anti-Communists. The uneasy equilibrium depended on their unwillingness to support either side to the hilt. This position proved untenable in a period of heightened international tension. By 1948 Burt discovered that the alternative to joining the anti-Communists was going down to defeat with the pro-Communist slate in the UAW. Faced with such a stark choice he went over to the anti-Communists. Even before Burt's decision, Conroy had adopted a strong anti-Communist attitude. At the height of the Cold War he denounced Soviet ambitions and the work of Communists in the unions in more vivid language than most of their opponents in the CCL used during the Cold War.

The debates in which Conroy figured prominently preceded elections to key posts in the CCL hierarchy. Every time a union leader closely associated with the LPP stood as a candidate for the presidency of the CCL, he received a lower percentage of votes than Nigel Morgan had gained in 1941.

Election	Number of votes	
1946	450 Mosher	198 C. S. Jackson
1947	500 Mosher	192 C. S. Jackson
1948	564 Mosher	154 C. S. Jackson
1949	503 Mosher	147 R. Haddow
1950	468 Mosher	72 R. Haddow
1951	507 Mosher	65 W. Stewart

The decline in Communist strength in these elections was due to two main factors. To begin with, the growing unpopularity of the U.S.S.R. and the LPP swayed a number of delegates who had previously voted for Communist or pro-Communist candidates at CCL conventions. Second, the suspension and expulsion of Communist-controlled unions from the CCL appreciably reduced the pool of delegates who could be relied upon to oppose Mosher because they were party members or supported the party in the unions.

By 1951 the Communists had lost a whole series of trade union positions across Canada, including many in the IWA and the UAW. A number of union officials who were members of the LPP were dismissed, or not re-elected when they offered their services at election time. Others abandoned their former loyalties and turned against the LPP, because they were disillusioned with Communism and the Communist party, as was the case with Pat Sullivan, secretary-treasurer of the TLC. When Sullivan was interned as a Communist in 1940, Buck praised him as "one of the most popular and effective union leaders in Canada." After Sullivan had issued a statement denouncing the leaders of a movement he had served to the best of his ability, the LPP dismissed him as a "contemptible traitor".[33] A number of Communists saved their union positions by making less dramatic statements than Sullivan's. Several found it advisable to lie low in the hope that their past would not be held against them. They waited for another day to display their true sentiments.

The federal government, on the other hand, made its attitude perfectly clear at the beginning of the Cold War. The authorities which had been favourable to this or that Communist initiative in the later stages of the Second World War, now took a jaundiced view of what the Communists were saying and doing in the unions.

Liberal spokesmen inside and outside Parliament welcomed the defeat of party members in union elections, and the end of Communist influence on the executives of the CCL and TLC. In an effort to reduce the role the Communists played in industry, mining and transportation, several union officials who held American passports were deported or prevented from re-entering Canada.[34]

The struggle against the Communists was not always fought along democratic lines. The Communist-run CSU, with over 7,000 members in 1948, was only destroyed after the federal government allowed Hal Banks to settle in Canada in 1949. By using methods not indicative of Canadian trade unionism at its best, the CSU was smashed. Sailors who were known Communists, or certainly staunch supporters of the CSU, were effectively prevented from obtaining employment on ships whose owners had signed a contract with the SIU, a rival of the CSU. The violence that erupted during the strikes organized by the CSU, or as a result of jurisdictional disputes between the CSU and the SIU, cost sixty CSU members a total of sixty-seven years in jail sentences. By 1950, the CSU had become a hollow shell and a symbol of the vicious struggle between Communists and anti-Communists. The secretary-treasurer of the CSU, T. G. McManus, carried on at his post until he switched from the LPP to Moral Re-Armament.

Several trade unions, however, refused or were unable to get rid of officials who were known to be Communists. Failure to act in response to directives from the CCL or TLC led to the suspension and expulsion of a number of unions. The CCL got rid of the IUMMSW, the UE, and the International Fur and Leather Workers Union. The TLC expelled a few unions on the west coast. Of these the most important was the United Fishermen and Allied Workers Union with over 7,000 members in 1954. In several instances, technicalities were used as a pretext to formalize the expulsion of these unions (for example, the UE was in arrears of the per capita tax to the CCL). Nevertheless, few had any illusions about what the real issue was.

The Communists fought attempts to drive them out of the unions in several ways. Communist publications bitterly attacked their opponents in print, accusing them of playing the capitalists' game and destroying the unity of the working class. They argued that the anti-Communist campaign was part and parcel of preparations to involve Canada in a war against the U.S.S.R. or China. Instead, they urged the workers to support the left-wing in the unions, or "progressives" as the Communists preferred to call their supporters.

The party leaders also called for the recruitment of many more workers into the LPP. In spite of repeated directives and the subsidizing of factory news bulletins, of which there were 29 in 1951[35], little progress was made, especially in factories and mines where a large number of workers was employed. In spite of exhortations from party headquarters the recruiting campaign petered out even before Stalin's death; although the LPP remained basically a party of workers and ex-workers—albeit of workers getting on in years. In 1951 workers represented 61 per cent, and trade unionists 37 per cent, of the party membership.[36]

At the height of the Cold War, in another effort to retain union influence, the LPP re-emphasized the importance of shop clubs as opposed to those based on geographical location. In 1948, 15 per cent of the LPP clubs belonged to the former category.[37]

Attempts to bring the LPP closer to the workers and thereby facilitate the work of party members in industry met with little success. No amount of prodding from above could convince party members in industry to proclaim their allegiance. The unpopularity of the U.S.S.R. and the LPP, and the fear of victimization, made many party members think twice before passing on the latest party directive or selling party newspapers to fellow workers. As party members grew inactive, or gave up their membership cards, shop clubs disintegrated or were forced to amalgamate into industrial clubs, which comprised party members employed in the same industry. Often distance prevented effective consultation, planning and co-ordination among party members who were thinly spread over a relatively wide area.

Aware of the dangers of isolation, and eager to return to the mainstream of the Canadian labour movement, the Communist-led unions periodically tried to rejoin the organizations which had expelled them. The campaign for readmission was fought, among other places, at annual conventions of the CCL and TLC. There the matter was raised by three groups of delegates: a handful of camouflaged party members; people who had been close to the LPP before the Cold War and who continued to follow the Communist line on some issues; and militants who prefaced their call for readmission with assurances that they were opposed to Communism. They argued that unionists should be free to speak their minds, and that it would be easier to deal with Communists when you "meet them face to face." All these groups were stronger in B.C. than elsewhere, although some of them represented UAW locals in Ontario.

There was little support for readmission because past Communist tactics and encroachments in the unions were not easily forgotten. To make sure that the Communists would never again present a major challenge in the trade union world, the anti-Communists imposed stiff conditions for readmission to the TLC and CCL. These were interpreted by the LPP and the Communist union officials as an invitation to capitulate. Understandably, they preferred to soldier on alone, in the hope that the unions they controlled would somehow survive as separate entities.

If frontal attacks failed to dislodge the Communists in the unions they controlled, their opponents used other methods to reduce these remaining concentrations of Communist strength in the unions. Anti-Communist unions would raid the membership of pro-Communist unions in the hope that a sufficient number of members would change sides and enable the raiding union to represent them in their dealings with employers and departments of labour. The struggle over union certification involved both political and jurisdictional questions. It consisted of a series of skirmishes as the two sides fought over this or that plant or mine.

The pro-Communists succeeded several times in beating off the raids sponsored by the United Steelworkers of America. Their ability to withstand the onslaught has been attributed to three factors. In the first place, they possessed sufficient organizational know-how and popularity among the minority of workers which took a close interest in union affairs. These unionists, who included some CCFers, remembered the record of Communist union officials in the struggle for better working conditions, and were unwilling to see their union merged into some large conglomerate like the United Steelworkers.

Second, the international unions which had not expelled their Communist leadership in the United States were able to assist their Canadian locals in the battle for survival. (The Communists faced a much more difficult task when they were under pressure from both the union headquarters south of the border and fellow-unionists in the Dominion). Before the Canadian authorities became alerted to the danger, American organizers of the IUMMSW were assigned to duty in Canada, where they helped to consolidate the Communist grip over that union. Earlier on, the CSU also profited from the assignment of American Communist cadres, although it was a Canadian union.

Finally, the business world did not display much eagerness in furthering the cause of anti-Communist unionists, except in the case of the CSU. Mosher was on strong ground when he complained that "certain employers are . . . willing to make agreements with Communist-dominated unions, simply because they can make a better bargain with a union which is on the defensive and trying at all costs to maintain its existence."[38]

It is difficult to say how far the struggle over workers in Communist-led unions affected the numerical strength of these unions. The available evidence indicates that the UE lost 12 per cent of its membership between 1949 and 1959, although the number of electrical workers in Canada expanded fairly rapidly in that period. On the other hand, the UE remained stronger than the rival International Union of Electrical Workers backed by the anti-Communists. The IUMMSW actually increased its membership by a third during the 1950s.

Losses in the trade union field sapped the strength and morale of the LPP. Equally painful were defeats in another area, from which the Communists had drawn much of their support ever since the foundation of the CPC. The attraction of Communism for some of the ethnic groups from eastern Europe declined appreciably compared to its strength during the war and during the early postwar years, when the Communist-inspired Canadian Slav Committee rallied many Canadians of East European origin who were glad to record their admiration for the Soviet struggle against Hitler and to preserve Slavic culture in Canada. At that time several prominent Ukrainian Canadian critics of the U.S.S.R. had abandoned their anti-Soviet stance.

The erosion of Communist strength in East European circles after 1945 was slow at first, but gained momentum as relations between the Soviet Union and the West deteriorated. The decline of pro-Communist sympathies was the result of several interconnected factors. One was the fact that the Communist mass organizations never monopolized the political and social life of any East European community, though they came fairly close to doing so in the case of the Finnish one in the 1920s. Even during the Popular Front days and the Second World War, some ethnic newspapers attacked Soviet policies and denounced the machinations of the CPC. This was particularly true of the Ukrainians in the Prairies, where a group of determined anti-Communists, several of whom had been prominent in the CPC (for example, D. Lobay and T. Kobzey), fought a bitter struggle against the ULFTA and its successor, the Association of United Ukrainian Canadians (AUUC). The existence of anti-Communist Ukrainians, who were and remain more critical of the U.S.S.R. than any Anglo-Saxon organization in Canada, must be borne in mind if one is to preserve a sense of proportion about Ukrainian support for the Communist movement.

Anti-Communist forces among Ukrainians and other ethnic

groups received strong reinforcements when over half a million refugees born in eastern Europe emigrated to Canada after 1945. Their sheer number, their experience of life under Nazi and Communist rule, and the level of education of some of these new Canadians, affected the balance of power in every ethnic community. By reinforcing existing non-Communist and anti-Communist organizations or creating new ones, by engaging in a variety of publishing and social activities, by holding mass meetings and demonstrations, and by pressuring Canadian politicians interested in their votes, they created alternative centres of power in Montreal, Toronto and the Prairies. At the same time they linked forces with others who had previously emigrated to Canada from eastern Europe and they attracted the support of some people who had gravitated towards Communist-led ethnic organizations. Not that the majority of new Canadians of East European extraction became, let alone remained, active in these anti-Communist associations. Most were only too eager to assimilate into Canadian society, retaining, however, their basic anti-Communist stance, which they did not hide from people they met. Their influence, in fact, must not be underestimated in any examination of the growing isolation of Canadian Communists.

The LPP also could do little against thousands of manual workers who had few illusions about life under a Communist regime. Nor did it strengthen its case by branding anti-Communist immigrants as "fascists". This description fitted only a minority of these East Europeans. The Communist press, for instance, did not increase its credibility by applying the term "fascist" to soldiers of the Polish Army who had fought hard against the Germans in Italy and preferred life in Canada to that in Poland.[39] Nor did the Communists gain much sympathy from their occasional brawls with anti-Communist Ukrainians.

The LPP could do no more. Natural causes had thinned the ranks of its ethnic organizations. So had the return of several thousand Communists and pro-Communists, mainly Croats, to eastern Europe after the end of the war. There was little infusion of new blood into the higher echelons of the Communist ethnic organizations, which, like the LPP, were run by small coteries of men who had been at the peak of their powers in between the two world wars. Not that leadership material among young Communists of East European descent was lacking. Few, however, were available, because most of these Communists had been absorbed into the English-speaking segments of the Communist movement, in line with a Comintern directive in 1928:

> The young generation which knows English should by no means be kept within the limits of Ukrainian work. The Ukrainian Communists who do not know English should be urged to learn the language as a means of taking part in the general life of the Party.[40]

The leaders of Communist ethnic organizations had to control a rank-and-file which, especially in the case of Jews, was getting increasingly prosperous. A number of party members of East European origin could now afford to leave those parts of Montreal, Toronto and Winnipeg where they had lived in the previous decades. A higher income enabled them to move out from those parts of the city where party influence was strongest, and settle in middle-class areas where other political and social values prevailed. Not that a change of residence and a higher standard of income always meant severing their association with a movement to which they had devoted many years. To this day the party relies more than is sometimes realized on people who have moved up the social ladder since 1945.

The dispersal of Communists and their sympathizers also put an end to those concentrations of ethnic voters who in the 1930s and 1940s had elected party members to school boards, municipal councils, provincial legislatures and, in one instance, to the federal parliament. Their change of neighbourhood increased the handicaps under which the LPP laboured in its efforts to use the forum provided by representative government, to demonstrate its leaders' fitness to hold public office, and to prove that the LPP was a force in Canadian politics. Only in that way could Canadians be convinced that a vote for a Communist candidate was not a wasted vote, a view that the Communists had to combat in every election campaign. The loss of aldermanic seats in Toronto and other cities in the late 1940s was a major blow to the prestige of the LPP and its ethnic organizations. Nothing could erase the impact of these defeats, though the party press did its best by drawing attention to an electoral victory at Clayton, Saskatchewan.

Without a fresh supply of recruits the elderly Communists had to redouble their efforts to preserve the ethnic organizations under their control and ensure the publication of newspapers in half a dozen languages. That they succeeded is no mean achievement, though the success is not entirely due to the energy, organizational skill and spirit of self-sacrifice of those who toiled on Canadian soil. In the struggle for survival in the East European communities, the Communists received little encouragement or praise from the party headquarters. John Weir, a leading Ukrainian Canadian Communist, noted that work in ethnic organizations, "rarely gets an acknowledgement, often is derided as secondary and unimportant."[41]

Communist defeats among ethnic groups and trade unions were not counterbalanced by the conversion of intellectuals. Although the Communists had always emphasized the need to rally manual workers, after the 1930s the intellectuals were by no means ignored. The Communist election platform in 1945 contained demands that might attract intellectuals or anyone who wanted higher cultural standards. It proposed the establishment of centres of "Culture and the Arts" across the country, and an extension of the services of the CBC, which "must be further democratized; it must become an active factor in the development and strengthening of the spirit of true Canadianism."[42]

These recommendations were made at a time when the LPP had a respectable number of intellectuals at its disposal. Many of them were self-educated, and most were unknown outside the Communist movement. J. S. Wallace was the senior bard of the Communist cause in Canada, while Pierre Gelinas was the best-known Communist intellectual in Quebec until he left the LPP in 1956. In several East European communities choirs, bands, orchestras, amateur theatricals and the literary pages in Communist newspapers and periodicals provided outlets for people eager to preserve and enrich their cultural heritage. Party leaders welcomed involvement in these cultural activities as a means of strengthening Communist influence among potential supporters of the LPP on election day.

It was only after the start of the Cold War that the LPP made a determined effort to develop what might be described as a Marxist-Leninist line in cultural matters. The time seemed propitious: various aspects of cultural life were attracting increasing attention and controversy, while American mass culture was meeting with growing opposition from Canadian intellectuals.

The first indication that the LPP was staking a claim as a guide and arbiter in the cultural sphere was an article by S. B. Ryerson in December 1947. Statements such as "the struggle against fascist reaction includes the field of culture and the arts," preceded the call "for more study of the problems of Canadian culture – more action and leadership on the cultural front."[43]

A more systematic and authoritative exposition of Communist objectives emerged from the third LPP convention in February

1949. The resolution "For a People's Culture" covered "cultural work both inside and outside the party in terms of theory, production and organization." The proposers admitted that "our Party has had no clear-cut policy on the question of Canadian culture." They warned, "We . . . are constantly exposed to the insidious poison of bourgeois propaganda." They insisted that "the task of the people themselves" is to "take up all that is healthy in our national culture and begin to build upon it a genuine people's culture." They proposed to "strengthen and encourage progressive cultural workers in their organizations," and called for the "production of skits, plays, exhibitions, composition, performance in the Party and the labour movement generally, but beginning primarily in the Party clubs."[44]

This growing Communist interest in cultural matters led to the establishment of an artists' group and a writers' group in Toronto. The latter produced a "peace play" and "agitprop sketches on assignments." Two years of intermittent cultural activity did not satisfy the LPP's theoretical organ. There were complaints that "we have made only the barest beginnings in complementing the decisions reached" in 1949. The same article blamed this state of affairs on the lack of sustained guidance from the national committee of the LPP, and criticized "the cultural workers themselves" for not "accepting the responsibility of fighting for the implementation" of the decision of the third party convention.[45]

To stimulate the "working class cultural fight against the culture sergeants of the Anglo-U.S. war camp," the fourth LPP convention (February, 1951), demanded that "cultural workers of the Party" should be "assisted to produce works along the themes of central party agitation." Cultural commissions were to be established in all centres. "Every avenue of attack on Yankee war culture" was to be "consistently explored, especially in the field of comic books, radio and motion pictures." Cultural activities in the Soviet Union, China and the People's Democracies in eastern Europe were to be popularized to a much greater extent than before; and the Massey Report was to be dealt with.[46]

Initial Communist reaction to the 1951 Report of the Royal Commission on National Development in the Arts, Letters and Sciences, headed by Vincent Massey, was highly unfavourable. John Stewart, secretary of the national cultural commission of the LPP, denounced the Royal Commission's "demagogic language and its phony 'Canadianism'" in an article headlined "Ideological Preparations for War". He claimed that the Report reflected "the economic, political and cultural crisis into which the war policies of the St. Laurent government have led Canada." After attacking

Prof. Underhill and Nathan Cohen, a critic who used to belong to the LPP, both of whom had expressed approval of the Report,[47] Stewart insisted that the Report actually "undermines" Canadian culture. According to him:

> only the working class can take on the real traditions of labour and struggle, the foundations of all true and great art, and build the real culture of Canada, English and French.[48]

The article ended with a number of LPP proposals, including:

> financial aid to advance the people's cultural development, such as aid to be administered by a National Arts Council, democratically elected through a conference of delegates from all cultural organizations desiring to participate, and fully representative of French and English Canada and the cultural organizations of national groups.[49]

In addition, Stewart called for the organization of an annual National Arts Festival, the building of community centres, more financial assistance to universities, university students, the CBC and the National Film Board. He supported the Report's recommendations for the extension of the National Gallery and National Museum and the building of a National Library. Finally, he advocated more cultural exchanges with countries run by Communist parties and invited "members of Canadian cultural organizations" to "break away from the festering influence of capitalist culture in Canada and move towards the working class."

Stewart's "dogmatic" criticism of the Massey Report aroused opposition in Communist ranks. The Montreal cultural commission of the LPP pointed out that he "hammers rather than convinces," and that the stand he had taken "would isolate us from cultural workers we seek to influence." Harry Fistell, editor of the *Canadian Tribune* in 1946, followed with a detailed refutation of Stewart's views. He criticized not only the original article on the Massey Report, but also questioned the wisdom of Stewart's attack on Prof. A. R. Lower in his article entitled "A Cultural Fifth Columnist". According to Fistell, this description of Lower made "several liberal University of Toronto professors . . . aghast . . . . Each, by the way, has donated something to the *Tribune* fund drive."[50]

Although Stewart acknowledged that he "fell to serious sectarian errors," and the theoretical organ of the LPP took care to point out that he did not speak on behalf of the LPP,[51] the damage had been done. In an attempt to remove the deplorable impression created by his articles, the leaders of the LPP convened the third national cultural convention at which Buck, Ryerson and Leslie Morris, the new chairman of the national cultural commission of the LPP, addressed over a hundred participants. The main resolution passed at the conference called on the LPP to "overcome all narrow approaches," and insisted that "we must not permit differences in viewpoint on artistic and political questions to stand in the way" of unity "in the fight for peace." The resolution pointed out that the draft of the new party program favoured,

> "The fullest promotion of Canada's own national forms of literature and art which expresses the democratic traditions of our people .... Out of the struggle for independence and Canadian democratic culture, there will emerge, under a People's Democracy, a people's culture based on socialist realism."[52]

A separate resolution on comic books demanded that the "attorney general in each province enforce the law as it exists and prosecute the publishers and distributors of obscene and brutalizing comic books."[53]

During the next few years the cultural policy of the LPP did not change. The same jargon was employed to raise the same issues. The same warnings against "sectarianism in the cultural work" were delivered. Little encouraging news was reported, except mounting opposition to many manifestations of American culture. This was accompanied by copious references to many aspects of the Canadian cultural scene. The praise of Canadian ballet and plays was often so generous that Fistell, just before his expulsion from the LPP, wrote: "Today the Party applauds everything—or almost everything—to which the label 'Canadian' is attached." He also argued that "the new bourgeois nationalism" in the cultural sphere "had attached the Party to its tail."[54]

In the meantime *New Frontiers*, the literary periodical launched in 1952, struggled along. It owed its existence to the fourth LPP convention which set aside "an initial budget not exceeding $500, to be financed and distributed by cultural events arranged by local cultural commissions and produced only as often as finances permit . . . "[55]

New Frontiers in the 1950s resembled its predecessor, *New Frontier*. Its contents reflected the concerns of the LPP: the struggle for peace and socialism, strong opposition to many aspects of American culture, and criticism of those whom the Communists held responsible for the neglect of literature and art in Canada. The national cultural commission of the LPP was the periodical's editorial committee.

A very dedicated woman was appointed editor. Born in England, educated at Oxford, and the wife of a professor at the University of Toronto, Margaret Fairley worked hard to ensure the magazine's regular publication and to proclaim, according to her obituary, "the Canadianism that suffused her heart and mind."[56] Her collaborators (people like Milton Acorn, Arthur S. Bourdinot, V. G. Hopwood, Jean-Jules Richard, George Ryga, W. E. Wilmott) included party members, as well as people who either sympathized with the views of *New Frontiers* or who merely sought an outlet for their own work. A great effort had to be made to keep *New Frontiers* going. As with other Communist endeavours, this quarterly lacked sufficient financial support. Events in eastern Europe in 1956 and the crisis in the LPP reduced its financial resources and the number of its contributors. In 1957 *New Frontiers* ceased publication.

At the same time the LPP drew up a realistic balance sheet of its activities in the realm of culture.

> While consistently opposing U.S. assaults upon Canada's culture and making modest contributions to democratic cultural life, as for example in Marxist literature, the debates about TV, radio and comic books, and by supporting activities in the labour movements such as writing, choirs, festivals, drama and dance groups, etc., the LPP's work has suffered from sectarian exaggeration of the place these occupy in the rising democratic consciousness.[57]

All in all, the political atmosphere grew distinctly hostile to the Communists as the 1940s gave way to the 1950s. As in Great Britain, so in Canada government action in some instances reinforced the weight of public opinion and turned decisively against the Communists. Steps were taken to ease out people with Communist views from sensitive positions in the federal civil service. The screening was not very thorough, nor was it marred by the abuses accompanying similar operations in the United States. It did not, for instance, prevent Herbert Norman from becoming head of the Canadian delegation at the United Nations and Ambassador to Egypt. According to Lester Pearson, his superior in the Department of External Afairs, Norman had associated with Communists during his student days. When a congressional committee in Washington began to investigate Norman's past and made certain charges[58] (which Pearson emphatically denied), he committed suicide. The Communists were not alone in arguing that he had been hounded to death.

Academics who were pro-Soviet and members of the LPP continued to teach at the universities. There were very few whose positions were threatened, let alone who were dismissed, for propagating pro-Soviet views which most of their colleagues found abhorrent, unscholarly or bizarre. Their isolation from the mainstream of academic thinking, and the unpopularity of the Soviet Union, induced many of them to express their views in a far more discreet form in the 1950s than they would subsequently in the 1960s.[59]

Lower down the pedagogic ladder, high school and elementary school teachers were not so fortunate in escaping the scrutiny of their colleagues and employers. Many school trustees were worried that party members would use the classroom to inculcate students with their opinions. A few teachers lost their jobs; rather more were harried, and found it advisable either to display greater prudence, or to seek employment elsewhere if they were not to abandon teaching altogether.

In the legal profession little overt discrimination occurred, although there was a considerable stir when the Bar Council of B.C. refused to admit a Communist in 1948. By the time Stalin died, most Canadian cities had a sprinkling of lawyers who supported causes with which the LPP was associated.

Nor did the arts remain immune from the ramifications of the Cold War. A minor sensation was caused in 1952 when the U.S. immigration authorities refused six members of the Toronto Symphony Orchestra permission to perform in Detroit. As a result the six lost their jobs, and the Communist press enjoyed a field day attacking the American government and the spinelessness of the management of the leading Canadian orchestra.

Party leaders and some activists were subject to a certain amount of surveillance by the RCMP. Police informers operated inside the LPP and its mass organization. In addition, the RCMP exchanged information with police forces in other countries, which were equally interested in keeping an eye on Communist activities and spy rings established in North America by the Soviet and East European governments. Occasionally the RCMP would be rapped in the House of Commons and the daily newspapers for its interference in the private lives of Canadian citizens, and for displaying what some Liberal and CCF MPs considered as excessive or misplaced zeal. All in all, such incidents were infrequent, and members of the LPP enjoyed a degree of privacy and freedom which their comrades in the United States, not to mention Stalin's victims in the U.S.S.R. and East Europe, would have envied.

The party continued to enjoy legal status although occasionally some MPs did advocate banning the LPP. The strongest pressure came from Social Crediters. Progressive Conservatives expressed similar desires. George Drew, while premier of Ontario and leader of the opposition in the federal Parliament, was a determined foe of the Communists. The Communists hated Drew and seldom missed a chance to attack him. In January 1946 the *Canadian Tribune* described him as "Public Enemy No. 1".

The MPs who called for a ban on the LPP reflected the views of some of their constituents. Certain organizations, including the Ontario branch of the Canadian Legion, came out in favour of declaring the LPP illegal. So did a motion at the annual convention of the TLC in 1952. After Bengough had castigated the Communists for their "treachery and duplicity", the resolutions committee of the TLC introduced a motion favouring the "outlawing" of the LPP-CPC and "of any organization aimed at destroying our democratic way of life."[60]

Only two of the eighteen speakers in the debate that followed were in favour of the motion. The others repeated the arguments which most of the delegates had heard at previous conventions. An underground Communist party would be more dangerous than the existing state of affairs. It would be unwise to have legislation banning a political party, because the same legislation could be applied against the trade unions themselves. The bulk of the delegates shared these sentiments and opposed the resolution in a hand vote. There can be no doubt that the outcome of the debate pleased the Communist leaders. They were relieved that the largest trade union organization in Canada had not followed in the footsteps of the Canadian and Catholic Confederation of Labour which had called for a ban on the LPP in 1946, 1947 and 1948.

The call for legislation against the LPP found little support among Liberal backbenchers in the federal Parliament. The most notable exception was Wilfred Lacroix, who strongly urged the outlawing of the LPP on several occasions during the Cold War. The Communists used his and similar proposals to remind Canadians that there were powerful forces in Canada that advocated the kind of repression that the Communists had endured after the First World War and in the early 1930s. Only a resolute struggle for civil liberties and the unity of democratic forces, the Communists insisted, would prevent persecution, which would not be confined to the LPP but would be extended against the labour movement as a whole. To fight those who were calling for a ban on the

LPP, the Communists launched the League for Democratic Rights in April 1950. Although its chairman was a K.C., the LDR never achieved the influence enjoyed by the CLDL. Only ten LDR branches were listed at the time of the second LDR convention in October 1951.[61]

The CCF, like the bulk of the Liberals, was opposed to any proposal to ban the LPP. Its election platforms in 1949 and 1953 reflected the views of CCF MPs in the federal Parliament. While drawing attention to the differences that separated the LPP from the democratic socialists, the CCF insisted that Communism could best be fought by correcting "those social and economic injustices and wrongs on which Communism thrives."[62]

Whenever the question of curtailing Communist activities was debated in the House of Commons, the federal government would point out that the situation was under control and that the Communists, however abhorrent their doctrines and identification with the Soviet Union, presented no serious threat to Canadian security in peacetime. The unwillingness of the Liberals to follow in the footsteps of Meighen and R. B. Bennett contributed to the weakness of vigilante groups in Canada. There were a few occasions on which irate citizens engaged in physical attacks on Communist leaders, or smashed property owned by the LPP in the English parts of Canada. The only major occurrence was in Windsor in 1947. On most other occasions the Communists were subjected to no more than robust heckling, which always included shouts of "Go back to Moscow." As a result the Communists and their sympathizers often found it difficult to get a quiet hearing, even when they succeeded in renting a hall. Some school boards, including that of Toronto, refused to give them facilities for meetings.

The Communists carried on with their work as best they could. Communist newspapers continued to appear, albeit with fewer pages and fewer contributors than before. Party conventions, closed to the press, met at fairly regular intervals. (Delegates of Communist parties in power were not granted visas to enter Canada to attend these conventions.) In between conventions and sessions of the national committee, Buck and some of his colleagues toured the country. They addressed small audiences, spoke on the radio, and granted interviews to cub reporters for non-Communist papers. Occasionally, they would travel to eastern Europe and the Soviet Union to attend party congresses, meet Soviet and other Communist officials, and take a vacation in some Soviet resort. A holiday in the U.S.S.R. was a prized fringe benefit to which members of the national and national executive committees of the LPP were entitled. On their return they would write articles favourable to the Soviet Union. On several occasions they complained about the thoroughness of the searches to which the Canadian customs officials had subjected them on their return to Canada.

At the grassroots level, party stalwarts paid their dues, attended club meetings, distributed leaflets, and attended demonstrations organized more often than not under the auspices of mass organizations rather than by the controversial and unpopular LPP. Students of the Communist movement easily recognized, among the demonstrators, the full-time party officials, who were eager to rally support and attract favourable publicity for the causes espoused by the LPP during the Cold War.

Much of the energy of the rank-and-file was devoted to activities associated with the party press in English and other languages. The newspapers in Ukrainian and Finnish were in somewhat better shape than the main vehicle of Communist propaganda in Canada. According to John Stewart, the editor of the *Canadian Tribune*,

> In its 17 years of existence, the *Tribune* has been read at one time or another by an estimated 75,000 subscribers . . . . Yet we have been able to retain scarcely 5 percent of these subscribers.

He attributed the failure to retain subscribers to a variety of causes. Among them was "the cold war, fear of discrimination" and the accusation that the weekly "is a 'Russian paper'." Moreover, the paper was "deadly dull, out of touch with reality, too political . . . too many unreadable articles." There was also the old complaint that the party leaders who decided on the policy and content of the paper could not make up their minds whether they wanted the *Tribune* to be a party organ, or a "labour paper" that would identify "with the working class and farm movement as a whole."

Since only 20 per cent of *Tribune* subscribers "renewed voluntarily" their subscriptions in response to mailed notices, the remaining 80 per cent had to be "called upon personally" to obtain the desired result. Party activists had to do that job, just as they were expected to find new subscribers and sell or distribute copies of the paper at "plant gates, parades, demonstrations, etc."

Advertisements, subscriptions and bundle sales met about 50 per cent of the costs of production. The rest had to be raised through the *Canadian Tribune*'s sustaining fund. The *Tribune*, however, was not the only Communist paper to rely heavily on donations. According to Stewart, "A quarter of a million dollars—

a heavy burden on a relatively small number of people" had to be collected annually for the LPP press.[63]

Every year party clubs were given targets of money to be raised. The best performers would receive favourable mention in party newspapers. Although most of the money was ostensibly raised to support the LPP newspapers in Toronto, Vancouver and Montreal, much of it reached other destinations. None other than the editor of the *Canadian Tribune* admitted in 1957:

> Frequently *Tribune* campaigns are used to raise additional money for party organizational work which in effect means that donations from *Tribune* supporters in the name of the *Tribune* are used by party organizations for other than *Tribune* work. While allowances should be made, it has gone beyond that.[64]

In addition to these never-ending fund raising campaigns, which imposed a great strain on dutiful party members, LPP officials made the rounds of businessmen and other pro-Communist sympathizers who were unwilling to associate publicly with the LPP. Such individuals had existed before the war, and they grew in number and importance after June 1941. They included educators, librarians, lawyers, doctors, and social workers, as well as civil servants in wartime Ottawa.

The Cold War thinned the ranks of these philanthropists, at the same time as party membership as a whole declined. To make up for the loss of revenue and pay for what remained a relatively expensive party apparatus, even more attention had to be devoted to fund raising. The extent to which this became the major preoccupation of party organizations was revealed during the destalinization crisis in Canada, when two LPP members wrote that in British Columbia,

> The activities of the clubs have been geared to maintaining the bureaucratic apparatus of at least eleven paid functionaries (including the *Pacific Tribune* staff). The political life of the clubs has been reduced to raising money.[65]

On several occasions members of the politbureau drew attention to this problem. In the heyday of Stalinism, Ryerson referred to the "financial load which sometimes seems to squeeze the breath out of Party organization." Harry Binder, the party treasurer in 1956, claimed that "our comrades have to spend the bulk of their time raising money. In most regions and provinces, campaigns for finances go on 12 months of the year." Norman Penner, the son of a successful Communist vote-getter in Winnipeg, declared several months later, "Our party has become a top heavy institution in which a tremendous effort is constantly required to maintain it."[66]

Fortunately for the LPP, there were also other ways of raising money. Commercial enterprises, run by party members for trade with eastern Europe provided an indirect source of revenue. Additional funds were obtained through bookstores, which gave employment to worthy party veterans and sold books printed in the U.S.S.R. in English, Russian and Ukrainian. Contributions to Soviet publications, and translations into Russian or Ukrainian of works by Canadian Communists helped to raise the income of those who enlightened the Soviet public about conditions in Canada.*

Whether even all these methods provided enough money for the salaries of party officials and the clerical staff, domestic and foreign travel, the printing of books, brochures and leaflets, the purchase of radio time, the renting of premises for public meetings, and granting of subsidies to various mass organizations remains a moot point. It is widely believed that funds from abroad have occasionally reached the Communists in Canada. What has changed over the years is the amount and the method used to channel these funds, since the days when the "American Agency" of the Comintern set aside $3,000 for the budding Communist movement in Canada, the Profintern sent 6,000 rubles to Canadian miners, and W. Z. Foster forwarded a large sum of money of the TUEL.[67]

The Canadian Communist leaders find nothing strange or demeaning in these tangible expressions of "international working class solidarity". Under different circumstances, they would themselves provide financial assistance to other Communist parties.† Not that many leaders of the LPP-CPC, or even many members of the politbureau, were familiar with the various kinds of aid they received from abroad. Such matters, like the links with the Soviet intelligence, were always kept highly confidential and were only

---

*No account of Communist fund raising would be complete without mention of the "beautiful red satin" cushion covers "with hammer and sickle and cut of Marshal Stalin" that LPP clubs advertised for $1.50. (*Canadian Tribune*, December 15, 1945.)

† In 1938 the CPC donated $392 to the Communist Party of Czechoslovakia and $250 to that of Cuba.

known to a tiny group of men of proven prudence and unswerving loyalty to the Soviet cause.

The discretion of this group enabled many Communist officials to argue in all honesty that stories of "Moscow gold" were a crude invention of rabid anti-Communists. They pointed out that their own modest salaries and the constant campaigns to raise money in Canada, were the best proof that the Canadian Communist movement was self-supporting, and relied solely on the financial sacrifices of its supporters and the business acumen of the people running its commercial enterprises.

Given the unfavourable image of the U.S.S.R. and the LPP at a time when most Canadians were experiencing levels of prosperity unheard of in the 1930s, many party members found it increasingly difficult to carry out their allotted tasks. Although a great deal of effort and ingenuity were put into the campaigns for peace and better working and living conditions, the results were disappointing.

Fewer and fewer party members were prepared to engage in what the Communist describe as "public work". As a result, canvassing and the door-to-door sale of party literature suffered. Few were prepared to speak out at meetings of organizations which Communists belonged to but did not control. The excuses made to the party leaders for this lack of enthusiasm were numerous. Some insisted that the time was not propitious for propaganda because of the corrupting effects of prosperity. The party would have to wait for a depression or a war before party activities could be resumed on a more ambitious scale. Others drew attention to the danger that a party member might lose his job if he became known as an activist. Others again could only be spurred into activity for a short period of time, unless the leaders supervised their performance very closely. Hence the party press repeatedly drew attention to the need to "check-up" on what the lower party echelons were doing in this or that Communist campaign.

Recruitment drives were another area of disappointment. Few new members joined and fewer still remained in the LPP. Periodically, the leaders investigated the reasons for this. In public they attributed the failure to replenish the ranks of the LPP, and the high turnover of party members, to the Cold War atmosphere in North America. They also claimed that potential party members, and people who actually took the plunge, were put off by the "character of our inner party life." According to Harry Binder, a prominent member of the politbureau, "Many workers are outside our ranks because they feel that they cannot be in the party" for financial reasons. Leslie Morris pointed out that the new member "is called upon almost to break with his past life in every respect and to assume a burden of work and finances that family life and finances forbid." Another Communist official drew attention to the fact that "many party members find life in the party something of a drudge" and quoted approvingly Edna Ryerson's statement: "There is not enough joy in our party."[68]

As weariness and doubt spread, thousands of Communists allowed their party membership to lapse. Their departure forced many clubs to amalgamate while others simply disintegrated for lack of determined Communists among their members. As the world became more and more hostile, the LPP assumed increasingly the characteristics of an inward-looking sect instead of the dynamic movement it had been in the 1930s.

Like other sects, the LPP had saints to revere, anniversaries to celebrate, martyrs to mourn, and a hierarchy of elders, acolytes and faithful. Marx, Engels, Lenin—and Stalin until 1956—were treated as the most profound of oracles, to be quoted whenever an argument needed buttressing or the rank-and-file were called upon to make new sacrifices. The meetings to commemorate the anniversaries of the Paris Commune, of the October Revolution and Lenin's and Stalin's birthdays, provided opportunities for getting together in a more formal and inspiring atmosphere than that which prevailed at the fortnightly meetings of party clubs, or at bazaars run for the *Canadian Tribune*. Although there were no Communist martyrs in Canadian jails, reference could still be made to Buck's imprisonment in the early 1930s, or to the Communists who were imprisoned—and in some cases tortured—in non-Communist societies and in Tito's Yugoslavia.

Many party members held Buck and his closest collaborators in high regard. Their faces were familiar to those seeking guidance and reassurance. Few could fail to be impressed by this group of ex-workers who displayed poise, polish and no mean oratorical talents, and who in public exuded self-confidence and faith in the Communist cause. They knew how to issue orders, cajole their followers, make their subordinates work hard, distribute tasks, blame and praise, and were never at a loss when something had to be explained. Once in a while they would admit that they too had erred in their assessment of some aspect of Canadian or world politics. Occasionally they displayed a *bonhomie* which many of their supporters found endearing, because it seemed genuine, and showed that the leaders had not lost the common touch.

News of major clashes within the leadership seldom reached the bulk of their followers. This also helped to increase the ordinary party member's admiration for Buck and his associates. Did not unity at the helm show that a working-class leadership and an organization based on "scientific socialism" were immune to the disputes and controversies that seemed endemic in the CCF?

The high esteem in which many party leaders were held made it easier for a small number of Communists to play a role that the party statutes had never envisaged for them. Increasingly they relied on co-optation to fill vacancies in party committees and commissions. Assignment to "tasks without consultation" was prevalent, while the executives of mass organizations lost much of their decision-making power to party committees established by the LPP to direct party work in such areas as ethnic groups, women, youth, among others.

These changes accompanied what a party resolution described as:

> The harmful tendency to exaggerate the role of full-time workers, to place the leadership, in practice, more and more in their hands through the Organization Committee. In practice, it has been difficult for workers in industry and women in the Toronto City Committee to play their full role.[69]

The full-time officials were, of course, selected by Buck and his closest collaborators. This provided them with extra powers to steer the LPP along the lines they considered essential. Not that they had much choice when recruiting suitable personnel. Many of the rank-and-file preferred the role of follower to that of apparatchik. Others were too old or lacked the minimum qualifications to serve as leaders at the city or provincial levels. Others again were eager to protect their own jobs and standing in the community. They preferred someone else to do the chores, assume the role of party spokesman and suffer the fate reserved for advocates of unpopular causes.

This state of affairs ensured that the more dogmatic Communists obtained important positions in the LPP. Given their temperament and experience as party bureaucrats, it is easy to see why in 1956-1957 they preferred the old certainties, defended by Buck with the support of the Soviet Union, to the iconoclastic proposals of those Communists who advocated major changes in the LPP, the U.S.S.R. and the international Communist movement.

The core of full-time officials made the crucial decisions without prior consultation with the rank-and-file. Little genuine debate on fundamental issues took place either inside or outside the convention halls. As a member of the politbureau admitted, "Often comrades who asked sharp questions have been dealt with unkindly and sometimes with administrative measures." A single slate of candidates for party offices confronted delegates to many party conventions. Attempts to add names to the single slate often resulted in a battle. There were few opportunities to review the work of this or that leader, unless the person in question had already been marked down for dismissal or expulsion. In 1957 Annie Buller complained that "years go by in some instances before we examine a comrade's work."[70]

These were not the only controls which the leaders used to maintain unanimity. There were others that had been tested and found useful over the years. If a party member lived in a place where there was a fair number of fellow Communists, as was the case in some metropolitan centres and mining communities, he would be part of a Communist sub-society with origins going back to the 1920s. Much of his leisure time would be spent among other party members and sympathizers, and in activities encouraged by the party leaders. At social functions run under party auspices he would relax in the company of women who shared his outlook to some degree at least. Marriage would sometimes cement closer relations between activists. The party press and periodicals would provide him with answers to many of the questions likely to bother or interest him. He would buy books recommended in Communist periodicals. To become a better Communist he would be encouraged to attend evening or weekend schools run by the LPP. He would be expected to join the appropriate trade union. He would be urged to join at least one mass organization. Everything would be done to convince him that he belonged to the most progressive organization in Canada, and that he was part of a worldwide movement on the march.

The Communist failure to win widespread support in Canada would be minimized or attributed to the fiendish scheming and unscrupulous propaganda of people who were fighting a losing battle against the forces of peace, progress and socialism, epitomized by the U.S.S.R. itself. Sooner or later Canadian workers, too, were bound to shed their "social democratic illusions" or abandon their allegiance to the "old line parties". Given the nature of the capitalist economy and the fighting spirit of the LPP, the argument went on, an evergrowing number of Canadians would inevitably rally 'round the Communists. Any kind of social protest, no matter how insignificant, and any evidence that capitalism was failing at home or abroad was inflated and used as proof that the postwar boom was about to end and that new struggles and victories were in sight.

There was little likelihood that party members could successfully challenge the leaders by advocating different policies, or by calling for new leaders at the helm of the LPP. Anyone who did so was branded one of the "agents of the class enemy." Attempts to recruit kindred spirits, who would be prepared to engage in group action within the LPP, led to the charge of "factionalism", one of the worst crimes a Communist could commit. The party leadership was on the lookout for any sign that their authority might be questioned. As soon as grounds for suspicion existed, a thorough investigation would be made to ferret out the guilty and unmask their accomplices inside and outside the LPP.

A special party commission would be established to deal with the case. Party members would be invited to submit evidence and the suspect would be ordered to appear before the commission. The zealots who manned these commissions created such a Star Chamber atmosphere that many suspects declined to take part in the proceedings, which comprised indictment, detailed interrogation and sentence.

Faced with the bleak alternatives of either leaving the LPP or staying on in the hope that things would somehow improve, party members reacted in two predictable ways. An increasing number dropped out. Others preferred to remain in the LPP. Force of habit, the friendships they had formed in the Communist movement, and their ultimate faith in the Communist cause, were stronger than the doubts that occasionally beset them.

Chapter 8

Destalinization in Canada

Stalin's death on March 5, 1953, sparked off a number of changes in the Soviet system of government and the international Communist movement. These reverberated throughout the world, and in 1956 shook the LPP to its core.

The first reaction to the news of Stalin's death was one of genuine grief at the loss of the man whom the leaders and rank-and-file of the LPP identified with the building of the first socialist state in the world and the Allied victory over Nazi Germany. As the national executive committee of the LPP admitted in 1957, "We made a most serious mistake in idealizing Stalin and in effect attributing infallibility to his ideas."[1] Buck declared in April 1956: "If we in Canada had reacted to that tragic event on the basis of what Stalin's work had contributed to Canadian democracy, tears probably would have been evident upon Canada's streets also."[2] Buck's statement cannot be attributed solely to his close identification with Stalin's policies for more than two decades. Salsberg, who had grave doubts about the treatment of Jews in Stalin's Russia, delivered a eulogy of the late Generalissimo in the Ontario legislature.[3]

Although Stalin had died, the LPP continued to follow the policies laid down by the CPSU for Communist parties in industrial societies. The struggle for peaceful co-existence between the U.S.S.R. and the U.S.A. continued to receive the highest priority. The ending of the arms race and the fight against colonialism were emphasized. Relations with democratic socialist parties were to be improved, and steps taken to co-operate with them in a variety of fields. The Communists were to work for the formation of left-wing governments, which they would join, and which would carry out major reforms in the political, economic and social spheres.

In Canada the Communists tried to stake their claim to being "the political spokesmen of labor and the farmers" by contesting the federal election in 1953 with a new slogan and a large number of candidates. The slogan *Put Canada First* reflected Communist thinking on a number of issues that had been discussed at great length ever since the party leadership had decided, in 1951, that the time had come to revise the 1943 program. The discussion began in earnest with the publication of the draft program in April 1952. Changes in Soviet foreign and domestic policies after Stalin's death influenced the course of the discussion in the LPP, as well as the contents of the final draft adopted in March 1954 at the national convention of the LPP.

This final document, as well as the debate which preceded it,[4] emphasized the need to regain Canadian independence lost to the United States as a result of the policies of the Liberals and the Tories, abetted by Social Credit and the CCF. The loss of independence, the Communists insisted, could be seen everywhere. In foreign affairs the Canadian government slavishly followed American initiatives, with disastrous results to Canada and the world. In the economic sphere subservience to the U.S. had led to the American takeover of key segments of the Canadian economy, to the neglect of secondary industries, to the failure to find markets in Asia and eastern Europe for grain and other Canadian exports, and to the delay in building an oil pipeline across Canada. In the world of labour American influence was responsible for the campaign against Communists and their sympathizers in the unions, for the failure of organized labour to protect the interests of workers, and for the high percentage of unorganized workers. Kowtowing to the Americans in all these spheres affected cultural standards in Canada. In that field, too, American influence was predominant and nefarious, preventing the emergence of a "people's culture", which alone could fulfil the needs of Canadians.

The struggle against American domination required, in the eyes of the Communists, the formation of a "people's coalition". The LPP was the only political party to advocate such an alliance. Little could be expected from the leaders of Social Credit or from those who were in charge of the CCF. Although the followers of these two parties reflected dissatisfaction with existing conditions and the old-line parties, the record of Social Credit in Alberta and of J. M. Coldwell, the CCF spokesman in the House of Commons, showed that they were at heart supporters of the very forces in society that were leading Canada to war and economic ruin.

The "people's coalition" would include CCFers and Social Crediters disillusioned with the record of their leaders. It would also be joined by an increasing number of trade unionists who suffered from the Liberals' economic policies. The middle class also would provide recruits, as more and more small business men became victims of big corporations, and as professional people realized the impasse into which Liberal policies were leading Canada.

The Communists claimed that the LPP offered a viable alternative, not merely to workers but to other segments of society as well. The very slogan *Put Canada First* implied the downgrading of the class struggle, and assumed the forging of an "alliance between working class and sections of employers whose interest temporarily merge."

This shift in Communist policy and tactics was neither unexpected nor confined to Canada. Once again, the Canadian Communists were echoing developments abroad. As Sam Lipshitz, a prominent official responsible for party work in the Jewish community, reminded his colleagues in 1956:

> 'Put Canada First' was developed directly and under the influence of Stalin's speech at the 19th congress of the CPSU 1952, in which he spoke of 'raising the banner of the nation', that was thrown overboard by the bourgeoisie.[5]

The attempt to channel anti-American feeling and rising Canadian nationalism in a direction favourable to the Communist movement was noticeable in the 1954 party program and the LPP election platform of 1953. The former document included a potted history of Canada, discussed the need for "a Canadian independent foreign policy of peace," dwelt on the "incomplete character of Canadian bourgeois democracy," urged the formation of a "democratic national front," and came out in favour of "a People's Democracy as a form of working class state" in Canda.

The ideas and jargon employed in the program reflected what the LPP theoreticians had absorbed from Soviet and Cominform publications and the theoretical organs of the American and British Communist parties. They argued that Canada, like other industrial societies in the West, was ripe for socialism, that only the working class could bring about the new society, and that physical violence need not necessarily precede the establishment of the workers' state in Canada. In private, however, many Canadian Communist leaders doubted whether a peaceful transition to socialism was feasible.

The LPP election platform in 1953 dealt with issues of immediate concern to would-be Communist supporters.[6] The opening sentence of *Put Canada First* declared that the LPP had "a new

national policy to make Canada truly great in a world of peace."
The remainder of the document comprised proposals that had figured in previous LPP statements: full employment; a 35-hour working week; "publicly-owned trans-Canada oil and gas pipelines";
the need to develop "basic and manufacturing industries in every
province"; guaranteed floor prices for all farm produce; a South
Saskatchewan River Dam. The food processing industries were
added to the list of industries to be nationalized. The section on
"Canadian culture" included the demand, "ban crime and horror
comics." "Tax the greedy, not the needy" cropped up under the
subheading "people's welfare, not warfare." The call for a
"Made-in-Canada Constitution" led on to a call to "strengthen
our democratic pride in Canada by the adoption of a Canadian
flag."

The 1953 election campaign of the LPP encountered three major
problems. In some instances, those who the leaders thought would
make suitable candidates declined an invitation to run because
they were afraid of losing their jobs. There was a larger number
who could not grasp the new party line. As Buck put it after the
election, "Phrases about creative Marxism don't mean much to a
comrade who doesn't fully understand the contribution to Marxism that is being praised." Worst of all was the unwillingness of a
number of Communists to agitate on behalf of *Put Canada First*.
These recalcitrants were mostly older workers of East European
extraction. Leslie Morris attributed their "hesitancy and reluctance in coming out to fight for Canada for fear of being accused of
'bourgeois nationalism' or 'leaving the rails of the class struggle'."[7]

And then there were unnamed "comrades" who wanted the LPP
to contest a relatively small number of ridings and support
"labor-farmer" candidates elsewhere. What such comrades for-
got was that before Stalin's death, party headquarters had shelved
the policy of "concentration" followed in the federal election in
1949. As early as September 1952, Buck had announced that the
LPP would field seventy or eighty candidates. In the end, the LPP
contested one hundred constituencies in seven provinces on
August 11, 1953. St. Laurent, the prime minister, and Coldwell,
the national leader of the CCF, faced LPP candidates in their respective ridings; George Drew, the Tory Leader, did not.

The LPP standard bearers included twenty-two women and
eleven "youth candidates". The remainder were mainly officials of
the various organizations comprising the Communist movement in
Canada: the LPP, ethnic associations, and trade unions under
Communist leadership. A doctor, a retired naval officer and several farmers and journalists also figured among the candidates.

The difficulties that the LPP encountered in its election campaign have to be weighed against several short-term advantages the Communists gained from operating on such an ambitious scale. To begin with, the election campaign helped to galvanize the party organization, which was inward-looking and quasi-dormant in many ridings. Second, a fairly large number of non-Communists were exposed to LPP slogans and arguments for the first time in several years. Third, electioneering helped the LPP to replenish its ranks, with the result that Ryerson could report "a five per cent overall increase in Party membership" in 1953.[8] Some of the recruits were former members rejoining the LPP; others came in for the first time. Although far fewer were recruited than the party leaders had hoped, they represented a welcome addition to an organization which had been getting smaller for years.

The overall election results, however, were disappointing, in view of the fact that the LPP campaign cost $100,000, included 750 radio broadcasts and meetings, and involved the distribution of 600,000 copies of the election manifesto as well as 1,500,000 copies of "other election literature."[9] Only 59,622 voters answered the call to elect LPP candidates, while 636,310 supported the CCF. The Communist vote was higher than the CCF's in only three of the ninety-one ridings contested by both parties. Two of these three constituencies were in Quebec, while the third was a rural riding in Alberta where a fairly high proportion of the voters was of East European extraction.

The ratio of votes per LPP member varied "from around a hundred to one in some constituencies to seven to one in others." In some ridings, where the LPP had few members and barely a rudimentary party organization, a sizable vote was registered. This was true particularly of several rural ridings in the Prairies, where the AUUC had branches. On the other hand there was a definite decline in the number of votes cast for the LPP in many urban constituencies, including the four Communist strongholds which the party leaders thought that they had a good chance of winning!

Election	Cartier Montreal	Spadina Toronto	Trinity Toronto	Winnipeg North
1945	10,413	10,050	7,488	9,116
1949	4,868	–	6,438	5,406
1953	896	1,938	1,725	2,515

Leslie Morris attributed "this serious blow to Party voting strength" to the "heavy decline of the Party vote among the Jewish and Slavic supporters."[10]

The leaders of the LPP analysed the election results at some length soon after the election. Morris defended the stand they had taken by suggesting that no other election tactics would have produced better results. What he did not dwell upon was the extent to which the LPP had overextended itself in 1953. This matter was brought up several years later when contributors to the *National Affairs Monthly* stated:

> We overextended ourselves . . . because of our impatience, our lack of concrete and careful examination of the possibilities . . . . the fact that we sowed illusions about the miracles that *Put Canada First* was going to do for our party made the pill even more bitter when the falsity of our position became revealed.[11]

There is plenty of evidence in support of this view. In the first place, many of those who joined the LPP during the election campaign left it again soon afterwards, thus demonstrating once more the proverbial difficulty of retaining new recruits. Second, the circulation of the *Canadian Tribune* suffered badly, and never recovered from the diversification of party activities in 1953. The attention normally given to securing the renewal of subscriptions went into electioneering. Since the weekly paper was the chief means of reaching Canadians, the ultimate result of the LPP election drive was to reduce the range of Communist influence. Finally, those who had serious doubts about the value of the *Put Canada First* slogan saw no reason to change their minds after the votes had been counted.

Disappointment over the election results was so great that the subject was raised again at the fifth LPP convention. A laconic passage in the main resolution referred to the "gap between the breadth of appeal of our policy and our acutely limited organizational strength."[12] The same document spoke of a plan to "nominate candidates in all federal and provincial constituencies." What this meant in practice was revealed in 1956: the National Committee toyed with the idea of competing with the CCF in every federal constituency in the next election.

The bold front put up by the LPP leaders in the election postmortems was reflected in their repeated calls to continue the struggle on the basis of *Put Canada First*. The slogan came under heavy criticism during the bitter intra-party debate after Khrushchev's denunciation of Stalin. Some members pointed out that the Tories, not the Communists, had reaped the benefits of Canadianism in the 1950s. They claimed that the LPP often looked like an ally of the Conservatives when it put forward proposals to counter growing American influence in Canada. Others argued that the downplaying of the class factor, implicit in the 1953 election slogan, represented a retreat from Marxism-Leninism and made it much more difficult to rally workers around the LPP. As a result, the LPP vegetated in the very areas from which the Communists should have drawn their main support. The LPP's neglect of the workers and their day-to-day struggles made the party more vulnerable when the LPP had to deal with all the problems that stemmed from destalinization in the U.S.S.R. Middle-class values had flourished in the LPP and provided a fertile ground for those who wanted to change the LPP's character.

The LPP's electoral defeats in 1953 forced the Communists back into obscurity, from which they did not emerge until 1956. In February 1956, Buck attended the public sessions of the twentieth congress of the CPSU in Moscow, in the course of which several Soviet leaders made cryptic remarks about the effects of the "cult of personality" in that country. The CPC had joined in the fulsome praise of Stalin, with the result that most Canadian Communists assumed that Stalin was an all-wise, highly benevolent leader, a man to be emulated in so far as ordinary humans were capable. Buck had been one of those who had taken a major part in promoting the cult of Stalin in Canada, with results that were not always beneficial to the Communist cause. In May 1956 he admitted that the "cult of the great man . . . marred our judgement and our ability to test the decisions that were made."[13]

Like the delegates of other Communist parties, Buck was not present at the closed sessions of the twentieth congress at which Khrushchev delivered his scathing denunciation of Stalin. When pressed by his colleagues about that speech, Buck claimed that the first intimation he had had of its contents was several weeks later in Warsaw. On other occasions he produced a different story with the result that his veracity was questioned by those who already had serious doubts about his fitness as party leader.

Before long the State Department in Washington published what is widely accepted as a fairly full and reliable text of Khrushchev's secret speech, and arranged for it to receive world wide publicity. The *Canadian Tribune* played its modest part by publishing the text on June 18, 1956.

In the words of an LPP document, Khrushchev's speech, "came as a shock for which we were wholly unprepared."[14] This was true even of members of the national committee, who, unlike those of the NEC, did not get from Buck the full text of Khrushchev's speech on his return from eastern Europe. Party members who would never accept non-Communist or anti-Communist versions of how Stalin treated his rivals, collaborators and compatriots, were overwhelmed by what Khrushchev had to report. In the past they had defended Stalin's drastic measures, using *Pravda's* arguments and phraseology. They had dismissed the evidence of Stalin's opponents as yet another capitalist or fascist fabrication. They had also accepted Stalin as a military genius, a view debunked by Khrushchev in his account of torture, incompetence and executions. The news was so momentous that many Canadian Communists felt confused and betrayed. As one activist put it,

> The real shock, as far as many of us are concerned, is the discovery that what held us together in the LPP in the past was not in the first place, the striving for socialism in Canada, but unlimited faith in the Soviet Union – and slavish adherence to the ideological lead of the CPSU. Now, for all but the most fanatical, there can never again be the unlimited faith in the Soviet party of any other CP.[15]

In the soul-searching that followed the publication of Khrushchev's secret speech, Buck and his associates offered no inspiring leadership. In fairness it must be pointed out that they faced a daunting task. Nothing in their careers as party officials had prepared them for a confrontation with bewildered and angry party members who suddenly realized that they had been duped for years. Buck tried to make the best of a bad job by claiming ignorance of much of what had happened in the Soviet Union, by agreeing with Khrushchev's denunciation of Stalin and by insisting that "deformations" of the socialist system during Stalin's last years did not mean that the Soviet Union had ceased to be a progressive and socialist society. At the same time Buck tried to reassure his followers by pointing out that Stalin's successors were taking steps to prevent the recurrence of one-man rule. The LLP should trust the CPSU, and concentrate on the struggle for peace and socialism in Canada.

As far as the Communist movement in Canada was concerned, Buck and those who shared his views admitted that Soviet precepts had been followed too closely, that in the process inner-democracy had suffered, and that the LPP had been insufficiently flexible in some of its policies. This self-criticism was coupled with the claim that the party line had been basically correct and that the LPP remained the avant-garde of the Canadian working class.

Buck's attempt to minimize his own political errors and avoid a thorough debate on Stalin's role was not successful. Gone were the days when critics like Harry Fistell could be drummed out of the party without a major debate. Events in eastern Europe had caused such a stir among Communists that opposition to Buck grew rapidly. His opponents included people who had previously concealed their personal doubts about the wisdom of many Soviet or LPP tactics, as well as members who displayed unforeseen political sensitivity after Khrushchev's speech. Among the latter were several disillusioned party officials who were merely looking for a good excuse to sever their connection with the LPP.

News of the persecution of Jews under Stalin compounded anxieties within the Communist movement and contributed a great deal to the LPP's disarray in the autumn of 1956. The shock was particularly great among party members of Jewish extraction, for they too had believed that anti-Semitism did not exist in the U.S.S.R. The Canadian Communists' faith in Stalin's leadership extended to the "uncritical acceptance of the dissolution of Jewish cultural organizations in the Soviet Union and the refusal to demand information as to why they were dissolved."[16] In 1956, however, Jewish Communist newspapers in Poland and New York published some very disturbing evidence of mistreatment of Jews in the Soviet Union and eastern Europe.

Among those who had suspected there was discrimination against Soviet Jews, long before it had become fashionable to raise the question in Communist ranks, was J. B. Salsberg, one of the ablest Canadian Communist leaders. Like so many other Jewish members of the CPC he came from a poor family. Unlike many others, he came to the CPC via the left-wing of the Poale Zion organization, and he had been a prominent trade unionist while still in his twenties. He and Buck did not see eye-to-eye during the party crisis in 1929, and Salsberg was actually expelled from the CPC after Buck had denounced him as "unprincipled". Before long Salsberg was back in the fold, and soon became the leading Communist expert on trade union matters. In that capacity he had more contacts with organized labour than his colleagues who were immersed in party work. He was also a very successful vote-getter in Toronto. Last but not least, he knew something about life in the Soviet Union, which he had visited in 1939 and 1955.

Aware of what had happened to Jewish cultural organizations and their leaders in the Soviet Union, Salsberg had raised in private a number of embarrassing questions while Stalin was still alive. Because of his refusal to accept and defend the position adopted by the majority of the LPP national committee on the question of Soviet Jewish writers and Jewish cultural organizations in the USSR,[17] he lost his seat in the party secretariat in 1953 and in the NEC in 1954. At one stage he was even in danger of losing his membership on the national committee, even though he never behaved as an ill-disciplined Communist eager to challenge publicly the defenders of Stalin's attitude and policy towards Soviet Jews before 1956.

Salsberg returned to the NEC in May 1956, when the LPP was busy trying to repair the damage caused by the revelation of Stalin's policies. With his stand vindicated by official Communist disclosures and by an LPP apology to him, Salsberg became the centre around which gravitated many of Buck's critics. The opposition against the veteran leader of the LPP remained inchoate and made no serious effort to form an anti-Buck faction in the party. However, they raised a number of fundamental questions which were debated at great length, particularly in Montreal and Toronto. In the meantime, normal party activities were badly neglected, while Communist newspapers and the *National Affairs Monthly* published articles, resolutions and letters-to-the-editor, all reflecting the wide range of views and proposals as well as the extent of the confusion and frustration among the leaders and the activists.

The wisdom of Khrushchev's denunciation of Stalin was not challenged except by some old party members in isolated communities in Alberta and B.C. In their last years these elderly members could not stomach the idea that Stalin was not the man they had believed in. Their criticism of Khrushchev was not echoed in public by members of the politbureau of the LPP who, like those of the French party, confined their complaints to the CPSU's failure to consult fraternal parties before Khrushchev's speech. Privately, however, many of those who sided with Buck during the crisis thought that Khrushchev had made a serious political error in attacking Stalin so brutally.

The controversy among party members centered on the relationship between the LPP and the CPSU and the advisability of making a clear break with the policies followed by the Communists in Canada since the foundation of the LPP. Buck's critics felt that the party had been too subservient, too inclined to accept on faith the Soviet version of men and events. The case of Tito was brought up as an example of the leadership's dependence on the CPSU. By praising Tito before 1948, denouncing him between 1948 and 1953, and finally declaring that the charges against him were false, the LPP had not enhanced its reputation as a reliable analyst.

Those who opposed Buck advocated a looser form of relationship with Moscow. They also insisted that a deeper study should be made of the conditions which had made it possible for the "cult of personality" to flourish, for thousands of Communists to be liquidated, and for Jews to be discriminated against in the Soviet Union.

The proposals they put forward for the day-to-day operations of the LPP varied a great deal. All the critics advocated limitations on democratic centralism, a considerable reduction in the number of full-time party officials, greater encouragement of rank-and-file involvement in the decision-making process, and the adoption of a friendlier attitude towards the CCF and other opponents of the status quo. They believed that these changes would make it easier for the LPP to play a role in Canadian politics. Some of the critics, however, became so pessimistic in the course of the debate that they doubted very much whether the LPP could ever really evolve.

Under the impact of Buck's refusal to modify his style of leadership and of the events in eastern Europe during and after the Hungarian revolution, Salsberg advocated a "new realignment of Marxist and socialist forces in Canada" because "The LPP, with its long history of subservience to the CPSU, its dogmatism, its sectarianism, its isolation from the masses and the distrust with which it is regarded cannot be transformed into . . . [a party] that will creatively apply all that is valid in the body of scientific socialist knowledge to Canadian conditions and chart our own Canadian path of socialism."[18]

As tempers flew and discussion became more acrimonious, Buck made fewer and fewer concessions to his critics. He referred less frequently to Stalin's crimes and to the mistakes the LPP had made under his leadership. Instead, he increasingly drew attention to what he considered were the full implications of his opponents' proposals for reforming the LPP. By October 1956 Buck was insisting, with some justification, that they wanted to destroy the very foundations of the Leninist type of party, something that he was not prepared to stomach. To defend what he and his supporters considered to be fundamental, Buck did not hesitate to denounce his critics as "revisionists", "liquidators", "do-gooders" and "rotten elements". The other side reciprocated with "dogmatists" and "sectarians".

One issue in particular contributed to the growing polarization of the LPP: the report of a party delegation to the U.S.S.R. To obtain guidance and seek information on the extent to which the CPSU had abandoned Stalinist practices, Buck, Kardash, Morris and Salsberg visited the Soviet Union in August 1956 and met several Soviet leaders, including Khrushchev. The statement issued by the NEC after the return of the delegation expressed satisfaction with the steps the CPSU was taking to overcome the "cult of personality". Although all the members of the NEC signed the document, Salsberg added the rider "that his vote be recorded in favour with certain reservations."[19]

Very soon the readers of Canadian Communist publications learned that the delegates had differed widely in their estimates of Soviet measures to deal with one-man rule and anti-Semitism. Salsberg, for instance, had gone away very disturbed after his talk with Khrushchev, who displayed great distrust of Jews and tried to ward off his visitor's anxieties with un-Marxian statements like "when a Jew sinks his anchor, there immediately springs up a synagogue."[20]

The journey to Moscow did not resolve the dilemmas faced by the LPP leaders as they grappled with the implications of destalinization. The ferment in the LPP actually grew fiercer during their absence. Dissatisfaction with Buck's attempts to divert attention from events in the U.S.S.R. and eastern Europe first assumed serious proportions in Montreal. To cope with the restlessness in that party organization, Buck and Salsberg left for Montreal immediately after the NEC had issued its report on the delegation's visit to the U.S.S.R.

At party meetings in Montreal Buck did not behave in a conciliatory manner. He questioned the right of party members to raise certain sensitive issues. The impression he left was so deplorable that Stewart Smith and Harry Binder, the party treasurer in 1956, were sent to Montreal to reassure party members and prevent them from leaving the LPP. They failed to stem the tide. Among the first to go was none other than Gui Caron, the provincial leader. He had come out strongly in favour of destalinization as early as April 1956. Disillusioned by Buck's response to questions and suggestions from fellow Communists, Caron resigned in October 1956, because he felt that the LPP was incapable of becoming "really Canadian and really democratic." Three members of the national committee who lived in Montreal followed Caron into the political wilderness in spite of numerous appeals to reconsider their decision. Several hundred party members in Montreal also left the LPP in their leaders' wake.

Other critics stayed on. Their strength in the NEC secured the passage of two controversial motions that greatly disturbed the pro-Moscow elements. The first authorized the dispatch of a telegram to the CPSU condemning Khrushchev's meddling in the affairs of the Polish United Workers' Party in October 1956.[21] The second, proposed by Norman Penner and carried by five votes to three with one abstention, called on Buck to give up the post of secretary-general in favour of a three-man secretariat which would prepare the ground for the national convention to be held in

January 1957. Penner justified the motion in a speech to the Toronto party organization. He insisted that a "real change in approach had to be signalized to the party if we were to end the sterility of the past 7 months, if we were to hold the Montreal membership, and if we were to make the strides forward urgently required."[22]

However desirable these objectives may have appeared to him and others at the time, his initiative harmed the cause he was associated with. By focusing on personalities rather than on issues, something that Salsberg wanted to avoid, Penner provided Buck with the argument that the struggle was essentially over personalities and that Buck's enemies wanted to supplant the secretary-general at the helm of the LPP and then to liquidate the party he had built up over the years. This argument swayed several party leaders who had not yet committed themselves fully to either side.

Although the NEC soon after rescinded unanimously the motion for Buck's resignation, the differences of opinion among the principal leaders were so great that a plenary session of the National Committee had to be called to resolve the deadlock. In addition to members of the NC, the meeting was attended by "members of all national sub-committees of the National Committee."[23]

In a marathon session which lasted from October 28 to November 9, the members of the NC reflected the lack of unanimity that was already evident in the NEC. They were unable to take a stand on Soviet intervention in Hungary, and a resolution setting the stand of the LPP on several major issues "was not even discussed." On two occasions Buck suffered humiliating defeats. "For the first time in the history of national committee meetings" his opening report was not adopted. Secondly, a written statement he introduced on the tenth day of the session "was so extreme that there was no one in the committee who was anxious to move or second its adoption" with the result that Buck had to withdraw it.[24]

All in all, the atmosphere in the NC was not conducive to cool reasoning or the emergence of a consensus. Charges and counter-charges fogged the debate, while contradictory news from Budapest, Moscow and Warsaw compounded the confusion. The days of debate and of jockeying for allies left their mark on the tense and increasingly tired debaters. The morale of some of Buck's critics fell when they learned of the second Soviet intervention in Hungary on November 4, 1956. They realized that repression in Hungary would hurt their cause too. To Communists everywhere the deployment of Soviet tanks in Budapest was a dramatic reminder of the limits of liberalization. For Buck, on the other hand, the tough Soviet stance was a source of encouragement to persevere in what he was already doing. He knew that in grave emergencies the CPSU expected unconditional identification with the U.S.S.R. As on other occasions, he was prepared to give proof of his loyalty in return for the support he needed. His rivals lacked his total commitment to the Soviet cause in 1956. The more perspicacious among them knew that they could expect little sympathy, let alone aid, from Moscow in their defiance of Buck and what he stood for.

Towards the end of the NC meeting the tide definitely turned in Buck's favour. The NC repudiated by eighteen votes to eleven, with one abstention, the NEC cable condemning Soviet interference in Polish affairs in October 1956. The quasi-unanimous decision of the NEC to resign also helped Buck. Buck, unlike Salsberg, favoured this method of breaking the deadlock. He knew that his followers were in the majority in the NC, and that they would elect those who more or less shared his views to the new NEC. He also expected the members of the new NEC to put an end to the kind of controversy that was tearing the LPP apart, and to guide the party back on course.

The election for the new executive was preceded by a call by Buck to choose those "who would fight the Right deviationists." His wish was granted. Those who shared his views were in a majority. Stewart Smith, who opposed Buck, was not re-elected; Salsberg tied for the last seat with two second-rank Communist officials. Although a way was found for him to join the NEC, he declined the honour. So did Binder and Norman Penner, who received more votes than Salsberg. Penner rejoined the NEC soon afterwards, and for a time tried to prolong the debate on the issues which concerned him so deeply, but before long he too realized that the LPP would not change while men with Buck's outlook ran the Communist movement.

The distribution of forces in the intra-party dispute in the autumn of 1956 showed that Buck was far stronger among party officials in western than in central Canada. The Communists of Ukrainian origin were solidly behind him, and were the first to call for the expulsion of the challengers of the established canons of Communist behaviour. From Vancouver McEwen supported Buck, wading in with a robust attack on Salsberg.[25] S. B. Ryerson, the party's best-known intellectual, also sided with Buck after returning from eastern Europe.

On the other hand, Buck was in a definite minority among articulate party members in Montreal, and he faced considerable opposition from holders of key positions in the Ontario and

Toronto LPP, the small Communist youth movement and pro-Communist Jewish organizations. Opposition from the rank-and-file diminished as the debate continued, and as bad news from eastern Europe piled up in the course of 1956. A sizable proportion of disillusioned members of the LPP lost interest in party affairs, more convinced than ever that the LPP had no future under leaders like Buck. They dropped out in increasing numbers, and no appeal could convince them that they should stay on at least until the forthcoming party convention, where the controversies would be thrashed out and solutions found to the problems that had baffled them for almost a year.

The turmoil in the party led to the postponment of the sixth national convention of the LPP from January to April 1957. This delay helped Buck to consolidate his position, and ensured that the delegates would ratify his victory. By holding out while the Soviet Communist line hardened and the "revisionists" took a beating in other Communist parties in the West, by appealing to old loyalties, and by presenting the issue as essentially one of "For or Against the Party," Buck rallied sufficient support to remain in charge of a battered organization.

Victory at the centre did not ensure immediate or full endorsement of his policies in two sensitive segments of the Communist movement. The enfeebled LPP organization in Montreal displayed signs of factionalism and insubordination, which the new provincial committee of the LPP hoped to quell by expelling several prominent Communists in 1958. Equally disquieting were rumblings in the United Jewish People's Order (UJPO), a pro-Communist benevolent organization founded under another name in the mid-1920s. Continued disagreements over the treatment of Jews in eastern Europe forced the NC of the LPP to devote attention to "the struggle for Marxism-Leninism among Jewish Canadians." In 1958 the NC passed a resolution referring to "cases of retreats and in some instances, capitulation before revisionist pressure and bourgeois nationalist ideas" in the struggle against Zionists. The "revisionists", led by Salsberg and Lipshitz, were accused of "constantly striving to water down the progressive character" of the UJPO and weaken its links with the LPP.[26]

All in all, the events in 1956 cost the LPP dearly. It lost experienced and dedicated leaders who could not easily be replaced. The Communist movement was much poorer after the departure of men like Harry Binder, Steve Endicott, Sam Lipshitz, A. A. MacLeod, J. B. Salsberg and Stewart Smith. Several of them were better known to party members, and non-Communists, than many of Buck's supporters.

Their departure also hurt the image of the LPP, since they had left it in the wake of disturbing revelations and bitter recriminations over anti-Semitism in the Soviet Union, lack of democracy in the LPP and Buck's dependence on Moscow. Such charges were all the more unwelcome because the LPP had always claimed to be the most democratic party in Canada, had insisted that in a socialist society like the Soviet Union anti-Semitism could not exist, and had categorically denied that the Soviet leaders interfered in the affairs of other Communist parties.

No less disturbing was the loss of a sizable number of party members, including new ones, and the collapse of numerous clubs scattered across Ontario and Montreal. Those who had stood by the LPP during the lean years of the Cold War now left it by the hundreds. Disillusionment with the Soviet Union, and Buck's refusal to mend his ways, drove many of them out of politics altogether. Others, unable to face the political wilderness and the loss of friends left behind, returned after a time to the LPP or one of its mass organizations. Still others found jobs in the expanding trade union movement. The Unitarian Church and the CCF-NDP provided another shelter. By and large those who joined the CCF-NDP supported the existing left-wing tendencies among democratic socialists and were active in the Waffle group in the 1960s. Some, after a period of political hibernation, emerged as spokesmen of the New Left, or of those sections of the peace movement that were not directly controlled by the CPC in the 1960s. Several of them devoted their undeniable talents to business affairs, where they were so successful that before long they joined the ranks of Canadian millionaires.

The career patterns of those who left the LPP in 1956-1957 confirmed the view that the Communist movement acted as a vehicle of upward mobility. As an organization eager to recruit workers and promote them in its hierarchy, the CPC-LPP taught managerial skills to several hundred Canadians of humble social background and little formal education. These skills stood them in good stead when seeking employment outside the Communist movement. In addition to those who got jobs in either the trade unions or the CCF-NDP, others found employment with professional organizations, newspapers, universities and provincial governments, including those of Ontario and B.C. Their new employers knew that many ex-Communists had something to offer, and that their knowledge and experience could be profitably used, because the individuals in question were not hidebound doctrinaires or narrow specialists ignorant of the world around them.

The bitter rift in the party, and the departure of so many prominent leaders and experienced militants, had immediate repercussions on the range of LPP activities. The number of full-time officials had to be scaled down, although not as severely as some of Buck's colleagues had feared in 1956. In 1958 there were only four full-time "political workers" at party headquarters, and "about a dozen" others across the country.[27] The *Canadian Tribune* was reduced from twelve to eight pages, while party members were urged in somewhat un-Marxist fashion: "no matter what views people have about the paper the main thing is to strive for an extension of circulation."* The *National Affairs Monthly* stopped publication in June 1957; six months later it was replaced by a thinner periodical. *The Marxist Review* lacked many of the Canadian contributors who had filled the pages of the LPP's theoretical organ at the height of the Cold War. Contributions from the Soviet Union continued to appear.

This lower profile was not the only factor preventing the LPP's speedy recovery. Many of its loyal members were better known for their devotion, and willingness to carry out routine tasks, than for their spirit of enterprise and ability to convince non-Communists that the LPP had a case at least worth listening to, and perhaps supporting. A party document in 1957 lamented the "tendencies to resist change and criticism," while Buck insisted that "we must overcome routinism ... [and] persistent attempts of sectarianism and of dogmatic attitudes."[28] All these factors contributed to "a serious falling off in our public work in many areas" as militants nursed their wounds and blamed "revisionists" for the LPP's condition.

Under these circumstances, the LPP could not participate in the federal elections in 1957 and 1958 on the same scale and with the same zeal as in 1953 or even 1949. On the other hand, the Communists campaigned on a platform that was not radically different from the old one. The proposals for peace, housing, agriculture, social legislation, constitutional reform and international trade followed the pattern established in 1945. In 1957 the LPP called for the nationalization of public utilities, banking and credit. The following year, the LPP reaffirmed its stand in favour of "a socialist Canada." In neither 1957 nor 1958 did their election manifesto contain the *Put Canada First* slogan, on which so many hopes had been built a few years before.

The Communists program appealed to very few voters. Only in

* *National Affairs Monthly*, February 1957, p. 1. According to its editor, the *Canadian Tribune* had a circulation of "less than 4,000." (*The Vancouver Sun*, March 8, 1957.)

Winnipeg North did the LPP standard bearer gain more than a thousand votes. Even in that riding, the Communist candidate received less than 4 per cent of the total votes cast.

	Number of candidates	Number of votes	Percentage of votes cast for the LPP candidate in Winnipeg North
1957	10	7,760	3.8
1958	18	9,869	3.3

The results of provincial elections in the late 1950s and early 1960s confirmed the isolation of the CPC, as the LPP was renamed in October 1959. Far fewer candidates were put up than in 1953-1955. The votes they received did not compare with those polled in 1943-1944 or immediately after Stalin's death. This was true in particular of Ontario, where the absence of Salsberg and MacLeod was keenly felt. Edna Ryerson, an effective Communist vote-getter, lost her seat on the Toronto School Board, partly because of the shame now attached to both Communism and Communists, and partly because the party machine was in disarray when she campaigned in 1956.

In the long run, the destalinization crisis in Canada was significant for two reasons. First, because it threw new light on the nature of the Communist movement and the outlook of its leaders. Second, because the repercussions of the crisis at home and abroad made it impossible for the Communists to profit from the malaise in Canadian politics in the 1960s. That decade offered a number of opportunities which the Communists could not exploit because they lacked the manpower and the prestige to compete successfully with other opponents of the status quo.

Chapter 9

Beyond the 1950s

The immediate task of the leaders of the LPP after the traumatic experience of 1956 was to arrest any further loss of membership. The haemorrhage was stopped at a figure never revealed by the LPP. Then came the slow and painful attempt to draw back, or replace at least some of those who had left the party in the late 1950s. In 1959 some progress had been made, and Communist publications could announce that membership had gone up by 15 per cent between May and October 1959. What that meant in actual numbers was never disclosed, because after 1946 the party press ceased publishing data on the numerical size of the LPP-CPC. This secretiveness is in marked contrast with the fairly copious information provided in *The Worker* in the 1920s. It indicates an unwillingness to supply information which might distress party members, discourage recruitment and make it more difficult for the CPC to find allies.

The small size of the CPC was not the only handicap under which the party laboured. No less disturbing was the announcement that the party's "average age is in the 50's."[1] Such a following could not undertake the strenuous work performed by the Communists in the 1920s and 1930s, nor did it attract young rebels into the Communist movement. Nevertheless, old age had one compensation: elderly and ailing party members were unlikely to challenge the authority or policies of their leaders, many of whom were as old if not older than their followers.

In January 1962 the members of the politbureau finally prevailed upon seventy-one-year-old Buck to give up the leadership of the CPC. No other Communist leader in the West had remained in charge of a Communist party for so long. Although he was elected chairman of the CPC and accorded the honours due to his age and former rank, Buck found it difficult to accept his new role. More than once he would express his fears about the direction in which the CPC seemed to be going under his successors.

The new Communist party leader was a native of South Wales, where he had worked in the coal mines before settling in Canada. Leslie Morris began his rise in the party in the mid-1920s. On his return from the Lenin School in Moscow he came into conflict with Buck and his associates, who at one stage wanted Morris tried by a party tribunal. Government persecution of the CPC patched up these differences, and Morris held a number of important positions in the party apparatus in Toronto and elsewhere. In 1940 he was one of those Communist leaders who stayed on in Canada, and he was very much involved in the day-to-day work of the illegal CPC.

Non-Communists remembered Morris as a man who knew how to maintain cordial relations with veteran prairie radicals, even during the worst days of the Cold War. Readers of the Communist press knew him to be one of the most effective Communist journalists in Canada. Among his colleagues he had the reputation of being a rather vain, weak man who tended to procrastinate until he was sure which policy would prevail in Moscow and where the majority in the CPC politbureau stood. Like other well-known Canadian Communists he had learned to control his doubts about several aspects of Soviet policy and Communist tactics in Canada.

Under his direction the party took steps to re-examine the character of Canadian society, the Communist role in Canadian politics and the relationship that had developed over the years between the CPC and CPSU. He proceeded very cautiously, partly because he was a prudent man, and partly because he could foresee the kind of reaction that any major changes would call forth in the CPC and the Soviet Union. Many of his closest collaborators were men who had publicly identified themselves with the CPSU in 1956, and saw no valid reason why they should abandon the old certainties. In Moscow, officials in the international department of the CPSU worried that the CPC might display fewer signs of fealty than in the past. They acted accordingly, and found some of Morris's colleagues who shared their fears.

When Morris died in 1964, Kashtan became secretary-general. Buck did not always get on well with Montreal-born William Kashtan, and the former leader found it difficult to endorse his election. This was all the more surprising as Kashtan seemed the strongest available candidate to members of the central and central executive committees when they examined the claims of the eligible candidates. Through much of the 1960s, Kashtan's problems were compounded by Buck's sniping. The former secretary-general's criticism could not be dismissed as the ramblings of an old man, disappointed at being passed over and eager to resume his old position. His colleagues knew of his standing in Moscow. Successive generations of Soviet officials, responsible for liaison with the two Communist parties in North America, had come to rely on his knowledge and dedication to what is called "proletarian internationalism" in Communist circles.

Nor was Buck alone in expressing doubts and fears about deviations from the path followed by the CPC under his leadership. Many shared his views to a greater or smaller extent. Some party officials who had won their spurs on the Prairies went further, and argued in favour of a tough stance, though in a less skilful manner than Buck. They, however, lacked his prestige and lost his protection when Buck had a stroke that left him incapacitated for any prolonged political activity. In November 1970 several of them were removed from the posts they held in the party headquarters at Toronto and were sent back to nurse their wounds in western Canada.

The CPC hoped to recover some of the ground lost in the late 1940s and the 1950s by exploiting the malaise in some segments of Canadian society. The party's stance on a variety of topics was explained in fairly detailed briefs to federal and provincial governments, and to government commissions set up to investigate specific problems. At the same time, the CPC passed resolutions and issued statements that had been discussed and approved at meetings of the central committee and at national conventions.

As in the previous decades, party members were invited to give their comments on many proposed policy statements. These comments appeared in an internal party bulletin and in pre-convention discussion sheets, which provided a lengthier, franker and more learned exposition of important issues than the articles in Communist weeklies. The range of views, proposals and complaints printed was greater than in the Stalinist era. On several occasions clashes between members of the politbureau could be deduced from the measured arguments and counter-arguments. These disagreements upset some veteran activists, who preferred the unanimity that prevailed in the LPP during Stalin's lifetime. They feared that public debate would harm the party, and that discussion would interfere with more important activities.

More public was the debate over the drafting and revision of the party program. In the final stages of the struggle against Salsberg and the "revisionists", Buck and his group decided to make the 1954 program of the LPP, *Canada's Path to Socialism*, "a more precise document, and to improve it by including many of the lessons of the past several years."

A draft of the new program was ready in 1958. It was discussed at some length before it was formally adopted in 1959 by the CPC under the title of *The Road to Socialism in Canada*. It contined no startling changes in Communist objectives and tactics, nor did the revised versions produced in 1962 and 1971.

The policies of successive federal governments were condemned, and there were warnings that economic conditions were bound to get worse unless the old-line parties adopted the proposals advocated by the Communists. Although the CPC continued to demand a socialist society, its spokesmen also called for the implementation of "immediate reforms" within the framework of the existing economic system. They insisted that a higher level of employment was possible if only the authorities followed a vigorous policy of public works and public housing and encouraged the growth of secondary industries.

The agricultural program of the CPC[2] was based on the "goal" of "maximum reduction". The Communists called for trade with "all countries", and subsidies and credits to "maintain agricultural prices." They came out in favour of a guaranteed net income of $4,200 per annum and demanded that the price of farm implements be controlled. The farmers were to be encouraged to pool their resources and knowledge, and steps were to be taken to provide better recreational, educational and hospital services in rural areas.

Aware that the federal government "dominated by monopolies" would ignore or dismiss out of hand these Communist proposals, and recognizing that the bulk of Canadian labour was not opposed to the status quo, the CPC urged the formation of a broad "anti-monopoly coalition" to fight for the reforms advocated by the Communists. The CPC continued to insist that it was in favour of the "parliamentary road to socialism," although party publications contained oblique references to "some comrades" who doubted whether a socialist society could be established without some violence. To reassure potential allies, Communist spokesmen emphasized their resolve to maintain a multi-party system and to protect civil liberties after the victory of the "anti-monopoly coalition" at the polls. In support of their case they referred to Communist parties in other Western societies which had similar programs and the same approach to civil rights.

Every meeting of the central committee and every party convention devoted a great deal of attention to the problems of launching this coalition. Although trade unions and farm organizations were expected to become an integral part of the broad popular movement, the Communists did not ignore the fact that little could be achieved in the English-speaking parts of Canada without the participation of the New Democratic Party (NDP). It could not be ignored both because of its electoral appeal and because of Soviet thinking in the 1960s. Soviet theoreticians, and those who followed their lead in western Europe, called for co-operation with socialists in industrial societies. They expressed the hope that economic realities and skilful Communist tactics would bring about collaboration between socialists and Communists in trade union affairs, as well as in municipal and parliamentary politics, culminating in left-wing governments which the Communists would join.

The Canadian Communists were in no position to disagree with the advice they received at the conferences and discussions they attended in eastern Europe and the U.S.S.R. Their main concern was to find ways and means of establishing close relations with the NDP. They did not formally apply to affiliate to the NDP, because the Communist leaders knew that the CPC stood no chance whatsoever of joining the NDP. Instead, the Communists advocated policies which they hoped would create a favourable climate of opinion for Communist initiatives among some segments of the NDP. References to the need for working class unity in the struggle against monopolies, a radical stance on the subject of nationalization and state intervention in economic affairs, demands for a neutral Canada and the call for increased trade with the Eastern Bloc were bound to have some effect on those NDP militants who already held similar views. The Communists also pressed their cause through personal contacts and by distributing Communist leaflets and newspapers outside NDP and trade union convention halls.

The Watkins Manifesto of the left-wing Waffle group within the NDP was welcomed by Kashtan "as a mirror of a rising socialist sentiment and an inevitable process of differentiation between right and left politics inside the NDP." He added, however, that the CPC did not "endorse the Manifesto" nor "advocate an uncritical attitude towards it," because "a movement for meaningful social change, if it is seriously to advance the struggle for policy, needs to unite with the revolutionary party of the working class, the party of scientific socialism, the Communist Party."[3]

His warning can best be understood in the light of his knowledge that the Waffle group was a magnet attracting at least some people who, if it had not existed, might have thrown in their lot with the CPC. No less annoying to the Communist leaders was the fact that the Waffle nucleus included Trotskyists, as well as ex-Stalinists – and their offspring – who left the CPC in 1956-1957 and were unlikely to urge the NDP and the Waffle group to collaborate with the very party they had left in disgust.

Kashtan and his colleagues knew that the NDP could not easily be pushed in the direction that the CPC thought was best for democratic socialists. Much would depend on the CPC becoming stronger and its members more skilful in applying the slogan of "unity and competition" with the NDP. Too great an identification with the NDP would sooner or later turn the CPC into another reformist socialist party, a fate to be avoided because, in Kashtan's words, "one reformist party is bad enough."[4] A stand-offish attitude, on the other hand, would perpetuate the existing isolation of the CPC, strengthen the already strong sectarian tendencies within the Communist movement, and make it impossible for the Communists to influence left-wing elements in the NDP. As Buck reminded his comrades in 1965: "It is largely from amongst this socialist left that our party will gain new members and supporters."[5]

The dilemma that the Communists faced in their approach to the NDP became acute at election time. Although the decision to contest this or that riding was left to provincial and constituency party organizations, the latter had to take into account the general line of the CPC as well as its limited manpower and financial resources. Hence it is not surprising that the Communists put up only a token number of candidates in federal elections. The wisdom of this decision was confirmed when the votes were counted. In every instance the Communist candidates did badly regardless of their ethnic or occupational background. Only North Winnipeg continued to provide the CPC with substantial though declining support.

	Number of candidates	Number of votes
1962	12	6,307
1963	12	4,162
1965	12	4,194
1968	14	4,505
1972	30	6,475

Communist explanations for the low vote differed. Some drew attention to the neglect of electioneering work. Others claimed that it was the result of the party's uncritical attitude towards the NDP. Others attributed the lack of support "to the level of political consciousness of the majority of the working class."

Where no Communist candidate stood, the local Communist organization used the election campaign to popularize the program and policies of the CPC. These included references to the need for an "anti-monopoly coalition" to fight big business and its representatives in Parliament. NDPers were urged to support the idea of such a coalition and encourage their leaders to do the same.

The campaign for closer relations between the CPC and NDP invariably raised the question of the attitude to be adopted towards NDP candidates in ridings not contested by the CPC. In only one of the four general elections in the 1960s did the CPC call on Canadians to support the NDP as part of the drive "to break up the role of the old line parties and to move Canada ahead." The Communist election platform in 1962 prefaced the invitation to vote NDP with references to the differences between the two parties over NATO, Canadian neutrality, the right of self-determination for Quebec, among others.[6]

The absence of clearcut directives in 1963, 1965 and 1968 gave some room for manoeuvre to those local party organizations that were eager to take a major part in the election campaign. The degree to which the Communists were prepared to throw their weight behind an individual NDP candidate in federal or provincial elections depended on that candidate's views on domestic and international problems. Critics of Soviet policy were considered unworthy of support; so were those democratic socialists who informed the press and the radio that they did not want to have anything to do with the Communists. On several occasions the Communist press attributed the narrow defeat of this or that NDP candidate to the line he had taken on the CPC, which had made it impossible for party members and sympathizers to support him.

The reaction of NDP candidates to Communist overtures varied as much as the amount of the support the Communists were prepared to give and the votes they could deliver. In some instances, NDP candidates accepted offers of assistance, hoping that the Communists would show discretion when campaigning on behalf of democratic socialists. Others publicly rejected Communist offers of assistance and took the opportunity of reminding the voters of the differences between the NDP and the CPC. In one case at least, an irate democratic socialist threatened to seek a court injunction to prevent Communist involvement in his election campaign. T. C. Douglas, the leader of the NDP, reflected the views of many democratic socialists when in 1962 he compared the Communist-NDP relationship to that of a flea living off a dog. Understandably, the Communists did not like the analogy. Leslie Morris did his best to answer the charge by writing, "We have no objection to being fleas if that would make the dog move in the right direction. Let us rather call ourselves gadflies."[7]

The Communist press reflected the Party's qualified support of a number of NDP initiatives, but there was also fairly frequent criticism of NDP leaders disapproved of by the CPC because of their stands on certain important issues in Canadian politics and international affairs.

The *Canadian Tribune* remained the chief vehicle for the transmission of the party line. The number of pages in the weekly was increased from eight to twelve in January 1961.* In Vancouver, the *Pacific-Tribune* published articles written on the west coast, as well as numerous contributions which appeared simultaneously in the *Canadian Tribune*. The Communist ethnic press displayed the same resilience with the result that in 1973 Communist newspapers appeared in eight languages besides English and French.

For those interested in a more sophisticated analysis of Canadian and world affairs, the Communists provided, starting in 1944, a review whose title changed several times before it finally became the *Communist Viewpoint* in 1969. Canadians could also buy the *World Marxist Review*, edited in Prague and printed in Toronto. Several East European legations and embassies in Ottawa sent out bulletins and periodicals in English. These depicted the working and living conditions in that part of Europe in lyrical terms. The U.S.S.R. received the same treatment in *Northern Neighbours*. All these publications published interviews with any Canadians, Communists or not, who visited eastern Europe and liked what they saw there.

The low circulation of the party press was paralleled by the small size of the CPC. Those in contact with the higher echelons of the party estimated the party membership at between 1,500 and 3,000 through most of the 1960s. To improve the situation, Kashtan and his colleagues urged party members and party clubs to play a bigger role both in community affairs and in non-Communist organizations. A fighting record, more frequent contacts with non-Communists, and a willingness to proclaim their loyalties, it was argued, were bound to attract a favourable response and increase

---

*According to a Soviet source, the *Tribune* had a circulation of 9,000, and *Vestnik*, the pro-Communist weekly in Russian, of 5,000. (N. Bogdanov and B. Viazeminskii, *Spravochnik Zhurnalista*, Leningrad, 1965, pp. 723, 734.)

the number of people who, if properly handled, might join the
CPC.

> We need to fight against any suggestion that our members can
> 'do better work' if they are not known as Communists. Peo-
> ple working ably and devotedly in the movements of the peo-
> ple enhance respect for their courage and integrity when they
> are recognized as Communists.[8]

These directives had only limited success. Party members had
suffered so many disappointments; few were eager to expose themselves to new rebuffs. One of the younger leaders of the CPC
reflected this malaise when he wrote, "The doubt that what we do
is vital has been seriously eroded over the past years. Doubt has
been cast on the ability of the party to surmount its difficulties."

Some people working actively in non-Communist organizations
gave up after a short time because they did not evoke the response
that they had been led to expect. Others, however, got so involved
in these organizations that they lost contact with the local CPC
clubs and were unwilling to carry out party directives. And there
were, as Kashtan pointed out,

> tendencies towards sectarianism with respect to the growing
> mass movements. This sometimes finds expression in a nega-
> tive attitude to movements led by others, be they bourgeois
> reformist, social reformist or petty bourgeois radicals. Instead
> of getting into those movements which have a wide following
> and striving to influence them in an anti-monopoly direction,
> we often take a standoffish approach to them, and criticize
> them from afar. This so-called purist approach will not influ-
> ence anyone and turn our party into a sect.[9]

Anti-Communism, though far less pervasive than at the height
of the Cold War, continued to plague those Communists who
agitated in a non-Communist milieu. Here and there, however, the
Communists succeeded in putting across their views, with the
result that a Communist leader could boast in 1969 that "scores of
resolutions that place these movements on record against the war
in Vietnam, for the recognition of China, for trade with the socialist countries, are the fruit of this constructive work."

But these limited successes did not lay the foundations of a
major increase in the numerical size of the CPC. Throughout the
1960s the party leadership insisted on two "areas of concentration": the working class and young people. The CPC made a spe-

cial effort in southern Ontario and among workers in six industries, "in a concentrated effort to build party organizations in the big plants."

Sending out special organizers, and involving party leaders in the recruitment campaign in the auto, electrical, construction, steel, transportation and service industries, brought slender results. In the Lenin Centennial Recruitment Drive in 1970 a mere forty persons throughout Canada joined the CPC by June of that year. It was left to a prominent Communist official to assure the central committee that "we have held our own." What he did not mention was that the number of recruits in 1970 was appreciably lower than during the Cold War. The LPP recruited 400 in 1952 and 489 between March and September, 1954.[10]

Stagnation and isolation from the mainstream of Canadian politics were partly attributed to the performance of party clubs, which the leaders felt did not display sufficient drive, burdened their members with too many duties, and did not engage in proper educational work to strengthen the political consciousness of dues-paying Communists. Some of those who joined the CPC were badly disappointed in their expectations. A resolution of the B.C. party convention in 1973 warned that "new people come into our Party with an image of a well-organized, self disciplined fighting organization. When they do not find this some become disillusioned and leave . . . ."[11]

The total number of party clubs remained a secret. The last available figure was for 1960. Then the CPC had about 150 clubs compared to "over 500" in the spring of 1946.[12]

As before, party clubs were unevenly distributed across the Dominion. In Quebec the clubs were largely confined to Montreal. East of Montreal there was only one club. The Toronto area had 61 clubs in 1949; in 1974 the *Canadian Tribune* reported the existence of 14 clubs in Metro Toronto. Even so, Toronto had more party members than any other city in Canada. In recent years a painstaking effort has been made to re-establish, in towns and mining centres, party clubs which disintegrated during the Cold War and the destalinization crisis in 1956-1957. In spite of modest successes, the CPC still has a long way to go, especially in Ontario. The situation in the Prairies is not more propitious, although the decline in the number of clubs is less obvious in Manitoba than elsewhere. All are in Winnipeg. In B.C. the party clubs are more evenly distributed across the province than elsewhere in Canada. They also contain a high percentage of manual and ex-manual workers. Less gratifying to the leaders is the fact that these clubs have among their members a high proportion of elderly workers and old age pensioners. By moving to the west coast they have depleted the ranks of party organizations in the less clement parts of Canada.

The leaders of the CPC checked on the performance of party clubs outside Toronto by going on speaking tours periodically. They were guests of honour and star speakers at public banquets to celebrate some memorable anniversary in the Communist movement, or to honour some worthy Canadian Communist. On such occasions they addressed small groups of elderly supporters interspersed with alert members of the RCMP in mufti, and a sprinkling of youngsters eager to see what a Communist looked like in the flesh. The leaders also spoke on the radio and occasionally appeared on TV. In addition to these public appearances special sessions were organized so that they could meet activists and middle-echelon officials. These meetings were invariably held in private. So were the provincial and national conventions of the CPC, which the representatives of the non-Communist press were not allowed to attend. In this respect the CPC differed greatly from most other political parties in Canada.

In view of the unpopularity of Communism and the CPC, the Communists conducted a lot of their agitation through CPC-controlled organizations or through associations in which party members had a foothold. In most instances Communist organizations in the 1960s were survivals from the time of the Cold War, if not earlier. The Communist members of these organizations carried out party directives and were expected to act as a group. They were, and remain, numerous among the organizers and the voluntary and clerical staffs of these organizations, which were sometimes chaired by non-Communists close to the CPC. The rank-and-file party members were strongly urged to join at least one of these mass organizations. The dutiful ones did so, to the detriment of their free time and their purse.

The range of activities of these organizations varied a great deal. Many of the associations existed only on paper, and displayed signs of life only when a telegram had to be sent or a statement made to show that the stand taken by the CPC and the U.S.S.R. met with the approval of a large number of organizations in which public-spirited Canadians were active.

Other mass organizations, however, had a life of their own. The largest were several ethnic and benevolent associations. Although far less significant than in the 1930s and 1940s, they represented one of the few areas where the CPC in the 1960s influenced the attitudes of thousands of Canadians, most of them elderly and of East European descent. Natural causes, the process of assimilation, and disappointment over policies followed by the Soviet government at home and abroad, have reduced the numerical strength of these organizations and their usefulness as "transmission belts".

The once-active Canadian Peace Congress was in its twilight years long before the CPC decided that Dr. James Endicott no longer deserved Communist support. His unwillingness to side with the U.S.S.R. in the dispute with China led to calls for his resignation and a visit by a member of the Soviet embassy in Ottawa.[13] By the beginning of 1972 the pressure on him was so strong that he and his wife resigned. They left the Canadian Peace Congress when it was at the nadir of its influence, but even in the 1960s it seldom enjoyed the influence of the other peace organizations which emerged in Canada after Stalin's death.

On several occasions party members sought a dialogue with these non-Communist peace organizations, joined them, and in a few cases obtained fairly responsible positions in them. The Communists' willingness to work hard, and the lack of staunch anti-Communists within these groups, made it easier for party members and sympathizers to play a role in them. Since the leaders of these organizations considered that the main task of the peace movement in North America was to fight for the reversal of American and Canadian defence and foreign policies, they gave the benefit of the doubt to the Soviet Union and the Canadian Communists, because they felt that the U.S.S.R. had a good case.

The Voice of Women was one of the peace groups that the Communists were interested in. It was the kind of organization that the CPC could not ignore in the party's repeated attempts to create a mass movement among women. Such a movement, the Communists argued, would depend to a large extent on the ability of the CPC to enrol more women and make better use of its woman power.

Although the nucleus of Communist pioneers in Canada included several dedicated women such as Rebecca Buhay, Annie Buller, Bella Gauld and Florence Custance, party work among women received low priority. The women's department at party headquarters was a one-woman affair in the 1920s and early 1930s. It failed to keep in touch with women party members, who, however, represented one-quarter of the total party membership in 1929. At least 90 per cent of these women were housewives who shared the ethnic backgrounds of their husbands.[14] Most of the Communist housewives were, according to a party document, "inactive, passive elements" in the CPC.

In the 1930s the percentage of women in the CPC fluctuated from 14 per cent in 1934 to 12 per cent in 1935, 15 per cent in 1937 and 14 per cent in 1938. It rose to 28 per cent in 1951. Although these percentages compared favourably with those for women in Communist parties in some other industrial societies, Buck and his colleagues were dissatisfied. Time and again they urged that a greater effort should be made to bring women into the CPC. They blamed husbands for not encouraging their wives to join, and they criticized party committees for not paying enough attention to agitation among women. "When the problem of work among women is brought up by male comrades, it is considered as a joke," acknowledged a party resolution in B.C.

Buck was equally critical of the work of women party members in the one organization which they either controlled or had a foothold in. The slogans of the Women's Labour League – "Protection of Womanhood", "Care of Motherhood" and "Co-operation instead of Competition" – were dismissed as "sentimental bourgeois slogans" when the party line hardened in 1929. At the same time women's pacifist organizations and advocates of family planning were attacked. The sixth convention of the CPC insisted that

> no propaganda on Birth Control, as a remedy of economic evils, be permissible and whatever articles written by women proletarians with an incorrect orientation have to be published, an editorial note, correcting the same, must accompany the article.[15]

In the early 1930s the Women's Labour League, led for a time by Alice Buck, the wife of Tim Buck, joined the WUL. During the Popular Front period, women party members were active in left-wing, liberal and peace organizations, and compaigned on behalf of the unemployed.

Early in 1947 the LPP sponsored the formation of the Congress of Canadian Women (CCW). The need for such an organization was made "very clear" to Mrs. Nielsen when she attended the founding convention of the pro-Communist Congress of American Women in 1946.[16] Like other mass organizations, the CCW held conventions to which observers were invited. The president of the CCW was a former CCFer. Mrs. Rae Lubbock sat as a CCF-MPP in the Ontario legislature in 1943-1945, and had been active in the Housewives Association before she allied herself with the Communists. The CCW took part in Communist peace campaigns and protests against poor housing, high prices and discrimination against women in industry. The LPP and the CCW produced several pamphlets and brochures describing the role of women in the U.S.S.R. They also stated their views on matters of primary interest to women and mothers. The Communists and their allies demanded equal pay for equal work, favoured the unionization of women workers, and advocated social legislation favourable to mothers and children.

On the subject of divorce and abortion the CPC had little to say. Occasionally, contributors to the *Canadian Tribune* would come out with statements critical of the divorce laws before the liberalization of 1968. They also felt that in some circumstances abortion was necessary. Unlike the Trotskyists, the LPP-CPC did not insist on "abortion on demand", nor did they devote much attention to "Women's Liberation". Instead, the Communists maintained that women could best achieve their objectives by taking part in the daily struggle of the working class, by joining the CPC and its mass organizations, and working for a socialist society in which women would enjoy equal status with men and realize their full potential.

The Communists' unwillingness to adopt the priorities and the agitational techniques of the most vocal elements of the women's liberation movement has been attributed to three factors. First, there is the widespread Communist belief that much of what passes for "Women's Lib" is a temporary phenomenon incapable of producing a solution to the real problems facing working-class women in our society. Second, many Communists were genuinely shocked by some of the arguments and objectives of the spokeswomen of women's liberation. The B.C. Party Women's conference in 1973 described "Lesbianism or Gay Liberation" as "simply an indication of the decadent society in today's capitalist part of the world," and warned that "the 'new morality' code of permissiveness and lack of responsibility increases the demand for abortion with little or no thought for the consequences."[17] Third, the leadership of some women's liberation groups contains a fair number of Trotskyists or ex-Trotskyists, a category of people whom the elderly men in charge of the CPC have never found easy to stomach.

The Communists' lack of sympathy for "Women's Lib" as that term is understood in non-Communist circles, considerably reduced whatever potential appeal the CPC may have had among non-conformist women. What proved even more disquieting to the party leaders was their inability to retain in the CPC a number of women comrades who transferred their energies and organizational skills to women's liberation groups in which several of them hold important positions.

Communists could also be found at the helm of several organizations catering for the unemployed and for tenants in apartment blocks. The latter succeeded in wresting major concessions from the government of B.C. The recipe for success here was the same as elsewhere. An issue that affected a large number of people; lack of sustained interest by other political parties in that particular issue; a sprinkling of party members prepared to do a great deal of unglamorous work; and the use of pressure group tactics in a mass society. Canvassing, petitions, public meetings and demonstrations, deputations to people in power, and access to the mass media, produced results and provided welcome publicity for the leaders of the campaign. Some of them used these activities on behalf of a segment of the population as a stepping stone to elected office at the municipal level.

In the world of labour the Communists continued to agitate in several ways. They kept up their opposition to compulsory arbitration, to the use of court injunctions in labour disputes, and to discrimination against women workers. They called for a higher minimum wage, a shorter work week and more social legislation. They gave publicity to strikers' demands and took part in some labour disputes, although not to the extent that the leaders of the CPC wanted.

The Communists also pressed hard for the removal of resolutions, oaths and policy statements that expressly prevented party members from holding executive posts in unions affiliated to the Canadian Labour Congress (CLC), formed in 1956 by the amalgamation of the TLC and CCL. A landmark in this struggle over the exclusion of Communists took place at the CLC convention in May 1968. Against the opposition of a former president of the USW local in Sudbury, the delegates voted by a large majority in favour of deleting from the CLC constitution the reference to "Communist" and "Fascist agencies", against which the CLC promised to protect the labour movement. The revised version merely referred to protection "from undermining efforts of all totalitarian agencies." The delegates also voted to delete from the oath which members of the CLC executive had to take, the passage in which the office holder declared that he was not

> associated with any group whatsoever which expounds or promotes or encourages any doctrine or philosophy contrary to or subversive of the fundamental principles and institutions of the democratic form of government in Canada.[18]

Many CLC affiliates adopted the same policy either before or after the crucial vote in May 1968.

Three factors combined to allow this major Communist victory at the CLC convention. In the first place, party members and sympathizers, including those who had lain low during the Cold War, did their best to create a climate of opinion that would be less unfavourable to the Communists. They emphasized the need for "working class unity" and accused their opponents of engaging in "MacCarthyism", "witch-hunting", "red scare tactics" and of playing the employers' game when they said anything against Communists or the CPC.

Secondly, the Communist campaign was helped considerably by the existence of an amorphous body of trade union activists who were receptive to some Communist arguments and slogans, and were prepared to fight alongside party members on convention floors in many parts of Canada. The strength of this shifting body of opinion cannot easily be assessed, although its existence has never been denied. It is part and parcel of the labour movement in Canada. Partly submerged at the height of the Cold War, these non-conformist radicals have been a source of embarrassment to both the CPC and the moderate trade union leaders. Neither side has been able to tame, let alone tap the energies of these radicals to the full. To the Communists they appear disparate left-wing elements who are welcome, though scarcely reliable, allies. To the present leaders of the CLC they are gadflies, and their association with Communists in their day-to-day activities is a reminder that the victories of the non-Communists during the Cold War were merely another round in the battle that has been going on ever since the Bolsheviks challenged the socialists in the West almost sixty years ago.

Finally, it must be remembered that the Communist campaign to lift the restrictions on Communists succeeded because the trade union hierarchy was no longer prepared to fight the Communists with the same vigour as it had shown in the late 1940s and through most of the 1950s. As William Dodge, executive secretary of the CLC, put it at the time of the 1972 convention of the B.C. Federation of Labour, "A couple or more Communists wouldn't make the difference."

The following day, a Communist was elected one of the vice-presidents of the B.C. Federation of Labour. He decided to run "when he heard" Dodge say that "he did not mind a few Communists in the federation."[19]

The fate of Communist-controlled unions outside the CLC remained an important source of controversy between pro- and anti-Communist unionists in the 1960s. According to a non-Communist source, these unions had 60,000 members in 1956;

according to a Soviet one, they had up to 70,000 members in the early 1960s.[20]

The strongest of these unions were the IUMMSW, the UE and the United Fishermen and Allied Workers Union. The Communist unions operated like other unions; some were perhaps more strike-prone than others. By and large, employers did not find it difficult to get along with Communist union officials. They were getting on in years, and did not want to provide a pretext for another major anti-Communist drive.

The Communist-led unions tried to negotiate their re-entry into the mainstream of Canadian labour. The CLC responded to feelers and formal applications with conditions designed to break the Communist grip over these unions. On several occasions these unions were told to merge with larger unions, where the Communists knew that they would not hold the levers of power.

It was only after Stalin's death that mergers took place. The first to be absorbed were some of the smaller unions that had been expelled from the TLC and CCL. Then the bulk of the IMMSW joined the anti-Communist United Steelworkers of America in 1967. The deals that preceded amalgamation contained provision for the employment of Communist union officials on the staff of the larger non-Communist union. The fact that several veteran Communist unionists found a niche under these arrangements inevitably led to the charge of "betrayal". Although party members working in these unions made the charge, they could not prevent CPC headquarters from welcoming the merger.

The United Fishermen found the merger terms unacceptable and preferred to apply for affiliation to the CLC. Its application had the support of many trade unions in B.C., where the Communists were regaining some of the ground lost during the Cold War. In 1972 the United Fishermen and the UE returned to the fold, in spite of misgivings several non-Communist union leaders expressed in public.

The successful campaign to enter the CLC increased the prestige of those Communist leaders, such as William Kashtan, who in the 1960s were sceptical of the proposal that the CPC should take the initiative to launch a new trade union centre along the lines of the WUL. Nor did they encourage those leftists who urged the CPC to support the formation of Canadian unions that would compete with the existing AFL-CIO unions. Those who favoured independent Canadian unions included Dr. Charles Lipton, a one-time member of the central committee of the CPC, and Kent Rowley, who was one of the leaders behind the formation of the Council of Canadian Unions.

Mindful of the damage caused by "dual unionism", and doubtful whether new independent unions could compete successfully with established international ones, the CPC preferred to concentrate its limited resources on agitation in the existing unions and on urging others to do the same. The CPC also voiced fairly frequent criticism of the CLC leaders and the international unions, accusing them of anti-Communism, failure to organize the unorganized workers, and subservience to employers and the AFL-CIO leadership. Instead, the Communists called for greater autonomy for the Canadian locals of the international unions and the CLC vis-à-vis the AFL-CIO. The demand for autonomy showed how carefully the elderly leaders of the CPC moved in a delicate area of great interest to them. A case can be made that in the 1960s the CPC was "tailing" behind the growing number of Canadian trade unionists who were increasingly dissatisfied with the way that the AFL headquarters and the American international unions made decisions on their behalf. Only in 1973 did the CPC come out unequivocally in favour of an " "independent" and "sovereign" Canadian trade union movement.[21]

Given the outlook of the Communist leaders in the 1960s, their attitude towards the Quebec-based Confederation of National Trade Unions (CNTU) becomes understandable. Although the CNTU was then growing rapidly, and was often more militant than the leaders of the AFL-CLC unions in Quebec, Kashtan opposed too close an identification with the CNTU at the expense of the international unions. Instead, he advocated collaboration between the CNTU and CLC unions which would culminate in a merger of these two union organizations in a single trade union centre in Quebec, which in turn would join a Canadian trade union centre independent of the AFL-CIO.

Quebec remained another area of major interest to the CPC. For decades the party insisted that the French Canadians were a separate nation and that they were grossly discriminated against. Comintern and Soviet publications expressed similar views; in 1929 the Profintern described French Canadians as the "most cruelly" exploited section of the Canadian proletariat."[22] However, the CPC did not accept the opinion of separatists and some Marxists that Quebec was a colony run by Anglo-Saxon Canadians.

Communist spokesmen argued that French Canadians would prefer to remain within the Confederation provided radical changes occurred. These, so far as the Communists were concerned, would have to include structural changes in the Canadian economy, as well as reforms that would take into account Quebec's history and special problems. The only proper solution was an agreement freely entered into by representatives of English-speaking and French-speaking Canada.

The Communist preference for a united Canada was defended on the ground that division along national lines was bound to weaken the labour movement and damage the struggle for a socialist Canada, while making it easier for the U.S.A. to extend its influence north of the border. Even after the FLQ kidnapped James Cross and murdered Pierre Laporte in 1970, Kashtan declared that "separatism would not be in the best interests of the national aspirations of the French Canadian people. Nor could a divided Canada be in the interests of the two nations."[23]

While supporting the idea of a united Canada, the CPC insisted in Leninist fashion that the French Canadians should be granted the right of self-determination, including the right to secession. The reference to self-determination began appearing in Communist documents in 1929 and the early 1930s. It does not figure in party pronouncements during the Popular Front period, nor after Hitler's invasion of the Soviet Union: it was felt at that time that the struggle for an independent Quebec would divert Canadians from their contribution to the worldwide struggle against Hitler, Mussolini and Japan. The Communists, like everyone else, knew that the nationalist elements in Quebec were at best lukewarm towards Canada's participation in a war against the two dictators. During and after the war the LPP repeatedly issued statements emphasizing the need for equal treatment of French Canadians. These demands were interspersed with the slogan "Maîtres chez nous", a slogan the Liberals adopted as their battle cry in the provincial election in 1960. In 1946, references to the right of self-determination, up to and including secession, reappeared in Communist publications, although at no time did the LPP advocate the break-up of Canada. Even when events in the 1960s showed the strength of Quebecois nationalism, the CPC made no concentrated effort to exploit separatist feeling. It thus ensured that the party in Quebec would remain – at least in the short run – a small, isolated protest movement drawing most of its strength from among those people who were not of French extraction.

Communist agitation among the Quebecois brought little but disappointment to the CPC leaders in Toronto. In the 1920s and early 1930s the Communists had to compete with Albert St. Martin, a court clerk who had been active in the Montreal locals of the SPC and SDPC before 1914. A strong critic of the Catholic Church, he was a self-styled Communist who actually applied for affiliation to the Comintern. His unorthodox approach to Communism and to organizational matters was unacceptable to the CPC, and led to complaints about St. Martin's "anarchist" and "anarcho-syndicalist" views. The CPC also opposed him in organizations like the Université Ouvrière and l'Association Humanitaire, in which various unorthodox ideas were expressed.

To encourage the formation of a Communist nucleus among the Quebecois, in 1927 the CPC formed the Club Educationnel Canadien-Français and subsidized *L'Ouvrier canadien* which was published irregularly between 1927 and 1931. During the Depression the CPC also sent several French Canadians to Comintern educational establishments in the U.S.S.R. It was not until the 1930s that the CPC began to make headway among French Canadians. Most of the recruits were unskilled and unemployed workers. A sprinkling of university graduates like Gui Caron, a great nephew of Louis Papineau, also joined the CPC in the days of the People's Front.

Their conversion to Communism did not put an end to the CPC's handicaps in Quebec. The Communists' obstacles included the low level of education of the French Canadian workers, many of whom were recent arrivals in the cities. The absence of a long tradition of working class militancy was another drawback to the formation of native proletarian cadres. While in the English-speaking parts of Canada the CPC relied considerably on immigrants from the British Isles and eastern Europe, in Quebec it had to start from scratch. Time and again it had to send Anglo-Saxons and East Europeans to Montreal to nurse the fledgling Communist organization among the Quebecois. The help they gave did not produce a major breakthrough, because few of the Anglo-Saxons and East Europeans were at home in the French-Canadian milieu. Fewer still spoke French well enough to pass for Quebecois on the rostrum or as canvassers.

Other disadvantages for the CPC were the unyielding opposition of the Catholic Church, the Padlock Act, and the unwillingness of most French-Canadian intellectuals to accept the CPC as an ally. In the Popular Front days the Communists could claim no more than a few contacts with young intellectuals on the fringe of the established parties. After the Hitler-Stalin pact the local Communists flirted for a time with French-Canadian nationalists opposed to conscription. Hitler's invasion of the U.S.S.R. forced the Communists to search for different partners. This time they found a more sympathetic ambience in Montreal. The Padlock Act was not enforced by the provincial Liberal government, which dissolved several police agencies which had previously kept an eye on the Communists. Pro-Soviet feeling in Montreal, and the unionization drive in Quebec, enabled the Communists to enlarge their influence and play a prominent role in the trade union movement. By 1945 the LPP had several hundred French Canadian members.

The LPP encouraged their involvement in the Communist movement. Special rules were passed to ensure that French Canadians would not be in a minority among delegates from Quebec at the national conventions of the LPP and CPC. A determined effort was made to promote Quebecois in the provincial party organization. This policy produced results that the LPP was to regret on several occasions.

Personal ambition and the lack of team spirit among French Canadian Communist leaders compounded the difficulties under which the LPP laboured in Quebec. The result was friction, the formation of factions and – in one instance – a major split in party ranks. The ostensible reason for this state of affairs was the relationship between party headquarters in Toronto and its Quebec wing. The French Canadian leaders in the LPP often felt that little progress could be made unless Buck granted them a higher degree of autonomy. Not that they wanted to liquidate the LPP, something they were sometimes accused of in the heat of controversy. In 1945 they actually rejected the proposal to turn the LPP in Quebec into an educational association, and to carry out the bulk of Communist activity through a broadly based party dedicated to social justice.[24]

The issue of autonomy for the Quebec wing of the LPP contributed to the dramatic walkout of Henri Gagnon and Everiste Dubé, a veteran Communist, at the provincial party convention in November 1947. Gagnon took with him a large number of Quebecois Communists and formed the Parti Communiste du Québec Français in 1948. The members of this splinter group were active in a number of fields and feuded with the LPP when they were not negotiating their re-entry into the mainstream of the Canadian Communist movement.

Equally damaging to the fortunes of the LPP was Duplessis's victory at the polls in 1944. The LPP put up few candidates in that election. The support the Communists gave to the provincial Liberals in several ridings was explained by Sam Carr in an article criticizing the "CCF's reckless anti-Liberal campaign." The Communists, on the other hand, "rose above narrow partisanship . . . guided . . . by the needs of the province and the people of Canada."[25]

In the wake of the Guzenko case in Ottawa, Duplessis once again applied the Padlock Act. Once again, the provincial and Montreal police harassed the Communists. Occasionally they would confiscate an issue of a Communist newspaper and raid meetings and offices of Communist organizations. Obstacles were placed in the way of Communists renting halls for public meetings. Attempts were made to prevent Communists from speaking on the radio, or Communist-led unions from receiving certification. At the height of the Cold War a determined effort was made to unseat a Communist alderman in Montreal. This effort succeeded when Duplessis introduced a bill in the Quebec legislature, specifically designed to oust the LPP representative. As a result of these anti-Communist measures, the LPP had to devote a great deal of energy, in and out of court, merely to preserve a semi-legal existence.

Although the Padlock Act helped to restrict the range of Communist activities in Quebec, it could not prevent the Montreal party organization from remaining the second largest in Canada. Ably led by Gui Caron and Harry Binder, the provincial organization of the LPP retained the allegiance of several hundred Quebecois and succeeded in forming several party clubs outside Montreal. Some of its candidates in provincial and federal elections polled more votes than their CCF opponents. In March 1956, Henri Gagnon and several of his associates rejoined the LPP in spite of misgivings about some aspects of the party program. Most of these hard-won successes were lost when later in the year many French and Jewish Communists left the LPP in disgust. Gagnon abandoned the LPP in 1958.

The desertion by French Canadian cadres, which the CPC-LPP had acquired and nursed at great cost, made it impossible for the Communists to make an appreciable impression on the Quebecois in the 1960s. The Communist failure to rally support in Quebec was a major weakness for an organization which claimed to represent the best elements of the working class in Canada, and to possess a scientific explanation of history. On the other hand, the Communist lack of influence in Quebec is not surprising if one remembers that the more respectable and intellectually better endowed democratic socialists also failed to make an impact on Quebecois politics.

When socialism began to gain ground among French Canadians, it came through neither the NDP nor the CPC. It reached Quebec via London and Paris, where a number of graduate students from Quebec became acquainted with the views of British Fabians and various groups of French Marxists and left-wing Catholics who occupied an uneasy position between the powerful French Communist party and the decaying Socialist party led by Guy Mollet. Marxism, as expounded in Paris, sounded attractive to those in need of an explanation for the backwardness of Quebec, and of a tool with which to modernize Quebecois society. It was these intellectuals who played an important role in stirring up public opinion against Duplessis and his successors. They also attacked the Quebecois Liberals for their subservience to Ottawa, and for their economic policies.

In this struggle the French Canadian intellectuals, who considered themselves Marxists or merely socialistically inclined, used slogans and arguments that had appeared in Communist publications at home or abroad. Like the CCF-NDP, they also attracted ex-members and sympathizers of the CPC in Quebec. These intellectuals formed study circles, published periodicals and talked to the local representatives of the CPC. The latter advocated "socialist unity" as the first step to a "genuinely broad national and democratic front," which would include the trade unions and the teachers, and "present a people's alternative to the bourgeois parties." In some instances, the CPC figured as one of the many groups participating in conferences and demonstrations held to denounce those in power in Ottawa and Quebec City.

For a short while the Communists felt that they were making progress. Sam Walsh, head of the party organization in Quebec, told his colleagues in 1965 that the "Communist Party is becoming accepted as part of the 'national liberation' front of Quebec by many groups, although there are still very serious reservations."[26] These reservations did not relate solely to the worldwide controversies that had contributed so much to the isolation of the CPC throughout Canada. In Quebec the task of the Communists was further complicated by the Communist attitude towards Canadian unity and the subordination of the Quebec wing of the CPC to the party centre in Toronto. Neither of these factors helped the "task of winning and holding French Canadian party members."

According to Walsh, the "root cause" lay in "our inconsistent and even timid defence of the right of French Canadians to self-determination." The fact that the CPC was "the only party in Quebec which has not got a distinctly or wholly independent Quebec structure" did not improve matters.

To strengthen the Communist appeal in a milieu that sounded so promising, the CPC decided in May 1965 to create, within the CPC, the Parti Communiste du Québec (PCQ). As the secretary of the CPC put it, the change "should undoubtedly help to extend" the party's "influence in the labour and democratic movement and among the genuinely national forces in Quebec." Electoral results showed that these hopes were premature. The occasional candidate put up by the PCQ in federal and provincial elections very seldom saved his deposit or gained more than a few hundred votes.

The struggle against the established order in Quebec and else-where contained strong anti-American undertones. Although the Communists always drew a distinction between what they called "progressive forces" in the United States on the one hand, and the powerful in Washington and Wall Street on the other, throughout the 1960s the CPC treated the U.S.A. as the leading imperialist power in the world, the rulers of which were capable of doing anything to thwart the awakening of the colonial peoples in the ex-western colonies, and to prevent the advancement of socialism.

The party continued to campaign for Canadian withdrawal from NATO and NORAD, called for Canadian neutrality, and hailed Soviet initiatives in the field of disarmament. During the Cuban missiles crisis in 1962, the CPC supported the Soviet government. It adopted a similar position at the time of the Six-Day War (1967) in the Middle East.

The sympathy of the Canadian Communists and the U.S.S.R. for the Arabs, and their strong criticism of the Israeli government, widened the gulf separating the CPC from the bulk of Jewish opin-ion in Canada. Nor did their pro-Arab attitude make it easy for the CPC to hold Jews in the party, or for party members to exert influence in organizations like the United Jewish People's Order. Prominent party members like Joe Zuken in Winnipeg criticized the Soviet attitude in the non-Communist press. Others who were active in pro-Communist Jewish Canadian circles took a far less critical attitude towards Israel than the central committee of the CPC. The latter, however, also came out in favour of the continued existence of Israel. This approach made it easier for the CPC to hold its members of Jewish descent, and through them to preserve tenuous links with the Jewish community, in which, however, the CPC exerts less influence today than ever before.[27]

Like other Communist parties in industrial societies, the CPC found it easier to back the CPSU and the U.S.S.R. in their dealings with the non-Communist world than with fellow-socialist states. This was shown in particular when the ramifications of the Sino-Soviet dispute, and the entry of Soviet troops into Prague (1968), spread to Canada.

The Canadian Communists admired the long struggle of their Chinese comrades against Chiang Kai-shek's Nationalists and the Japanese. They gave publicity to that struggle, and at least one Canadian Communist worked in the Comintern apparatus in the Far East during a crucial period in the history of the Chinese

Communist movement. Better known is the contribution of Dr. Norman Bethune, a member of the CPC and a veteran of the Spanish Civil War, who died from blood poisoning while treating Chinese Communist soldiers in 1939. Today he is one of the most venerated foreigners in the People's Republic of China.

The CPC hailed the victory of the Chinese Communists as a major blow against imperialism and capitalism, and called for the recognition of Mao Tse-tung's government. His writings appeared in bookstores run under CPC auspices. The worsening relations between Moscow and Peking affected the CPC when the Chinese began to distribute in Canada several pamphlets that were the stock in trade of the Chinese Communists in their attack against the Soviet leaders.

In an effort to prevent further deterioration in Sino-Soviet relations, two CPC leaders visited Peking in 1963. In their conversations with their Chinese hosts, Leslie Morris and William Kashtan found "no meeting of minds." The Chinese advocated revolutionary action, argued that the main centres of discontent were in the underdeveloped world, and insisted that Communists in industrial societies could best serve the common cause by supporting those already engaged in revolutionary activities in underdeveloped societies. They also suggested to their guests that the Communists in Canada should hang the democratic socialists.[28]

Distressed by what they had learned, the two CPC delegates returned to Canada via Moscow where they described their experiences to Khrushchev. After the trip to Peking and Moscow, the CPC continued to support the Soviet Union against Mao, whose policies at home and abroad were criticized in Canadian Communist publications with the same arguments as were used by the CPSU.

In the controversy with the dominant wing of the Communist Party of China, Buck, Morris and Kashtan carried the bulk of the elderly rank-and-file of the CPC. Little overt opposition was noticeable until a group of militants in Vancouver was expelled from the CPC in 1964. Led by Jack Scott, a native of the British Isles and a former shop steward, they formed the first of several Maoist organizations in Canada. The Progressive Workers Movement (PWM) attacked the CPC for its lack of revolutionary drive and its identification with Soviet "revisionism". At the same time the monthly *Progressive Worker* denounced American imperialism and advocated the formation of a new trade union centre independent of the AFL-CLC. The CPC retaliated by calling for the "isolation" of the PWM.

Before long the PWM was rent by dissension and had to take

second place to other Maoist groups with a similar program. The most articulate of these groups, the Internationalists, was founded in Vancouver in 1963. It consisted largely of students, some of whom were recent immigrants to Canada. In 1970 the Internationalists provided the nucleus for the Communist Party of Canada (Marxist-Leninist). The chief characteristics of this group were frequent purges in their ranks, the youth of its leaders and militants, a fervent belief in the applicability of Mao Tse-tung thought in Canada, a vocabulary based on the *Peking Review*, and a high degree of intolerance of other left-wing views and organizations. The hostility of these young Maoists extended to the Canadian Party of Labour, which for a time championed the Maoist cause in the Sino-Soviet dispute and in which several former U.S. citizens were active.

The Maoists won their chief successes in the very areas where they encountered no serious opposition from the CPC. On some campuses they achieved a certain amount of notoriety in confrontations with the university authorities. In Quebec they put up more candidates and won five times as many votes as the CPC in the 1972 federal election. Among the growing number of Chinese, East Indians and Blacks in Canada, the Maoists were more active and gained more support than the CPC. The CPC, in spite of its opposition to racial discrimination and its advocacy of reforms to improve the lot of the average immigrant from the Third World, failed to make the kind of headway that the Communists had achieved among Finns and Ukrainians in the 1920s. In the ranks of organized labour the Maoists were easily defeated by the more experienced and far more numerous trade union leaders associated with the NDP and the CPC.

The emergence of the Maoists was paralleled by the growing influence of the Trotskyists. Years of uphill struggle, of patient agitation and periodic attempts to infiltrate the CCF-NDP, at last began to show results in the 1960s. In the metropolitan centres the League for Socialist Action (LSA) and the Young Socialists attracted teenagers, students and young graduates, who were prepared to fight for a socialist Canada and an independent and unilingual Quebec. They took an active part in the campaign for peace in Vietnam, for major educational reforms at the universities, for abortion on demand, and for the rights of homosexuals, sponsored by the Trotskyist *Labor Challenge*. Although the turnover of supporters remained high and the LSA was not the only spokesman of the Trotskyist cause in Canada, Trotskyist agitation angered many democratic socialists and Communist veterans. The latter knew that Trotskyist strength lay in the very age groups where the CPC had been notoriously weak since the beginning of the Cold War.

Events in Czechoslovakia in 1968 provided additional ammunition for the Trotskyists and Maoists, and imposed new strains on the leaders of the CPC who were groping for a way to rejuvenate the party and re-establish its influence. The difficulties they experienced in agreeing on a Communist approach to Canadian problems were compounded by their realization that success or failure in Canada, and the image of the CPC, could not be divorced from what the U.S.S.R. and the pro-Moscow Communist parties were doing in other parts of the world.

Some party leaders were prepared to identify themselves completely with the U.S.S.R. in public. They were appalled when on several occasions the CPC and mass organizations indulged in mild criticism of some aspect of Soviet nationality policy. They were annoyed when those of their colleagues who also had the reputation of being die-hards found it politic not to express their views in a manner that was fashionable under Stalin. Both these groups of leaders distrusted prominent Communists who were seeking a way of turning the CPC into an organization that would be less closely identified with the CPSU, and bolder in its search for allies among non-Communist opponents of the Establishment in Canada.

Czechoslovakia became a battleground over which the leaders clashed, even before the entry of Soviet troops into Prague in August 1968. To some extent, Canadian Communist appreciation of developments in Prague depended on the dispatches sent by John Boyd, a well-known member of the CPC in the 1960s. He had been secretary of the pro-Communist Canadian Slav Committee after the war, editor of the *Canadian Tribune* after 1956, and a member of the politbureau of the CPC before he became associated with the editorial board of the *World Marxist Review* in Prague. The articles he wrote for the *Tribune* displayed broad sympathy for Dubcek's efforts to liberalize the Communist regime in Czechoslovakia. At first, Boyd's dispatches received great publicity in the *Tribune*, which published them under such headings as "Program strengthens socialist relations" and "differing views and ideas."

Before long, however, key members of the CPC realized that the CPSU was becoming increasingly upset by the course of events in Prague. Prominent Canadian Communists who went to eastern Europe that summer soon became aware of how suspicious the Soviet leaders were of Dubcek's intentions. Hence the unwillingness of the CPC to establish close contacts with their Czechoslovak colleagues.

As soon as Soviet troops entered Prague on August 20, 1968, the politbureau of the CPC criticized the Soviet move and called for "an early withdrawal of all foreign troops" from Czechoslovakia. The communiqué attributed the unhappy state of affairs in Czechoslovakia "not only to the intrigues of enemies of socialism but, facilitating these, the presence of unresolved problems of socialist development and socialist democracy."[29]

For the first time since 1956 the CPC came out unequivocally against a major aspect of Soviet foreign policy. No sooner had the CPC made its views known than the party leadership began to retreat from its position. By October 1968 a communiqué, issued over the signature of the central committee, reversed the politbureau's original stand. It rejected those aspects of the August 21, 1968 communiqué which gave "expression to the false position that the entry of Warsaw Pact troops into Czechoslovakia was not in the interests of socialism."[30]

These communiqués reflected tensions and disagreements within the CPC. The first communiqué was a compromise, because there were members of the politbureau who wanted to condemn Soviet intervention in stronger terms. They echoed the views of several other Communist parties, which adopted a more critical stand on the subject of Soviet policy in Czechoslovakia than the CPC's. The second communiqué in October 1968 represented a shift of emphasis which once again was not confined to the CPC. In Canada, however, it represented an attempt to align the CPC with the CPSU. It was also a concession to the die-hards, who shuddered at the thought of the CPC opposing the Soviet Union. According to a leading party official who shared these sentiments, a "wave of membership meetings across the country" demanded "a clear statement in support" of Soviet intervention in Czechoslovakia.[31]

Soviet policy in the neighbouring Ukraine proved to be another source of embarrassment to Kashtan and his colleagues. The high proportion of Ukrainians in the CPC, and their financial sacrifices for the Communist movement, assured the spokesmen of these Ukrainians an important role in the party. They often acted as watchdogs, and as a powerful pressure group which ensured loyalty to the CPSU. Not that the Ukrainian Communists always found it easy to identify with certain trends in the CPC. In 1928 the leaders of the ULFTA complained at the Sixth Congress of the Comintern about their treatment from Buck. Although the matter was patched up, thanks to the plan to involve Ukrainian Communists in agitation outside the Ukrainian community, friction arose again in the mid-1930s. This time a former secretary of the Ukrainian Agitprop Committee of the CPC complained about

Soviet policies in the Ukraine. T. Kobzey and his associates were expelled from the CPC and denounced in the party press.

In the next three decades there were few overt signs of dissent among Ukrainian Canadian Communists, although M. Popovic had doubts about the Stalinist version of the Great Purge. Their immunity to Salsberg's arguments in 1956 was so total that one of the most prominent Communists of Ukrainian extraction could boast,

> We are proud . . . there have been no resignations from membership or positions among membership, that our members have not succumbed to pressures of hysteria and liquidationism.[32]

In the mid-1960s, however, disagreements among Ukrainian Communists in Canada broke out openly. Once again, events outside Canada were the cause of the crisis. In the heyday of destalinization in the U.S.S.R., Soviet spokesmen admitted that there had been breaches of "socialist legality" in the Ukraine, and that a number of Ukrainians, including faithful party members, had lost their lives due to the "cult of personality." Such statements confirmed what anti-Communist Ukrainians in Canada had stated more than once in arguments with their pro-Communist compatriots. Worse was to follow when a disillusioned veteran of the CPC returned from Kiev.

John Kolasky had been selected to attend the Higher Party School of the central committee of the Communist Party of the Ukraine in 1963. Disturbed by living and working conditions and shocked by the extent of russification in the Ukraine, he protested; he was arrested and expelled from the U.S.S.R. in 1965. On his return to Canada Kolasky described his experiences. With the help of printed material which he smuggled out of the Soviet Union, he wrote two books to prove his contentions.

Kolasky's revelations added to the soul-searching already going on among pro-Communist Ukrainians in Canada. He touched a sore point, since one of the strongest planks of Communist propaganda among Ukrainian Canadians was the Soviet encouragement of Ukrainian culture, something that the Communists liked to contrast with the policies of tsarist Russia and Poland.

For a time the leaders of the CPC tried to ward off the demands of several prominent Ukrainian Canadian Communists to send a delegation to investigate the situation on the spot. When the pressure became irresistible, the CPC leaders suggested a compromise solution. They accepted the idea of a delegation to the Ukraine, but arranged for it to include Buck and William Ross, the leader of the CPC in Manitoba, in addition to Communists of Ukrainian extraction.

After spending three weeks in the U.S.S.R. in 1967, and talking to Soviet leaders in Kiev and Moscow, the delegation submitted a report, which was not published in the *Canadian Tribune*, but only in an internal bulletin distributed to party members.[33] The report agreed indirectly with some of the charges Kolasky had made. When Soviet pressure failed to prevent the publication of the report, twenty-eight well-known Soviet Ukrainians signed a letter which was published in the Ukrainian-language-weekly *Zhyttia i slovo* in Toronto. They denied the charges made by the visitors, and drew attention to the fact that anti-Communist Ukrainians were using the delegation's report in their campaign against the U.S.S.R. In October 1969 the CPC took an important step to placate the CPSU. The central committee of the CPC withdrew the report of the delegation to the Ukraine "as an official document of the Party."

This move did not end the secret debate that had been going on since 1956 in Ukrainian Canadian circles associated with the CPC. A growing number of Canadian tourists returned with stories that did not convey a picture of progress, happiness and material abundance in the Soviet Ukraine. Many of them also brought back the news that they were not allowed to visit their relatives in the Ukrainian countryside. The point was made often enough to induce some delegates to AUUC conventions to complain about restrictions on the movement of tourists in the Ukraine.

The reaction of the Ukrainian Canadian Communists to these conflicting reports depended to a large extent on the positions they held in the CPC and the mass organizations for Ukrainians. While Salsberg and his friends took with them many party members of Jewish extraction when they left the CPC in 1956-1957, the Ukrainian rank-and-file of the CPC and AUUC was by and large inclined to accept the official Soviet version. The sceptics were prominent members of the mass organizations. In private several of them continued to press for further investigations, and challenged the explanations given by party headquarters in Toronto and Kiev.

The CPC, however, did not retaliate with expulsion, except in the case of Kolasky. The party could not afford drastic solutions, because the dissenters still held a lot of influence among Ukrainians and they had not indulged in public criticism of the U.S.S.R. Nevertheless, there was a movement to bring these Ukrainians to heel. Several of Buck's followers from the Prairies expressed such sentiments, but they were hardly representative of the higher echelons of the CPC. Kashtan and his associates wanted to avoid further loss of membership and subscriptions to the party treasury. To achieve this, they had to manoeuvre carefully between competing pressure groups. They also had to deal with missives from the CPSU, and not very subtle moves by members of the Soviet embassy in Ottawa. The Russians were eager to promote to key positions in the CPC and the mass organizations, the Ukrainian Canadian Communists who had given proof of loyalty to the Soviet cause.

The continued identification of the CPC with the U.S.S.R. and the party's isolation in Canadian politics had two major results in the 1960s. It led to the resignation of several intellectuals whom the CPC could ill afford to lose. Unlike the intellectuals who broke with the Communist movement in 1956-1957, these intellectuals left the CPC quite undramatically. Some merely declined to stand for re-election to leading party bodies in 1969, and then allowed their membership to lapse. In very few instances did the CPC broadcast the fact that they had left its ranks, let alone expel them for political deviation, although their departure was the result of growing political differences over a number of years. The disagreements revolved around the relationship between the CPC and the CPSU and Communist tactics in Canada. The critics advocated looser links with Moscow and a stance such as the Italian Communist Party seemed to have achieved in its dealings with the CPSU. The CPC's domestic policies also came under fire; at least one of those who gave up his party membership was in favour of a more sympathetic attitude towards French Canadians fighting for an independent Quebec.

Those who left the party included two former members of the politbureau: John Boyd and S. B. Ryerson. Boyd was of Ukrainian extraction, had spent over thirty years in the Communist movement, and had worked for almost as long on the staff of Canadian Communist newspapers. Ryerson held a number of important positions in the party apparatus in Montreal and Toronto. For a time he also had been associated with the English edition of the organ of the Cominform in Bucharest. To most non-Communists he is best-known as the most sophisticated Marxist historian in Canada, the author of several books which threw new light on the forces which helped to shape the Dominion of Canada.

The continuing identification of the CPC with the U.S.S.R. in the 1960s also made it more difficult for the Communists to appeal to the young. Despite the malaise among politically conscious students in the 1960s, the CPC was unable to replenish its ranks, though the party leaders displayed some interest in the young even after the dissolution of the YCL in 1942.

The YCL was replaced by a Labor Youth Federation in the later stages of the war. Early in 1945, the LPP toyed with the idea of launching a more broadly based youth organization as part of the Liberal-Labor Coalition proposal. Steps were taken to form a Federation of Democratic Youth.[34] The plan was shelved in the wake of Duclos' attack on Browder.

In 1945 the Labor Youth Federation became the National Federation of Labor Youth (NFLY). For three years the NFLY was largely a federation of the youth sections of mass organizations, like the AUUC, the Finnish Organization and the United Jewish People's Order. In 1948 the NFLY was transformed into an organization based on individual membership. Young workers provided half the members, and high school students most of the remainder. University students associated with the Communist movement enrolled in the LPP clubs established on several campuses. They took an active part in student politics and were elected to mock parliaments on half a dozen campuses.

Elsewhere, young Communists engaged in various activities. They sold the *Champion*, the organ of the NFLY, for a time ran a youth parliament in Toronto, played a prominent role in several strikes and helped to build a railway in Yugoslavia before Stalin's denunciation of Tito. In addition, the NFLY placed

> considerable emphasis upon Marxist book-learning, political action in line with (and often identical to) the campaigns of the LPP, frequent meetings, monthly dues, heavy financial commitments, etc.

> In 1953 this type of organization was seen to be incompatible with the interests of Canadian socialist-minded youth, and a change was made in this 'party like' concept of the NFLY.

An attempt was made

> to bring into the organization many young people who are not necessarily interested in studying Marxism or participating in political campaigns, but who are interested in the NFLY program and activities. This was done by "lightening" the conditions of membership, by providing activities and by making clubs more attractive.[35]

These changes did not "result in a rapid and constant growth of the NFLY." Instead it continued to decline. It had 2,500 members in 1947, about 800 in 1951-1952 and 600 on the eve of the party crisis in 1956. It was left to Bill Willmott, one of the more able NFLY leaders, to lament the fact that "we remain" [in 1956] an insignificantly small organization."

He advocated in place of the NFLY a more widely-based youth organization to foster patriotism and to compete

> with the best in other organizations: song groups of high calibre, sports teams, dances, etc. . . . our concept of campaigns should be changed, with a more flexible attitude towards forms and less pressure to carry out any one form, and more modest goals in each campaign. Most important of all, membership should not include acceptance of a Marxist interpretation of events, a condition that is not stated, but is in the conception of membership that many have.[36]

By the time the theoretical organ of the LPP published these proposals, the NFLY, like the LPP, was in turmoil. Its secretary, Steve Endicott, and his predecessor Norman Penner, sided with Buck's opponents during the crucial confrontations in the autumn of 1956. So did a number of young Communists, mainly in Montreal and Toronto, who left the Communist movement in disgust.

The NFLY never recovered from the crisis. After an unsuccessful attempt to operate under the label of "Socialist Youth League", the YCL was launched again in May 1960. Frequent name changes did not increase the appeal of the Communist youth movement. Its ineffectiveness did, however, make it a source of controversy and recrimination in Communist ranks.[37] Some members blamed the state of the YCL on party officials, who neglected "youth work" and ignored the efforts of young Communists. Others complained that the party's attitude to its youth organization was wrong. Several felt that, given the temper of the Canadian youth, a YCL closely associated with the CPC could not obtain appreciable support. A veteran Communist pointed out that there were comrades who asked why so few youngsters were eager to join the CPC while the New Left had no difficulty in recruiting supporters. Hard-liners were sceptical of attempts to build a broadly based youth movement in which non-Marxists would be welcome. Some activists claimed that the creation of special youth clubs divided the party along age lines. Kashtan at one stage attributed the YCL's lack of appeal to the "too conservative" image of the CPC.

Although the "youth question" was the subject of many discussions, informal or otherwise, and although the party bulletin *Viewpoint* aired a variety of proposals which were tried out in turn in the 1960s, the leaders of the CPC found it difficult to decide on how to proceed. In 1964-1965 they allowed the central apparatus of the YCL to disintegrate. No sooner had the YCL disappeared for all practical purposes than the CPC began insisting on the need for "a turn to the youth" and urged the rebuilding of the YCL. The pressure to do so was evident, especially after the entry of Soviet troops into Prague. Some of the younger Communists who criticized Kashtan on several other issues opposed this Soviet move. Among them was the editor of *Scan*, the YCL organ, who was also a member of the central committee of the CPC. When he and several middle-rank Communists on the west coast were expelled from the CPC in the autumn of 1968, the *Pacific Tribune* accused him of removing "without authorization . . . a substantial sum of money and the mailing plates of the magazine."[38]

The leader of the CPC was aware of the difficulties faced by the party in its agitation among the young. He warned the delegates to the twentieth party congress in 1969 that the task of "building" a Communist youth organization "will not be easy."[39] His statement came at the end of a decade which saw a rapid increase in the number of students, including those specializing in the social sciences or exposed to some of the rudiments of Marxism, and the appointment of a significant number of university teachers who were highly critical of the established order. All these factors offered fertile ground for anyone wanting to question the basic assumptions of Canadian society and to advocate some form of socialism. The arrival of thousands of young Americans during the same decade strengthened the propensity to emulate American protest movements, which engaged in direct confrontation with the authorities in universities and elsewhere.

The CPC welcomed these stirrings at the universities, although, according to Kashtan, "our Party has been slow in understanding the underlying factors which give force to the growing rebellion among students." The questioning of Canada's role in NATO, growing disenchantment with U.S. foreign policy and American politics in general, and widespread opposition among young Canadian intellectuals to American economic and cultural penetration, followed to some extent the approach pioneered by the CPC.

What was galling to party leaders and veterans was the fact that the overwhelming majority of those who denounced capitalism and the political system in North America were not associated with the CPC and showed no inclination towards joining it. Those who did not support the Maoists or Trotskyists sympathized with some segment of the New Left. The publications of the New Left drew their inspiration either from non-Soviet Communists like Che

Guevara, or from thinkers and militants who were not active in the pro-Moscow Communist parties in the 1960s. Some of these thinkers, like Herbert Marcuse, had even been attacked in Communist publications in the U.S.S.R. at the same time as in pro-Soviet journals in the West.

The spokesmen of the New Left concentrated most of their fire on the economic and political Establishment in North America. Occasionally the U.S.S.R. would be attacked for its nuclear tests, for interfering in the affairs of East European countries, and for its unwillingness to give more concrete aid to revolutionary forces fighting the United States and its allies in the underdeveloped parts of the world. Economic reforms in the Soviet Union received short shrift, because they were regarded by the New Left as a concession to the consumer society which the radicals disliked in the New World.

Another source of controversy between the CPC and the New Left was the failure of many radical students to look on the working class as the vanguard of any meaningful movement for social change. Even more disturbing to the Communists was the unwillingness of most New Leftists to accept the need for a Leninist type of party, let alone to recognize the CPC as the vehicle for the social and economic transformation of Canada. In so far as the New Left paid any attention to the CPC, which was very seldom, it was merely to deplore the chances that the CPC had missed in previous years and to castigate the Communists for their constant support of Soviet policies.

These disagreements, compounded by differences of age and life style, contributed to the CPC's difficulties in meeting the challenge of the New Left. Communist attitudes towards the New Left veered from dogmatic rejection of the proposals put forward by those who were neither Maoists not Trotskyists, to what was described by a leading Communist official, in a veiled attack on his colleagues, as " . . . the mistaken view that out of the New Left forces the party would grow in numbers and influence and the only obstacle to this was 'our ingrained sectarianism'."[40]

Torn by conflicting proposals for "youth work", enmeshed in its own past and half-aware that the inchoate New Left represented a wide range of shifting attitudes, the CPC found it impossible to rally these people who were among the most strident Canadian opponents of the status quo and most eager to confront anyone considered to be a representative of the Establishment.

The main hope of the CPC lies in the probability that North American society will continue to breed articulate radical students, and that developments in North America will sooner or later bring about a differentiation in their ranks. A growing number of these young people, the Communists believe, will realize that a closely knit organization based on the principles of Marxism-Leninism is absolutely necessary to create socialism, and will accept the CPC as that organization. Modest increases in the numerical size of the YCL in the early 1970s offered a glimmer of hope to those party members who were well aware of the Communist failure to make an impact among students in the 1960s.

Conclusion

The Communist movement in Canada has been in existence for over fifty-five years. During that time it has sometimes been driven underground, while on other occasions it has operated as a political party with major electoral ambitions. At one time or another it has been active in practically every part of Canada west of Ottawa. It has also made periodic attempts to establish a network of party organizations in the Maritimes and Quebec. It has sold or distributed party literature in large quantities. Its leaders have spoken on the radio and addressed crowds varying in size and enthusiasm. In one way or another most Canadians outside the Maritimes and Quebec have been exposed to at least some Communist slogans and have had the opportunity of buying Communist publications.

The reactions of people who have come into contact with the Communists have varied a great deal. Most of them have been nonplussed or unimpressed, and given no further thought to the party and its program. Others have developed more definite views on the subject of the CPC, ranging all the way from dismissing Communists as "mugs and thugs" to the more flattering definition of the CPC as the "vanguard of the Canadian working class".

Those who were prepared to probe deeper before making up their minds about the CPC were invariably struck by the effort involved in launching and maintaining a viable Communist movement in Canada. No other political party in Canada expected its leaders and members to sacrifice so much of their time, energy and income. In return, the CPC offered few material incentives to most of its members, and little favourable publicity. Communists had to defend unpopular policies which repeatedly antagonized their compatriots when not leaving them indifferent. They were also kept busy on humdrum tasks which often produced mediocre results and provided few opportunities for self-aggrandizement outside the Communist party.

These sacrifices imposed such a strain on a person's energy, freedom, family life and powers of imagination that only a minority of party members was willing to make the necessary effort over a long period of time. Most others displayed less zeal, or simply left the party in disappointment over what they had seen and what was expected from them.

Those who remained in the party were moved by other considerations. The most important was a faith which was religious in its intensity. Moscow, as a leading Communist put it, was their "Mecca", the Bolshevik revolution the harbinger of things to come, and victory in Canada not too far away. A prominent Communist in Alberta reflected this optimism when he confessed, in 1929, that "the nearness of the world revolution" was "a fairly general existing opinion" for "a number of years, at least for the first few years of the C.P. of C."[1]

The Depression provided another incentive to persevere. The breakdown of the old order seemed so obvious that, with a bit of imagination, party members could compare the situation in North America in 1931-1932 with that in Russia before the Bolshevik takeover. A member of the politbureau in the early 1930s expressed this mood when he wrote, "Were it not for a 'perspective', I should feel like taking up a homestead."[2]

The successful struggle against Hitler, and Communist victories in eastern Europe and Asia, provided additional evidence that socialism was supplanting capitalism, and that the world was moving in a direction desired by Canadian Communists. Sooner or later changes in Asia and Europe were bound to affect the nature of society in North America and the ratio of forces in Canada. This faith buoyed up the Communists when the tide was running against them during the Cold War. According to one of their Ontario leaders, after the Second World War they talked "about '10 years' to a socialist Canada."[3]

This faith in the inevitability of their victory was sustained by two factors. To begin with, most Communist leaders were self-taught men who thought that they had found, in the Marxist-Leninist doctrine, an explanation for, and a solution to, both their own problems and the world's ills. They absorbed what they could of the doctrine by hurriedly reading pamphlets and editorials, by attending party schools and by listening to speeches delivered by people sharing their own social and educational background. The material at their disposal may have seemed biased, simplistic and dreary to a scholar in his study; but to party officials and aspirants to party office this material confirmed what they already vaguely believed in, and provided them with additional arguments as they went about their daily work.

Their outlook can best be understood if one bears in mind that they did not consider themselves as merely members of a small party fighting an uphill battle, but as part and parcel of a world-wide movement that had many victories to its credit. McEwen explained this mood succinctly in a letter to his friends in Vancouver after watching the parade in Moscow on the anniversary of the October Revolution.

> When we meet, as we often do, in good comrade Betty's room, we sometimes go away feeling we are only a small group of people who like to be together, but do not cut much ice in the scheme of things. A day in the Red Square banishes all such gloomy notions.[4]

They were convinced that the Bolsheviks had built the prototype of a society in every way superior to what any Canadian government had done, or was likely to do, regardless of whether the old-line parties or the democratic socialists were in power. The achievements of the Bolsheviks were always contrasted with the failure of successive federal governments to deal with pressing Canadian problems.

Second, the CPC was able to strengthen this belief in the uniqueness of the Soviet experiment through its party network and mass organizations. Its greatest victories were won among the unassimilated and poor East Europeans, living in isolated communities west of Ottawa, or leading a ghetto-like existence in certain metropolitan centres before the days everyone owned a TV and car. To them the CPC was not merely a party that would solicit their votes at election time and attack the powerful all the year round: it was also a movement which enriched their lives through a variety of cultural and recreational activities, which enabled them to maintain a link, however tenuous, with the part of Europe they came from, and which protected them, or at least gave the impression of defending them, in a society that seemed alien and harsh.

The leaders of the CPC attached a great deal of importance to extra-parliamentary activities. They realized that however great the emphasis on electioneering, that alone would not bring about the desired end. They knew from their own experience that the CPC could only broaden its narrow popular base by displaying great drive and imagination in the "day-to-day struggles of the masses." The CPC, after all, won its most durable successes when it succeeded in merging into the communities where it agitated, when it became part of the ethnic scene, when it defended those segments of society, urban or otherwise, which felt deprived or ignored by more conventional forces in Canadian politics.

A disposition to accept simple explanations and solutions, and a readiness to apply certain organizational precepts borrowed from abroad and largely alien to the Canadian political system, created a Communist sub-culture in some parts of Canada. Its members led lives different from those of most Canadians. The attention they paid to events outside Canada, their sustained interest in public affairs, and their involvement in various organizations, set them as much apart from the non-Communists in whose midst they lived as did the views propagated by the Communists.

To the outside world the members of this sub-culture presented a brave front, regardless of whether they pursued popular or unpopular policies. They claimed they had the answers, the organizational know-how, and the men to resolve the dilemmas and cope with the crises that confronted Canadian society. The self-confidence they displayed in public stood them in good stead, until Khrushchev decided to lift the veil from Stalin's record. The ramifications of destalinization speeded up the decline of the Communist movement in Canada, reducing it to a group of elderly and middle-aged men and women. In spite of bickerings over tactics and personalities, they stuck together because they had a great deal in common. Faith in the Soviet Union remained an important factor; force of habit was another. Hostility to the outside world was a third. And then there were memories of exploits in past days when they had made several notable constribstions to the lives of thousands of Canadians.

To begin with, it was largely under the impact of events in Russia between 1917 and 1920 that immigrants from eastern Europe became for the first time a definite force in Canadian politics, a force that neither the federal government nor the politicians in Winnipeg, Regina and Edmonton could afford to ignore, however much they disliked the attitudes and activities of these pro-Communists. It was through the Communist movement that thousands of East Europeans broadened their horizons in Canada and acquired skills which, though rudimentary in many instances, enabled the immigrants to play a modest role in public life and community affairs as members, and later on as ex-members, of the CPC.

The Communists taught them the advantages of group action in a mass society, the importance of applying pressure through certain channels, the need for organization, punctuality and planning. The party gave them confidence by encouraging them to write articles for the Communist press, to speak at public meetings, and to perform simple tasks in various committees set up by the CPC to mobilize its forces and find allies. The acquisition of these skills speeded up their integration into capitalist society, increased their upward social mobility, and enriched their daily lives. They gained a feeling of accomplishment when they spoke under Communist auspices, and when non-Communists stopped to listen, argue or agree with them, supporting them at election time or marching behind them in demonstrations.

The feeling of accomplishment, and of occasional euphoria when success seemed to warrant it, could not prevent doubt from creeping in during those frequent periods when, even with the best will, little could be done, although party leaders were insisting on greater efforts and were searching for scapegoats. Members responded to these pressures and investigations from above in two ways. Some, regardless of ethnic origin, displayed renewed zeal. Others showed less interest in their party assignments, with the result that those in charge were confirmed in their suspicions that the person under investigation was failing or unreliable.

The suspect and the disenchanted often sought consolation in drink, the scourge of many a disappointed leader and militant whose political future was uncertain and whose days in the Communist movement were numbered. Once they left the CPC, there was a wide choice of roads to follow. A few found solace among the Trotskyists, others in the CCF-NDP. In many instances so great was their disappointment that nothing would induce them to make new sacrifices for any public cause.

Their reasons for disappointment with the CPC covered a wide spectrum. People who had accepted the Communist explanation for the CPC's isolation from the mainstream of Canadian politics, and the reasons for the party's identification with the U.S.S.R., were often deeply disturbed by the cliquism, wire-pulling, spitefulness and abuse of authority existing at every level of the Communist movement. Although these phenomena were not confined to Communist parties, they contributed to the high turnover of party members and the small numerical size of the CPC.

Many of those who joined the CPC did so because they thought, or were led to believe, that the Communists were different from and superior to other mortals. They were disagreeably surprised when many manifestations of human frailty seemed more pronounced in the CPC than in other organizations. The party's hierarchical structure, its highly ambitious goals, drastic changes in the party line, and the heavy pressure to donate time and money, created tensions which in turn produced uncomradely behaviour and contributed to many desertions.

Others left simply because they were bored. The sight of the same old faces at party meetings in often dingy surroundings, the sound of the same voice expounding at great length the rudiments of Marxism-Leninism, the constant references to what Marx, Engels and Lenin had written, and the dreary jargon used to explain developments at home and abroad, drove hundreds of members away from the party.

Not that a prolonged stay in the Communist movement was something that could easily be erased from one's mind, even if one quickly found other friendships, causes and interests. For years to come many an ex-Communist was influenced by what he had learned as a party member about the nature of industrial society, its evolution, the impact of imperialism, the role of a political organization. The knowledge gained as a member of the CPC affected the stand that many took in public affairs after leaving the Communist movement.

Although scepticism had replaced faith, many ex-Communists retained their social conscience, which led them into involvement in community affairs, the trade unions and the CCF-NDP. Often their preference for gradual reforms marked their break with Stalinist theories and practices they had resolutely defended in the past. By and large, the ex-Communists who did not abandon politics altogether tended to support movements of social change. In many instances their influence after leaving the CPC-LPP was greater than it had been when they were Communist activists and leaders. By joining the NDP and placing their organizational know-how at its disposal, and at that of the trade union movement and certain pressure groups, they enabled other critics of the status quo to challenge established institutions and conventional wisdom with greater skill and self-confidence. This contribution cannot be acknowledged by the CPC because the failure to retain the membership of people nursed and trained in the party raises too many awkward questions for party spokesmen.

Another Communist contribution to the quality of Canadian life was the campaign on behalf of the unemployed. In the early stages of the Depression, the CPC was the only Dominion-wide political party which consistently fought alongside and on behalf of the unemployed, drew attention to their plight and demanded some action. The CPC-led campaign forced the authorities to grant more relief and to introduce unemployment insurance legislation.

Less dramatic but equally important was the Communist role in the unionization drive in the 1930s, which employers and various layers of government opposed. More than once, Communist initiatives, zeal and organizational talents enabled the trade unions to survive and enrol more members. Ironically, the pioneering work of the Communists helped to strengthen their rivals. Building on foundations laid in many instances by party members, the unions were able to attract hundreds of thousands of workers and take the credit for better working and living conditions across Canada.

Over the years the Communists have made a number of other claims. They have insisted that they were the first to give warning about the American takeover of the Canadian economy, the first to draw attention to the less edifying aspects of American foreign policy, the first to suggest that the BNA Act be freely re-negotiated by the representatives of English and French-speaking Canada, the first to campaign for this or that piece of social legislation.

Although some of these claims cannot be dismissed out of hand, the fact remains that the CPC failed to generate much interest and support when it raised these and other controversial issues. Growing awareness of these issues only came when they were raised by less radical critics, associated in many instances with the CCF-NDP, who roused public opinion and obliged the federal government to act. In the debates and campaigns which preceded government action, the original Communist initiative was seldom noted; groups and individuals opposed to the Communists received the credit. In many instances the non-Communists could argue in all honesty that they had reached certain conclusions independently of the Communists, whose viewpoint and proposals were unknown to them.

The reasons for the Communist failure to change Canadian society become obvious considering the severe handicaps under which the Communists always operated. The ethnic composition of the party, the inability to strike deep roots among trade unionists in the 1920s, the failure to retain that nucleus of intellectuals who served the party faithfully until the events of 1956, all this reduced the CPC-LPP to what Salsberg described as, "by and large . . . a party of restricted groups and of specific electoral areas, of little islands in the great national scene."[5]

The established order did its best to ensure that the Communists would never become a major force in Canadian politics, nor, except in the latter stages of the Second World War, a leading force among Canadian labour. Anti-Communist propaganda, the harrying of activists, the victimization or threat of victimization of militants in some walks of life, and legal action, helped to minimize the Communist movement.

Government measures against Communists, however, also

divided informed public opinion and led to controversies inside Parliament and out. They also raised the question of the extent to which Canadian political institutions lived up to the democratic ideal proclaimed by those in office. On several occasions confrontation with the Communists exposed the dilemma of those who thought that liberal democracy faced a stark choice of either doing nothing, and watching helplessly while the Communists undermined the Canadian political system and society, or of resorting to repressive measures against a small minority which did not share the same values as the great majority of the nation. By their reliance on coercion, these moderates revealed the limitations of their own liberalism, and their lack of faith in the ability of Canadians to cope with a genuinely revolutionary challenge by democratic means. The fact that the CPC strongly supported the U.S.S.R. clouded the issue of civil rights. It enabled anti-Communists, eager to ban the CPC, to argue with some justification that the CPC was not an ordinary political party, and that it should be treated as an outpost of an ambitious great power.

The Communists contributed to their own isolation by needlessly antagonizing a wide spectrum of Canadian opinion. Often they only realized what damage they had done after it was too late. Nor did they improve matters by sometimes treating various different shades of public opinion as one hostile bloc united in their desire to crush the Communists and the U.S.S.R. It was only after the Comintern line had changed that Buck could warn his colleagues, "We cannot afford to lump all capitalist parties and movements into one heap."[6]

Communist jargon, many of their slogans, the sudden shifts in the party line, and their attempts to control any organization they could lay their hands on, repelled many people. Others were dissuaded from joining by the CPC association with and glorification of the Soviet Union. This was so pronounced a trait that some observers have attributed Communist defeats to the party's identification with a foreign power. Many ex-Communists would agree with this explanation. They remember only too well the shouts of "Moscow gold" or "Soviet agents" when they canvassed or spoke at public meetings.

On the other hand, the association of the Canadian Communists with the U.S.S.R. was in many ways beneficial to the struggling Communist movement. Excluding financial assistance, the magnitude of which is uncertain, the CPC derived several advantages from being part of a dynamic worldwide movement. It could bask in the glory of the Soviet Union whenever the U.S.S.R. presented an attractive face to the western world. It could point out that its own proposals were not utopian because they had already been tried out and proved to work in the "socialist sixth of the world." Some of its leaders were educated in establishments run by the CPSU. Although the training they received was often inappropriate under Canadian conditions, they gained insight into a society virtually unknown to most Canadians.

More important perhaps was and is the Bolshevik insistence on certain organizational patterns such as democratic centralism, the system of cells, party fractions in mass organizations, the need for a nucleus of full-time officials, and the involvement of Finnish and Ukrainian Communists in the broader context of the Canadian Communist movement. It is doubtful whether the CPC would have achieved such success as it did achieve, if it had not made great use of the experience of the CPSU and employed its limited manpower accordingly. The Comintern emphasis on extra-parliamentary activities, and on Popular Front tactics, also helped the CPC to strike deep roots and to blend into the Canadian scene.

It is a moot point, however, whether CPSU advice compensated for the grave errors committed by the CPC when it applied, or thought that it was applying, the advice and directives it received on other issues and occasions. More than once the Canadian Communists adopted Bolshevik policies, tactics and assessments of trends in the world economy that were highly controversial, to say the least. Attempts to transplant to North America plans and forecasts prepared by people unfamiliar with conditions in Canada often had damaging consequences.

All the major crises that shook the CPC-LPP and divided its leadership, all the losses of membership and influence, were caused by events and changes in other countries and other Communist parties. The electoral performance of the CPC-LPP depended as much on what the U.S.S.R. did and stood for at the time, as on what the Canadian Communists had done or proposed to do at the riding or ward levels. Forecasts transmitted from Moscow and refurbished by leaders and theoreticians in Toronto, seldom increased the credibility of Communist propaganda in Canada. An Anglo-American war did not break out in 1929, a major slump did not materialize in the late 1940s, the Soviet Union did not provide its citizens with a standard of living superior to that of the leading industrial societies in the 1960s, the "monolithic unity" of Communist parties did not survive Stalin's death.

Few Canadian Communist leaders were in a mood to question Soviet policies and prognostications in public, or to urge their supporters to do so. Buck epitomized their attitude when he settled an argument with Salsberg with the words, "What is good for the

Central Committee of the CPSU, is good enough for me."[7] Set in their ways, the elderly leaders of the CPC carried on as best and for as long as they could. Petty intrigues, as they jockeyed for positions and favours, occupied much of their time. As always, they basked in any Soviet successes, and defended Soviet policies more or less convincingly.

Their reliance on the Soviet model and Soviet initiatives has been criticized by their opponents in the political arena and by those who left the CPC-LPP in despair. And yet it must be remembered that the Communists did not pioneer in left-wing circles this reliance on Messiahs and foreign panaceas. Before 1914 small groups of socialists in Canada looked for inspiration and guidance south of the border, to a Daniel De Leon, to a Eugene Debs or to Bill Hayward. Many immigrants from the United Kingdom admired Keir Hardie. What was new in the case of the Communists was the degree to which they were prepared to worship foreign leaders, support policies decided abroad, and ignore important evidence until foreign Communists took the initiative to draw attention to it.

The only alternative to identification with the U.S.S.R. would have been a determined attempt to break, or at any rate considerably loosen, the close ties between the CPC and the CPSU. Such a policy would have created so much turmoil and confusion among Canadian Communists that the idea was never seriously entertained by most leaders of the CPC-LPP. Nor did the ex-Communists' repeated failure to form a strong revolutionary Marxist organization independent of Moscow encourage those who toyed with that idea in North America.

Identification with the CPSU thus became a mixture of conviction, habit and self-interest, buttressed by the realization that the CCF-NDP had largely pre-empted the field of left-wing politics. No matter how hard they worked, the Communists found it difficult to compete with the socialists. Whatever they had tried, had failed. They applied for affiliation to the CCF, only to be rebuffed. They tried to outdistance the CCF with electoral promises and a fairly large number of candidates in some federal and provincial elections. Great was their disappointment when the votes were counted. For a short period they were prepared to give qualified support to the Liberals in order to further the Communist cause and to "by-pass" the CCF. The "Liberal-Labor Coalition" proposal exposed them to ridicule from both left-wing and right-wing socialists and did not help their claim that they were opposed to old-line parties. The only other policy they could have adopted would have been the dissolution of the CPC-LPP and the entry of its members into the CCF-NDP. This the Communist leaders refused to countenance, because it would have meant the end of the Communist movement in Canada, and a dramatic denial of everything they had said and done since the early 1930s.

Not that the CPC had much room for manoeuvre, once it became known that the CCF, unlike the Socialist Party in the United States, would remain a force in Canadian politics and that few prominent socialists were prepared to collaborate with the Communists on major issues. By and large the leaders of the CCF-NDP looked upon the CPC as a mischievous if not an alien element in the ranks of the Canadian left and trade union movement, as a group of men and women who could not be trusted because they were devious and their first loyalty was to a foreign power. J. S. Woodsworth held that belief from the early days of the CCF. Others accepted his interpretation with varying degrees of alacrity. After the Hitler-Stalin pact in 1939, most democratic socialist leaders displayed a fair degree of suspicion of the Communists and of Communist tactics, which they felt were bound to damage the unity, image and electoral appeal of the CCF-NDP.

The socialists' unwillingness to accept the Communists as partners had repercussions far beyond the ranks of the Canadian left. If the CPC could not influence the socialists to any extent, how could the Communists hope to make an appreciable impact on the much larger body of voters who supported the old-line parties and were far less open to proposals for major social and economic reforms?

Lack of major Communist victories in the trade unions in the 1950s and most of the 1960s, and failure to bring about a rapprochement between the CPC and the CCF-NDP, relegated the CPC to a position of a virtual outcast, publishing newspapers which few people wanted to buy, holding on precariously to a few unions, and controlling a number of ethnic organizations of elderly people. It was left to a party veteran, S. B. Ryerson, to remind his comrades in 1969 that "we at best are no more than a barely marginal force."[8]

Faced with such a bleak situation, the Communists leaders have consoled themselves and their followers by drawing attention to the more attractive episodes in the party's past, as well as to the problems and crises in the non-Communist world. They also declare that the CPC could regain the influence it once wielded, if only members used the right tactics and displayed the zeal for which the militants were known in the 1930s. This hope cannot be dismissed as bombast or wishful thinking of people trying to convince themselves and others that most of their efforts have not been in vain and that a bright future awaits the CPC. The history of Communism in Canada shows that the party is capable of rapid recovery and that it can make an impact in those areas where it meets no strong opposition from other groups concerned with moving Canadian society in a direction that will give less scope to private enterprise, and de-emphasizing the role of forces, institutions and organizations which shaped the course of Canadian history before 1939.

Whether the Canadian Communists will forge ahead or remain an obscure sect will depend on three factors: events abroad, over which Canadians have little control; forces that the CPC can set in motion; and the alternatives which the democratic socialists and the more traditional elements in Canada will offer in an increasingly complex society. The Communists understand this as clearly as do their political opponents.

Bibliography

The largest collection of unpublished Communist documents available to the public is in the Public Archives of Ontario. It consists of the CPC archives seized by the police when they raided the party headquarters in Toronto in August 1931. The material is particularly useful for the period 1929-1931, although documents for the earlier period are also included.

The Communist press provided the author with the main source of documentation on the state of the Communist movement, its objectives and enemies. By and large *The Worker* (1922-1936) is more illuminating than the *Daily Clarion* (1936-1939), *The Clarion* (1939), *The Toronto Clarion* (1940-1941), *Canadian Tribune* (1940-1974), and the *Daily Tribune* (1947). The Communist newspapers in Montreal and Vancouver are useful sources regarding Communist activities in Quebec and B.C. The Communist ethnic press is more diverse and extensive than Communist dailies and weeklies in English. Increasingly the ethnic press echoed what the organs of the CPC had already published in English. Nevertheless it cannot be ignored by students of East European communities in Canada.

The theoretical organs of the CPC-LPP (*National Affairs Monthly, Marxist Review, Horizons, Marxist Quarterly, Communist Viewpoint*), contain fairly detailed analyses of various aspects of life in Canada. They also deal with organizational and ideological questions of interest to party officials and activists. A franker discussion of these problems is available in the internal bulletins of the CPC-LPP: *Party Organizer, Communist Review* and *Party Builder* in the 1930s, *Club Life* in the early days of the LPP and *Viewpoint* in the 1960s and early 1970s.

Although incomplete and edited for public consumption, the proceedings of some party conventions and meetings of the central committee throw additional light on the CPC-LPP. In many instances they include the text of the main resolutions passed by the convention and the speeches by senior party officials.

The proceedings of Comintern and Profintern congresses and sessions of their executives frequently included interesting contributions by delegates of the CPC and Canadian pro-Communist labour organizations. These are more revealing than the bland reports delivered by the representatives of the CPC-LPP at party congresses and conferences of Communist parties in eastern Europe after 1945.

The leaders of the CPC contributed articles to newspapers and periodicals published under the auspices of international organizations which reflected the Soviet viewpoint. Of these the most important are *International Press Correspondence* (London, 1922-1938), *Rundschau* (Basel, 1932-1939), *Die Welt* (Stockholm, 1939-1943), *World News and Views* (London, 1938-1954). *For a Lasting Peace, For a People's Democracy* (Belgrade, Bucharest, 1947-1956), played the same role at the height of the Cold War. To some extent *World Marxist Review* (Toronto, 1958-) is a successor to *Die Kommunistische Internationale* (Petrograd, Berlin, Paris, Stockholm, 1919-1941) in which there are few contributions from Canada. *Krasnyi Internatsional Profsoiuzov* (Moscow) and *Internatsional Molodezhi* (Moscow) contain articles on Communist agitation among the workers and the young in Canada in the interwar years.

The leading organs of the CPSU (*Agitator, Kommunist, Partinaya Zhizn, Politicheskoe Samoobrazovanie*), have also published contributions by Canadian Communists. Soviet learned journals have from time to time analysed the evolution of the Canadian economy and Canada's relations with the U.S.A. and Britain. A study of Soviet attitudes towards Canada remains to be written.

Communist activities among the young can be traced through Communist newspapers devoted to the younger generation: *Young Worker, New Advance, Champion, Advance*, and *Scan*.

The non-Communist reaction to the CPC-LPP can best be studied through trade union publications, *The Winnipeg Free Press*, and the three Toronto dailies: *The Globe and Mail, The Star* and *The Telegram*.

The number of monographs on the history of the CPC-LPP is very small. The CPC published *Power to the People. Fifty Years of Pictorial Highlights of the Communist Party of Canada, 1921-1971* (Toronto: Progress Books, 1971). Buck's version of events is recorded in *Thirty Years, 1922-1952; the story of the Communist movement in Canada* (Toronto: Progress Books, 1952), *Canada and the Russian Revolution* (Toronto: Progress Books, 1967), and

Lenin and Canada (Toronto: Progress Books, 1970). They are the work of a participant eager to inspire his followers and castigate his opponents, particularly Maurice Spector. More autobiographical are his contributions to *Rabochii klass i sovremennyi mir* (Moscow), nos. 1 and 2, 1972.

Three other Communists published their memoirs. Tom McEwen concentrates on the 1920s and the early 1930s in *The Forge glows Red* (Toronto: Progress Books, 1974). A. E. Smith's *All My Life* (Toronto: Progress Books, 1949) contains much material on the CLDL. *Recollections of the On-To-Ottawa Trek* (Toronto: McClelland and Stewart, 1973) by Ronald Liversedge is a vivid account of the life and struggles of a staunch party member who was active among the unemployed in B.C. during the Depression. The appendix to his memoirs consists of a number of valuable documents on the On-To-Ottawa Trek. They are edited by Victor Hoar, also the author of *The Mackenzie-Papineau Battalion* (Toronto: Copp Clark, 1969), the best study of Canadians who fought in the Spanish Civil War. J. A. (Pat) Sullivan's *Red Sails over the Great Lakes* (Toronto: Macmillan, 1955) is the reminiscences of an ex-Communist union leader.

Three Communists have had very sympathetic biographers. Tom McEwen's *He Wrote for Us* (Vancouver: Tribune Publishing Company, 1951) deals with William Bennett; Catherine Vance chronicled the life of Bella Gauld in *Not by Gods but by People* (Toronto: Progress Books, 1968) and Ivor Mills wrote of his father, H. E. Mills, in *Stout Hearts stand Tall* (Vancouver, 1971).

For an anti-Communist view of the CPC, see Watson Kirkconnell, *Seven Pillars of Freedom* (Toronto: Burns and MacEachren, 1952). Much more scholarly is William Rodney, *Soldiers of the International – A History of the Communist Party of Canada, 1919-1929* (Toronto: University of Toronto Press, 1968).

Martin Robin, *Radical Politics and Canadian Labour* (Kingston, Ont.: Industrial Relations Centre, Queen's University, 1968) includes valuable material on the Communists in the CLP. For additional material on the same subject, see the annual reports on Labour Organization in Canada published by the federal Department of Labour in Ottawa. Walter Young's *The Anatomy of a Party – The National CCF* (Toronto: University of Toronto Press, 1969) has an illuminating chapter on the relations between the CCF and the CPC-LPP. It is largely based on the CCF records and the Woodsworth papers in the Public Archives in Ottawa. Gerald Caplan provides a useful account of the Communist impact on the fortunes of the Ontario CCF in *The Dilemma of Canadian Socialism – the CCF in Ontario* (Toronto: McClelland and Stewart, 1973).

Stuart Jamieson surveys some of the problems posed by the Communists in the trade unions in *Industrial Relations in Canada* (Toronto: Macmillan, 1957). Charles Lipton's *The Trade Union Movement of Canada, 1827-1959* (Montreal: Canadian Social Publications Limited, 1968) is the work of a man who spent many years in the Communist movement and who is very critical of the role played by the international unions in Canada. For detailed accounts of the efforts of the CCL leaders to restrict Communist influence during and after the Second World War, Gad Horowitz, *Canadian Labour in Politics* (Toronto: University of Toronto Press, 1968) and Irving M. Abella, *Nationalism, Communism and Canadian Labour* (Toronto: University of Toronto Press, 1973) are indispensable.

Communist attempts to rally prairie farmers are discussed in Duff Spafford's article on the left-wing in Saskatchewan in Norman Ward and Duff Spafford (eds.), *Politics in Saskatchewan* (Toronto: Longmans, 1968) and in my contribution to David J. Bercuson's *Western Perspectives*, vol. 1 (Toronto: Holt, Rinehart, and Winston, 1974).

G. Mowatt, *History of the Canadian Peace Movement until 1969* (St. Catharines, Ont.: Grape Vine Press, 1969) is sympathetic to the efforts of the LPP and Dr. Endicott.

For Communist accounts of their attempts to influence Canadians of Russian and South Slav extraction, see G. Okulevich's *Russkie v Kanade* (Toronto: Izdanie Glavnogo Pravleniia Federatsii Russkikh Kanadtsev, 1952), and E. Jardas' article in P. Moraca (ed.), *Cetrdeset Godina*, vol. 1 (Belgrade: Kultura, 1960). The literature on the ULFTA and AUUC is fairly extensive. M. Popovich wrote several useful articles on Ukrainians in Canada in *Robitnicho—Farmers' kii Kalendar na Perestupnii Rik 1928* (Winnipeg: Robitnicho—Farmers'ke Vidavchiche Tovaristvo, 1928). Peter Krawchuk's *Na Novii Zemlii* (Toronto: Eveready Printers Ltd., 1958) is a detailed account of the pro-Communist Ukrainians in Canada. Paul Yuzik's *The Ukrainians in Manitoba* (Toronto: University of Toronto Press, 1953) is still the best non-Communist study of the Communist impact on a Ukrainian community.

Several M.A. theses defended at Canadian universities reflect the growing interest in the Communist movement in Canada. The most valuable of these are Douglas Rowland, "Canadian Communism – the post Stalinist phase" (University of Manitoba, 1965), and Marcel Fournier, "Histoire et Idéologie du groupe canadien-français du Parti Communiste, 1925-1945" (Université de Montréal, 1969).

Notes

Abbreviations

A Democratic Front	*A Democratic Front for Canada. Reports, Speeches, Resolutions at the Thirteenth Session of the Dominion Executive, Communist Party of Canada, June 1938* (Toronto, 1938).
Abella	I. M. Abella, *Nationalism, Communism and Canadian Labour* (Toronto, 1973).
Buck	Tim Buck, *Thirty Years, 1922-1952. The Story of the Communist Movement in Canada* (Toronto, 1952).
Carr	Sam Carr, *Communists at Work* (Toronto, 1937).
CI	*The Communist International between the Fifth & the Sixth World Congresses, 1924-1928* (London, 1928).
CT	*Canadian Tribune*, Toronto.
CU	*The Canadian Unionist*, Ottawa.
DC	*Daily Clarion*, Toronto.
Horowitz	Gad Horowitz, *Canadian Labour in Politics* (Toronto, 1968).
IPC	*International Press Correspondence*, London
Kommunisticheskii Internatsional	*Kommunisticheskii Internatsional pered VII Vsemirnym Kongressom. Materialy* (Moscow, 1935).
LG	*The Labour Gazette*, Ottawa.
NAM	*National Affairs Monthly*, Toronto.

Ninth Plenum	*Towards a Canadian People's Front. Reports and Speeches at the Ninth Plenum of the Central Committee, Communist Party of Canada, November 1935* (Toronto, 1935).
PAO	Public Archives of Ontario. Attorney General's Department, Province of Ontario, Record Group. Communist Party of Canada records.
Report	*Report of the Sixth National Convention, the Communist Party of Canada, held May 31st, to June 7th, 1929* (Toronto, 1929).
Rodney	William Rodney, *Soldiers of the International. History of the Communist Party of Canada, 1919-1929* (Toronto, 1968).
WNV	*World News and Views*, London.
Young	W. D. Young, *The Anatomy of a Party: the National CCF, 1932-1961* (Toronto, 1969).

Chapter 1: Sources of Canadian Communism

1. *Cotton's Weekly* (Cowansville, Que.) August 21, 1913. Membership rose to over 4,500 by the end of the year. *Ibid.*, March 19, 1914.
2. *Ibid.*, August 21, 1913.
3. *Ukrains'ka radians'ka entsiklopediia*, vol. 15 (Kiev, 1964), pp. 108, 220.
4. *Rabochii Narod* (Winnipeg), July 13, 1918.
5. Department of Labour of Canada, *Ninth Annual Report on Labour Organization in Canada (For the Calendar Year 1919)*. (Ottawa, 1920), p. 39.
6. *The Workers' Guard* (Toronto), November 12, 1921.
7. *Ibid.*
8. *NAM*, August 1946, p. 241.
9. The most detailed account of the origins of the CPC is in *Rodney*, pp. 28-36. For the Communist version, see Buck's reminiscences in *Rabochii klass i sovremennyi mir* (Moscow), no. 1, 1972, pp. 126, 128-129, and his *Canada and the Russian Revolution* (Toronto, 1967), pp. 83-86, and *Lenin and Canada* (Toronto, 1970), pp. 19-28.
10. Department of Labour of Canada, *Twenty-first Annual Report on Labour Organization in Canada (For the Calendar Year 1931)* (Ottawa, 1932), p. 166.
11. *Western Clarion* (Vancouver), May 1, 1920, and February 1, 1921.
12. *Ibid.*, March 16 and April 1, 1921.
13. *Ibid.*, February 15, 1921.
14. *Ibid.*
15. *Ibid.*
16. *Ibid.*
17. For the founding convention at Guelph, see *Rodney*, pp. 37-40.

Chapter 2: The 1920s

1. *NAM*, August 1946, p. 241.
2. *The Workers' Guard*, January 14, 1922.
3. *B.C. Federationist* (Vancouver), October 14, 1921.
4. *Western Clarion*, November 1, 1921.
5. *The Workers Guard*, February 11, 1921.
6. *Ibid.*, December 17, 1921.
7. PAO, Box 8, Envelope 7, 8 C 0570.
8. *OBU Bulletin* (Winnipeg), May 18, 1922.
9. *Ibid.*, April 4, 1922.
10. Communist Party of Canada, *Why every Worker should join the Communist Party* (Toronto, 1930), p. 10.
11. PAO, Box 1, Envelope 3, Letter of August 3, 1929.
12. Communist Party of Canada, *Why every Worker, op. cit.*, p. 10.
13. *Buck*, pp. 29-30.
14. *NAM*, August 1946, p. 277.
15. *The Militant* (New York), June 1, 1929.
16. *IPC*, August 9, 1929, p. 815.
17. PAO, Box 8, Envelope 4, 8 C 0158.
18. *Ibid.*, Box 8, Envelope 7, 8 C 0476.
19. *The Worker* (Toronto), March 15, 1923.
20. *Report*, p. 65.
21. *The Worker*, February 2, 1926.
22. *Ibid.*, May 9, 1925.
23. *Ibid.*, October 8, 1927.
24. Department of Labour of Canada, *Seventeenth Annual Report on Labour Organization in Canada (For the Calendar Year 1927)* (Ottawa, 1928), pp. 170-171; *Agrar-Probleme* (Berlin), no. 1, 1928, pp. 205-207.
25. *Canadian Labour Monthly* (Toronto), April 1928, p. 18.
26. *The Worker*, March 15, 1923.
27. *Rodney*, p. 163.
28. Trades and Labor Congress of Canada, *Report of the Proceedings of the Thirty-Eighth Annual Convention* (Ottawa, 1922), p. 114.
29. *CI*, p. 354.
30. *Ibid.*
31. Department of Labour of Canada, *Fourteenth Annual Report on Labour Organization in Canada (For the Calendar Year 1924)* (Ottawa, 1925), p. 144.
32. Tim Buck, *Steps to Power* (Toronto, 1925), p. 36.
33. Department of Labour of Canada, *Seventeenth Annual Report, op. cit.*, pp. 168-170.
34. *The Canadian Labour Monthly*, November 1928, p. 42.
35. PAO, Box 8, Envelope 7, 8 C 0610.
36. *The Worker*, March 15, 1923.
37. *Ibid.*
38. *Ibid.*, May 4, 1929.

39. *CI*, p. 356.
40. *Mezhdunarodnoe profdvizhenie za 1924-1927 gg. Otchet ispolbiuro IV kongressu Profinterna* (Moscow, 1928), p. 362.
41. *The Worker*, August 28, 1926.
42. For the rationale, see *Ibid.*, August 1, 1922.
43. *Ibid.*, April 17, 1926.
44. Department of Labour of Canada, *Fifteenth Annual Report on Labour Organization in Canada (For the Calendar Year 1925)* (Ottawa, 1926), p. 146.
45. *The Worker*, January 9, 1926.
46. Department of Labour of Canada. *Sixteenth Annual Report on Labour Organization in Canada (For the Calendar Year 1926)* (Ottawa, 1927), pp. 194-195.
47. *Ibid.*, p. 196.
48. *The Worker*, July 9, 1927.
49. *Ibid.*, November 19, 1927; Martin Robin, *Radical Politics and Canadian Labour, 1880-1930* (Kingston, Ont. 1968), pp. 264-265.

Chapter 3: "Class against Class"

1. Buck gave his version of the struggle against Spector's pro-Trotsky views in *Lenin and Canada*, pp. 47-65.
2. *The Worker*, December 1, 1928.
3. *The Communist International* (New York), April 1938, p. 368.
4. *The Militant*, June 1, 1929.
5. *The Worker*, December 1, 1928.
6. *Ibid.*, April 27, 1929.
7. PAO, Box 8, Envelope 4, 8 C 0140.
8. *The Worker*, December 29, 1928.
9. *Report*, p. 65.
10. *Ibid.*, pp. 80, 129; Box 8, Envelope 6, 8 C 0269; *The Worker*, July 6, 1929.
11. PAO, Box 1, Envelope 4, 1 A 0719.
12. *CT*, September 15, 1945.
13. *Pravda* (Moscow), January 6, 1971.
14. *Kommunisticheskii Internatsional*, p. 383.
15. PAO, Box 1, Envelope 3, 1 A 0731.
16. *Ibid.*, Box 8, Envelope 5, 8 C 0266.
17. *Ibid.*, Box 8, Envelope 6, 8 C 0325 and Envelope 7, 8 C 0477.
18. *Ibid.*, Box 8, Envelope 7, 8 C 0454.
19. *Ibid.*, 8 C 0593.
20. *Resolutions of Enlarged Plenum of Communist Party of Canada – February 1931* – (Toronto, 1931), pp. 6-7, 9, 10.
21. PAO, Box 1, Envelope 7, 1 A 0510.
22. *Ibid.*, Box 8, Envelope 7, 8 C 0462.
23. *Ibid.*, Box 4, Envelope 37, 4 A 2433.

24. *Ibid.*, Box 8, Envelope 7, 8 C 0462.
25. *Ibid.*
26. *Ibid.*, Box 8, Envelope 6, 8 C 0325.
27. *Ibid.*, Box 4, Envelope 38, 4 A 2654.
28. *The Worker*, January 3, 1931.
29. *Communist Review*, nos. 8-9, December 1934-January 1935, p. 9.
30. *The Worker*, April 25 and June 27, 1931.
31. *Ibid.*, March 9, 1929; PAO, Box 8, Envelope 5, 8 C 0265.
32. PAO, Box 1, Envelope 10, 1 A 0494.
33. *Ibid.*, Box 2, Envelope 16, 2 A 1014.
34. *Kommunisticheskii Internatsional*, p. 385.
35. *The Worker*, March 16, 1929, and August 25, 1934.
36. *The Communist International*, no. 18, September 20, 1934, p. 717.
37. Department of Labour of Canada, *Twenty-fourth Annual Report on Labour Organization in Canada (For the Calendar Year 1934)* (Ottawa, 1935), pp. 138-139.
38. *CU*, May 1933, p. 197.
39. PAO, Box 3, Envelope 30, 3 A 2253 and 2267.
40. *Ibid.*, Box 1, Envelope 4, 1 A 0244.
41. *Ibid.*, Box 3, Envelope 34, 3 A 2310.
42. *The Worker*, October 22, 1932.
43. *Krasnyi Internatsional Profsoiuzov* (Moscow), nos. 1-2, January 1932, p. 65.
44. *The Worker*, January 24, 1931; PAO, Box 8, Envelope 6, 8 C 0307.
45. *The Worker*, October 3, 1931.
46. *Rundschau* (Basel), September 24, 1935, p. 2136.
47. PAO, Box 9, Envelope 8, 9 C 0788.
48. *IPC*, May 7, 1931, p. 440.
49. *Bulletin of the WUL* (Toronto), No. 9, April 28, 1931.
50. *Kommunisticheskii Internatsional*, p. 385.
51. *The Vancouver Sun*, April 5, 1935.
52. Ronald Liversedge, *Recollections of the On-To-Ottawa Trek* (Toronto, 1973), p. 98.
53. PAO, Box 1, Envelope 10, 1 A 0520.
54. *Ibid.*, Box 1, Envelope 10. J. M. Clarke's letter of December 17, 1930.
55. *Ibid.*
56. *Ninth Plenum*, p. 137.
57. PAO, Box 28, Envelope 4, p. 421; *The Furrow* (Winnipeg), June 1931.
58. *Ninth Plenum*, p. 135.
59. *The Worker*, August 29, 1931.
60. *Ninth Plenum*, p. 130.
61. *Ibid.*
62. *Ibid.*, p. 42.
63. PAO, Box 8, Envelope 7, 8 C 0474 and Box 9, Envelope 11, 9 C 1110.

64. *RILU Magazine* (London), nos. 1-2, February 1932, p. 83.
65. *Canadian Labor Defender* (Toronto), May 1930, August 1930 and March 1934; *The Worker*, March 26, 1932.
66. PAO, Box 3, Envelope 27, 3 A 1658; Box 8, Envelope 6, 8 C 0339.
67. *The Globe* (Toronto), November 10, 1932.
68. *Manitoba Free Press* (Winnipeg), February 26, 1932.
69. *CT*, May 2, 1942.
70. *Kommunisticheskii Internatsional*, p. 384.
71. PAO, Box 9, Envelope 8, 9 C 0668.
72. *Communist Review*, nos. 8-9, December 1934 – January 1935, p. 39.
73. *Resolutions, op. cit.*, p. 7.
74. *Carr*, p. 15.
75. *The Worker*, October 8, 1935.
76. *Ninth Plenum*, pp. 81, 83.
77. *Ibid.*, p. 17.
78. *Ibid.*, p. 206.
79. *Ibid.*, p. 83.

Chapter 4: Towards a People's Front

1. *IPC*, October 7, 1935, p. 1289, and November 21, 1935, p. 1544.
2. *Towards Democratic Unity for Canada. Submission of the Dominion Committee, Communist Party of Canada, to the Royal Commission on Dominion-Provincial Relations* (revised ed.), (Toronto, n.d.).
3. *Workers Voice* (Toronto), March 20, 1937.
4. *The Commonwealth* (Vancouver), May 17, 1935.
5. *The Worker*, January 13, 1934.
6. *Ibid.*, July 7, 1934.
7. *The Commonwealth*, May 17, 1935.
8. *Ninth Plenum*, p. 26.
9. *DC*, March 1, 1937.
10. *Ninth Plenum*, p. 91.
11. Tim Buck, *What we propose* (Toronto, 1936), p. 50.
12. *Ninth Plenum*, p. 106.
13. *The Communist International*, September 1936, p. 1224.
14. *Ninth Plenum*, pp. 22-23.
15. *DC*, October 30, 1937.
16. *IPC*, December 24, 1937, p. 1390.
17. *DC*, September 30, 1937.
18. *Ibid.*, April 20, 1937.
19. *People's Weekly* (Edmonton), August 6, 1938.
20. The best account of the split in the Ontario CCF is in G. L. Caplan, *The Dilemma of Canadian Socialism – The CCF in Ontario* (Toronto, 1973), pp. 50-63.
21. *DC*, August 9, 1937.

22. Tim Buck, *The Road Ahead* (Toronto, 1936), p. 51.
23. *Carr*, p. 35.
24. *DC*, April 2, 1938.
25. *Ibid.*, April 27, 1938.
26. *Ibid.*, June 4, 1938.
27. *People's Weekly*, July 23, 1938.
28. *DC*, June 13, 1938.
29. *Ninth Plenum*, p. 70.
30. *The Communist International*, April 1938, p. 365.
31. Buck, *The Road Ahead*, p. 19.
32. *A Democratic Front*, p. 13.
33. *Ibid.*, pp. 24-25.
34. Buck, *What we propose*, p. 70.
35. *The People's Advocate* (Vancouver), March 10, 1939.
36. *DC*, June 9, 1939.
37. *The Clarion* (Toronto), August 26, 1939.
38. *NAM*, December 1948, p. 341.
39. *Ninth Plenum*, p. 109.
40. *Carr*, p. 38.
41. *A Democratic Front*, p. 133.
42. *The Party Builder* (Toronto), no. 1, March 1938, p. 3.
43. *A Democratic Front*, pp. 49-50, 133.
44. *Ibid.*, p. 50.
45. S. Smith, *A Manual on Party Branch Work* (Toronto, 1939), p. 3.
46. L. Morris, *A Handbook of Party Education* (Toronto, 1939), pp. 6-7.
47. *Carr*, p. 31.
48. *A Democratic Front*, p. 43.
49. *Ibid.*, pp. 44, 45.
50. *Ibid.*, p. 46.
51. *Ibid.*, p. 64.
52. *Kanadskii Gudok* (Toronto), July 16, 1932; *DC*, March 10, 1938.
53. *Kanadskii Gudok*, April 8, 1932; G. Okulevich, *Russkie v Kanade* (Toronto, 1952), pp. 135, 185.
54. P. Moraca (ed.), *Cetrdeset Godina. Zbornik secanja aktivista jugo-slovenskog revolucionarnog radnickog pokreta*, vol. i (Belgrade, 1960), p. 390.
55. *Ninth Plenum*, p. 184.
56. PAO, Box 8, Envelope 7, 8 C 0546.
57. *The Worker*, June 29, 1929.
58. For a Soviet critique of the YCL, see *Internatsional Molodezhi* (Moscow), June 1930, pp. 70-75.
59. *Ninth Plenum*, p. 94.
60. *A Democratic Front*, p. 124.
61. *New Advance* (Toronto), July 1938, p. 16.
62. *DC*, February 24, 1937.
63. *Masses* (Toronto), April 1934.
64. *DC*, August 16, 1937.

65. *Rundschau*, March 14, 1935, p. 697; *DC*, November 11, 1937.
66. *NAM*, September 1946, p. 281.
67. *The Communist International*, September 1936, p. 1225.
68. *Rundschau*, September 24, 1935, p. 2136.
69. *CU*, May 1935, p. 321; *The Worker*, May 23, 1935.
70. *NAM*, February 1957, p. 3.
71. *Ninth Plenum*, p. 37.
72. T. A. Ewen,*Unity is the Workers' Lifeline* (Toronto, n.d.), p. 29.
73. *WNV*, January 29, 1938, p. 79.
74. *Parliament must act to provide one million jobs! Proceedings of the central committee meeting, Communist Party of Canada, Toronto, June 6-7-8, 1970* (Toronto, 1970), p. 18.
75. *The Worker*, April 21, 1934.
76. *DC*, October 11, 1938.
77. *The Communist International*, April 1938, p. 365.
78. *Young*, pp. 267-268.
79. *NAM*, February 1957, p. 12.

Chapter 5: From an "Imperialist" to a "Just" War

1. *The Clarion*, August 26, 1939.
2. *Ibid.*, September 9 and 16, 1939.
3. *CT*, March 30, 1940.
4. *The Toronto Clarion*, May 10, 1940.
5. *Ibid.*, April 5, 1941.
6. *The Clarion*, March 23, 1940.
7. *WNV*, December 12, 1939, p. 1172.
8. *Ibid.*
9. *The Toronto Clarion*, May 1, 1940.
10. *Rabochii klass i sovremennyi mir*, no. 2, 1972, p. 155.
11. *The Toronto Clarion*, January 20, 1941.
12. *Ibid.*, September 26, 1940.
13. *Buck*, pp. 166-167, 179-183.
14. *The Toronto Clarion*, December 9, 1940.
15. *The Communist* (New York), December 1940, p. 1109.
16. Political Committee of the Communist Party of Canada, *Federal Election Manifesto* (1940), p. 2.
17. *Ibid.*, p. 22.
18. *WNV*, March 1, 1941, p. 142.
19. *New Advance*, January 1940, p. 15.
20. *Ibid.*, April 1940, p. 21.
21. *CT*, July 20, 1940.
22. *Abella*, pp. 41-70, 113-114, provides a useful account of Communist activities in unions not affiliated with the TLC between the outbreak of the Second World War and Hitler's invasion of the U.S.S.R.
23. *CU*, September 1940, p. 91.

24. *Abella*, p. 52.
25. *Ibid*., pp. 66-68.
26. *CU*, May 1941, p. 302.
27. *CT*, April 18, 1942.
28. *Ibid*., November 10, 1945; *NAM*, May 1948, p. 164.
29. Tim Buck, *Organize Canada for Total War* (Toronto, 1942), p. 23.
30. *New Advance*, September 1942, p. 18.
31. *CT*, February 6, 1943.
32. *The Report of the Royal Commission appointed under Order in Council P.C.411 of February 5, 1946, to investigate the Facts relating to and the Circumstances surrounding the Communication, by Public Officials and Other Persons in Positions of Trust of Secret and Confidential Information to Agents of a Foreign Power* (Ottawa, 1946), pp. 105, 116.
33. *Pacific Advocate* (Vancouver), July 28, 1945.
34. *Program of the Labor-Progressive Party* (Toronto, 1943); *Constitution and By-Laws of the Labor-Progressive Party* (Toronto, 1943).
35. *Constitution and By-Laws of the Labor-Progressive Party*, p. 7.
36. *Horowitz*, p. 85.
37. *Ibid*.
38. *The People* (Vancouver), September 11, 1943.
39. *CT*, September 11, 1943.
40. *The Canadian Forum*, June 1944, p. 56.
41. *CT*, March 14, 1942.
42. *Abella*, pp. 80-85.
43. *CT*, April 15, 1944.
44. *Ibid*., August 5, 1944; *NAM*, September 1944, pp. 167, 168.
45. *CT*, December 9, 1944.
46. *Ibid*., January 13, 20 and 27, 1945.
47. *Young*, pp. 276, 277.
48. *Cahiers du Communisme* (Paris), No. 6, April 1945, pp. 21-38.
49. *The LPP and Postwar Canada* (Toronto, 1945), p. 29.
50. See *The LPP and Postwar Canada* and the *Pacific Advocate* for July-September 1945.
51. *CT*, November 17, 1945.

Chapter 6: Spies and Others

1. *Ibid*., January 15, 1944.
2. *Ibid*., August 4, 1945.
3. *The LPP and Postwar Canada*, pp. 17-21, 63, 72-75.
4. *Ibid*., p. 73.
5. *The Report of the Royal Commission, op. cit.* p. 714.
6. *CT*, February 23, 1946.
7. *Ibid*., March 2, 1946.
8. *NAM*, April 1957, p. 11.
9. *Daily Tribune* (Toronto), November 3, 1947.

10. *NAM*, August 1947, p. 218.
11. *Ibid.*, p. 216.
12. For the text of Buck's speech, see *Ibid.*, February 1948, pp. 36-61.
13. *Ibid.*, p. 69.
14. *Ibid.*, December 1948, pp. 349, 350.
15. *CT*, January 24, 1949.
16. *Ibid.*, February 21, 1949.

Chapter 7: The Cold War

1. *NAM*, December 1956, p. 10.
2. L. Morris, *Challenge of the '60s* (Toronto, 1964), pp. 4-5.
3. *NAM*, February 1951, p. 86.
4. *For Peace, Progress, Socialism* (Toronto, 1946), p. 41.
5. *For a Lasting Peace, For a People's Democracy* (Bucharest), May 15, 1949.
6. *Hansard. Debates of the House of Commons, 1960 Session*, vol. VI (Ottawa, 1960), p. 6354.
7. *CT*, December 22, 1952.
8. *The Financial Post* (Toronto), May 6, 1950.
9. *NAM*, March 1951, p. 42.
10. *Young*, p. 281.
11. *Ibid.*, p. 282.
12. *NAM*, October 1951, pp. 7, 8.
13. H. A. Logan, *Trade Unions in Canada. Their Development and Functioning* (Toronto, 1948), p. 343; *Horowitz*, pp. 125-130; *Abella*, p. 163.
14. *LG*, November 1950, p. 1812.
15. *Report of the Proceedings of the Sixty-second Annual Convention of Trades and Labor Congress of Canada* (Ottawa, 1948), pp. 264-266, 267-271.
16. *Report of the Proceedings of the Sixty-third Annual Convention of the Trades and Labor Congress of Canada* (Ottawa, 1949), pp. 314, 337.
17. *LG*, December 1948, pp. 1369, 1373.
18. *Ibid.*, March 1949, pp. 243-244.
19. *Ibid.*, p. 244. See also Bengough's letter to members of the TLC, *The Trades and Labor Congress Journal* (Ottawa), March 1949, pp. 11-13.
20. *CT*, April 2, 1951.
21. The TLC Executive Council statement on the expulsion of the CSU is in *The Trades and Labor Congress Journal*, June 1949, pp. 13-14.
22. *LG*, November 1949, p. 1354.
23. *Report of the Proceedings of the Sixty-fourth Annual Convention of the Trades and Labor Congress* (Ottawa, 1950), p. 314. For the debate on Communism, Communists and the CSU, see *Ibid.*, pp. 55-62, 229-252, 254-259, 313-316, 373-374.

24. PAO, Box 4, Envelope 35, 4 A 2387.
25. For the debate on Communism and Communists, see *Report of the Proceedings of the Sixty-fifth Annual Convention of the Trades and Labor Congress of Canada* (Ottawa, 1951), pp. 205-215, 221-222.
26. *LG*, November 1947, pp. 1578-1579.
27. *Ibid.*, December 1948, p. 1359.
28. *Ibid.*, p. 1361.
29. *Ibid.*, November 1949, p. 1368.
30. For a brief account of the struggle on the West Coast, see I. Abella's article "Communism and anti-Communism in the British Columbia Labour Movement, 1940-1948" in David J. Bercuson (ed.), *Western Perspectives*, vol. 1 (Toronto, 1974).
31. *Horowitz*, pp. 86-89, 108-117, 121-122.
32. *Ibid.*, p. 118.
33. *The Communist* (New York), December 1940, p. 1100; *NAM*, April 1947, p. 100.
34. *Abella*, pp. 156-158.
35. *NAM*, October 1951, p. 63.
36. *Ibid.*, p. 39.
37. *Ibid.*, July-August 1948, p. 222.
38. *CU*, October 1951, p. 299.
39. *NAM*, July 1946, p. 199.
40. PAO, Box 8, Envelope 4, 8 C 0159.
41. *NAM*, March 1957, p. 15.
42. *A Better Canada—To Fight For—To Work For—To Vote For* (Toronto, 1945), p. 25.
43. *NAM*, December 1947, pp. 378, 379, 380.
44. *Ibid.*, March 1949, pp. 102, 103.
45. *Ibid.*, February 1951, p. 61.
46. *Ibid.*, March 1951, p. 77.
47. *Ibid.* See the obituaries of Cohen in the May-June 1971 issue of the *Canadian Jewish Outlook* (Toronto), and in the April 1971 issue of *Fraternally Yours* (Toronto), a bulletin published by a group of ex-Communists who left the LPP in the 1950s.
48. *NAM*, September 1951, p. 43.
49. *Ibid.*, p. 51.
50. *Ibid.*, February 1952, p. 57.
51. *Ibid*, September 1951, p. 36, and November 1951, p. 48.
52. *Ibid.*, July 1952, pp. 48, 49.
53. *Ibid.*, p. 50.
54. *Ibid.*, Mid-March 1954, p. 60.
55. *Ibid.*, March 1951, p. 77.
56. *Horizons* (Toronto), No. 25, spring 1968, p. 2.
57. *NAM*, January 1957, p. 5.
58. William Rusher, *Special Counsel* (New Rochelle, N.Y., 1968), pp. 183-234.
59. *Communist Viewpoint* (Toronto), March-April 1971, p. 64.

60. *Report of the Proceedings of the Sixty-seventh Annual Convention of the Trades and Labor Congress of Canada* (Ottawa, 1953) pp. 12-13, 324-327.
61. *CT*, November 5, 1951.
62. D. Owen Carrigan, *Canadian Party Platforms, 1867-1968* (Toronto, 1968), p. 204.
63. *NAM*, March 1957, p. 10.
64. *Ibid.*, For an attempt to refute Stewart, see *Ibid.*, May 1957, p. 14.
65. *Ibid.*, March 1957, p. 3.
66. *Ibid.*, March 1951, p. 44; May-June 1956, p. 65; January 1957, p. 9.
67. *Rodney*, p. 36; *Mezhdunarodnoe profdvizhenie*, op. cit., p. 538; PAO, Box 10, envelope 17, 10 C 1795.
68. *NAM*, February 1956, p. 15, and May-June 1956, pp. 65, 67.
69. *Ibid.*, April 1952, p. 61.
70. *Ibid.*, February 1957, p. 15.

Chapter 8: Destalinization in Canada

1. *NAM*, January 1957, p. 5.
2. *Ibid.*, April 1957, p. 3.
3. *CT*, March 16, 1953.
4. *Canadian Independence and a People's Parliament—Canada's Path to Socialism* (Toronto, 1954); *NAM*, September 1952, pp. 18-23; November 1952, pp. 55-63; December 1952, pp. 38-48; January 1953, pp. 48-55; February 1953, pp. 40-45; March 1953, pp. 35-51; April 1953, pp. 45-53; September 1953, pp. 44-51; February 1954, pp. 33-34; Mid-February 1954 Supplement, pp. 9-32; March 1954, pp. 23-63; Special Mid-March 1954 issue.
5. *NAM*, March 1957, p. 8.
6. *Ibid.*, June 1953, pp. 9-13.
7. *Ibid.*, November 1953, p. 23.
8. *Ibid.*, May-June 1954, p. 49.
9. *Ibid.*, November 1953, p. 12.
10. *Ibid.*, p. 15.
11. *Ibid.*, May 1957, pp. 19, 21.
12. *Ibid.*, May-June 1954, p. 74.
13. *CT*, May 7, 1956.
14. *NAM*, January 1957, p. 1.
15. *Ibid.*, February 1957, p. 14.
16. *Ibid.*, January 1957, p. 6.
17. *CT*, July 16, 1956.
18. *NAM*, February 1957, p. 4.
19. *Ibid.*, October 1956, p. 16.
20. *Vochenblatt* (Toronto), December 6, 1956.
21. *NAM*, January 1957, p. 7.
22. *Ibid.*, December 1956, p. 6.
23. *Ibid.*, November 1956, p. 1.

24. *Ibid.*, January 1957, p. 8.
25. *Ibid.*, April 1957, pp. 4-5.
26. *Marxist Review* (Toronto), October-November 1958, pp. 27, 28.
27. *Ibid.*, April-May 1958, pp. 17, 19.
28. *CT*, October 19, 1959.

Chapter 9: Beyond the 1950s

1. L. Morris, *Challenge of the '60s*, p. 27. "In Toronto 80% of our members are over 40 years of age." *Discussion* (Toronto), No. 5, Mid-March 1964, p. 8. A working paper on party organization discussed by the central committee of the CPC in April 1968 admitted that "the age composition of our party remains highly unsatisfactory." *Viewpoint* (Toronto), November 1968, p. 17.
2. *Viewpoint*, June 1966, pp. 63-65. For a more detailed description of Communist agricultural policy, see William C. Beeching, *Farmers! Fight For Your Future* (Toronto, 1971).
3. *Defeat the Government's Austerity Program. Proceedings of the Central Committee Meeting, Communist Party of Canada, Toronto, October 4-5-6, 1969* (Toronto), p. 7.
4. *Parliament must act, op. cit.*, p. 12.
5. *Viewpoint*, January 1965, p. 28.
6. D. Owen Carrigan, *op. cit.*, p. 261.
7. *CT*, January 29, 1962.
8. *Viewpoint*, June 1966, p. 50.
9. *Defeat the Government's Austerity Program, op. cit.*, p. 9.
10. *Parliament must act, op. cit.*, p. 18; *NAM*, May 1953, p. 37 and October 1954, p. 32.
11. *Report. 20th B.C. Provincial Convention. Communist Party of Canada. March 24-25, 1973* (Vancouver, 1973), p. 5.
12. Interview with Nelson Clarke. *The Financial Post*, December 10, 1960.
13. *The Globe and Mail*, December 23, 1971, and January 12, 1972.
14. *Report*, p. 90.
15. *Ibid.*, 71.
16. *CT*, March 30, 1946.
17. *Women in Today's World. B.C. Party Women's Conference. October 1973* (Vancouver, n.d.), pp. 7, 8.
18. Canadian Labor Congress, *7th Constitutional Convention. Report of Proceedings* (Toronto, 1968), pp. 66-67; *The Globe and Mail*, May 9, 1968.
19. *The Vancouver Sun*, November 9 and 10, 1972.
20. *Revoliutsionno-istoricheskii kalendar. Spravochnik 1966* (Moscow, 1965), p. 189.
21. *CT*, April 25, 1973.
22. PAO, Box 9, Envelope 15, 9 C 1461.

23. William Kashtan, *The Fight for Democracy and Social Advance* (Toronto, 1970), p. 20.
24. *The LPP and Postwar Canada*, p. 99.
25. *NAM*, September 1944, p. 174.
26. *Viewpoint*, May 1965, p. 27.
27. Editorials, articles and letters-to-the-editor in the Canadian Jewish weekly *Vochenblatt* mirror the predicament of party members and sympathizers interested in the future of Israel and the fate of Jews in eastern Europe.
28. Communist Party of Canada, *Questions for Today* (Toronto, 1964), p. 104.
29. *CT*, August 21, 1968.
30. *Ibid.*, October 9, 1968.
31. *Convention '69* (Toronto), no. 4, March 25, 1969, p. 24.
32. *NAM*, March 1957, p. 14.
33. For an account of the case, see *The Ottawa Journal*, February 12, 1968. For a critique of the delegation's report by a Ukrainian Canadian Communist leader, see *Viewpoint*, November 1968, pp. 20-22.
34. *CT*, February 17 and March 31, 1945.
35. *NAM*, October 1956, p. 5.
36. *Ibid.*
37. *Discussion*, no. 2, Mid-January 1964, pp. 10-12; *Viewpoint*, May 1964, pp. 17-18; *Convention '69*, no. 2, February 26, 1969, pp. 1-2, 12-14, and no. 3, March 14, 1969, pp. 13-15, p. 28.
38. *Pacific Tribune* (Vancouver), January 3, 1969.
39. *'69 Convention. 20th Convention, Communist Party of Canada, April 4-6, 1969. Resolutions, Reports, Policy Statements* (Toronto, 1969), p. 15.
40. *Convention '69*, no. 4, March 25, 1969, p. 24.

Conclusion

1. *The Worker*, March 9, 1929; PAO, Box 1, Envelope 5, 1 A 0285.
2. PAO, Box 1, Envelope 10, Letter to J. M. Clarke, January 7, 1931.
3. *NAM*, October 1956, p. 10.
4. *Ibid.*, December 1954, p. 51.
5. *Ibid.*, February 1957, p. 3.
6. Buck, *The Road Ahead*, p. 17.
7. *NAM*, February 1957, p. 3.
8. *Convention '69*, no. 2, February 26, 1969, p. 19.

Index

Abella, I. M., 193
Aberhardt, William, 84, 95, 108-111, 113
Acorn, Milton, 206
All-Canadian Congress of Labour, 46-47, 68-69, 72, 73, 74, 89, 131-132, 135, 147
Alter, V., 162
American Federation of Labor, 4, 30, 44-46, 132, 134, 147, 186, 188-190, 252, 253, 260
American Youth Congress, 124
Anglo-American Secretariat, 22-23, 58
Armstrong, Max, 60
Association Humanitaire, 255
Association of United Ukrainian Canadians, 199, 222, 265, 267
Avrom (Yanovsky), 127
Axelson, Carl, 40, 83

Ban the Bomb Petition, 184-186
Banks, Hal, 196
Barrett, Silby, 147
Bartholomew, Hugh, 24, 30
B. C. Federation of Labour, 18, 193-194, 251
B.C. Federationist, 18, 24
B.C. Workers' News, 130
Beder, E. A., 128
Bedacht, Max, 27
Bell, Tom, 11, 13
Bellamy, Edward, 3
Bengough, Percy, 188, 189, 190, 208
Bennett, R. B., 68, 78, 81, 89-90, 94, 112, 113, 157, 209
Bennett, William, 24
Bespalko, John, 83
Bethune, Norman, 260
Binder, Harry, 211, 213, 229, 231, 232, 257
Bland, Salem, 128
Blatchford, Robert, 3
Boilermakers and Iron Shipbuilders Union, 160
Bourassa, Henri, 11
Bourdinot, A. S., 206
Boychuk, John, 11, 27, 87
Boyd, John, 262, 266
Branch and Neighbourhood Councils, 75

Brewin, F. A., 151
British People's Convention, 145
British Socialist Party, 3
Brotherhood of Railway Carmen of America, 52
Browder, Earl, 28, 29, 42, 45-46, 111, 164-165, 267
Bruce, Malcolm, 16, 60, 87, 93
Buck, Alice, 248
Buck, Tim, 11, 13, 16, 21, 24, 27, 28, 31, 42, 43, 44, 45-46, 47, 48, 55, 56-63, 65-68, 70, 85, 87, 88, 89, 90, 93, 95, 97, 101, 109, 111, 112, 113, 122, 124, 136, 140, 142, 143, 144, 149, 150, 151, 152, 158, 161, 162, 164, 165, 167, 171, 177, 179, 181, 182, 186, 195, 205, 214, 215, 218, 221, 224-234, 236-238, 241, 248, 256, 260, 263, 265, 268, 279, 280
Buhay, Mike, 11, 60, 62
Buhay, Rebecca, 11, 247
Bukharin, N. I., 54
Buller, Annie, 216, 247
Burford, W. T., 135
Burt, George, 194

Cacic, Tom, 65-66, 87, 88
Callaghan, Morley, 151
Canadian and Catholic Confederation of Labour, 208
Canadian Congress against War and Fascism, 127-128
Canadian Congress of Labour, 147-148, 151, 157, 160, 186, 191-198, 250, 252
Canadian Farmers' Educational League, 40
Canadian Federation of Labour, 135
Canadian Forum, 105, 158
Canadian Friends of Soviet Russia, 10
Canadian Labour Congress, 250-253
Canadian Labour Defence League, 34, 89, 90, 107, 209
Canadian Labour Party, 51-53, 67, 102
Canadian League against War and Fascism, 91, 105, 128
Canadian League for Peace and Democracy, 128-129
Canadian Party of Labour, 261
Canadian Peace Congress, 184-185, 247

Canadian People's Movement, 145, 148
Canadian Seamen's Union, 142, 188-190, 196, 198
Canadian Tribune, 61, 142, 146, 151, 157, 161, 163, 167, 172, 173, 175, 179, 184, 204, 208, 210-211, 214, 223, 234, 243, 249, 262, 265
Canadian Workers' Ex-servicemen's League, 91
Canadian Youth Congress, 105, 124-125, 146
Canadian Youth Congress against War and Fascism, 124
Cannon, J. P., 55
Caron, Gui, 229, 255, 257
Carr, Sam, 63, 66, 87, 93, 99, 106, 117, 142, 152, 161, 165, 169, 171, 172
Cascaden, George, 13
Cecil-Smith, E., 99
Champion, 267
Chiang Kai-shek, 58, 128, 259
China, 51, 58, 125, 183, 184, 203, 244, 247, 259-260
Churchill, Winston, 158
Clarion, 130, 140, 142
Clarke, J. M., 41, 82
Clarté, 130, 142
Club Life, 176
Cohen, Nathan, 161, 204
Coldwell, J. M., 102, 129, 151, 159, 163, 177, 178, 187, 219, 221
Cominform, 182, 220, 266
Comintern, *see*, Communist International
Committee for Industrial Organization, 134, 147
Committee to Aid Spanish Democracy, 105, 131
Communist International, 13, 16-23, 24, 25, 26, 27, 29, 30, 31, 34, 40, 41, 44, 45-46, 48, 53, 54, 55, 57, 58-60, 62-65, 66, 67, 71, 73, 74, 77, 78, 86, 87, 89, 91, 92, 96-97, 98, 106, 124, 126, 127, 129, 131, 132, 137, 140, 145, 170, 177, 200, 212, 253, 255, 259, 279, 280
Communist-Labor Total War Committee, 152
Communist Party of America, 12, 13, 21
Communist Party of Canada—and: Anglo-Saxons, 24, 25, 35-37, 49, 66, 77, 119-120, 122; Croats, 121;
200; Doukhobors, 121; East Europeans, 24, 33, 35-38, 49, 65, 67, 120-122, 131, 155, 169, 199-200, 221, 222, 247, 274-276; Finns, 24, 35-38, 57, 59, 62, 65, 66, 120, 122, 199, 261, 280; Jews, 35-36, 38, 57, 94, 122, 201, 222, 226, 231, 257, 259, 265; Quebec and Quebecois, 35, 50, 57, 58, 97, 149, 185, 242, 253-258; Russians, 121-122; Ukrainians, 24, 35-38, 39, 57, 59, 62, 66, 67, 94, 120-121, 199-202, 231, 261, 263-266, 280; Yugoslavs, 66, 121-122; attitude towards: BNA Act, 50, 278; Canadian independence, 46, 57-58, 63-65, 219; Canadian Labour Party, 51-53, 57, 67, 102; Co-operative Commonwealth Federation-New Democratic Party, 52, 93-95, 98-108, 115, 157, 158-163, 167, 169, 176, 177-179, 183, 185-186, 191, 192-193, 215, 219, 223, 228, 281, 282; culture, 202-206, 219, 221; farmers, 39-41, 81-85, 239; intellectuals, 126-129, 202-206, 266, 278; Liberals, 8, 9, 51, 94, 106, 112, 113, 157, 158, 162-163, 164, 169-170, 175, 176, 177, 183, 186, 187, 207, 208-209, 219, 258, 267, 281; Section 98 of the Criminal Code, 15, 50, 89, 90, 91, 94, 107, 113; small businessmen, 97, 220; Social Credit, 84, 94, 106, 108-111, 115, 125, 128, 160, 208, 219; Tories, 9, 51, 87, 89-90, 94, 106, 112, 113, 157, 158, 162, 186, 208, 219, 221, 223-224; trade unions, 27, 29-30, 42-49, 57, 71-74, 117, 131-135, 146-148, 156-157, 159-160, 186-198, 250-253, 277-278; unemployed and unemployment, 16, 23, 68, 74-81, 176, 277; women, 34, 154, 247-249; workers, 41-49, 57, 69-74, 131-135, 141-142, 149, 186-199, 224, 244-245, 250-253; young people, 123-126, 145-146, 154, 232, 244, 267-271

convention: founding (1921), 21;
    4th (1925), 52; 5th (1927), 38;
    6th (1929), 59-60, 248; 8th
    (1937), 109; 20th (1969), 269
convention, Labor Progressive
    Party: 1st (1943), 152, 158; 2nd
    (1946), 176; 3rd (1949),
    202-203; 4th (1951), 204; 5th
    (1954), 219, 223; 6th (1957),
    229-230, 232
convention, Workers' Party of
    Canada: preliminary conference
    (1921), 27; founding (1922),
    28-30, 42
finances, 36, 40, 65-66, 68, 174-175,
    187, 211-213
foundation of the : Communist
    Party of Canada, 21; Labor
    Progressive Party, 152; Workers'
    Party of Canada, 27-30
in: Alberta, 32, 33, 39, 49, 66,
    109-111, 227; B.C., 32, 33, 47,
    49, 59, 66, 117, 119, 121, 134,
    152, 165, 211, 227, 245-246,
    248,249,250,252; Manitoba
    32, 66, 67, 68, 119, 137-138,
    245; Maritimes, 35, 78, 119,
    272; Nova Scotia, 32, 33, 47,
    49; Ontario, 32, 33, 67, 78, 119,
    120, 231, 233, 235, 245;
    Quebec, 33, 35, 67, 78, 113-114,
    119, 123, 143, 162, 245,
    253-258, 272; Saskatchewan,
    32, 66, 67, 110, 113, 176
membership, 35, 39, 57, 66, 77, 87,
    90, 106, 115-119, 175-176, 190,
    197, 214, 222, 232, 233-234,
    236, 243-246, 256
organization, 27, 31-33, 38, 57, 101,
    153-155, 215, 275, 280
press, 27, 39, 121, 130-131, 142,
    209, 210-211, 223, 243
program, 21, 27, 31, 50, 100,
    152-153, 168, 176, 182,
    220-221, 238-239
recruitment, 34, 36, 66, 77,
    175-176, 196-197, 213-214, 222,
    236, 244-245
strikes, 35, 47-49, 69-71, 72, 79,
    133, 174
"Z" Party, 31
Communist Party of Canada
    (Marxist-Leninist), 261

Communist Party of China, 260
Communist Party of Cuba, 212
Communist Party of Czechoslovakia,
    212
Communist Party of Great Britain, 140
Communist Party of the Soviet Union,
    62, 224, 225, 227, 229, 237, 259,
    262, 263, 265, 281
Communist Party of the United States
    of America, 5, 22, 31, 49, 57, 59,
    64, 93, 164, 182
Communist Party of Spain, 129
Communist Political Association, 164
Communist Review, 67
Communist Viewpoint, 243
Confederation of Catholic Unions, 135
Confederation of National Trade
    Unions, 253
Congress of American Women, 248
Congress of Canadian Women, 248
Conroy, Pat, 148, 192, 194
Co-operative Commonwealth
    Federation, 52, 55-56, 84, 89,
    93-95, 98-108, 115, 128, 144, 147,
    148, 150, 156, 157, 158-163, 167,
    169, 170, 176, 177-179, 183,
    185-186, 187, 191, 192-193, 207,
    209, 215, 219, 223, 228, 233, 258,
    261, 276, 277, 278, 281, 282
Co-operative Commonwealth Youth
    Movement, 123-125, 146
Cotton's Weekly, 4
Councils for the Defence of
    Foreign-Born Workers, 89
Croll, David, 106,
Cross, James, 254
Custance, Florence, 11, 12, 21, 25, 27,
    247
Czechoslovakia, 259, 262-263

Daily Clarion, 110, 130, 133, 173
Daily Tribune, 173-175
De Leon, Daniel, 3, 21, 281
Debs, Eugene, 3, 21, 281
Dodge, William, 251
Douglas, T. C., 105, 125, 128, 129, 242
Draper, D. C., 86
Drew, George, 177, 178, 208, 221
Dubcek, Alexander, 262
Dubé, Evariste, 256
Duclos, Jacques, 164, 267
Duplessis, Maurice, 111, 112, 113-114,
    162, 177, 256-257, 258

Elections, Civic, 135-137, 156, 181-182

Elections, Federal: 1925, 52; 1926, 50, 52; 1930, 94; 1935, 93-95, 99; 1940, 144; 1945, 163, 167-169; 1949, 221; 1953, 221-224; 1957, 234-235; 1958, 234-235; 1962, 241-242; 1963, 241-242; 1965, 241-242; 1968, 241-242; 1972, 241-242

Elections, Provincial: Alberta (1948), 178; B.C. (1934), 137; B.C. (1941), 158; Manitoba (1936), 137-138; Ontario (1934), 91; Ontario (1937), 106, 137; Ontario (1943), 160; Ontario (1945), 163; Ontario (1948), 178; Quebec (1944), 162, 256; Saskatchewan (1938), 110; Saskatchewan (1944), 160; Saskatchewan (1948), 178

Fairley, Margaret, 206
Farmer-Labour Party, 52
Farmers' Union of Canada, 83
Farmers' Unity League, 82-85, 91, 155
Federation of Democratic Youth, 267
Federation of Ukrainian Social Democrats, 8
Finnish Organization, 9, 35, 36, 37, 62, 83, 267
Finnish Social Democratic Party, 8
Fistell, Harry, 204, 205, 226
For a Lasting Peace, For a People's Democracy, 182
Foreign Enlistment Act (1937), 130
Foster, W. Z., 42, 164, 212
Franco, Francisco, 129-130
Freed, Norman, 112, 136
French Communist Party, 227, 257
Friends of the Mackenzie-Papineau Battalion, 129
Friends of the Soviet Union, 34
Furrow, The, 40, 84

Gagnon, Henri, 256, 257
Gardiner, Robert, 78
Garland, E. J., 102
Gauld, Bella, 247
Gelinas, Pierre, 202
Glace Bay Gazette, 161
Glambeck, John, 40
Gordon, King, 100-101, 102
Guevara, Che, 270
Guzenko, Igor, 171, 172, 180, 256

Haddow, Robert, 195
Hall, Frank, 189
Hardie, Keir, 281
Harrison, Caleb, 21
Hayakawa, S. I., 127
Hayward, William, 281
Heaps, A. A., 68, 94, 103, 112
Hepburn, Mitchell, 111, 112, 125, 133, 151, 158
Herridge, W. D., 113
Hill, T. A., 27, 87
Hitler, Adolf, 96, 97, 125, 128, 139, 140, 141, 142, 143, 144, 145, 148, 149, 150, 158, 182, 199, 254, 255, 273, 282
Hopwood, V. G., 206
Housewives Association, 248
Hungary, 228, 230
Hunter, Peter, 124
Hyde, Laurence, 127

Independent Labour Party of Manitoba, 68
Industrial Banner, 61
Industrial Workers of the World, 3, 4-5, 10, 16, 20, 47, 61
International Brigades, 129, 149
International Fur and Leather Workers Union, 157, 196
International Union of Electrical Workers, 199
International Union of Mine, Mill and Smelter Workers, 157, 192, 193, 196, 198, 199, 252
International Woodworkers of America, 148, 157, 193, 194, 195
Internationalists, 261
Irvine, William, 52, 105, 128
Israel, 259
Italian Communist Party, 266

Jackson, C. S., 148, 192, 195
Japan, 125, 128, 139, 254
Jensen, Carl, 27, 29
Johnstone, Jack, 90
Jolliffe, E. B., 102

Kardash, William, 83, 165, 228
Kashtan, David, 146
Kashtan, William, 123, 125, 176, 237, 240-241, 243, 253, 254, 260, 263, 266, 269
Kautsky, Karl, 19

Kavanagh, Jack, 16, 19, 24, 25, 27, 28, 43
Kemal, Mustapha, 58
Kennedy, Leo, 127
Khrushchev, N. S., 138, 223, 224-229, 260, 275
King, Mackenzie, 58, 68, 78, 89, 94, 112, 125, 131, 140, 146, 157, 158, 160, 162, 163, 167, 177
Kirkconnell, Watson, 151
Klein, A. M., 127
Knight, Joe, 13, 16, 24, 25, 28
Kobzey, T., 199, 264
Kolasky, John, 264-265
Kolisnyk, William, 136
Korea, 183, 184, 190
Krestintern, *see* Peasant International

Labor Challenge, 261
Labor College, 10
Labor Educational League, 10
Labor Progressive Party, *see* Communist Party of Canada
Labor Youth Federation, 267
Lacroix, Wilfred, 208
Lakeman, J., 25
Laporte, Pierre, 254
Laxer, R. M., 178
League for Democratic Rights, 209
League for Socialist Action, 261
Lenin, V. I., 6, 9, 10, 14, 17, 18, 19, 21, 23, 25, 29, 51, 64, 102, 165, 177, 214, 277
Lenin School, 56, 63-64, 237
Leopold, J., 15, 87
Lewis, C. Day, 127
Lewis, David, 102, 105-106, 110, 137, 146, 151, 156, 158, 160, 162, 177, 183
Liberal Labor Coalition proposal, 162-163, 169-170, 175, 176, 267, 281
Lipshitz, Sam, 220, 232
Lipton, Charles, 252
Litterick, J., 137-138
Livesay, Dorothy, 127
Lobay, Daniel, 199
Lovestone, Jay, 57
Lower, A. R., 204
Lubbock, Mrs. Rae, 248
Lumber Workers Industrial Union, 49

Macdonald, John, 11, 16, 21, 23, 27, 44, 51, 53, 56-60, 62, 65, 66, 68, 86, 97, 143
Mackenzie-Papineau Battalion, 129
MacLachlan, J. B., 93, 132
MacLeod, A. A., 128, 156, 232, 235
Macpherson, C. B., 127
Mahoney, William, 193
Manion, R. J., 112
Mao Tse-tung, 260, 261
Maoists, 260-261, 262, 269, 270
Marcuse, Herbert, 270
Margolese, J., 62
Marshall Plan, 183
Martin, Paul, 125
Marx, Karl, 15, 26, 214, 277
Marxist Review, 234
Masses, 127
Massey, Denton, 125
Massey, Vincent, 203
McKean, Fergus, 164-166, 167
McNaughton, Andrew, 163
McEwen, Tom, 73, 75, 78, 87, 92, 93, 128, 134, 144, 167, 231, 274
McInnis, Angus, 94, 103, 107
McInnis, Grace, 146
McManus, T. G., 196
McNamee, L. P., 83
McNeil, Grant, 102
Meighen, Arthur, 112, 209
Millard, C. E., 147, 148, 150, 160, 178, 191, 194
Mills, H. E., 83
Mine Workers Union of Canada, 49, 132
Moore, Tom, 43
Morgan, Nigel, 148, 160, 167, 195
Moriarty, William, 11, 19, 27, 60, 62
Morris, Leslie, 60, 61, 63, 92, 101, 109, 110, 123, 131, 144, 148, 159, 164, 169, 175, 186, 205, 213, 221, 228, 236, 237, 243, 260
Morton, Elizabeth, 128
Mosher, A. R., 131, 135, 147, 148, 160, 191, 192, 195, 198
Murphy, Harvey, 193
Murphy, J. T., 45
Mussolini, Benito, 96, 125, 128, 139, 254

National Affairs Monthly, 158, 174, 223, 227, 234

National Council for Democratic Rights, 151
National Federation of Labor Youth, 267-268
National Unemployed Workers' Association, 75
Navis (Navizivs'kii), John, 11
New Advance, 126, 150
New Democracy, 113, 164
New Democratic Party, 233, 257, 258, 261, 276, 277-278, 281-282
New Frontier, 127, 205
New Frontiers, 205-206
New Left, 233, 268, 269-270
New Masses, 127
Nielsen, Dorise, 144-145, 148, 152, 170, 248
Non-Contributory Unemployment Insurance Bill, 78
Norman, Herbert, 206
North Atlantic Treaty Organization, 183, 184, 242, 259, 269
Northern Neighbours, 243

OBU Bulletin, 30, 72
Official Secrets Act (1939), 172
On-To-Ottawa Trek, 78-81
One Big Union, 16, 24, 25, 28, 29-31, 47
Ouvrier canadien, L', 255

Pacific Tribune, 211, 268
Padlock Act, 113, 125, 255, 256-257
Parr, Jack, 127
Parti Communiste du Québec, 258
Parti Communiste du Québec Français, 256
Pattullo, T. D., 112
Pearson, Lester, 185, 206-207
Peasant International, 41, 65
Peking Review, 261
Peel, F. J., 27, 62
Penner, Jacob, 29
Penner, Norman, 212, 229-230, 231, 268
People's Front, 96-114, 119, 123, 132, 135, 144, 153, 177, 248
People's League, 109
Philpott, Elmore, 107
Pierce, G., *see* Smith, Stewart
Polish United Workers Party, 229
Popovic, Matthew, 11, 25, 29, 87, 93, 264

Powell, G. F., 109
Pratt, E, J., 127
Pravda, 225
Pritchard, W. A., 21, 27
Profintern, 13, 24, 25, 30, 49, 59, 65, 73, 74, 77, 88, 212, 253
Progressive Art Club, 91, 126
Progressive Farmers' Educational League, 39-41, 81
Progressive Party, 52
Progressive Worker, 260
Progressive Workers Movement, 260
Put Canada First, 219-221, 223-224, 234

Reconstruction Party, 94, 105
Red International of Labour Unions, *see* Profintern
Relief Camp Worker, 76
Richard, J. J., 206
Road to Socialism in Canada, 239
Roebuck, Arthur, 91, 106
Roosevelt, F. D., 158, 165
Rose, Fred, 156, 158, 161, 170, 171 172
Ross, William, 265
Rowley, Kent, 252
Roy, M. N., 45
Royal Canadian Mounted Police, 15, 21, 22, 80, 170, 207, 246,
Russell, R. B., 28-31, 135
Ruthenberg, C. E., 13
Ryerson, Edna, 214, 266
Ryerson, S. B., 126, 152, 179, 202, 205, 211, 231, 235, 282
Ryga, George, 206

Sacco-Vanzetti case, 51
Salsberg, J. B., 132, 136, 137, 152, 156, 218, 226-232, 235, 264, 278, 281
Scan, 269
Scott, Charlie, *see* Jensen, Carl
Scott, F. R., 123, 151, 178, 260
Scott, Jack, 260
Seafarers' International Union, 188, 196
Shoesmith, R., 62
Sifton, Clifford, 151
Simpson, James, 53, 61
Sims, Charles, 86, 152
Smith, A. E., 89, 91, 93, 107, 126, 150

Smith, Stewart, 56-57, 59-61, 63-64, 84, 86, 89, 90, 95, 96, 98, 100, 103, 106, 111, 119, 128, 132, 136, 142, 165, 175, 229, 231, 232

Social Democratic Federation, 3

Social Democratic Party of Canada, 2, 3-4, 5, 6-7, 8, 10, 24, 29, 61, 254

Socialist Labor Party, 2, 3, 21, 24

Socialist Party of America, 3, 21, 282

Socialist Party of Canada, 2, 3-4, 5, 6-7, 12, 13, 16, 17-21, 24-27, 29, 30, 61, 73, 90, 254

Socialist Party of North America, 2, 6, 24, 61

Socialist Youth League, 268

Sommerville, Norman, 268

Soviet Union, *see* Union of Soviet Socialist Republics

Spector, Maurice, 11, 13, 21, 23, 35, 52, 55, 56, 57-58, 60, 68, 97

Spencer, H. E., 102

Spry, Graham, 101, 102

Stalin, J. V., 54, 55, 57, 106, 138, 165, 182, 208, 212, 214, 218, 221, 223, 224-225, 227, 238, 262, 267, 275, 280, 282

St. Laurent, Louis, 151, 203, 221

St. Martin, Albert, 254-255

Stevens, H. H., 94

Stewart, John, 203-204, 210

Stewart, William, 195

Strachey, John, 108

Stubbs, L. St. George, 185

Student Christian Movement, 125

Sullivan, J. A. (Pat), 157, 188, 195

Theatre of Action, 127

Tito, Josip Broz, 170, 214, 227, 267

Trade Union Educational League, 40, 42-43, 61, 68, 73, 212

Trade Union Unity League, 73, 132

Trades and Labor Congress, 4, 30, 43-47, 53, 68, 69, 72, 73, 74, 84, 89, 128, 131-132, 147, 151, 157, 160, 186, 188-191, 208, 252

Trotsky, Leon, 18, 55, 170

Trotskyists, 55-56, 60, 89, 98, 101, 106, 124, 132, 133, 241, 249, 261-262, 269, 270, 276

Tuomi, William, 83

Ukrainian Labor Farmer Temple Association, 9, 36, 37, 39, 62, 83, 84, 85, 121, 142, 150, 263

Ukrainian Labor Temple Association, 9

Ukrainian Social Democratic Party, 8

Underhill, Frank, 105, 128, 204

Unemployed Councils, 75

Unemployed Worker, The, 76

Unitarian Church, 233

United Church of Canada, 110

United Communist Party of America, 12

United Automobile Workers of America, 157, 195, 197

United Electrical, Radio and Machine Workers of America, 148, 157, 193, 196, 199, 252

United Farmers Educational League, 82

United Farmers of Alberta, 40, 78, 81, 83, 84, 89, 99

United Farmers of Canada (Saskatchewan Section), 40, 41, 81, 82

United Farmers of Manitoba, 40, 81

United Farmers of Ontario, 106

United Fishermen and Allied Workers Union, 196, 252

United Front, 22, 31, 81, 101, 104, 111

United Jewish People's Order, 172, 232, 259, 267

United Mine Workers of America, 132

United Steelworkers of America, 198, 250, 252

Union of Soviet Socialist Republics, 9, 13, 34, 50, 51, 55, 56, 62, 83, 123, 139, 140, 141, 148, 149, 158, 170, 171, 172, 173, 177, 180, 181, 182-183, 184, 187, 189, 191, 195, 196, 197, 199, 203, 208, 209, 212, 213, 215, 216, 218, 224, 225, 226, 233, 234, 240, 246, 247, 248, 254, 255, 259, 260, 262, 263, 264-266, 270, 276, 279-280

Université Ouvrière, L', 255

Vaara, A., 62

Vancouver Labour Council, 193

Vapaus, 39, 120

Vestnik, 243

Voice of Labour, 130

Voice of Women, 247

Waffle group, 233, 240-241

Wallace, J. S., 126, 202

Walsh, Sam, 240

Watkins Manifesto, 240
Weir, John, 63, 136, 202
Weinstone, William, 13
Wells, A. S., 18, 24, 25
Western Clarion, 4, 18, 19, 20, 26
Wheat Pools, 41
Wiggins, W. E., 40, 83, 84, 144
Williams, G. H., 41, 82, 110
Willmott, W. E., 206, 268
Winnipeg General Strike, 14-16, 28
Women's Labour League, 34, 74, 248
Woodsworth, Kenneth, 125
Woodsworth, J. S., 52, 68, 98-104,
    106-107, 124, 137, 146, 282
Woodworkers Industrial Union of
    Canada, 194
Worker, The, 39, 40, 43, 49, 53, 56, 64,
    73, 74, 75, 81, 83, 84, 98, 102, 108,
    130, 136, 236
Workers' Alliance, 10, 29
Workers' Economic Conference
    (1932), 76
Workers Guard, The, 12, 27
Workers' International Revolutionary
    Party, 12

Workers' Party of America, 31
Workers' Party of Canada, *see*
    Communist Party of Canada
Workers' Theatre, 126, 127
Workers' Unity League, 71-75, 88, 90,
    92, 131-132, 248, 252
World Marxist Review, 243, 262

Young Communist International, 59,
    124, 125
Young Communist League, 33, 59, 92,
    120, 122-125, 142, 267, 268-269,
    270
Young Pioneers, 33-34
Young Socialists, 261
Young Men's Christian Association,
    146
Young Men's Hebrew Association, 146
Young Women's Christian
    Association, 146
Young Workers League, 33

Zhyttia i slovo, 265
Zuken, Joe, 259